DATE DUE

DE 20 01			
DE 6 01			
DE 19 01			
JE 4 03			
DE 11 08			

Kate:

THE JOURNAL OF A CONFEDERATE NURSE

A Postwar Photograph of Kate Cumming

(Reproduced from the frontispiece of her *Gleanings from Southland*)

✠✠

THE JOURNAL

OF A CONFEDERATE NURSE

by Kate Cumming

edited by

Richard Barksdale Harwell

———◆———

LOUISIANA STATE UNIVERSITY PRESS

Baton Rouge

✠✠

THIS BOOK IS DEDICATED TO N. C. C.

PREFACE

IN THE SPRING of 1866 John Esten Cooke was soliciting material for a book he proposed to publish the next fall, a book to be called "Heroic Women of the South." It would be "a full and reliable record of the noble actions of Southern Women—their charities, self-sacrifice, and heroic courage and devotion—during the trying scenes of the late war. . . . For such a volume, ample material exists: and the writer urges upon his countrymen the importance of recording the facts upon the imperishable tablets of history. They are fresh in the memory to-day, as in every heart: but, a few years hence they will have passed into obscure tradition, and the coming generations will grow up in ignorance of these exhibitions of a grand devotion—as much the pride and glory of the South, as the courage of her sons upon the field." [1]

Cooke never published his proposed volume—surely not from a lack of material, more likely from being overwhelmed by a super-abundance of material. But the record of Southern women in the War is not lost. Indeed, it lives in some of the finest memoirs and personal narratives of that period: in Mary Boykin Chesnut's *Diary from Dixie*, Phoebe Yates Pember's *A Woman's Story*, Constance Cary Harrison's *Recollections Grave and Gay*, Mary Louise Wigfall Wright's *A Southern Girl in '61*, Sallie A. Brock Putnam's *Richmond During the War*, Kate Stone's *Brokenburn*, Sarah Morgan Dawson's *A Confederate Girl's Diary*, Parthenia A. Hague's *A Blockaded Family*, Dolly Lunt Burge's *A Woman's War Time Journal*, Mary A. H. Gay's *Life in Dixie During the War*, and Eliza Frances Andrews' *The War-Time Journal of a Georgia Girl*. And these are only samples from an extensive list of women's narratives of the War.

High on any such list should be Kate Cumming's *A Journal of Hospital Life in the Confederate Army of Tennessee*. Miss Cumming's narrative was among the first of the printed records of women's part in the War. But, obscurely published in 1866, it has been too little known, and its present price on the rare-book market prohibits wide

---

[1] Broadside dated "Winchester, Va., May, 1866." In private hands.

familiarity with the original edition. It has been my pleasure to edit it for presentation to a new and, it is hoped, wider audience.

The editorial mechanics have been kept as simple as possible. Occasional lapses into faulty grammar have been allowed to stand, but mispellings of proper names have been, where possible, corrected in brackets after their first occurence and silently corrected in subsequent use. When it has been possible to fill out names indicated (as was often the case) by Miss Cumming only by an initial, the names have been given in full without remark. Exceptions have been made in a few cases where it was apparently the author's intent to hide a name by the use of the initial only. These exceptions are indicated by square brackets.

The length of the original publication has necessitated some reduction of it. Miss Cumming quoted poetry at the drop of a cliché. Most of her quotations have been excised, but enough have been retained to hold the flavor of the original. A few short passages of religious musings (similar to passages retained) have been omitted, and a few discursive anecdotes of no point to the main line of her journal have been eliminated. Likewise, the length of the narrative has required that explanatory notes be kept to a minimum. The editor has attempted to restrict the notes to those which add to the medical and social history that the journal reflects. The many opportunities for notes on military and political history have purposely been passed over; such material is so readily available that it has seemed wise to emphasize less widely known aspects of the War. Many names could be identified by explanatory notes. This, however, would clutter the pages to little effect. Instead, the names that can be traced have been extended in the index, and only a few doctors and others of primary importance in Miss Cumming's story individually noted.

The editor's thanks are due Professor T. Harry Williams of the History Department of Louisiana State University, the library of Emory University (and especially to Miss Ruth Walling, paragon of reference librarians), the Birmingham Public Library, Dr. W. Stanley Hoole of the University of Alabama Library, Miss Mildred Jordan of the Abner W. Calhoun Medical Library at Emory University, Dr. Genevieve Bixler of the Southern Regional Education Board, Miss Eleanor Brockenbrough of the Confederate Museum in Richmond, Mr. Nelson Coffin, Jr. of Columbus, Georgia, Mr. McDonald Wellford and Dr. Beverley R. Wellford of Richmond, Virginia, Mr. John Cook Wyllie of the University of Virginia Library, the Library of the Boston Athenaeum, and—particularly—Mr. James I. Robertson, Jr. of Danville, Virginia, and Decatur, Georgia.

RICHARD BARKSDALE HARWELL

Chicago, Illinois
March 1959

TABLE OF CONTENTS

ILLUSTRATIONS

EDITOR'S INTRODUCTION

KATE CUMMING was a lady. Hardships and menial work, the disapproval of friends and family were her lot as a matron in the Confederate hospitals. But work, nor strain, nor the consciousness of disapproval could divert her from the life she conceived her duty. As much as any soldier, she contributed to the cause of the Confederacy. In risking the disdain of those who needed to prove themselves ladies by refraining from hard or unpleasant tasks she proved herself the finest kind of lady.

When the states of the South seceded in 1860-61 there was too little preparation for the actualities of war. Least of all was there preparation for an adequate hospital service for the army. What need an elaborate hospital corps for a war which would be decided in a few battles and in a few short months? Nor had medical service attained the stature it reached before later wars. Medical progress since 1865 has been so tremendous that it is difficult to realize the state of medical practice in 1861. " The Civil War," wrote George W. Adams in 1940, " was fought in the very last years of the medical middle ages. . . . Physicians trained in the old attitudes were trying desperately to meet the gigantic problems of military medicine and surgery with such means as they could command." [1]

As the War dragged into years and the toll of battles mounted toward an incredibly high total, an effective medical corps for the Confedcracy had to be improvised. From a paper organization, based on the medical department of the prewar United States army, the Confederate medical service developed into a well-knit, surprisingly efficient corps. Deprived of supplies, Confederate doctors substituted. Lacking resources, they used whatever they had. Driven by defeat from one post to another, they developed flexibility. The object was the provision of medical service. This object they accomplished. " That they came nearer to success than any previous ' doctors in uniform ' is a fact that was lost sight of in the blaze of medical progress that came in the seventies and eighties," declared Mr. Adams.[2]

Even more than the Army of Northern Virginia, the Confederate

---

[1] George Worthington Adams, " Confederate Medicine," *The Journal of Southern History*, VI (1940), 151.

[2] *Ibid.*

ix

Army of Tennessee was a great laboratory of medical innovation. It was in the hospitals of this army that Kate Cumming recorded her observations as a hospital matron (executive nurse). It was of these hospitals that Dr. S. H. Stout, their remarkable director, could somewhat over-confidently assert: "The Medical Department in the field and hospitals retained its organization intact and unbroken to the end of the war. So efficient was it that during Johnston's and Sherman's campaign, Johnston's army was probably strengthened by it to an extent equal to a full division of fighting men. This was done by the organization and mobilizing of the hospitals in a manner so unique that its like was unknown in any previous war." [3] When Dr. Stout made this statement in a reminiscent address in 1902 he doubtless viewed his wartime achievements through the rose-colored glasses of memory, but there was a strong basis of fact in his claim.

Kate Cumming was a part of this, and it is her record of Confederate hospital life that is reprinted here. Though sometimes burdened with detail, her journal is a forthright, interesting, and informative account of a minor, but important, facet of Confederate army life. Professor E. Merton Coulter writes of it: "As a realistic description of the Confederate hospital service, this journal is of first-rate importance." [4] It fully deserves to rank with the best of Confederate personal narratives.

Miss Cumming was born in Edinburgh, Scotland, in 1835.[5] As a child she moved with her family to Montreal and thence, after a few years, to Mobile. There she grew up, to all intents a Southerner, but very conscious of her Scots background. At the outbreak of the War she was a comfortably situated young lady of Mobile. In 1860 Mobile was the second cotton port of the United States, and "the numerous hands through which the cotton passed . . . were the means of making money plentiful. . . . This flush of money caused an easy and rather indolent manner of living, which was enjoyed by the Southerner with a zest scarcely understood by the more hardy people of the North." [6] But the old Mobile was not to last long. The Presidential canvass of 1860 presaged an eventful decade. "Like all Southern women, being perfectly satisfied with our rights, we thought it extremely unladylike to meddle with politics. I cannot tell why,

[3] Samuel Hollingsworth Stout, "An Address Concerning the History of the Medical Service in the Field and Hospitals of the Army and Department of Tennessee," *Southern Practitioner*, XXIV (1902), 447.
[4] E. Merton Coulter, *Travels in the Confederate States* (Norman, Okla., 1948), 61.
[5] This date is given in T. W. Herringshaw's *Herringshaw's Encyclopedia of American Biography* (Chicago, 1898), 269, and is accepted by the Library of Congress for use in its catalog. Miss Cumming's obituaries, however, in the Birmingham *News* and the Mobile *Daily Item* for June 7, 1909, give her age as eighty. This would make the year of her birth 1828 or 1829.
[6] Kate Cumming, *Gleanings from Southland* (Birmingham, 1895), 17.

but during that campaign we zealously entered into all concerning it. . . . In the parlor, on the promenade, at balls and parties, and indeed everywhere, the subject of conversation was politics. We read with avidity the political speeches made North and South, and commented unsparingly upon their merits. We would leave our most important work to attend a speech or procession." [7]

Before it changed Mobile life, the coming of the War accelerated it. The War was a romantic fillip. Fireworks and impromptu celebrations had greeted the secession of South Carolina. When Virginia cast her fate with her sister Southern states in April 1861 " All business was suspended, and young and old, rich and poor, gave themselves up for a grand carnival of rejoicing." [8] Miss Cumming spent a long and pleasant visit aboard the ship *Oconaster* in the spring of 1861 and eventually saw her mother and two sisters off to England aboard her. She was left in Mobile with her father and brother, the two David Cummings, to meet a new sort of life that none of them was prepared for or expected.

Concerts and theatricals for the benefit of the troops marked the first months of war. Troops were gaily fêted as they left for the Virginian front. " Oh! but we were full of zeal and patriotism in those days! " [9]

Battles and wounds and defeats and deaths changed the gaiety to dread and fear. " We had a long, dreary and anxious summer. The city was in a most defenceless state, and could easily have been captured . . . Our people were determined not to give it up without a struggle, so we did not know how soon the war ships would pass Fort Morgan, and throw shells into our midst. . . . Everything was arranged for sudden flight to the woods." [10] The effects of war were making themselves felt.

Illness kept Miss Cumming inactive for several months. As she was recuperating she heard a report of an address at Saint John's Church by the Reverend Benjamin M. Miller, an old friend of her family, in which he called on the ladies to go to the front to nurse the sick and wounded. Miss Cumming's family disapproved of her being a part of such a project and she at first limited her participation to assisting those who were leaving for the hospitals in gathering blankets, quilts, and delicacies for the troops. About forty ladies had volunteered their services and planned to go to northern Mississippi or to Tennessee under the chaperonage of a Mrs. Ogden, the widow of a United States army major. Miss Augusta Jane Evans, who at twenty-seven had already achieved an enviable reputation as the South's leading authoress, was among those volunteering. She wrote a friend in March of 1862 that she was " very busy making all arrangements to leave home at any moment when I am notified that my services are needed

[7] *Ibid.*, 19.   [8] *Ibid.*, 21.   [9] *Ibid.*, 27.   [10] *Ibid.*, 32.

elsewhere" and added "we are organizing a corps of nurses for the hospital . . . I have determined to devote myself to the hospital." [11]

The decisions of both Miss Evans and Miss Cumming were reversed. Miss Evans did not go to the front. Miss Cumming did. "The last regiment that we went to see off," she wrote, "was the Twenty-first Alabama. Many of the men we had known from boyhood, had been schoolmates and been associated together at Sunday school and church. I resolved then and there that if Mr. Miller would take me, I would go with him and do my best. I had never been inside of a hospital, and was wholly ignorant of what I should be called upon to do, but I knew that what one woman [Florence Nightingale] had done another could."[12] She overcame the opposition of her father but could not extinguish that of her brothers-in-law. One declared that no sister of his should take such a step, the other that "nursing soldiers was no work for a refined lady." The pioneer work of Florence Nightingale was still fresh in the public mind and particularly in the Cumming household. The mother and sister of one of the sons-in-law had served with Miss Nightingale in the Crimea. But the young Southerner pointed out that Miss Nightingale had served a rich and powerful government and that the Confederacy could not give such assistance as she had been given. "All of this made me more determined than ever. If our government was too poor to assist us, there was the more need of assisting it. And, as to the plea of its being no place for a refined lady, I wondered what Miss Nightingale and the hundreds of refined ladies of Great Britain, who went to the Crimea, would say to that! " [13]

After weeks of preparation and waiting, Mr. Miller rushed into the Mobile churches on the evening of April 6, 1862, to announce to the congregations that the crisis had come, that his party of volunteers would leave on the next morning. While the battle of Shiloh was still in progress, these ladies headed north, considerably more willing than able to serve as Confederate hospital nurses.

Confederate hospital service was a harder life than Miss Cumming bargained for, but she stuck it out. Most of her fellow volunteers in Mr. Miller's party soon gave up the work, but she continued in the hospitals at Corinth and Okolona until midsummer and, after a few weeks in Mobile, again offered her services in those at Chattanooga. After Confederate laws were changed in the fall of 1862 to permit the employment of women in hospitals she was regularly enlisted in the Confederate medical department.

If the state of the medical profession was generally backward at the beginning of the War, the status of nursing as an auxiliary calling was practically nonexistent. Miss Nightingale had been internationally

---

[11] William Percy Fidler, *Augusta Evans Wilson, 1835–1909, A Biography* (University, Ala., 1951), 91.

[12] Cumming, *Gleanings from Southland*, 37-38. [13] *Ibid.,* 38.

celebrated for her contribution with the British army, and her methods had been called to the attention of Americans through the publication of her *Notes on Nursing: What It Is, and What It Is Not* in New York in 1860. But the ambition of a few women to engage in professional nursing service was more than counterbalanced by the opposition within the medical profession to such a course. The North was first to see the advantages of regularizing the position of female nurses in the hospitals. On June 10, 1861, Dorothea L. Dix was appointed Superintendent of Female Nurses of the Army of the United States. Miss Dix was assigned the responsibility of assembling and training a corps of army nurses. She was not, however, supported with authority commensurate with her responsibility. The authorities lacked faith in her, and she eventually proved to be more authoritarian than authoritative in her administration. The nurses themselves, however, gained status despite both public and medical prejudice and eventually made up a highly creditable corps. The early circulars promoting Miss Dix's work read in part: "No women under thirty years of age need apply to serve in government hospitals. All nurses are required to be very plain looking women. Their dresses must be brown or black, with no bows, no curls, no jewelry, and no hoop skirts." [14] There were eager volunteers and the Union soon had organized and trained in the rudiments of nursing a corps of two thousand. Among them were Clara Barton, later the organizer of the American Red Cross, and Louisa May Alcott, who wrote a narrative of her wartime nursing career as well as her more famous *Little Women*.

The South was slow in recognizing the desirability of women as regular members of the medical department of the army. For a year and a half the women worked in the hospitals only as volunteers, and few of them had undergone any but home training. It was not until September 1862 that Congress granted them official status. But the women themselves had not been behindhand, and the services they had performed on a volunteer basis had trained them for fuller service as enrolled members of the Confederate Medical Department.

Dr. S. H. Stout, later Medical Director of Hospitals of the Army and Department of Tennessee, was the surgeon in charge of the Gordon Hospital in Nashville in 1861. He was not fully convinced of the usefulness of women in the hospitals until he saw the work of the Confederate ladies among the wounded following the battle of Shiloh. In his own personal narrative he declared, "Then, and ever after throughout the war the women of the South, whether rich or poor, educated or uneducated, whenever or wherever they were in the vicinity of the sick or wounded, whether separated from their commands, suffering on the battlefield or languishing in the hospitals,

[14] Isobel Stevenson, "Nursing in the Civil War," *Ciba Symposia*, III (1941), 921-22.

never hesitated to go to their relief. Aged and stately matrons, youthful and inexperienced maidens, who perhaps had never left home the distance of a mile without an escort, undauntedly entered hospital wards or visited in out of the way places sick and wounded Confederate soldiers and administered to them. The soldiers of the war in the Crimea were comforted and cared for by a single Florence Nightingale, and the story of her good works has gone sounding down the pages of history, honoring one great and good woman for her work of love; but the Florence Nightingales who ministered to the comfort of sick and wounded Confederate soldiers, if a roll of these deserving women and young maidens could be made, could be counted only by the hundreds of thousands." [15]

More specifically of the women who were regularly enrolled as hospital matrons he asserted: "Mrs. Gilmer, Miss Cumming, and Mrs. Newsom, were the first refined, intellectual, self-denying ladies, who, in the midst of the suffering soldiers, served at their bunkside at night as well as day. Their self-denying and heroic benevolence inspirited many other educated and refined ladies to imitate their examples. It was not long after I was assigned to the directorship of the hospitals, before they were nearly all supplied, when circumstances permitted[,] with matrons of like character, who resided in the hospital buildings, and were equally as devoted and self-denying in their attention to the wounded.

"The gratitude of the soldiers was always manifest whenever these matrons, who were *internes*, came into the wards. For they served them as amanuenses by writing letters to the families and friends of the disabled. They prayed for and with them when requested. They cooked appropriate and delicate food for them when needed. They wiped the sweat from the brows of the dying and closed the eyes of the dead. Often entrusted to send the last messages of the dying to their families and friends at home, those faithful matrons never failed to perform their promises." [16]

By law, the matrons were obliged "to exercise a superintendence over the entire domestic economy of the hospital, to take charge of such delicacies as may be provided for the sick, to apportion them out as desired, to see that the food or diet is properly prepared, and all such other duties as may be necessary." Certainly enough work to fill a twenty-four-hour day. But the matrons were authorized assistant matrons "to superintend the laundry, to take charge of the clothing of the sick, the bedding of the hospital, to see that they are kept clean and neat, and perform such other duties as may be necessary," as well as ward-matrons, whose duties "shall be to prepare the beds and bedding of their respective wards, to see that they are kept clean

[15] Stout, "Some Facts of the History of the Organization of the Medical Service of the Confederate Armies and Hospitals," *Southern Practitioner*, XXV (1903), 156.
[16] *Ibid.*, 523.

and in order, that the food or diet for the sick is carefully prepared and furnished to them, the medicine administered, and that all patients requiring careful nursing are attended to, and all such other duties as may be necessary." [17]

This law did much to bring system to the entire hospital service of the Confederacy. And the experience of the first year of the War soon resulted in better administered hospitals. After the fall of Nashville in early 1862 Dr. Stout had been transferred to Chattanooga and had organized the hospitals there on a high level of efficiency. Dr. Stout was a real medical pioneer. Removed by distance and by difficulty of communications from rigid control by the Surgeon General's Office at Richmond, he was relatively free to develop the hospital organization most suited to his needs. In addition to making wise use of women in the hospitals, Dr. Stout added much to the comfort of his patients by effective control of the hospital funds—to the point of establishing a regular system of foraging and bartering for supplies. By purchasing a printing press for the exclusive use of his office and printing blank forms on it, he was able to save thousands of dollars that could be devoted to increasing the soldiers' comfort. He devised an architectural arrangement of his hospital wards that promoted maximum efficiency and comfort within each building. His most far-reaching innovation was the establishment of the hospitals in his department on a truly mobile basis. In Richmond there were more than fifty establishments designated as "hospitals," but the principal and lasting ones were those which were soon congregated into one great collection of buildings on Chimborazo Heights. In the Army of Tennessee they were scattered across hundreds of miles as they retreated before Sherman. Mobility of the hospitals was necessary for tactical reasons, and it was effective in placing the patients in the localities that were best able to furnish supplies.

The long trek of the Confederate hospitals began as early as 1862 when units were established in Cleveland, Tennessee, and Ringgold, Rome, and Dalton, Georgia. By the middle of the next year the hospitals had spread farther south into Georgia: at Kingston, Cherokee Springs, Catoosa Springs, Tunnel Hill, Marietta, and Newnan, and Dr. Stout's command had been enlarged to include Atlanta. Retreat and reorganization brought hospitals in his department as far east as Madison, Athens, and Augusta. The campaign towards Atlanta necessitated the removal of the hospitals south of that city. By July 1864 they were scattered among Athens, Augusta, Barnesville, Columbus, Covington, Forsyth, Fort Gaines, Greensboro, Griffin, LaGrange, Macon, Madison, Milner, Newnan, Oxford, Thomaston, and Vineville. Soon establishments at Americus and Cuthbert were necessary to take care of the units threatened by the Federal advance. There were prison

[17] C. S. Statutes, 1st Cong., Sess. II, Ch. 17, 1862.

hospitals at Macon and Andersonville, and a hospital for the Georgia militia at Milledgeville. By early fall they had spilled over from Georgia into Auburn, Eufaula, Montgomery, and Notasulga in Alabama.[18]

It was the mobility of the Confederate hospitals that kept them in existence at all, but repeated moves contributed little to the health and comfort of the patients. Medical Inspector E. N. Covey reported to Richmond in September 1864: "Nearly ever since I began my tour of Inspection, the Hospitals of this Department have been in a migratory state, and I have been fully able to appreciate both the trials of the Med. Officer and the hardships of the sick soldier; both of which have been trying in the extreme." [19] Inspector Covey urged consolidation of the hospitals and better quartermaster service for them. It is doubtful that consolidation would have improved efficiency or that, at this point, it could have been effected. The mobile system had proved its worth, if only as the lesser evil. But better quartermaster service would certainly have helped. Dr. Covey was seeing the mobile system only after it had been overextended when he, truthfully, wrote: "The entire line of Hospitals on the Atlanta Road, from Augusta to West Point, has been abandoned. Of course all the points North of this Road have been rendered useless to us, either by the occupation by the Enemy or their proximity to his lines. This has necessitated the still greater scattering of, the already too much scattered, Hospitals, and squatting them in little towns, where every available house from a common Grocery to the town church has been taken for their purposes, and in most instances building[s] so taken have been entirely unfit for the treatment of the sick and wounded." [20]

[18] Flewellen Hospital, Manuscript Order Book. In private hands.

[19] E. N. Covey, ALs, September 8, 1864, unaddressed copy sent to Dr. Stout. In Stout Papers (Emory). Dr. Stout carefully preserved the manuscript records of his command and held them intact until his death. It was from this source that his articles about his Confederate service were written. Long after his death the records were considerably dispersed and substantial collections of them are now at the University of Texas, Emory University, and the Tennessee State Library. Smaller collections are owned by Mr. W. E. Thomas of Medford, Oregon, the Confederate Museum, and the Virginia Historical Society. Some single pieces are in scattered collections. "Inasmuch as the records of the Surgeon General's office were burned at Richmond in April, 1865," wrote Dr. Stout, "these official papers are of inestimable value to science and to history." Stout, "Reminiscences of Medical Officers of the Confederate Army and Department of Tennessee," *St. Louis Medical and Surgical Journal*, LXIV (1893), 228-29. Although a large part of the medical records at Richmond were lost much more material than is generally believed to be available on Confederate medicine is at hand in the Stout Papers, records in the Confederate Museum and the National Archives, a few hospital record books, accounts of individuals, and the articles published by Confederate veterans in a number of Southern medical journals. An excellent general history, scholarly in its treatment and thorough in its scope, is H. H. Cunningham's *Doctors in Gray: The Confederate Medical Service* (Baton Rouge, 1958).

[20] *Ibid.*

The continued movement of the hospitals, however, was a necessity, not a choice. By October 1, 1864, they were all ordered to Columbus, Georgia, and two weeks later to Opelika, Alabama. With a stop at Tuscumbia, Alabama, headquarters were moved to Macon, Mississippi, by late November, and individual hospitals were scattered as far as Burnsville, Corinth, and Meridian, Mississippi, and Pulaski, Tennessee. Headquarters were moved back to Columbus, Georgia, on January 25, 1865, and back to Atlanta in early April. There the hospital service of the Army of Tennessee saw the end of the War, and the last official order of the medical department was issued from Atlanta April 27, 1865.[21]

President Jefferson Davis paid tribute to the efficiency of the whole Confederate medical service in saying: " The only department that was not demoralized was the Hospital Department which was well in hand and doing efficient service until the end of the war." [22]

Miss Cumming's narrative covers, of course, only a portion of the hospital system of the Army of Tennessee, itself only a portion of the whole Confederate hospital complex. But her experiences were typical of the service of the hospital matrons, and her journal is the fullest and best record of such services. It was published shortly after the end of the War, in the first rush of Confederate narratives into print. Introducing her preface with the usual apology that her journal had not been written for publication, she went on to declare: " [The author's] journal, which was written with the feelings which the scenes naturally called forth, is given without alteration. She has endeavored to give a true and impartial record of what came under her own observation. What is recorded on the authority of others may be taken for what it may be considered to be worth. In the matter of dates she is not, perhaps, in every instance accurate, though in general they will be found correct." [23]

References in her introduction to Henry Wirz's trial indicate that the manuscript of her journal was turned over to the printer in the fall of 1865, too soon for a full rewriting after the close of the War. There are no indications that the original manuscript was doctored for publication, and errors in grammar and misdated entries are evidence to the contrary. The journal was published by John P. Morton and Co. in Louisville and by William Evelyn in New Orleans in 1866 under the cumbersome title *A Journal of Hospital Life in the Confederate Army of Tennessee from the Battle of Shiloh to the End of the War: With Sketches of Life and Character, and Brief Notices of Current Events During That Period.*

Perhaps the publication of her book was too close to the events

[21] Flewellen Hospital, Manuscript Order Book.
[22] Stevenson, " Nursing in the Civil War," *loc. cit.*, 902.
[23] Cumming, *A Journal of Hospital Life . . .* (Louisville, New Orleans, 1866), 5.

Miss Cumming recounted. Perhaps its value was overlooked in the long flow of Confederate personal narratives. It never achieved the circulation it deserved and in recent years has been more often known as a book quoted than as a book read. Of the three personal narratives of hospital service in the Army of Tennessee it is by far the best. Mrs. S. E. D. Smith's *The Soldier's Friend*[24] embodies some useful and interesting facts of hospital work in North Georgia, Covington, and Cuthbert, but her narrative is obviously ghost-written and misses the personal touch with which Miss Cumming's abounds. Mrs. Fannie A. Beers was in service with Miss Cumming at Chattanooga and Newnan. She tells of her experiences at these and other Confederate hospitals in her *Memories*,[25] but her account was written too long after the War to be of much direct value. The reader of Miss Cumming's story is sometimes overwhelmed by the quantity of different names in it, but the exactitude of her details and the fullness of her record impart an unusual sense of immediacy to her narrative. She did not write with the flair for words or the instinct for the revealing anecdote that mark Phoebe Pember's charming recollection of hospital service at Chimborazo,[26] but her account is more illuminating by its telling more of the actual workings of the hospitals. Miss Cumming herself undertook a reworking of her journal in a second book published as *Gleanings from Southland* in 1895. But *Gleanings from Southland* is a poor shadow of the original narrative. She shortened the original by more than half and pared from it many of its most striking passages. The spirit of reconciliation which marks it, though representative of a noble motivation, cancels the lively defiance and courage so notable in the first version.

After the War Miss Cumming returned to Mobile. In 1874 she removed with her father to the new city of Birmingham and identified herself with church and cultural activities there. She taught school and music and was especially active in the Episcopal Church of the Advent. In her last years she took part in the work of the United Daughters of the Confederacy and the United Confederate Veterans. She never married. She died June 5, 1909, at Birmingham and was buried two days later from her beloved Saint John's Episcopal Church in Mobile.[27] The living memory of her work in the Confederate hospitals had passed into obscure tradition, recalled only by devoted patients who survived her. But she had left for all time, for each renewal of interest in her time, a printed record that is forever as fresh as the day it was written.

[24] Mrs. S. E. D. Smith, *The Soldier's Friend* (Memphis, 1867).

[25] Mrs. Fannie A. Beers, *Memories: A Recollection of Personal Experiences During Four Years of War* (Philadelphia, 1889). Cited hereinafter as *Memories*.

[26] Phoebe Yates Pember, *A Southern Woman's Story* (New York, London, 1879).

[27] Obituaries in the Birmingham *News* and Mobile *Daily Item* of June 7, 1909; undated clippings in the George Ward scrapbooks at the Birmingham Public Library.

KATE CUMMING'S ITINERARY

IN THE CONFEDERATE HOSPITAL SERVICE

1862

April 7	Left Mobile for the battlefields
April 8	Arrived at Okolona, Mississippi
April 11	Arrived at Corinth, Mississippi
May 27	Returned to Okolona
June 18	Arrived in Mobile
August 28	Left Mobile for Chattanooga, travelling via Montgomery, West Point, Georgia, and Atlanta; arrived at Chattanooga August 30 and sent to Ringgold, Georgia
September 4	Visited Chattanooga for the day
September 10	Arrived at Dalton, Georgia
September 16	Arrived at Chattanooga

1863

January 17	Left Chattanooga for Mobile, travelling via Atlanta and Montgomery; arrived at Mobile January 19
February 5	Left Mobile to return to Chattanooga, travelling via Selma (February 7), Montgomery (February 8), and Atlanta (February 9); arrived at Chattanooga February 10
July 22	Arrived at Kingston, Georgia
July 30	Visited Rome, Georgia, for the day
August 7	Returned to Chattanooga
August 12	Arrived at Cherokee Springs, Georgia
September 7	Left Cherokee Springs for Newnan, Georgia, travelling via Dalton and Atlanta; arrived at Newnan September 9
September 28	Left Newnan to visit hospitals at Ringgold and in the field till October 3; returned via Marietta (October 4 and 5) and Atlanta; arrived at Newnan October 5

1864

January 29	Left Newnan for Mobile; arrived at Mobile January 31 and returned to Newnan "some few days" before March 3
May 16	Visited Atlanta; returned to Newnan May 17
May 20	Visited Atlanta for the day
August 15	Left Newnan for Americus, travelling via West Point, Opelika, Alabama; Columbus, and Macon (August 17) ; arrived at Americus August 19
November 27	Left Americus for Gainesville, Alabama, travelling via Butler, Georgia (November 28), Columbus (November 29 and 30), Montgomery (November 30 to December 5), and Selma (December 7) ; arrived at Mobile December 9; did not continue to Gainesville

1865

February 28	Left Mobile to return to Georgia, travelling via Montgomery (March 4), Columbus (March 5), and Macon (March 6 to 8) ; arrived at Griffin, Georgia, March 8
May 4	Left Griffin for Newnan, travelling via Atlanta; arrived at Newnan May 5
May 17	Left Newnan to return to Mobile, travelling via West Point, Tuskegee, Alabama (May 22 to 26), and Montgomery; arrived at Mobile May 27

Kate:

THE JOURNAL OF A CONFEDERATE NURSE

AUTHOR'S INTRODUCTION

FOR GIVING the following pages to the public some apology may be due. When the war closed, human nature like, I felt a great thirst for revenge. I should, indeed, not have liked it had I been told so then; but I can look back now and feel how just would have been the charge.

I thought I could hear with calmness, nay, even pleasure, that the French, or any other nation, had desolated the North as the South has been. Since then a better feeling has arisen; and, while arranging my journal for the press, the vivid recollections of what I have witnessed during years of horror have been so shocking, that I have almost doubted whether the past was not all a fevered dream, and, if real, how I ever lived through it.

These notes of passing events, often hurriedly penned amid the active duties of hospital life, but feebly indicate, and only faintly picture, the sad reality. I now pray, and will never cease to pray to the end of my days, that men may beat their swords into plowshares and their spears into pruning-hooks, and that nation may not lift a sword aginst nation, nor learn war any more.

It is with the hope that the same feeling may be aroused in every reader that I present this volume to the public.

The southerner may learn a lesson from the superhuman endurance of the glorious dead and mutilated living who so nobly did their duty in their country's hour of peril. And the northerner, I trust, when he has brought in review before him the wrongs of every kind inflicted on us, will cry, Enough! they have suffered enough; let their wounds now be healed instead of opening them afresh.

I have another motive in view. At the present moment there are men on trial for ill-treating northern prisoners. This is to me the grossest injustice we have yet suffered.[1] I would stake my life on the

---

[1] The trial of Henry Wirz, superintendent of the Confederate prison at Andersonville, began August 23, 1865, and continued until, on October 24, he was sentenced to death. He was hanged November 11, 1865, at Washington. The proceedings of the Military Commission were published as Henry Wirz, *defendant, Trial of Henry Wirz* (Washington, 1868).

Dr. Joseph Jones accused the Commission of "excluding all portions of my

truth of every thing which I have related, as an eye-witness, in the following pages. I have used the simplest language, as truth needs no embellishment. May I not hope that what I have related in regard to the manner in which I saw prisoners treated will soften the hearts of the northerners toward the men now undergoing their trial, and make them look a little more to themselves?

We begged, time and again, for an exchange, but none was granted. We starved their prisoners! But who laid waste our corn and wheat fields? And did not we all starve? Have the southern men who were in northern prisons no tales to tell—of being frozen in their beds, and seeing their comrades freeze to death for want of proper clothing? Is there no Wirz for us to bring to trial? But I must stop; the old feeling comes back; these things are hard to bear. People of the North, the southerners have their faults. Cruelty is not one of them. If your prisoners suffered, it was from force of circumstances, and not with design.

I know that the women of the South will think I have said too much against them; but let them remember that I, too, am a woman, and that every slur cast on them falls on me also. Will the neglect of the suffering, which I have but too faintly sketched, not serve to make them resolve in future to do better; and, like the lady in the dream, say

" The wounds I might have healed—
The human sorrow and smart;
And yet it never was in my soul
To play so ill a part:
But evil is wrought by want of thought,
As well as want of heart." [2]

I feel confident that very much of this failure is to be attributed to us. I have said many a time that, if we did not succeed, the women of the South would be responsible. This conclusion was forced upon me by what I could not but see without willful blindness. Not for one moment would I say that there are no women in the South who have nobly done their duty, although there was an adverse current, strong enough to carry all with it. Whole books might be written, recounting heroic deeds and patient suffering, amid trials seemingly impossible to endure. The names of Newsom, Hopkins, Gilmer, Evans,

---

testimony which related to the distressed condition of the Southern States, and the efforts of the medical authorities to relieve the sufferings of the prisoners of war " and of " deliberately endeavor[ing] to arouse the hatred of the entire North against . . . the medical officers of the Confederate army." He declared, " The grand object of the trial and conviction of Henry Wirz was the conviction of President Davis, Gen. Robert E. Lee and other prominent men of the Confederacy, in order that ' TREASON MIGHT BE RENDERED FOREVER ODIOUS AND IN-FAMOUS.' " *Medical and Surgical Memoirs* (New Orleans, 1876–90) , III, pt. 1, 399.
[2] Thomas Hood, " The Lady's Dream," stanza 16.

Harrison, Walke, Monroe, and I might mention a host of others, will live in the hearts of the people of the South as long as there is a heart here to beat.

Let us cease to live on the surface; let us do and dare—remembering, if we are true to ourselves, the world will be true to us. There is one very important work before us—a work all will sympathize with and aid. The war has left thousands of our men almost as helpless as they were in infancy. Had we been successful, our government would have done its duty in providing for these men. As the case now stands, there will be very little care bestowed on them. Is nothing to be done for these heroes? It is not charity to care for them, but a sacred duty.

In bringing before the minds of the public, as I have, that I am a native of the " land of the mountain and the flood," there is a motive. All true, honest southerners, I feel confident, will acknowledge that I have not exaggerated the evils that existed in the South. To say I did not feel the wrongs of the South as deeply as any native would be far from the truth. God knows how my heart has bled for them;. though many a time, when I have seen her people proving recreant in her hour of trial, I have said that I was thankful I could claim another land; forgetting, in my blindness, that she had her traitors as well as we. And let her not, when she compares the struggle of the two for independence, forget that there is such a thing as comparisons being odious. Were Scotland brought over here and placed in our midst, we should scarcely heed it, from the small surface she would occupy.

We have a territory equal in extent to Great Britain, France, Italy, Germany, and Spain, and not one tenth of the population to defend it. The enemy could come in with his immense armies at any point. That is why the flanking movement succeeded so well.

When the war broke out, I looked around for a parallel, and naturally my native country and her struggle came up first. Since I have been mingling with the southern people, I have found that I was far from being the only one who was claiming that land of romance and chivalry. It was impossible to go any place without meeting her descendants; and, thanks to Walter Scott and Burns, they had any other wish but that of disclaiming her.

I have never seen Scotland to remember her, but have read much about her mountains, glens, and lakes, and I can not see how they can surpass in grandeur and beauty those we have here; and had we only the writers, gifted with the fire to sing, as none but Scotia's bards have done, in her praise, they would find beauties here as boundless as our empire.

Many will say that it is impossible that the South can ever prosper in union with the North. For centuries, not four years, England and

5

Scotland, on the same island, a small rivulet dividing them, fought against each other with a ferocity such as no two nations ever exhibited. In 1603 the throne of England became vacant by the death of Queen Elizabeth. The next and nearest heir was James VI of Scotland. He ascended the English throne. The two nations from that time were united in all save the name. In 1707 the Act of Union was passed, and the two nations formed what is now Great Britain.

Many years have elapsed since that union. Is a Scotchman to-day an Englishman? or, *vice-versa*, an Englishman a Scotchman? All know they are as distinct in nationality as the first day they were united. Where is there such a union for harmony? Not on this earth.

Scotland has lost nothing in grandeur or might since then. Her seats of learning can compete with any in the world. Where is there a nation that can boast of more brilliant lights, both civil and military? Is not her literature spread broadcast over the whole earth? But not even in all these does her greatness consist. The " Cotter's Saturday Night " gives them to us in graphic terms, and

> " From scenes like these old Scotia's grandeur springs,
>   That makes her loved at home, revered abroad:
>   Princes and lords are but the breath of kings,
>   ' An honest man's the noblest work of God! ' " [3]

Let us learn a lesson from these facts, and, as I said before, look to ourselves.

Many a man, whose name is now a shining light, never would have been heard of had not misfortune come upon him. The misfortunes did not make him great; his greatness was there before, but it had been pampered in luxury. If the southern people ever were a great people they will show it now. In the whole world there is not such a favored spot as the South. It is an

> " Empire mightier than the vast domain swayed once by vicious Cæsars! "

That is why the North fought so hard to keep us with her. We have every climate necessary for the well-being of man; we have prairies, mountains, lakes, rivers, and a soil inferior to none. Is this fair heritage to become a howling wilderness, because a people we dislike will have us unite with them whether we will or no? Let us imitate them in what is worthy of imitation. They are enterprising and industrious: we need both. We have much to be proud of. We have men who may be likened to the great Washington, without any disparagement to him: Davis—for I feel certain that not a hair of

[3] Robert Burns, " The Cotter's Saturday Night," stanza 19.

6

his head will be harmed [4]—Lee, Johnston, and many others. And have we not our dead? if dead we may call them, for

"To live in hearts we leave behind is not to die!"

O, let us give up this terrible strife! A truly great man does not know revenge; his soul rises above it as something fit for meaner minds. So with nations. Leave our statesmen to settle our difficulties; and let us remember those exquisite lines of Goldsmith, written after he had walked the weary world round in search of happiness, and returned to his native land:

> "How small, of all that human hearts endure,
> That part which laws or kings can cause or cure!
> Still to ourselves in every place consigned,
> Our own felicity we make or find;
> With secret course, which no loud storms annoy,
> Glides the smooth current of domestic joy.
> The lifted ax, the agonizing wheel,
> Luke's iron crown, and Damien's bed of steel,
> To men remote from power but rarely known,
> Leave reason, faith, and conscience all our own." [5]

---

[4] At this time President Jefferson Davis was confined at Fortress Monroe, Virginia.
[5] Oliver Goldsmith, "The Traveller," ll. 429-38.

7

I: OKOLONA, CORINTH

April 7, 1862.—I left Mobile by the Mobile and Ohio Railroad for Corinth, with Rev. Mr. Miller and a number of Mobile ladies.[1] We are going for the purpose of taking care of the sick and wounded of the army.

As news has come that a battle is now raging, there are not a few anxious hearts in the party—my own among the number, as I have a young brother,[2] belonging to Ketchum's Battery,[3] who I know will be in the midst of the fight, and I have also many dear friends there.

A gentleman, Mr. Skates, has heard that his son is among the killed, and is with us on his way to the front to bring back the remains of him who a short time since formed one of his family circle. May God give strength to the mother and sisters now mourning the loss of their loved one! May they find consolation in the thought that he died a martyr's death; was offered up a sacrifice upon the altar of his country; and that, when we have gained our independence, he, with the brave comrades who fought and fell with him, will ever live in the hearts and memories of a grateful people! I can not look at Mr. Skates without asking myself how many of us may ere long be likewise mourners! It is impossible to suppress these gloomy forebodings.

[1] Probably Benjamin M. Miller, rector of Christ Church, Church Hill, Mississippi. He is the only Miller listed among the "List of the Clergy" in the Protestant Episcopal Church in the Confederate States. General Council, *Journal . . . 1862* (Augusta, Ga., 1862).

[2] David Cumming, Jr. Farrow & Dennett, *firm, Directory of the City of Mobile, 1859* (Mobile, 1859).

[3] Ketchum's Battery (later Garrity's Battery) was organized at Mobile in May 1861. From Shiloh through Nashville it was in every important engagement of the Army of Tennessee. William H. Ketchum was succeeded after his death by William H. Homer, later by James Garrity. William Brewer, *Alabama: Her History, Resources, War Record, and Public Men . . .* (Montgomery, 1872), 696. (Hereinafter cited as Brewer, *Alabama.*) In the course of her journal Miss Cumming mentions many other Alabama units: the Third, Fourth, Sixth, Eighth, Ninth, Eleventh, Twelfth, Seventeenth, Twenty-first, Twenty-second, Twenty-fourth, Twenty-ninth, Thirty-second, Thirty-sixth, and Thirty-eighth infantry regiments and Fowler's, Lumsden's and Tarrant's batteries. Short sketches of these are included in Brewer's book.

9

About midnight, at one of the stations, a dispatch was received prohibiting any one from going to Corinth without a special permit from head-quarters. Our disappointment can be better imagined than described. As military orders are peremptory, there is nothing for us to do but to submit. Mr. Miller has concluded to stop at one of the small towns, as near Corinth as he can get, and there wait until he receives permission for us to go on.

April 8.—Arrived at Okolona, Miss., this morning. We are still sixty miles from Corinth. When we alighted at the depot, we were told that there were no hotels to go to. As it had been raining for some time very hard, all about us looked as cheerless as possible. Our prospects, as may be supposed, were gloomy enough. While in this perplexity, each one giving an opinion as to what we had best do, word was brought us that the citizens of the place, hearing of our arrival and mission, had opened their houses for our reception, and many sent carriages to take us to their homes.

As the good people of Mobile have provided us with comforts and delicacies of all kinds for the soldiers, our failure to reach Corinth is a sad disappointment. The stories which we hear of the suffering and almost starving condition of our men aggravate it still more.

The people here can tell us little or nothing about the battle, except that one has been fought. How our forces have come out of it, they have not learned.

Several of our party, myself included, are domiciled with an excellent family by the name of Haughton, consisting of an old lady, her young daughter Lucy, and two pretty girls, her granddaughters. They are extending to us true southern hospitality.

We were all exhausted by loss of sleep, disappointment, and anxiety, and hence did not go to the cars when they passed at 11 A. M. Mrs. Haughton's two granddaughters went down, and, upon their return, informed us that the cars were filled with the wounded on their way to Mobile and other points. Among other items, there is a report that Captain Ketchum is killed, and all his men are either killed or captured; that the Twenty-first Alabama Regiment has been cut to pieces. I was never more wretched in my life! I can see nothing before me but my slaughtered brother, and the bleeding and mangled forms of his dying comrades, and the men of the gallant Twenty-first Alabama, whom I had seen leave Mobile but a few weeks ago so full of life and hope—many of whom were mere boys. The battle was fought at Shiloh, about twelve miles from Corinth. We had gained a victory, but at a great sacrifice. I tried to comfort myself and trust in God, assured that he was doing all for the best. O, if they would only let us go on! I feel certain that we could help the poor wounded sufferers.

It is raining in torrents. Nature seems to have donned her most

10

somber garb, and to be weeping in anguish for the loss of so many of her noblest sons.

About midnight a train came down. I jumped up, and awoke Miss Mary Wolf. Hurriedly dressing ourselves, we took a servant and started down to see if we could hear any thing. I felt confident we should meet other ladies there as anxious as ourselves. I was not mistaken, for we had not gone far when we met a number returning from the train. It was a car sent down to get negroes to build fortifications.

April 9.—I have been to the cars. Saw Mr. John Maguire, a member of Ketchum's Battery. He is wounded. The company has had one man killed—John Ashby—who fell fighting at his post, and some seven or eight wounded.

The Twenty-first Alabama Regiment suffered pretty badly. I have letters for two of its members. One of these, Charles Farrow, I am told, is a prisoner; the other, John Ortella, a native of Italy, is killed. Poor fellow! I saw a letter written by him a few weeks since to a friend, in which he requested her to pray for him, as he had not time to pray for himself.

Mrs. Walker, one of the ladies who came with us from Mobile, has heard that one of her sons is badly wounded, and a prisoner. Dr. Walkely is on the train, and has with him the dead body of his only son, a member of the same regiment. He left Mobile with us a volunteer surgeon, little dreaming the fate of his boy! I spoke to him, but his lip quivered so with emotion that he could not answer me.

The train was filled with wounded. All told terrible tales of the scenes in Corinth, which only served to make us more miserable. We have had a frightful battle. It was fought on the 6th and 7th inst. The first day our army drove the enemy back near the Tennessee River, within range of their gunboats. On the second they were heavily reinforced, and we retired. Nearly every state in the Confederacy is draped in mourning for the loss of their loved ones, and the whole country has to weep over the death of the good and great general, Albert Sidney Johnson [Johnston], who was in command. His loss is a sad one. His place can not be easily filled. I have been told that it was his death that caused the last day's failure. He had planned the battle, and there is no doubt that, had he lived, he would have succeeded in executing it successfully. He has died the death of a soldier and conqueror, battling for the right. He is doubly a martyr, as he had not only the bullets of the enemy to contend with, but the shafts of envy which were hurled at his fair fame by his own countrymen. They say that he was wounded while recklessly exposing himself. But, ere his noble spirit took its flight, he had the proud satisfaction of seeing the enemy driven back in dismay and confusion. May his soul rest in peace! It has gone where it will be judged, not

11

as man judges, but by the heart alone. Let his faults lie with him in the grave; be it our duty to do honor to his many virtues.

General Gladden of Louisiana is mortally wounded; Colonel Blythe of Mississippi is killed. Mobile has to mourn the loss of some of her bravest and best—Major Armstead, young Maguire, Anderson, Marshall, Spear, Burns, Cummins, Herpin, Ledyard, and others, are names never to be forgotten. . . .

I spoke to John Maguire, and reminded him of that day, one year ago, when he participated in one of the finest displays of which the city of Mobile boasts—the Firemen's Anniversary.[*][4]

A number of ladies have come from Natchez, Miss., to join us. They have also been cared for by the good people of the place.

After we returned to Mrs. Haughton's, I was quite amused in listening to her granddaughter's account of a visit which they had just made to the hospital. It seems that the surgeons entertain great prejudice against admitting ladies into the hospital in the capacity of nurses. The surgeon in charge, Dr. Caldwell, has carried this so far that he will not even allow the ladies of the place to visit his patients. These young ladies went over with some milk and bouquets, and were not permitted to present them in person to the patients, but had to give them to the doctor. So they told him they knew the reason; he wanted all the *good things* for himself. The doctors, one and all, are getting terrible characters from the ladies; even good Dr. Nott of Mobile is not spared.[5] I only wish that the doctors would let us try and see what we can do! Have we not noble examples of what our women have done? For instance, Mrs. Hopkins, in Virginia, and, I have no doubt, many others. Is the noble example of Miss Nightingale to pass for nothing? I trust not. We need not aspire to be Miss Nightingales, or Mrs. Hopkinses; still we can contribute our " two mites."

We have with us two very excellent ladies—Mrs. Hunter and her

* The 9th of April is the anniversary of the organization of the fire department. Two of the companies, the Creole and Neptune, date their origin from 1819. This department has for its members men of the highest standing. On this anniversary, the engines are decked most gorgeously, and dressed with flowers. One year ago to-day the companies vied with each other in their efforts to make the finest display. The whole department exhibited more energy than was its wont. The war spirit had just been aroused on account of the north holding, as a right, what we deemed our own—Fort Sumter—and our people, awakened as if from a lethargy, determined to throw heart and soul into the contest.

[4] A list of the fire companies with their officers is given in Farrow & Dennett, appendix, p. 47.

[5] Dr. Josiah Clark Nott was one of Mobile's most eminent citzens. Famous in his own time as a physician, he is now best remembered as the author of pioneer works on anthropology: *Types of Mankind* and *Indigenous Races of the Earth.* He was instrumental in the establishment of the Medical School of Alabama in Mobile in 1858. Dr. Nott lost two sons during the War. Brewer, *Alabama,* 407-408.

daughter—refugees from Missouri. They were in a hospital at Nashville when the city was taken possession of by the enemy, and have been relating their experience, which is very interesting.

April 10.—This morning we were informed that we could go to Corinth, as the order did not apply to us. With joy we hailed the news! It was still raining, but we did not mind that. When we reached the depot, Mrs. Ogden informed me that Miss Booth was sick—too much so to leave this morning. As we left Mobile together, I felt it my duty to remain with her.

I met at the depot Dr. Anderson of Mobile; and was quite amused at a remark which he made to some ladies who were telling him how badly Dr. Caldwell had acted, in not permitting us to visit his hospital. In his usual humorous manner, he said, "What can be expected from an old bachelor, who did not appreciate the ladies enough to marry one?" He also said that he did not think any hospital could get along without ladies. So we have one doctor on our side.

I rode in a carriage with Rev. Mr. Clute, the Episcopal minister of the place, to Mrs. Henderson's where Miss Booth was staying. Mrs. Henderson was glad to see me. She is a very intelligent lady, and quite handsome. Her sister, Mrs. Young, living with her, is a highly accomplished musician—plays upon the harp and piano beautifully. She sang some very fine Scotch songs for me. We had a long talk about Scotland. They are of Scotch descent. I felt quite proud of the manner in which they spoke of that land of heroes. It is my native land; and although raised in this, and never personally having known any other, I will not forget the country of my forefathers—the land of Wallace and Walter Scott. I have always found that the southern people speak in praise of it, and the noble deeds for which it is famed, and more now than ever, as we are undergoing the same ordeal through which she so nobly passed in her great struggle for independence: all trust that we may show a like spirit, and meet with like success. The husbands of both these ladies are in the army.

This is a very wealthy portion of Mississippi, and food of all kinds seems to be plentiful. At Mrs. Haughton's we had sweet potatoes as a substitute for coffee, and it was very nice. Mrs. Haughton informed us that she did not intend to use any other kind while the war lasted.

April 11.—Miss Booth and myself arrived at Corinth to-day. It was raining when we left Mrs. Henderson's, and as her carriage was out of repair, she sent us to the depot in an open wagon. We enjoyed the novel ride, and began to feel that we were in the *service* in reality. My heart beat high with expectation as we neared Corinth. As I had never been where there was a large army, and had never seen a wounded man, except in the cars, as they passed, I could not help

13

feeling a little nervous at the prospect of now seeing both. When within a few miles of the place, we could realize the condition of an army immediately after a battle. As it had been raining for days, water and mud abounded. Here and there were wagons hopelessly left to their fate, and men on horseback trying to wade through it. As far as the eye could reach, in the midst of all this slop and mud, the white tents of our brave army could be seen through the trees, making a picture suggestive of any thing but comfort. My thoughts wandered back to the days of ancient Corinth, and the time it was besieged by the brave and warlike Romans, when the heroic Greeks had to succumb through the fault of their commander. I think of this only in contrast; for the Federals are as unlike the former as our fate will be unlike that of the latter. We have not a Diæus commanding, but the dauntless Beauregard and patriotic Bragg, who, knowing their rights, dare and will maintain them, though the whole North be arrayed against them. I am certain of one thing: that neither the Roman nor Greek armies, brave as history has portrayed them, were composed of more high-souled and determined men than those of ours.

Corinth is at the junction of the Memphis and Charleston and the Mobile and Ohio Railroads, about one hundred and twenty miles east from Memphis, and three hundred miles north from Mobile.

The crowd of men at the depot was so great that we found it impossible to get to our place of destination by ourselves. Mr. Miller was not there to meet us. I met Mr. George Redwood of Mobile, who kindly offered to pilot us. We found Mr. Miller and all the ladies busy in attending to the wants of those around them. They had not been assigned to any particular place, but there is plenty for them to do. We are at the Tishomingo Hotel, which, like every other large building, has been taken for a hospital. The yellow flag is flying from the top of each. Mrs. Ogden tried to prepare me for the scenes which I should witness upon entering the wards. But alas! nothing that I had ever heard or read had given me the faintest idea of the horrors witnessed here. I do not think that words are in our vocabulary expressive enough to present to the mind the realities of that sad scene. Certainly, none of the glories of the war were presented here. But I must not say that; for if uncomplaining endurance is glory, we had plenty of it. If it is that which makes the hero, here they were by scores. Gray-haired men—men in the pride of manhood—beardless boys—Federals and all, mutilated in every imaginable way, lying on the floor, just as they were taken from the battle-field; so close together that it was almost impossible to walk without stepping on them. I could not command my feelings enough to speak, but thoughts crowded upon me. O, if the authors of this cruel and unnatural war could but see what I saw there, they would try and put a stop to it! To think, that it is man who is working all this woe upon his fellow-man. What can be in the minds of our enemies, who are now arrayed against us, who have never harmed them in any way, but simply claim our own, and nothing more! May God forgive them, for surely they know not what they do.

This was no time for recrimination; there was work to do; so I went at it to do what I could. If I were to live a hundred years, I should never forget the poor sufferers' gratitude; for every little thing, done for them—a little water to drink, or the bathing of their wounds—seemed to afford them the greatest relief.

The Federal prisoners are receiving the same attention as our own men; they are lying side by side. Many are just being brought in from the battle-field. The roads are so bad that it is almost impossible to get them moved at all. A great many ladies are below stairs: so I thought that I had better assist above. The first thing which I did was to aid in giving the men their supper, consisting of bread, biscuit, and butter, and tea and coffee, without milk. There were neither waiters nor plates; they took what we gave them in their hands, and were glad to get it. I went with a lady to give some Federal officers their supper, who were in a room by themselves; only one or two of them were wounded. One, a captain from Cincinnati, had a broken arm. Before I went in, I thought that I would be polite, and say as little as possible to them; but when I saw them laughing, and apparently indifferent to the woe which they had been instrumental in bringing upon us, I could not help being indignant; and when one of them told me he was from Iowa, and that was generally called out of the world, I told him that was where I wished him, and all like him, so that they might not trouble us any more.

April 12.—I sat up all night, bathing the men's wounds, and giving them water. Every one attending to them seemed completely worn out. Some of the doctors told me that they had scarcely slept since the battle. As far as I have seen, the surgeons are very kind to the wounded, and nurse as well as doctor them.

The men are lying all over the house, on their blankets, just as they were brought from the battle-field. They are in the hall, on the gallery, and crowded into very small rooms. The foul air from this mass of human beings at first made me giddy and sick, but I soon got over it. We have to walk, and when we give the men any thing kneel, in blood and water; but we think nothing of it at all. There was much suffering among the patients last night; one old man groaned all the time. He was about sixty years of age, and had lost a leg. He lived near Corinth, and had come there the morning of the battle to see his two sons, who were in the army, and he could not resist shouldering his musket and going into the fight. I comforted him as well as I could. He is a religious man, and prayed nearly all night.

15

Another, a very young man, was wounded in the leg and through the lungs, had a most excruciating cough, and seemed to suffer awfully. One fine-looking man had a dreadful wound in the shoulder. Every time I bathed it he thanked me, and seemed grateful. He died this morning before breakfast. Men who were in the room with him told me that he prayed all night. I trust that he is now at rest, far from this dreary world of strife and bloodshed. I could fill whole pages with descriptions of the scenes before me.

Other ladies have their special patients, whom they never leave. One of them, from Natchez, Miss., has been constantly by a young man, badly wounded, ever since she came here, and the doctors say that she has been the means of saving his life. Many of the others are doing the same. Mrs. Ogden and the Mobile ladies are below stairs. I have not even time to speak to them. Mr. Miller is doing much good; he is comforting the suffering and dying, and has already baptized some.

This morning, when passing the front door, a man asked me if I had any thing to eat, which I could give to some men at the depot awaiting transportation on the cars. He said that they had eaten nothing for some days. Some of the ladies assisting me, we took them hot coffee, bread, and meat. The poor fellows ate eagerly, and seemed so thankful. One of the men, who was taking care of them, asked me where I was from. When I replied Mobile, he said that Mobile was the best place in the Confederacy. He was a member of the Twenty-first Alabama Regiment; I have forgotten his name. I have been busy all day, and can scarcely tell what I have been doing; I have not taken time even to eat, and certainly not time to sit down. There seems to be no order. All do as they please. We have men for nurses, and the doctors complain very much at the manner in which they are appointed; they are detailed from the different regiments, like guards. We have a new set every few hours. I can not see how it is possible for them to take proper care of the men, as nursing is a thing that has to be learned, and we should select our best men for it—the best, not physically, but morally—as I am certain that none but good, conscientious persons will ever do justice to the patients.

Sunday, April 13.—Enjoyed a very good night's rest upon some boxes. We all slept below stairs, in the front room—our baggage separating us from the front part of it, which is the clerk's office, and sleeping apartment of some dozen men. It was a laughable sight to see Father Miller fixing our beds for us. Poor man! He tried so hard to make us comfortable. Some slept on shelves. I slept so soundly that I did not even dream, as I was completely worn out with the labor of the day. I could realize how, after a hard day's marching or fighting, a soldier can throw himself upon the ground, and sleep as soundly as if he was on a bed of down. A number of persons arrived last night, looking for their relations. One very pretty lady, with her parents, is in search of her husband, a colonel, who is reported badly wounded. I have since heard that she has found him at a farm-house, and he is much better off than she had been informed. Her mother, on leaving, presented me with some very nice sperm-candles.

I have just seen my brother. He looks rather the " worse for wear." But, thank God, he is safe! This was his first battle, and I have been told that "he was brave to a fault." The company distinguished itself on that eventful day; and Mobile may well be proud of the gallant men who compose it.

I have been told by a friend that the night of the first day's battle he passed by a wounded Federal who requested him to bring him some water from a spring near. On going to it, he was much shocked to see three Federals lying with their heads in it. They had dragged themselves to the spring to slake their thirst, and there they had breathed their last. There is no end to the tales of horror related about the battle-field. They fill me with dismay. . . .

The confusion and want of order are as great as ever. A great many doctors are here, who came with the men from the different regiments. The amount of good done is not near what it might be, if things were better managed. Some one is to blame for this state of affairs. Many say that it is the fault of Dr. Foard,[6] the medical director. But I suppose that allowance must be made for the unexpected number of wounded. I trust that in a little time things will be better.

One of the doctors, named Little, of Alabama, told me to-day that he had left his young wife on his plantation, with more than a hundred negroes upon it, and no white man but the overseer. He had told the negroes, before he left, if they desired to leave, they could do so when they pleased. He was certain that not more than one or two would go.

I have conversed with some of the wounded prisoners. One of them, quite a young man, named Nott, is very talkative. He says that he dislikes Lincoln and abolitionism as much as we do; declares that he

---

[6] Dr. A. J. Foard had first been assigned to duty with General Braxton Bragg's troops at Pensacola in April 1861. He later served as Medical Director under Bragg, Johnston, and Hood. Joseph Jones, " Roster of the Medical Officers of the Army of Tennessee . . . ," *Southern Historical Society Papers*, XXII (1894), 203. Dr. Stout wrote of him: " The successful organization of the medical services in the field and the hospitals of the Department of Tennessee, was effected by his wisdom, untiring attention to duty, his sincere sympathy with the often over-worked medical men under his direction, his patience in instructing the many medical men who entered the service without any knowledge of army regulations, and his judicious, careful study of their merits." " Some Facts . . . ," *Southern Practitioner*, XXIV (1902), 105. Dr. Foard was Medical Director of the Army of Tennessee. Dr. Stout was Medical Director of Hospitals. Its field hospitals had still a third Medical Director. The medical service in the other armies of the Confederacy were organized in the same pattern.

is fighting to save the Union, and nothing more. All of them say the same thing. What a glorious Union it would be!

Quite a number of bunks arrived to-day, and we are having the most severely wounded placed on them. I am so glad, as we can have some of the filth taken off the floors. A doctor requested me to go down stairs and see if there was a bunk with a Federal upon it, and if so have him taken off, as he had a badly wounded man that needed one. I went and asked Mrs. Royal, from Mobile, whom I had heard talk very bitterly. She knew of one, but would not tell me where it was. Her true woman's nature showed itself, in spite of her dislike. Seeing an enemy wounded and helpless is a different thing from seeing him in health and in power. The first time that I saw one in this condition every feeling of enmity vanished at once. I was curious to find out who the Federal was, and, as Mrs. Royal would not tell me, I went in search of him. I found him with but little trouble; went to the men who were upon the bunks, and asked them where they were from. One, quite a youth, with a childish face, told me that he was from Illinois. I knew in a moment that he was the one. I asked him about his mother, and why he had ever left her. Tears filled his eyes, and his lips quivered so that he was unable to speak. I was deeply moved myself, spoke a few words of comfort, and left him. I would not have had him give up his bunk for the world. Poor child! there will be a terrible day of reckoning for those who sent you on your errand, and who are the cause of desolating so many hearts and homes.

As I was passing one of the rooms, a man called me, and begged me to do something for him and others who were with him. No one had been to see them that morning, and they had had no breakfast. I gave them something to eat, and got a nurse to take care of them. About eight were in the room, among them Mr. Regan of Alabama and Mr. Eli Wasson of Texas, both of whom had lost a leg. I paid these special attention, as they were worse than the others . They were very grateful and thanked me all the time. Mr. Wasson said that he knew that he would get well now. They are both unmarried, and talk much of their mothers and sisters, as all men do now. " Home, sweet home," is the dearest spot on earth to them, since they are deprived of its comforts. Mother, wife, and sister seem to be sweeter to them than any words in the English language.

We eat in the kitchen, surgeons and all. It is not the cleanest place in the world, and I think, to use a Scotch phrase, would make even Mrs. McClarty " think shame." Hunger is a good antidote for even dirt. I am aware that few will think so except those who have tried it.

April 15.—Enjoyed a very good night's rest in a crowded room. Had part of a mattress upon the floor, but so many were upon it that for half of the night I was under a table.

My patients are doing well. My own health is excellent. While I was down stairs this morning a gentleman requested me to give him something to eat for some fifty or sixty wounded men whom he had in his care. He had nothing for them, but was expecting something from his home in Tennessee. It would be some days before he could get it. Mrs. Ogden gave them what she could. He informed us that his name was Cannon; that he was a doctor, and a clergyman of the Episcopal Church. He said that if our men were not better treated than at the present time, it would be the means of demoralizing them more than the enemy's balls.

While passing through the large ward yesterday, a young man lying upon the floor called me, and asked me if I did not recollect him. His name was Shutterlee; he was from Mobile, and a member of the Twenty-first Alabama Regiment. I remembered that I had often seen him, when a little boy, playing with my brother. Poor fellow! he was badly wounded, and suffered a great deal. I asked him if I could do any thing for him. He told me that Mrs. Lyons of Mobile was taking care of him, but wished me to write to his mother, and inform her where and how he was, which I lost no time in doing.

Mr. Wasson is cheerful, and is doing well; tells me much about his home in Texas and the nice fruit there; says that I must go home with him, as his family would be so glad to see me.

Mrs. Lyons is sitting up day and night, attending to some eight or nine patients. One of them is shot in the face, and has it covered with a cloth, as it is so lacerated that it presents a most revolting aspect. Mrs. Lyons is also taking care of some prisoners. There is a Federal surgeon named Young waiting on them. I have been told that Dr. Lyle, one of our surgeons, refused to attend them, as he had just lost two brothers in the war, and has heard that his father is a prisoner. His feelings are such that he is fearful he might not do justice to the sufferers. If there were no other surgeons here, he would endeavor to do his duty by them.

April 16.—Mr. Miller, Mrs. Ogden, and nearly all the ladies from Mobile left for Columbus, Miss. I remained, with Mrs. Glassburn, from Natchez. My brother is here, and I have become so much interested in some of the wounded that I could not leave them. Mrs. Ogden was completely worn out; and it is not much to be wondered at, as she, with the rest of us, has had to sleep in any and every place; and as to making our toilet, that was out of the question. I have not undressed since I came here.

This morning, while the ladies were preparing to leave, as their goods and chattels were all mislaid, much noise prevailed in finding them. I was annoyed, as I knew that many of the wounded were within hearing. I thought that it was not strange that surgeons should prefer to have Sisters of Charity to nurse their sick, for they know

19

how to keep quiet. To add to the noise there were a number of washerwomen who had come from New Orleans. A doctor, who I was informed was Dr. Foard, the medical director, was assigning them to the different places in the hospitals. If Pope had been there, I think that he could have made a few additions to his " Ode to Silence."

I dislike very much to see some of the ladies go, as they have been very kind to the sufferers, and I know that they will miss them very much. They go to Columbus, Miss., where are a great many of the wounded. I daily witness the same sad scenes—men dying all around me. I do not know who they are, nor have I time to learn.

April 17.—I was going round as usual this morning, washing the faces of the men, and had got half through with one before I found out that he was dead. He was lying on the gallery by himself, and had died with no one near him. These are terrible things, and, what is more heart-rending, no one seems to mind them. I thought that my patients were all doing well. Mr. Wasson felt better, and knew that he would soon go home. I asked the surgeon who was attending him about his condition, and was much shocked when I learned that neither he nor Mr. Regan would live to see another day. This was a sad trial to me. I had seen many die, but none of them whom I had attended so closely as these two. I felt toward them as I do toward all the soldiers—as if they were my brothers. I tried to control my feelings before Mr. Wasson, as he was so hopeful of getting well, but it was a hard task. He looked at me once and asked me what was the matter; was he going to die? I asked him if he was afraid. He replied no; but he was so young that he would like to live a little longer, and would like to see his father and mother once more. I did what I could to prepare him for the great change which was soon to come over him, but I could not muster courage to tell him that he was going to die. Poor Mr. Regan was wandering in his mind, and I found it useless to talk to him upon the subject of death. I managed to get him to tell me his mother's address. He belonged to the Twenty-second Alabama Regiment.

About dark a strange doctor was visiting the patients. When he came to Mr. Wasson, I was sitting by his bedside. He asked me if this was a relative. I informed him that he was not, but I had been attending to him for some days, and he now seemed like one. Mr. Wasson looked at him and said, " Doctor, I wish you to tell me if I am going to die." The doctor felt his pulse and replied, " Young man, you will never see another day in this world." A pallor passed over his countenance, and for a little while he could not speak. When he did, he looked at me and said, " Sister, I want to meet you in heaven," and then requested me to get a clergyman to visit him. There happened to be one in the hospital. I sent for him, and he prayed and talked with him for some time. Mr. Wasson then asked me if I could not let his brothers know his condition; he had two or three in Corinth. A friend who was with him did all in his power to inform them, so that they could see him before he died, but it was of no avail. They were sick, and we could not ascertain in what hospital they were confined. He was much disappointed in not seeing them. He then asked me to write to his mother, who lives in Grimes County, Texas. He desired me to inform her that he had made his peace with God, and hoped to meet her in that land where all is peace and happiness. He would have rejoiced to have seen her and the rest of his dear relatives before leaving this world, but the Lord had willed it otherwise, and he was resigned.

April 18.—I remained with Mr. Wasson all night. A child could not have been more composed. He told me how good the Lord was in giving him such peace and strength at the last hour. About 4 o'clock A. M. he insisted that I should leave him, as I required rest. He begged so hard that I left him for a little while. When I returned he had breathed his last. One of his companions was with him, and was very attentive—told me that he died as if he was going to sleep. . . .

Mr. Regan died this morning; was out of his mind to the last. . . .

It does seem strange that, amid all the terrible scenes of destruction that we are daily witnessing, we think as little of death as ever, and act as if it was something that might happen to others, but never to ourselves. . . .

Mrs. Lyons left this morning for home. She was very sick; and one of the doctors informed her, if she did not leave immediately, she would certainly die. I know the men whom she has been nursing will miss her very much, as she has been so attentive to them.

While I was giving some sermons to the men to read, I met with Dr. Foster of Natchez, Miss., who is here for the purpose of taking home some wounded men. He looked at the sermons. They were preached by Rev. Dr. Pierce on last fastday, in St. John's Church, Mobile.[7] The first warned us not to put our trust in any thing earthly, but in Him alone who sitteth in the heavens; and, as just as our cause was, if we trusted in man alone, it would come to naught. The other said, as we profess to be a Christian nation, we should act with that forbearance toward our enemies which Christians should always manifest; and, wronged and abused though we be, we must not hate. This task is a hard one; so the author advises us to have hourly upon our lips the language of his text: "Lead us not into temptation, but deliver us from evil." After examining them, Dr. Foster asked me to get some copies for him, as he thought that they would be the means of doing much good in the army.

[7] Henry Niles Pierce, *Sermons Preached in St. John's Church, Mobile, on the 13th of June, 1861, the National Fast Appointed by His Excellency Jefferson Davis* . . . (Mobile, 1861) .

Dr. Smith has taken charge of this hospital. I think that there will be a different order of things now. He is having the house and yard well cleansed. Before this, it was common to have amputated limbs thrown into the yard, and left there.

Mrs. Glassburn and myself started to go to College Hospital, when we met the doctor who spoke to my patient last night, and he went with us. His name is Hughes—is from Lexington, Ky. The walk was very pleasant. Met a general and his staff. The doctor thought it was General Polk—our bishop-general, as he is called. We called at a shed on the way; found it filled with wounded, lying on the floor; some men attending them. All were in the best of spirits. Mrs. Glassburn promised to send them some of our good things. When we arrived at the hospital, we were charmed with the cleanliness and neatness visible on every side. The Sisters of Charity have charge of the domestic part, and, as usual with them, every thing is *parfait*. We were received very kindly by them. One was a friend of Mrs. Glassburn. She took us through the hospital. The grounds are very neatly laid out. Before the war it was a female college. I saw, as his mother requested, Mr. John Lyons, who is sick; he is a member of Ketchum's Battery. The wounded seem to be doing very well. One of the surgeons complained bitterly of the bad management of the railroad, and said that its managers should be punished, as they were the cause of a great deal of unnecessary suffering. They take their own time to transport the wounded, and it is impossible to depend upon them. That is the reason why we see so many sick men lying around the depot. Crossing the depot upon our return, we saw a whole Mississippi regiment sick, awaiting transportation. They looked very badly, and nearly all had a cough.

April 19.—Had quite a number of deaths up-stairs to-day. Jesse H. Faught, Walker County, Ala., and John M. Purdy, Morgan County, Tennessee, were of the number. The latter had his brother with him, who is much grieved because he can not inform his mother of the death of her son, as his home is in possession of the enemy. Another man, by the name of Benjamin Smith, from Memphis, Tenn., and a member of the Sixth Tennessee, Volunteers, died. When I went to see him, I found him in the last agonies of death. I was informed that he was a native of Canada. He was scarcely able to speak; when he did so, he asked me to write to his sister, Mrs. H. Hartman, Arovia, Canada West. I regretted that I did not see him sooner, and felt grieved to see him die so far away from home and kindred—I will not say among strangers—none are who are fighting with us in our sacred cause. May his soul rest in peace! He has lost his life in defense of liberty—that of which his own country is so proud—and when maidens come to deck the graves of our southern patriots, they will not forget one who sacrificed all for them. I have only written the names of those whom I can recollect; many a poor fellow dies of whom I know nothing.

Mrs. Gilmer is leaving us. I am informed that she has done much for the soldiers, having been in hospitals from the commencement of the war. She returns to her home in Memphis. It is rumored that we are going to evacuate that city, and she wishes to see her family before the enemy reaches it.

I received a letter, and a box filled with eggs, crackers, and nice fresh butter, from Miss Lucy Haughton. She also sends a lot of pickles, which the men relish very much. I hope all the ladies in the Confederacy will be as kind; if they could only witness one-half the suffering that we do, I know they would be. I have sometimes felt like making a vow to eat nothing but what was necessary to sustain life till the war is over, so that our soldiers can have the more. When the men are first brought to the hospital, they eat all they can get, but in a few days their wounds begin to tell upon their systems; their appetites leave them, and it is almost impossible to get them to eat any thing. None but those who are the most severely wounded are left here; all are carried to the rear as soon as they are able to be moved.

A young man, by the name of Farmer, of the Sixth Kentucky Regiment, died down-stairs a day or two ago. He is reported to have been very rich. His brother-in-law, Rev. Mr. Cook, was with him, and intends taking his body to his own home in Tennessee, as the young man's home is in the hands of the enemy. I have made the acquaintance of two of his friends, Mr. Chinn and Lieutenant Minor, both from Kentucky. I feel sorry for all from that state, as it has behaved so badly, and for those who are in our army, as they have given up their all for the cause.

I was shocked at what the men have told me about some dead Federals that they saw on the battle-field. They say that on the bands of their hats was written, "Hell or Corinth;" meaning, that they were determined to reach one of the places. Heaven help the poor wretches who could degrade themselves thus. I can not but pity them, and pray that God will turn the hearts of their living comrades. Can such a people expect to prosper? Are they really mad enough to think that they can conquer us—a people who shudder at such blasphemy; who, as a nation, have put our trust in the God of battles, and whose sense of the magnanimous would make us scorn to use such language?

I was much amused to-day at an answer that a Federal captain gave to one of our doctors. The doctor asked him how many men the Federals lost at the battle of Shiloh. He answered, not more than eight hundred. The doctor turned away from him without speaking. I laughed, and said that proved them greater cowards than ever; for if that was the case, why did they not take Corinth, as they had come there for that purpose. I do hope that we will let the Federals have the honor of telling all the untruths, and that we will hold to the truth, let the consequences be what they may—remembering that " where boasting ends true dignity begins." The captain is an intelligent man, and was an editor of a newspaper in Cincinnati. The rest of the officers who were in the room with him have left, except a lieutenant, who is sick.

April 22.—All the patients are being sent away on account of the prospects of a battle; at least, those who are able to be moved.

We have had a good deal of cold, wet weather lately. This is the cause of much sickness. Dr. Hereford, chief surgeon of Ruggles's brigade, has just informed me, that nearly our whole army is sick, and if it were not that the Federals are nearly as bad off as ourselves, they could annihilate us with ease. The doctor related an incident to me, which I think worthy of record. Before the battle of Shiloh, as the brigades and divisions were in battle array, with their banners flaunting in the breeze, Dr. Hereford discovered that General Ruggles's brigade had none. He rode up to him and asked him the reason; just at that moment a rainbow appeared; the general, pointing to it with his sword, exclaimed, " Behold my battle-flag! "

Every one is talking of the impending battle with the greatest indifference. It is strange how soon we become accustomed to all things; and I suppose it is well, as it will do no good to worry about it. Let us do our duty, and leave the rest to God.

It is reported that Fremont is about to reinforce the Federals; I am afraid that it will go hard with us.

April 23.—A young man whom I have been attending is going to have his arm cut off. Poor fellow! I am doing all that I can to cheer him. He says that he knows that he will die, as all who have had limbs amputated in this hospital have died. It is but too true; such is the case. It is said that the reason is that none but the very worst cases are left here, and they are too far gone to survive the shock which the operation gives the frame. The doctors seem to think that the enemy poisoned their balls,[8] as the wounds inflame terribly; but I scarcely think that they are capable of so great an outrage. Our men do not seem to stand half so much as the northerners. Many of the

[8] There is no authenticated case of the use of poisoned balls by either the Union or the Confederate army. Dr. R. Murray, Medical Director of the District of Ohio of the Federal army, wrote in his report after the battle of Shiloh: " It is remarkable that the conical balls extracted, both from our own wounded and the Confederates, were, in almost every instance, bent and twisted, and, in some cases, split. They must be made of softer material than the European minié balls; or, probably the difference may be owing to ours being molded and not pressed." U. S. Surgeon General's Office, *The Medical and Surgical History of the War of the Rebellion* . . . (Washington, 1870) , I, pt. 1, appendix, 39.

doctors are quite despondent about it, and think that our men will not be able to endure the hardships of camp-life, and that we may have to succumb on account of it; but I trust that they are mistaken. None of the prisoners have yet died; this is a fact that can not be denied; but we have had very few of them in comparison with the number of our own men.

April 24.—Mr. Isaac Fuquet, the young man who had his arm cut off, died to-day. He lived only a few hours after the amputation. The operation was performed by Surgeon Chaupin of New Orleans, whose professional abilities are very highly commended. Dr. Hereford was well acquainted with Mr. Fuquet and intends to inform his mother of his death.

It is reported that an engagement is going on at Monterey. A wounded man has just been brought in.

The amputating table for this ward is at the end of the hall, near the landing of the stairs. When an operation is to be performed, I keep as far away from it as possible. To-day, just as they had got through with Mr. Fuquet, I was compelled to pass the place, and the sight I there beheld made me shudder and sick at heart. A stream of blood ran from the table into a tub in which was the arm. It had been taken off at the socket, and the hand, which but a short time before grasped the musket and battled for the right, was hanging over the edge of the tub, a lifeless thing. I often wish I could become as callous as many seem to be, for there is no end to these horrors.

The passage to the kitchen leads directly past the amputating room below stairs, and many a time I have seen the blood running in streams from it.

There is a Mr. Pinkerton from Georgia shot through the head. A curtain is drawn across a corner where he is lying to hide the hideous spectacle, as his brains are oozing out.

April 25.—A rainy, gloomy day, and well accords with the news just heard. New Orleans is in the hands of the enemy. The particulars have not reached us, but I sincerely trust that it was not given up without a great struggle. What a severe trial this will be to the proud people of that place—to have their fair city desecrated by the tread of such a vandal foe. I trust that the day is not far distant when they will be compelled to leave much quicker than they came into it.

Quite a number of General Price's army came last night. They are from the states of Missouri, Arkansas, Texas, and Louisiana, and as brave and daring a set of men as the world has ever seen. I feel that we are now safe in Corinth, and that Fremont may bring as many of his abolition horde as he pleases; they will meet their match.

Troops are coming in from all quarters. A day or two since a regiment arrived, and camped in front of our windows. The men were nicely dressed, and displayed a flag, of which they appeared very proud.

25

They attracted the attention of a number of ladies—and there was many a conjecture as to where they were from. To-day I learned that it was the Twenty-fourth Alabama Regiment, from Mobile. A number of the officers went to Virginia, as privates, in the Third Alabama.

I am getting along very well now. Miss Henderson from Mobile, and Mrs. Noland from Natchez, and myself are the only ladies attending the men up-stairs. There were two others, but Dr. Smith discovered that they had no business here, and sent them off. Mrs. Noland and Miss Henderson are very devoted nurses. Miss Henderson is paying a great deal of attention to a young man by the name of Jones. He is badly wounded in the leg, and the doctors think that he will lose it. Mrs. Noland has some patients very badly wounded, of whom she has taken as much care as if they were her own children. She has a son in another part of the army, and says that, if any thing happens to him, she knows that some good woman will do the same for him that she is now doing for others.

With a few exceptions, all the ladies are doing good service. It is said that there is always a black sheep in every flock: we have ours. We have been eating our meals lately in a small room opening into a large ward. This morning, while at breakfast, I was not a little astonished to hear a very pretty widow say that she had never enjoyed herself so much as she had since she had been here; that, when she left home, she was told that she must try to catch a beau—and she had succeeded. The doctors, I thought, looked amazed, that any woman, at such a time, and in such a place, should be guilty of such heartlessness. Enjoyed herself! when it was impossible to look one way or the other without seeing the most soul-harrowing scenes that it has ever been the lot of mortals to witness; and at that moment the groans of the suffering and dying were entering the room. I looked at the sentinels who were at the door; they, I thought, looked as shocked as we. I trust that such women are very rare.

April 26.—The day has cleared off beautifully. The news of the fall of New Orleans is confirmed. There was no fighting in the city. The forts were taken, and the gunboats came directly up, and threatened to shell it unless it was immediately surrendered. There were so many women and children in it that the authorities were compelled to surrender without striking a blow in its defense. Its loss is a severe one to us, as it commanded the passage of the Mississippi River, and the gunboats can ascend the river and capture any place they wish. I have been told that our forces destroyed all the sugar in the city at the time of the surrender. I do hope that this is true, as I had rather refrain from its use all my life than that the enemy should have it.

Three men have just had limbs amputated. This is so common that it is scarcely noticed. How my heart sickens in contemplating the horrors with which I am surrounded! Our sins must have been great to have deserved such punishment.

Sunday, April 27.—Mr. Johnson and my brother called on me this morning, and we took a walk round Corinth. The day is very beautiful. Nature is putting forth her glories, and smiling, as if in mockery of the passions which are raging in the heart of man, whom God has made a " little lower than the angels," and who would be so if sin did not deface him. Here are two immense armies, ready at any moment to rush upon each other, and deal death and destruction around them.

We visited one of the hospitals, in a church. Dr. Capers was the surgeon in charge; he is from Mississippi. He was very kind, and took us all through it, and showed us some of the most emaciated human beings that I ever beheld. He informed us that they were thus reduced by drinking poisoned whisky, a sad commentary on the maker and vendor. But what will man not do for the god, Mammon? Ruin his fellow-mortals, soul and body!

The hospital was in good order, and the patients looked cheerful. An Irish lady is in it. She is from Louisiana, and, from all I hear, has done much good in the service. She is a woman of strong nerve. She told me that, on the night following the battle of Shiloh, she visited the battle-field in search of her son, who she thought was killed or wounded, but he was neither.

As we have no chaplain, we have no service. I read the Bible and other books to the men, and they are much pleased to have me do it. I have met with none who have not respect for religion. They are mainly Baptists, Methodists, and Presbyterians, and some few Roman Catholics. A young man by the name of Love is here, badly wounded. He is from Texas, and informed me that he was one of nine brothers in the service. Three, I think, were killed in the battle of Manassas. He wishes that he were better, so that he could go into the army again.

April 29.—About one hundred sick men were brought in last night, on their way to another hospital. We gave them coffee, bread, and meat, with which they were much pleased. Some of them were too sick to eat this, so we gave these the few eggs we had.

General Sterling Price, with a part of his army, has arrived. He is in this hospital. We were all introduced to him. He gave us his left hand, as his right was disabled from a wound received at the battle of Elkhorn. I told him that I felt that we were safe in Corinth now, since he and his brave followers had arrived. He gave me a very dignified bow, and, I thought, looked at me as if he *thought* that I was talking a great deal of nonsense. He was not behind his sex in complimenting the ladies for the sacrifices they are making in doing their duty. I have heard so much of that lately, that I sometimes wonder if the southern women never did their duty before. I meant what I said to the general, and I felt quite proud of the honor I enjoyed in shaking hands with him whose name has become a household word with all admirers of true patriotism, and whose deeds of heroism in the West have endeared him to his followers, so that they look on him more as a father than any thing else.

27

In the afternoon he visited the patients. Many of them were men who had fought under him, and all were delighted to see him. One of them, Captain Dearing, was wounded at the battle of Shiloh. He was quarter-master in Blythe's Mississippi Regiment, and when the battle came off could not resist the temptation of engaging in it. He is badly wounded in two places, but is doing well. He is from Kentucky, but is a native of the Emerald Isle. I can not help contrasting these men with those born in the South, they seem to be able to endure physically so much more than the southerners. We have had quite a number of them, and I do not recollect that any have died.

April 30.—I saw General Price when he rode to camp. I think he is one of the finest looking men on horseback that I have ever seen. I have a picture of Lord Raglan in the same position, and I think that he and General Price are the image of each other. I showed the picture to some of the doctors, and they agreed with me. General Price is in bad health, but could not be induced to stay longer with us, as his abode is with his soldiers in the camp, where he shares their sorrows and joys. It is this that has so endeared him to them. Missouri may well be proud of her gallant son.

The hospital is nicely fixed up; every thing is as neat and clean as can be in this place.

Mrs. Glassburn has received a great many wines and other delicacies from the good people of Natchez. I believe they have sent every thing—furniture as well as edibles. We have dishes in which to feed the men, which is a great improvement. The food is much better cooked. We have negroes for cooks, a good baker, a nice dining-room, and eat like civilized people. If we only had milk for the patients, we might do very well.

There is a young man here taking care of his brother, who is shot through the jaw. The brother procures milk from one of the farm-houses near, and had it not been for this I believe the sick man would have died of starvation. We have a few more such, and they have to be fed like children. One young man, to whom one of the ladies devotes her whole time, has had his jaw-bone taken out. We have a quantity of arrow-root, and I was told that it was useless to prepare it, as the men would not touch it. I thought that I would try them, and now use gallons of it daily. I make it quite thin, and sometimes beat up a few eggs and stir in while hot; then season with preserves of any kind—those that are a little acid are the best—and let stand until it becomes cold. This makes a very pleasant and nourishing drink; it is good in quite a number of diseases; will ease a cough; and is especially beneficial in cases of pneumonia. With good wine, instead of the preserves, it is also excellent; I have not had one man to refuse it, but I do not tell them of what it is made.

Our army is being reinforced from all quarters. The cars are coming and going constantly, and the noise is deafening. It is a blessing that

28

our men are not nervous, or the noise would kill them. We are strongly fortifying this place. I hope we will soon gain a victory; but our forces can not tempt the Yankees to fight.

We are told by Dr. Smith to do what is necessary for the prisoners, but talk as little as possible to them.[9] The captain from Cincinnati is still here; a very sick lieutenant is in the same room. I believe he is one of the captain's officers. I have to attend him. A few mornings since, when I was visiting him, the captain stated that there was good news in the papers. (He is allowed to read all the southern papers.) I asked what it was. He answered that a proposition had been made for the exchange of prisoners; and that it came from our side. I remarked that all humane proposals came from our side; and that I did not think that his would be magnanimous enough to accept it. He said he hoped they would, so that he could see his home once more. I pray so too, as I know that our men who are prisoners have been enduring extreme hardship.

Every one is still down-hearted about New Orleans, as its fall has divided the Confederacy by opening the Upper Mississippi River to the enemy. All praise the spirited answer given by the mayor when ordered to surrender the city. He said that the citizens of New Orleans yielded to physical force alone, and that they still maintained their allegiance to the Confederate States; and upon refusal to pull down the state flag from the city hall, Commodore Farragut threatened to bombard the city. The mayor replied, the people of New Orleans would not degrade themselves by the humiliating act of lowering their own flag, and that there was no possible way for the women and children to leave; so he would have to do his worst. We can not but admire such spirited behavior; but it is nothing but what I expected from the proud Louisianians. Indeed, I had no idea that they would give up their much-prized city as easily as they did, but thought that it would have to be taken street by street. When all is known, I trust that the people will not be blamed. A number of Louisiana troops are here, who are much enraged about it. General Lovell, who was in command, is severely censured, but I trust he is not in fault.

We are still busy; wounded men are constantly brought in. To-day, two men had each a leg amputated. It is supposed that both will die.

General Van Dorn, with a number of his troops, has just arrived.

May 1.—A bright, beautiful day. I do not feel well. Every one is complaining; quite a number of the ladies and doctors are sick.

---

[9] From the other side of the lines Surgeon Murray wrote: "Nearly one thousand of the Confederate wounded fell into our hands, and I am happy to say that our medical officers and men showed them the same attention that they did our own; indeed the men were more ready to nurse and to attend to the wants of the enemy than to our own men. I regret to say, that they showed the utmost apathy and indifference to the suffering of their fellow soldiers, and were, with difficulty, forced into doing them any service, while their curiosity and wish to converse with the wounded Confederates, in some measure, overcame their inertness." *Ibid.*

Corinth is more unhealthy than ever. The cars have just come in, loaded outside and inside with troops. They are Price's and Van Dorn's men, and are from Texas, Arkansas, Louisiana, and Missouri. Poor fellows! they look as if they had seen plenty of hard service, which is true. They are heroes of Oakhill, Elkhorn, and other battles. I have been informed that in their marches through the West they have endured all kinds of hardships; going many days with nothing but parched corn to eat, and walking hundreds of miles, through frost and snow, without shoes. Those on the outside of the cars carried an old shattered flag, of which they seemed to be very proud. I was much astonished that the men who were at the depot did not give these war-worn veterans and their flag one cheer of welcome. I had hard work to keep from giving them one myself. I thought that the southern people were more demonstrative, and I remarked so to a gentleman who was standing near me. He replied that we had become so much accustomed to these things that we did not mind them.

The two men who had their limbs amputated yesterday died during the night. Decatur Benton, from Decatur County, Ala., died to-day. He was wounded at the battle of Shiloh. He had erysipelas upon his head and face, and had been out of his mind some time before his death. He was in his seventeenth year.

May 2.—Mr. Ogden, a member of Captain Ketchum's Battery, called on me this morning. He has been discharged from that company, and is going to Mobile to join the engineering department; the one in which he served while in the British army. From all I can learn, he has been a brave and good soldier.

In the afternoon, Mr. J[ohnson] called; he, Miss [Henderson], Dr. Herrick, and myself went to pay a visit to the Twenty-first Alabama Regiment. After spending some time in trying to discover its where-abouts, we learned that it was too far distant for us to go. We had a very pleasant ramble in the woods. I had no idea that the country around Corinth was so pretty—it being quite hilly. . . .

A company of " dire artillery's clumsy car," not " tugged by sluggish oxen," but drawn by fine-looking horses, passed us. The scene was an impressive one. Nature looked so calm, as if in contrast with the terrible war-monsters before us. I could not look at them without thinking that, ere long, they might be belching forth their iron hail; dealing death and destruction; bringing woe to many a heart and household. General Polk and his staff passed; he looks every inch a soldier. I am told that he is much beloved in camp.

May 3.—A very warm day. I am obliged to stop writing some letters, as I hear heavy cannonading; the sound makes me quite nervous; this is the first time that I have ever heard firing in battle. I suppose my brother is in it.

Seven o'clock P. M., and a number of wounded have just been

30

brought in. There was a skirmish at the intrenchments. My brother is not hurt, or I should have known it by this time.

Sunday morning, May 4.—I have just seen Generals Price and Van Dorn review their troops. They were at too great a distance to distinguish the different regiments; but the sight was quite imposing, as column after column marched along, with their flags flying in the breeze. But little glitter was worn on the dress of the men; they did not need it; we all knew that they carried with them hearts that all the power of the foe could neither bend nor break, and without which all glitter and gold are mere dross. The cavalry appeared splendid; no knights of olden time rode their horses with loftier mien than did these warriors. I enjoyed the scene until the ambulances passed in review, with their white flags, denoting their use. This cast a blight over the whole.

Evening.—Our troops are returning. They offered battle to the foe, but, as usual, it was not accepted. They never will fight when there is any thing like an equal force to oppose them.

It has turned cold and rainy. We have just been looking at some of our troops, who are camping on a hill within sight of the hospital. They have no tents or shelter of any kind, and look very deplorable. It makes us miserable to look at them; but we can not aid them in any way.

I have spent the day talking and reading to the men; they like to hear us read to them, but they do not seem to care much for reading themselves. Mr. McLean of Mobile has given me a number of copies of the Illustrated London News, with a full account of the Crimean war. I thought if any thing would interest them these would; but they look at the pictures, and throw them down as unworthy of notice. They seem to have no ambition to know any thing outside of their own country. I regret this, as we are all creatures of imitation, and if we do not know how others have suffered and fought for freedom, we will not know how to imitate them. . . .

May 5.—Mrs. Ogden is here with four Mobile ladies; the others have returned to their homes. The ladies who are with her are Mrs. May, Miss Wolf, Miss Murphy, and Mrs. Millward. They are on their way to Rienzi to attend the patients. I am glad that they are going, as they will be the means of doing much good.

We have a boy here, named Sloan, from Texas, and a member of the Texas Rangers. He is only thirteen years of age, and lost a leg in a skirmish. He is as happy as if nothing was the matter, and he was at home playing with his brothers and sisters. His father is with him, and is quite proud that his young son has distinguished himself to such a degree, and is very grateful to the ladies for the kind attention which they bestow upon him.

A few days ago a number of wounded men were brought in. In

31

going round, as usual, to see if I knew any one, I saw a man who seemed to have suffered a great deal. His eyes were closed, and while I was looking at him he opened them, and said, with a feeble voice, " Is not this a cruel war." I requested him to keep quiet. As I left him, a gentleman approached me and remarked, " I see that you have been talking to my friend. He is going to die, and we can ill spare such men. He is one of the bravest and best men in the army." He informed me that his name was Smith, and at the time of the fight was acting quartermaster of the Twenty-fifth Tennessee Regiment, and that he was also a Methodist minister. After I had given him a cup of tea, I asked one of the surgeons what he thought of his condition. He replied that I could do what I pleased for him, as he could not possibly live more than twenty-four hours. After he was shot, he carried a wounded man off the battlefield. He himself was then placed on horseback. The horse, being wild, threw him. He was then placed in a wagon, and carried some four or five miles, over an extremely rough road. From all this he lost much blood. Notwithstanding the opinion of the surgeons, he is improving.

I have just received a box of " good things " for the patients from the kind people of Mobile. My friend, Mr. McLean, has sent his share. I am so grateful for them. If they only knew or could realize one half the suffering that we daily witness, they would do more.

Poor Mr. Jones, the young lad whom Miss Henderson is attending, has had a leg amputated to-day. He conversed very calmly about it before it was done, and seemed to think that he would not survive the operation. He has told Miss Henderson all about his people, and what she must tell them if he should die. She has nursed him as carefully as if she had been his own sister. He loved to have some of us read the Bible to him.

We have no chaplain to attend the sick and dying men; they often ask for one. I have thought much of this, and wonder why chaplains are not appointed for the hospitals. I think that if there is one place more than another where they should be, it is one like this; not for the dying alone, but for the moral influence it would exert upon the living. We profess to be a Christian people, and should see that all the benefits of Christianity are administered to our dying soldiers.

May 6.—Mr. Jones is dead; he was eighteen years of age. He died the death of a Christian; was a brave soldier; true to his God and country. Miss Henderson sat up all night with him. She is endeavoring to procure a coffin for him. We have none now in which to bury the dead, as the Federals have destroyed the factory at which they were made. At one time, I thought that it was dreadful to have the dead buried without them; but there is so much suffering among the living, that I pay little heed to those things now. It matters little what becomes of the clay after the spirit has left it. Men who die as ours do, need " no useless coffin " to enshrine them. . . .

May 7.—A beautiful day. The troops are marching in the direction of Rienzi; it is supposed that the enemy are trying to flank our army, but I do not fear while we have such vigilant generals as Beauregard and Bragg to watch them.

I had a slight quarrel with our ward-master. One of the men, lately wounded, was in a room where were some who had occupied it since the battle of Shiloh. One of them—a mere boy—was wasted to a skeleton; his back was covered with bed-sores. Poor child! he was very fretful. I observed that it annoyed the new patient, and requested Dr. Allen, who is very kind to the soldiers, to allow me to have him removed to a room by himself. He kindly gave his consent. While doing it, the ward-master objected; but as I had obtained leave, I had him removed, and he commenced to improve immediately.

I have been through the ward to see if the men are in want of any thing; but all are sound asleep under the influence of morphine. Much of that is administered; more than for their good, and must injure them. I expressed this opinion to one of the doctors; he smiled, and said it was not as bad as to let them suffer. . . .

May 8.—A number of men, wounded in a skirmish, have been brought in to-day. The surgeons dressed their wounds; there is always plenty for us to do without that. We wash their hands and faces, which is a great treat to them, as they are covered with dust; we bathe their wounds, which are always inflamed, and give them something refreshing to drink.

O, I do feel so glad that I am here, where I can be of some little service to the poor fellows; and they are so grateful for every little attention paid them.

We get up before sunrise in the morning; take a cup of coffee, as the doctors inform us that unless we do so we will be sick. We then give the men their "toddy"; wash their faces and hands, and then furnish them their breakfast.

May 9.—A great many wounded men, both Federal and Confederate, were brought in to-day. About twenty-five of ours were shot through mistake. A fine-looking Federal captain is wounded in three or four places. His head and face are tied up, and he can not speak. He has a Bible, on the back of which is printed the Union flag. Some of us were looking at it; one of the ladies remarked that it was still sacred in her eyes. This astonished me, after the suffering which we had seen it the innocent cause of. I said that it was the most hateful thing which I could look at; as every stripe in it recalled to my mind the gashes that I had witnessed upon our men. I have conversed with a number of the prisoners; they all express the same opinion as the others, that they dislike Lincoln and the abolitionists as much as we do, but they are fighting for the Union. What a delusion!

I am no politician. I must own to ignorance in regard to federal or state rights; but I think I have a faint idea of the meaning of the word

" union." According to Webster and other authorities, it is concord, agreement, and conjunction of mind. We all know how little of that and happiness exists in a forced union of man and wife, where there is neither love nor congeniality of feeling. Can these men really think it when they say it? Are they so blind as to think, even if they succeed, that it can ever bring happiness to them or us? Is it not exactly the same as the case of the marriage state? They must strike out the word union, and have in its stead monarchy or anarchy; one of these, perhaps, would be better. Why, the Czar of Russia lays no higher claim to the right to rule his empire than do these men the right to govern us. Again, supposing they do succeed in subjugating us, have they forgotten that such a thing is not on record, where the Anglo-Saxon race has ever been held in bondage? Why, it would be as much to their disgrace as ours. Are we not the same race? Let them ask themselves what they would do were the case reversed; were we the aggressors, and demanded of them what they now demand of us. I think we all know their answer. It would be that given by the immortal Washington to the haughty monarch of England, when he attempted to make slaves of men who had determined to be free. Grant that we had no lawful right to secede; that I know nothing about, and never was more grieved than when I knew that we had done so; not from any wrong or unlawfulness, but from the fact that, united, we were stronger than we would be when separated; and I also feared the bloodshed which might ensue. If we were sinners in that respect, what were our forefathers when they claimed the right to secede from the British crown? Calling it fighting for the Union, is about as false as the love of the abolitionist for the negro, and we all know what that is. No happiness can exist in union without concord; and there can be no concord where any two people are so diametrically opposed to each other. All this I have repeated to them often, but I might as well have saved myself the trouble, for they are as blind to reason as any bigoted, self-deluded people ever were.

I was introduced to General Hindman, who dined with us to-day. He is still lame from a wound received at the battle of Shiloh. He is a peculiar-looking man; his hair is light and long, floating around his shoulders. I always imagine, when I see a man with his hair so long, that there is a vacancy in his cranium. I believe that it is Shakespeare who says that what a man lacked in brains he had in his hair. As the former is an article that we have much use for, and whose workings are much needed at present among our leading men, I can not but regret that outward indications in this instance were unfavorable. But perhaps this is only my prejudice against foppishness and every thing effeminate in men. General Hindman may be an exception to this rule, and I trust he is.

May 10.—The hospital is again filled with the badly wounded. There is scarcely an hour during which they are not coming in from skirmishes. I sat up all night to see that the nurses performed their duties properly, and assisted in bathing the wounds of the men. They all rested quite well, excepting one, who was severely wounded in the hand. He suffered a great deal. One died suddenly this morning. I gave him his toddy; he was then quite cheerful; and I went to give him his breakfast, but his bunk was empty—he was dead and gone. He was wounded in the arm. The doctor desired him to have it amputated, which he would on no account permit. The result was hemorrhage ensued, and he bled to death before assistance could be rendered. I did not learn his name, nor any thing about him.

These things are very sad. A few evenings since, Dr. Allen was conversing about the horrors with which we are surrounded. He remarked that it was hard to think that God was just in permitting them. " Shall we receive good at the hands of God, and shall we not receive evil? " We, as a nation, have been so prosperous, that we forget that it was from him that we derived our benefits. He often sends us sorrows to try our faith. He will not send us more than we are able to bear. How patiently the soldiers endure their trials! Who dare say that strength is not given them from on high? Let us do our part, and, whatever happens, not lose trust in him, " for he doeth all things well "; and, in the language of Bishop Wilmer, " May the trials through which we are passing serve to wean us from the world, and move us to set our affections on things above! " " May we bear the rod, and him who hath appointed it! " Dr. Allen was some time with General Floyd, in Western Virginia, and remarked that he had seen nothing here to compare with what the men endured there. They were in the mountains, where it was impossible to get any thing for them.

We gained quite a victory yesterday. Price's and Van Dorn's troops were engaged. We saw them as they marched out in the morning. They crossed a bridge opposite our bed-room window.

Sunday, May 11.—A very hot, sultry day. I am very tired, as I have all to attend, the other ladies being sick; many of the nurses are sick also. It is more unhealthy now than ever, and unless some change takes place I fear that we will all die.

As there is much noise and confusion constantly here, it is almost impossible to collect one's thoughts. I miss the calm of the holy Sabbath more than any thing. I have read and talked to the men, and it astonishes me to see how few are members of the Church. They all seem to think and know that it is their duty to belong to it, but still they remain out of it. How much more will they have to answer for than those who have never known God, and have not enjoyed the privileges of the gospel. " He that confesseth me before men, him will I confess before my Father which is in heaven."

May 12.—Two men died this morning, Mr. Adams and Mr. Brennan, from Coffee County, Alabama. Mr. Brennan was wounded. As a friend, Mr. Adams came to nurse him. Both were taken sick this morning, and died after a few hours' illness.

We have the same sad scenes to witness as ever—sick and wounded men lying on the platform at the depot, night and day, and we are not allowed to take them any thing to eat. Dr. Smith is obliged to prohibit it, as it is contrary to orders, and he has not the food to spare for them.

A terrible circumstance happened a few nights since. Our druggist, Dr. Sizemore, went out about 9 o'clock to see some one. When within a short distance from the hospital he heard groans; went to the place from which they proceeded, and found a box-car, that had been switched off the track, filled with wounded men, some dead and others dying, and not a soul with them to do any thing for them. The conductor was censured, but I think whoever sent the men off are in fault for not sending proper persons to take care of them. If this kind of treatment of our brave men continues much longer, I fear that we will have none to fight for us, for such a total disregard of human life must have a demoralizing effect. If we had many more such kind-hearted officers as Dr. Smith, our men would suffer little through neglect. None leave this hospital without he is certain they can go comfortably, and have plenty of nourishment to last them on their journey. I have seen him, many a time, go to the cars himself, to see that they were properly put in. I am informed that he spends every cent of his pay for their comfort. He will reap his reward.

May 13.—Our troops have gone out this morning to endeavor to tempt the enemy to fight, but they will not leave their intrenchments. It is reported that they have been heavily reinforced, but, with all that, I have no doubt that if they would only fight our men would whip them.

We have a member of the Twenty-first Alabama Regiment from Mobile, who was badly wounded at the battle of Shiloh. There is no hope of his recovery. Every thing has been done for him that it is possible to do. He is a sad spectacle; he is so worn and wasted. He is a German, and can not understand any thing said to him by us. He has no relatives in this country.

Conversing with one of the patients, a very intelligent gentleman, I asked him what he thought of President Davis. He thought that he was a good man, but not the one for the place. I did not ask him his reason for this opinion. He is the first man that I have heard say this, and I hope that he is mistaken, as at this time the country needs a great man at its head.

May 15.—Heavy firing was heard to-day, and I felt certain that a battle had commenced. I was in the kitchen when I first heard it, and was compelled to stop what I was doing, as the sound makes me unfit for any thing.

May 16.—The fast-day set apart by the President. I hope that it will be duly observed. I believe that it is well kept in the army. There has been no show of keeping it in this hospital; the old excuse is given—" too much to do."

A few evenings since we came very near being burned out. While the ladies downstairs were making pads for the wounded expected next day—we use hundreds of them daily—the cotton took fire and communicated to some of the ladies' dresses. A gentleman extinguished it before any serious damage occurred. I was attending some patients at the time, and was certain from the noise that the enemy had come to storm the hospital, for which I was laughed at considerably.

Dr. Griffin of Kentucky and Dr. Benedick of New Orleans are both sick.

Sunday, May 18.—A very hot day. Our patients are nearly all gone. Captain Dearing left to-day. He is in a fair way to recover. He was one of the worst of the wounded. Three of the ladies are very sick. Miss Marks is not expected to live. She has made up her mind to that effect, and is perfectly resigned. She is a member of the Episcopal Church.

May 19.—A gloom seems to hang over every body, as if something dreadful was going to happen. No news of a battle yet. It would not surprise me if none took place here. We will be compelled to leave soon, as this place is becoming daily more sickly.

Mr. Smith has just left for one of the hospitals below. He is rapidly improving. So much for the opinions of doctors! but the best of us may be mistaken sometimes.

May 21.—News has just reached us that the battle has commenced in earnest. A number of our surgeons have been ordered to the battle-field. May God give us the victory! I feel confident that if we could gain one here the war would soon be over, and that we would be recognized by foreign nations. I can not see why they do not now recognize us. We certainly can and will be free. My only wish for them to do so is to stop bloodshed, as I think, if they would do it, the North would be compelled to let us alone.

I have just been informed that the Yankee gunboats have passed Fort Morgan. I hope, if true, that Mobile will be laid in ashes before the foot of the vandal foe is permitted to desecrate it. They have not the same excuse that the people of New Orleans had—a large population of women and children; and then we have an outlet which they did not have.

Miss Marks is still very low. I feel very sorry to see her die in this terrible place; but it matters little where we die, so that we are prepared.

May 22.—No battle occurred yesterday. Every one is confident that if the enemy would only fight, we would *whip them soundly.* They are digging intrenchments closer and closer, and could shell Corinth at any hour. Some are not more than two and a half miles from us. We are beginning to feel a little nervous at the prospect of a shell

37

waking us up some morning; certainly not a pleasant one to contemplate.

A prisoner is here, who eats at the table with us. He is a Presbyterian minister. He makes some very provoking remarks. Dr. Smith has advised us to take no notice of them, and say as little as possible. This appears hard, as nearly every one at the table has suffered some wrong at the hands of him and his people; nearly all their homes are in the hands of the enemy.

Dr. Sizemore has just received word of a young brother who has died in a northern prison, and of the ill treatment of the chaplain of his regiment, an inoffensive old man of more than seventy years, who had gone with the regiment more as a father than any thing else. This old man was imprisoned as if he were a common felon. Dr. Sizemore, knowing all this, has to endure the presence of this man, and see him treated as if he were one of our best friends. I must say that we are carrying out the commands of our blessed Savior; and how proud I am of it! May we be enabled to do the same to the end; and, above all things, not to retaliate upon the innocent, for God has said, " Vengeance is mine, and I will repay." I was seated next to the prisoner to-day. He says that he is an Englishman. I would like to think that he is telling an untruth, as few Englishmen side with tyranny. But I expect that he has been long enough with the Yankees to imbibe some of their barbarous notions. He expressed the opinion that the southern people were not united. I remarked that if he would go through the state of Mississippi alone, he would change his mind, as I believe that if the men did not fight, the women would. But there will be no need of the latter, as the men will not fail to do their duty.

We requested Dr. Smith to permit us to pay him back for the impertinent remarks he had made to us. He granted permission, and stated that he would reprimand us in his presence. As soon as the foe made his appearance, some of the ladies commenced on him. Dr. Smith said, " The ladies are very hard on you." He replied with a very submissive air, " If it pleases them, I have no objection." Mrs. Glassburn, who was at the head of the table, observed, " It does not please us; but I will tell you what will: when we know that every Yankee is laid low in the ground, then we will be pleased indeed." He made no reply, and must have felt the force of the remark. At any other time it would have been a barbarous one; but at the present it was charitable, and one that we all felt, if realized, would not only be a blessing to us, but to humanity.

May 23.—Have had two very nice men here, wounded—a doctor and a captain. They are friends of Mrs. Glassburn. Dr. Smith sent them to Rienzi, where the Mobile ladies are. Mrs. Glassburn visited them, and came back perfectly delighted with the hospital arrangements there. She says that Mrs. Ogden is an excellent manager. I am glad of this, as she has had a great deal of opposition from surgeons, as all of the ladies have who have desired to go into hospitals. I can not see what else we can do, as the war is certainly ours as well as that of the men. We can not fight, so must take care of those who do.

I think as soon as surgeons discover that ladies are really of service, that prejudice will cease to exist. The patients are delighted to have us, and say that we can cause them to think of the dearest of places to them now—home.

Miss Marks is a little better, and has been sent to Okolona. The other two ladies who were sick have returned to Mobile.

Every corner of the hospital is clean, and ready for patients. The last of my patients died this morning. He was a German, named Ernest; was wounded at Shiloh. He wandered a good deal in his mind; but just before he died he sent for Dr. Smith, and requested him to write to his wife, and send her all the money he had. She lived on Magazine Street, New Orleans.

One of the saddest sights witnessed are two Federals, who have been here since the battle of Shiloh. One has had his arm, the other his leg amputated. They are seventeen and eighteen years of age, respectively. They look very pitiful, dying among strangers, far away from their homes and relatives. They have been cared for the same as our own; but that is not all that is wanted. They need sympathy, and of that character which it is impossible for us to extend to them, as they came here with the full intention of taking all that is dear to us. They may have been conscientious, and thought that they were doing their duty, but we are of a different opinion, and it will be some time before we change. They will soon die; both are religious. I never look at them without thinking of the thousands of our poor men who are in the same condition in the North. I do sincerely trust that they are as well treated as these poor fellows have been.

Dr. Nott, with several other surgeons, has examined the hospital. He looked well. He has lost a son in the war.

Sunday, May 25.—A bright, beautiful day, but very cold. We have been compelled to have fires in our rooms. Last evening I saw the ubiquitous chieftain, John H. Morgan. He is colonel of a Kentucky regiment, and one of the bravest and most daring of men. It was late when I saw him; so could not judge of his appearance. He had a crowd of admirers following him; he is fairly worshiped. Dr. Smith has just been telling us that he would not be surprised if we had to leave Corinth at a moment's notice, as there is danger of being shelled at any time. For some days back, stores have been moved to the rear in large quantities, which he thinks indicates an evacuation, or important move of some kind.

May 26.—This morning I visited Mrs. Williamson and Mrs. Crocker, who came from Mobile with us. They are in a hospital at the Corinth House. I saw a Mrs. Newsom.[10] I do not recollect that I was ever more

[10] Mrs. Ella King Newsom (later Trader) is the best known of the hospital matrons of the Army of Tennessee. She was born in Brandon, Mississippi, the

struck with a face at first sight than hers. It expressed more purity and goodness than I had ever seen before. . . .

I asked Mrs. Williamson who she was. She informed me that she was a rich widow from Arkansas, and had surrendered all the comforts of home to do what she could for the suffering of our army. She had been with it from the commencement of the war, and had spent a great deal of money. Mrs. Williamson also informed me that her face did not belie the goodness and purity of her heart; and that she was a Christian in the truest sense of the word. I hope that we have many such among us. I can not imagine why it is that I have heard so little about her. Is it because goodness and beauty are so common that Mrs. Newsom is not worth talking about, or is it that we do not properly appreciate what is good and lovely? As soon as Miss Nightingale went to the Crimean war, the whole world resounded with her praises; and here I have been nearly two months, and have scarcely heard Mrs. Newsom's name mentioned.

May 27.—We are all packed up, and intend leaving this morning. Mrs. Glassburn and nearly all the ladies are going to Brookhaven. I intend going to Okolona, and there remain until I learn in which direction the army will move.

We have seen many sad sights and much suffering since we came to this place; still, I shall ever look back on these two months with sincere gratification, and feel that I have lived for something.

The surgeons, one and all, have proved themselves kind and attentive to the brave men whom they have had under their care. The hospital is in perfect order, ready for the reception of patients. I visited Corinth Hospital this morning; they were not thinking of leaving, and had quite a number of wounded men. There I met Mrs. Palmer of Mobile, who had a son in the Twenty-first Alabama Regiment. She had visited the camp the day before with refreshments for the soldiers. She informed me that there were numbers of sick yet in camp, and if we left, she could not conceive how they could be moved.

---

daughter of Baptist minister T. S. N. King. She was raised in Arkansas and married Dr. Frank Newsom. Widowed before the outbreak of the War, she was in 1861 superintending the education of her younger sisters at Winchester, Tennessee. She soon volunteered her services and her considerable means to the use of the hospitals of Memphis. After an apprenticeship there, she began at Bowling Green a career of war work which took her through the major campaigns of the Army of Tennessee. Through her social position, her effective personality, and her acceptance as an equal by the general officers with whom she was associated (General W. J. Hardee in particular), she was—much in the Nightingale tradition —a powerful influence in furthering the status of nursing in the Confederacy. Brief sketches of her appear in Matthew Page Andrews' *Women of the South in War Times* (Baltimore, 1920), 131-44, and in Miss Cumming's *Gleanings from Southland*, 271-75. J. Fraise Richard's *The Florence Nightingale of the Southern Army* (New York and Baltimore, 1914) is wholly about her. None of these treatments, however, is a satisfactory coverage of her career.

‡‡

II: OKOLONA

‡‡

May 28.—Arrived at Okolona yesterday. I am staying at Judge Thornton's. The place is much changed since we were last here; it is filled with refugees, and sick and wounded soldiers. Mrs. Thornton has every corner of her house filled with the latter. I am informed that all private dwellings in the place are in the same condition.

Two ladies came from Corinth with me. The cars were very much crowded. I heard a gentleman, who sat near me, recite a poem to his friend, and say that he hoped that our people would be imbued with the same patriotic spirit that was in it. I took the liberty of asking him what it was. He informed me that it was the Battle of Killie-crankie, and could be found in Aytoun's " Lays of Scottish Cavaliers." This gentleman was from Missouri, and had been with the army of General Price during its campaign in the West. The tales he related of the sufferings of these gallant men were heartrending. For weeks they marched through frost and snow, with scarcely any thing to eat; the wounded and sick were left on the road side, and if cared for it was by mere chance. The men scarcely know what to do with themselves now, as they are in heaven compared to where they had been. He told me that in visiting the hospitals in Memphis, when he saw the great care which was bestowed upon our men, contrasted with the scenes which he had witnessed in the wilds of Missouri and Arkansas, it made him sad. He related one incident which affected him more than all others. A man was dying—one of the noblest looking that he had ever seen. A lady was bending over him, causing him to repeat the Lord's Prayer, as he had doubtless done a thousand times, when a child, at his mother's knee. The whole scene was one of the most impressive that he had ever witnessed. He said that he had never been so deeply impressed with the grandeur and beauty of this prayer. I could have listened all day long, hearing him tell of the daring exploits of Price and his gallant army.

The weather is oppressively warm, and I do not feel very well; but hearing that John Morgan was to pass, I could not resist the temptation of seeing so great a lion; for he is one of the greatest of the age. I was introduced to him by Mrs. Jarboe. I remarked to him that I regretted returning home without seeing Kentucky; that I had left home with the intention of seeing Cincinnati before I went back. He spoke very hopefully, and said that I would be there soon, as ere long the way would be open for all southerners. I then stated that I hoped to hear much of him, and the good that he would do our cause. He replied that he wished that he might hear of himself twenty years hence. I answered that if prayer would save him, he would be preserved, as I knew that many were offered up for him, along with those for the rest of our brave defenders. He is extremely modest. I paid him one or two compliments—deserved ones—and he blushed like a schoolgirl. He has a fine, expressive countenance; his eye reminded me of a description of Burns by Walter Scott. He related one or two of his adventures, and his eyes "fairly glowed with animation." He told us about a train of cars which he had captured in Tennessee, and that the ladies on the train were as frightened as if he intended to eat them. He said, "You know that I would not do that." He related a very amusing adventure he had had lately at Corinth. He made a call on General Buell in disguise. In the course of conversation with General Buell, he informed him that John Morgan was in Corinth. General Buell answered that he knew better; that he knew where he was; he was in Kentucky. Morgan has great command over his features; can disguise himself, and go where he pleases without being discovered.[1]

When the train left, the men gave him three cheers. He looked abashed, and blushed again. Mrs. Thornton said that she had rather see him than any of our great men.

May 29.—In company with a lady, I visited the General Hospital. Dr. Caldwell has improved much since my last visit here, as he granted us permission to go through it, and has *condescended* to have one lady—Mrs. Woodall—in his hospital. I was introduced to her, and tendered my services, but she did not accept them. I should not think that it was possible for her to do one third part of the work necessary. I am told that there are no less than two thousand patients in the place.

Quite a number of new buildings have been erected—large wooden

[1] Miss Cumming seems to have been completely captivated by General Morgan. That she followed his subsequent career with constant interest is apparent from later entries in her journal. The story of his conversation with General Buell is not supported in Basil W. Duke's *History of Morgan's Cavalry* (Cincinnati, 1867), though Duke does say, "Once or twice Captain Morgan passed himself as a Federal officer, in close vicinity to their camps, but this ruse could not be repeated often with success." p. 95. He tells a somewhat different story of the capture of the train, 165-66. Mrs. Irby Morgan, a kinswoman of the General, relates his anecdote of the train in much the same words as Miss Cumming on pp. 77-79 of her *How It Was* (Nashville, 1892). Sally Rochester Ford gives a fictional version of the incident in her *Raids and Romance of Morgan and His Men* (2d ed., Mobile, 1864), 107-109. The story of Morgan's later raid into Indiana and his subsequent capture and escape from the Columbus, Ohio, prison is related in a Confederate version in Samuel Chester Reid's *A Full Account of the Capture and Wonderful Escape of Gen. John H. Morgan, with Captain T. Henry Hines . . .* (Atlanta, 1864).

42

sheds, well ventilated, and capable of holding from twenty-five to thirty patients each. The part which we visited looked very well, but there is certainly room for improvement. We were shown the bread which the patients eat; it was black and sour; but as Mrs. Woodall has been here but a few days, she has not had time to improve matters. It is said that an improvement is visible already.

We met a young man from Alabama at the doctor's office, by the name of Harry Gordon. He was attending his captain, who was very sick, and was acquainted with my brother, whom he had seen a few days before. We met many of our old patients in the hospital, who were delighted to see us. There is a great lack of shade-trees, and it is a serious want.

It is impossible to learn any thing relative to our army at Corinth.

It is reported that the Federals have taken Booneville, burned the depot, captured two hundred of our men who were very sick, and that quite a number of sick were burned. This last I scarcely think possible. I can not think that the enemy are capable of any thing so cruel. Rumor is busy with her many tongues. I am anxious to learn the truth. Mrs. Ogden is about ten miles beyond Booneville; I hope nothing has happened to her.

May 31.—I went to the cars this afternoon to see if I could hear any thing of Mrs. Ogden and her party. I met Dr. Wm. Hughes. He informed me that Corinth was evacuated, and that we had saved almost every thing. This move is thought to be a master-stroke; the enemy have been working so long digging intrenchments, losing numbers of lives, and expending millions of dollars, all for nothing. Very little fighting took place. The place was shelled, but scarcely any one was hurt. The evacuation was done so quietly that the enemy knew nothing of it until the last man was out of Corinth. Their march into it must have been very unlike the triumphal march of the Romans into ancient Corinth, for there was nothing for them to exult over save bad water and a desolate place.

Dr. Hughes asked me if I knew of any place where he could pro-cure something to eat and a night's lodging. I informed him that I thought Mrs. Thornton would receive him.

Numbers of men are continually coming, begging for a mouthful to eat, which is very distressing. Some have arrived who were at Booneville. I asked them to give me a correct account of that affair. They informed me that the enemy behaved very well, and gave them all plenty of time to move from the depot before they fired it; that there were some dead bodies in a car near, and they might have been burned, but no lives were lost. Our men got off, as our cavalry came on the enemy and made them run. They informed us that many of our sick doubtless died in the woods. . . .

The men who imparted this information looked completely ex-hausted. They said that they had not tasted food for four days, and indeed they looked like it. After dark, while we were on the gallery, a man approached, and asked us to give him something for two badly wounded men under his charge. He desired a stimulant. I had a bottle of wine, which I gladly gave him. Dr. Hughes found that the wounded men were from Missouri, and old acquaintances, and said that he was too tired to go down and see them, but would do so in the morning.

While at the train this afternoon, I saw a number of men taken off the cars and laid on the platform; some were dead, and others sick or badly wounded. They were wrapped in their blankets, and put down as if they were bundles of dirty rags. No one seemed to notice them. O, how my heart sickened as I looked at the sight! Surely things could be better managed. Some one is to blame for this ill treatment of these brave men.

June 1.—Mr. Miller called early this morning, and informed me that Mrs. Ogden and the ladies were in a car at the depot. I went down immediately. They were not there, but the sick and wounded were, whom I had seen taken off the cars last night. I asked if there were none to care for them. I was informed that there was no one, and that they had not even had a drink of water. The sun was shining directly upon some of them. An immense train of cars was on the road. I went further down, with the hope of finding Mrs. Ogden, and at almost every step I saw sick and wounded men lying all over the ground. I came up to a group of officers who were having their breakfast cooked. I asked them if they could tell me what this meant. They replied that they had left Corinth in such a hurry that it could not be avoided. I told them that I thought it could, and that the doctors were to blame. To this they made no reply. Perhaps they were doctors, and I do not care if they were.

I at last came up with Mrs. Ogden and her party. They were almost starving; they had been three days on the cars. Mrs. Woodall sent them some coffee. They were on the way to some place in Alabama. I was introduced to Dr. Childs from Mobile, and several others, but do not recollect their names.

Dr. Hughes has brought his wounded friends up here. Both are very young men, named Curly and Oliver. Mr. Curly is badly wounded in the foot, and Mr. Oliver has lost one of his. Both were wounded by the same shell, while sitting talking to each other, the day before Corinth was evacuated. They are members of Lucas's Battery, Price's army.

Mrs. Thornton was busy last night until 12 o'clock cooking for the starving soldiers who come begging her for food. This morning she sent her two little boys around the country, requesting the citizens to send in food to the car-loads of men who were at the depot. She then made soup and other things, which she carried to them herself.

I went to church this morning. Service was held in a warehouse

44

The Evacuation of Corinth

RULES OF THE ACADEMY HOSPITAL.

Assistant Surgeons.

Each Assistant Surgeon will be held strictly responsible for everything pertaining to the comfort and welfare of his patients, the administration of diet and medicines, proper attention of nurses, cleanliness of bedding, clothing &c. He will visit his wards twice a day regularly (morning and evening) and, as much oftener during the day and night as the condition of his patients may require. He will answer all calls promptly and instruct his Head Nurses where he can be found when his services are required at unusual hours. He will, in no case, absent himself without permission and then not until arrangements are made for the proper care of his patients until his return. He will be in his wards at each meal-time and see that the diet prescribed is furnished, is in sufficient quantity, is properly prepared, and is given to the patients in the proper manner. Very sick or badly wounded patients will claim his special attention in this respect. He will adopt any means he may deem necessary to secure his patients against unkindness, neglect, or inattention, on the part of nurses. Disorderly or reprehensible conduct on the part of nurses or patients he will report promptly to the Surgeon in Charge. All prescriptions of diet and medicines will be re-written in full each day and not "continued." No "mixtures" will be prescribed but each prescription written in full.

Prescriptions will, at all times, be subject to scrutiny (and alteration when deemed necessary) by the Surgeon in Charge, who is alone responsible for the practice of the Hospital. Each morning after his regular round the Assistant Surgeon will return to the office a list of patients under his care capable of "duty," "guard duty," and "police duty." From these lists the Officer of the Day will organize the necessary squads.

Wardmasters.

Wardmasters will have subordinate control of the nurses. They will continually keep supervision over them in the discharge of their duties and report any dereliction to the Surgeon in Charge.

Nurses.

1. The nurses will be divided into two reliefs; the 1st watch from 6 to 12, the 2d from 12 to 6 o'clk.

2. There will be a Head Nurse to each watch, who will administer the medicines prescribed and distribute the diet according to the list made by the Assistant Surgeon. The Assistant Nurses will be under his immediate control.

3. Neglect of duty, inattention, unkindness to patients, disorderly or insubordinate conduct, will be promptly punished.

4. No nurse or other subordinate shall absent himself from the Hospital without a written pass signed by the Surgeon in Charge.

5. The wards shall be kept scrupulously clean and, at all times, well ventilated. The floors shall be scrubbed or dry-rubbed and swept, bedding changed or arranged, and everything put in order between the hours of 5½ and 6½ o'clock in the morning—both watches assisting in this labor.

6. Every nurse will attend roll-call twice a day—at sunrise and sunset.

7. Head Nurses are responsible for the condition of their wards and the conduct of their Assistants.

Patients.

1. No disorderly conduct tolerated.

2. Smoking and chewing tobacco strictly forbidden in the wards.

3. Lounging on the beds, spitting on the floors, in the halls or on the stoves, forbidden.

4. Convalescents will spread up their own beds.

5. Convalescents are required to do light duty about the hospital.

6. Patients shall observe directions given to them by the Nurses or Wardmasters, always behaving respectfully towards them.

7. Patients will report to the Surgeon in Charge or to the Assistant Surgeon in charge of the ward, any unkindness, inattention or neglect on the part of nurses.

8. No baggage allowed in the wards.

9. No patient will leave the Hospital without a written pass signed by the Surgeon in Charge.

10. Every patient will be at his own bed while the Assistant Surgeon is making his rounds.

11. No liquor allowed in the wards except as prescribed.

MEALS.—Breakfast at 6½ o'clock, A. M.; Dinner at 12 o'clock, M.; Supper at 6 o'clock, P. M.

FRANK HAWTHORN, Surgeon in Charge.

Approved:—S. H. STOUT, Medical Director Hospitals.

Rules for a Hospital of the Army of Tennessee
(Reproduced from a unique copy at the library of the
University of Texas)

belonging to Judge Thornton, as every church in the place has been taken for hospitals. I heard a very good sermon from a Baptist preacher.

June 2.—News has been received from Virginia that we have gained a great victory, which I hope is true. Mrs. Thornton has two sons, who she expects were in the battle. Of course she is anxious about them, but does not act as many would—sit down and forebode the worst—but goes cheerfully to work, attending to the wants of those around her, with a firm trust that if her sons are wounded some good woman will be there to care for them.

Visited a hospital, of which the ladies of the place have special charge. They cook and prepare all the delicacies, and provide every thing at their own expense. It did me good to see the quantities of milk and good butter.

Miss Marks is here, and is improving. She is at a house called a hotel; the sole one the place affords. It is a perfect shanty.

June 3.—I have been visiting some wounded men who are in the houses of citizens. Dr. Slaughter was wounded at the battle of Shiloh; has not yet recovered from his wounds. His father is attending him.

I sat up all night with a very sick child belonging to a lady by the name of Murdoch. The poor little thing suffers a great deal; the mute appeals for aid, which you have no power to extend, are truly touching; and I think I felt as bad, if not worse, at the sight of this child's sufferings, as I ever did at the sight of any of the sick or wounded whom I saw at Corinth. . . .

June 4.—This place is filled with strangers; the rear of the army being here—quartermasters, commissaries, etc. Mrs. Thornton's house is like a hotel; the men walk into it without asking any questions, sit down at the table, take what they want, and some times they pay. Mrs. Thornton has not the heart to prevent it, as the men seem to be so hungry.

Dr. Hughes introduced me to Colonel Hunt, of the Ninth Kentucky Regiment. He is a very handsome man, and is an uncle of John Morgan's.

June 6.—The enemy are still in Corinth, and are fortifying it. They do not seem inclined to follow us.

I have just received a letter from my brother, who is in camp near Baldwin.

June 7.—Colonel Williams, quartermaster for Price's army, and two young men, his assistants, are boarding here. They have a small room for their stores, for which they are very thankful, as the place is so crowded.

One of the young men who is with the colonel is an Episcopalian. To-day he informed me that Mr. Clute intended having service in the open air, as his church, along with the others, has been taken for a hospital.

Whitsunday, June 8.—This morning I went to church with my Missouri friend, Colonel Williams's assistant, and quite an amusing incident happened. I had seen and spoken to him a number of times, but did not know his name. We see so many persons here that it is impossible to remember their names. I recollected, while walking with this gentleman, that I was ignorant of his name, and asked him what it was. He laughed so heartily that he could scarcely tell me. Surely these are strange times. We never think of requiring an introduction to a soldier, as we have perfect confidence in them. To be in our army is a passport. The men are all gentlemen—at least I have found them so thus far. The one I was then walking with was not an exception. His name is Curtis. He was a captain in Price's Missouri State Guard, and was with it at the time it was captured. He is now with Colonel Williams on General Price's staff.

We called on Mr. Clute, who was glad to see me. He kindly inquired after Mrs. Ogden, and all the other ladies. I was introduced to Mrs. Clute, and she and I raised the tunes. The services were held under a large oak-tree, and the scene was quite romantic. Mr. Clute preached an excellent sermon on the subject for the day.

June 10.—Mrs. Thornton, Miss Groom, and myself visited some wounded and sick men, who are in tents. They were lying on the ground—some of them without even a mattress. They were all cheerful and contented, with the exception of one—a colonel—who grumbled a great deal at every body. This is something so unusual—a complaint from any of the men—that we asked Mr. Crutchfield, his nurse, about his case. He informed us that he was an old bachelor, who has been very sick, and having none of the soothing influences of home on which to think, his illness rendered him cross. The men in the tents were all from Missouri and Arkansas. Good Mrs. Thornton wanted to have some of these poor fellows taken to her house, but it was already full.

The two young men from Missouri are still with her, and many others. As soon as her patients are well enough to be moved, some kind friends from the country take them to their homes. The change is very beneficial to them. But it is only those who are out of the surgeon's hands who can go.

We are all very busily employed making clothes for the soldiers, which is the only kind of work we do now.

Major Proctor of Kentucky is here. A few days ago, in the course of conversation, I told him I had often heard his state spoken of in glowing terms by a particular friend—a Scotchman. On telling Major Proctor about my friend, he said, "I know who you mean—George Donaldson"; and sure enough, he was the same. Major Proctor is the owner of the Diamond Cave in that state, and Mr. Donaldson had remained at his house for months at a time, while exploring the geological wonders of Kentucky. Major Proctor is with General Hardee. He has two step-sons, named Bell, with John Morgan.

There was quite a common incident occurred last evening, but I can not avoid making a note of it. As the cook put her pail, in which was the night's milk, down on the ground, and turned around to shut the gate, a soldier snatched it up and carried it off. So we were minus milk for supper. Mrs. Thornton said she expected he needed the milk more than we did, and if he would only bring back her bucket, she would not mind; so this morning the bucket was brought back. This is not called stealing, but *pressing*.

Mrs. Thornton is very lenient with the soldiers. She says perhaps her boys in Virginia are helping themselves in the same way, and, if in need, are perfectly right. The great trouble here seems to be the scarcity of water. Every one has a cistern, but as there has been no rain for some time many of them are dry. The soldiers seem to think it very hard that they can not get enough water. This is the poorest country for water I have ever been in. There seem to be no natural springs like those that abound in Alabama.

I have been informed by some of the soldiers that, on their march from Corinth, they had paid for water to drink. I trust that this is not true, although I have no reason to doubt those who told me.

I can understand how a man could refuse to give water to a large party of men, as he had but little, and they so many; but how he could sell it to them is one of the mysteries. But I must not forget that, even in this generous, warm-hearted country, there are men sunk so low with their love for lucre, that for it they would sell honor, country, and their very souls. . . . I, however, trust such men are rare among us.

I have been told much about the suffering of our men in Corinth for the want of water. Many a time they drank what their horses turned from in disgust. They made holes in the mud, and drank the water formed in them. The Federal army did not suffer as much, as they had the Tennessee River to draw from. They will suffer now, as they are moving their army further from the river. I hope and trust that they may get so far in that they will not be able to get back.

Many think that this last move of ours is a wise one, as the enemy will be drawn so far from his base of supplies that he will be compelled to either fight or retreat. The army is anxious he should do the former.

Every one is discussing the merits of our respective commanders, Bragg and Beauregard. The latter has been one of my idols, and I must confess that I do not like the idea of having it so soon cast down. The tide is running in favor of Bragg. It is now said, if he had had his way at Shiloh, we would have gained a complete victory.

The soldiers tell us that General Bragg is a strict disciplinarian, and, were we to credit one half of the stories told about him, we would

47

think him a perfect monster of cruelty. It is said he makes a perfect pastime of shooting the men, and that not long ago he had one shot for killing a pig. I made particular inquiries regarding this matter of a friend whom I knew to be acquainted with the facts. He informed me that on the retreat from Corinth there had been some men shot, but they were regularly tried by a court-martial.

Before the army left Corinth orders were read to every regiment, informing the men that they must on no account fire off their guns while on the march, and telling them of the penalty incurred by the disobedience of these orders. Many of our men disregarded them, and I am told that quite a number were thus accidentally wounded. The man who was shot for killing a pig, also killed a negro, besides openly disobeying orders.

For my own part, I can not think it is right to take the life of a fellow-mortal unless it is for a flagrant crime, and I do wish that some other mode of punishment could be adopted. These are things I try not to think about.

I am glad I have got what I suppose is the right story about General Bragg.

June 12.—I took a horseback ride, in company with Miss Clute and Captain [Curtis]. I had a chance of seeing a little of this prairie country. This is said to be one of the richest portions of Mississippi. I am very fond of a mountainous country and dense forests; so the scenery had little charms for me, although I could not but look with pleasure on the fine wheat and corn fields, which are here in abundance. The enemy say they will starve us into submission. I do not think we run much risk of starving, with such fields as these.

We had a pleasant ride. The captain is a fine-looking man, and, as a matter of course, is fully aware of the fact, as all *good-looking men are*. He had told Judge Thornton that he was a married man. As his manner does not indicate that he is, we think that he is only saying this for a joke; so we concluded to take him at his word, and treat him as such. The tables are completely turned, and nothing he can tell us to the contrary will make us change our minds. It worries him not a little to think that he should be so *ignominiously* laid on the shelf.

Mr. John Fowler from Mobile is here, taking care of his brother, who is quite sick. The latter is a captain in the Twenty-fourth Alabama Regiment. He is at a private house. I called on him, and he told me that the march from Corinth was terrible—enough to kill any one. I intend going home in company with these gentlemen. Mr. Miller has been here, and informed me that Mrs. Ogden and nearly all the other ladies from Mobile have gone home.

The wounded and sick at Mrs. Thornton's are doing well. The Missourians are both improving. Mr. Curly has his brother with him, who takes care of both.

A lady called, a few days ago, to see Mr. Oliver. She is the wife of

General Price's chief surgeon. She told us that the last lady she spoke to before leaving Missouri was Mr. Oliver's mother, who begged her, if any harm befell her son, to attend him. She could not help shedding tears when she saw the plight he was in. But he does not seem to mind it, and is, like all the others, perfectly cheerful and resigned. He does not seem to suffer near so much as his friend. His foot has been amputated above the ankle, while Mr. Curly is wounded through the center of the foot, and it is a very painful wound.

When I first came here there was a very sick captain from Alabama. I made him a nice drink, thinking it would be a treat; but he did not like it, and took no pains to conceal his dislike. Miss Groom remarked that, if I had made it for some Frenchmen who are in the house, they would have taken it for politeness' sake, whether they liked it or not.

I hear many complaints about the bad treatment our men are receiving in the hospitals. I have been told that many a day they get only one meal, and that of badly-made soup, and as badly-made bread. I have asked some of the ladies of the place as to the truth of these reports, and have been informed that they are only too true.

The citizens have done what they could for them, and they are still doing; but there are so many that they require a great number to take care of them—more than there are at present.

If our government can not do better by the men who are suffering so much, I think we had better give up at once. But when I recollect how much mismanagement of this kind there was in the British army at the commencement of the Crimean war, it is not much to be wondered at if we, a people who have been living in peace so long, should commit errors at first.

Trinity-Sunday, June 15.—Mr. Clute preached an excellent sermon on the Trinity. I have seen a good deal of Mr. and Mrs. Clute, and am much pleased with both. I could not help being a little astonished at the poor-looking house they live in; and I am told that Mr. Clute scarcely gets enough money to live on. Surely this rich place ought to be able to support their pastor better. I thought we were bad enough in the city in supporting the gospel, but the people in the country seem to be more remiss in that respect than we are. I am afraid I will have to believe, what I have often been told by people from the old country, that we have not enough of religion among us to support its teachers.

This evening I visited a very nice family where there were two very pretty girls, both quite young. I was surprised when all took out bottles of snuff and commenced *dipping*. There were many lamentations at the high price of snuff. These ladies chewed this horrid stuff with as much zest as a man would his tobacco; indeed, I think I would much prefer the latter, though both are most disgusting. It is a common practice among the ladies in this state to " dip " snuff, and I am told it is the same in the other southern states.

49

June 16.—A few days ago Mrs. Thornton received news that her eldest son had been wounded in the late battle near Richmond. She is a good deal worried about him, but bears the news with fortitude. She is one who would think life a disgrace, received as the price of liberty. She is very hopeful as to his being well cared for, and is certain that some good woman is administering to his wants in that grand old patriotic state—Virginia. We hear much about the kindness of the people there to the sufferers.

June 17.—Last evening Judge Thornton heard that his wounded son would be up by the evening train. He, Miss Groom, and myself went down to the train, but he was not there. As we were going down a guard stopped us; he said the ladies could pass, but not Judge Thornton, and as we could not go without him we were in quite a dilemma. The guard put us all right by telling Judge Thornton to go off the road, and round a tree which was near, as he had no jurisdiction over any place but the main road.

I intend leaving to-day for home. Mr. Fowler's brother is much improved in health, and is able to be moved. I regret leaving my kind friends, and all of the patients. The Missourians have got to feel as if they were my brothers.

III: MOBILE

✠✠✠

June 18, 1862.—I arrived in Mobile this morning, about 9 A. M., accompanied by Mr. John Fowler and his brother. We had a hard time getting down, as the train was very much crowded. Indeed, I scarcely know how I managed to get on it, as the guard tried to prevent us; my friends, Dr. Hughes and Captain Curtis, *threw* me on, minus half of my baggage. I stood on the steps of the car for a little while, when one of the soldiers inside, with true southern gallantry, insisted on my taking his seat. As the car was filled with sick and wounded men, I was unwilling to do so; but from his importunity I was compelled to accept. The intention was a good one, and I received it in the spirit with which it was given, but I did not relish the change. The car was so close and crowded that I could scarcely breathe. I was seated with some very nice men from Missouri, but they certainly had not made use of a certain aqueous fluid that morning in making their *toilets*. As that liquid is scarce in Mississippi, I excuse them. One seemed anxious that I should have a *lock* of his *hair*, as he combed and scattered it around me. Another one bought some plums, and put them in a very *greasy* hat, some of which he very kindly offered me, and for politeness' sake I took them. I had to hold my head out of the window to get fresh air. To add to all, we had no water.[1]

General B[eauregard] was on the train. He and his *staff* had the ladies' car and the baggage-car next, which was the cause of our being so crowded. I could not help wondering what had become of our boasted *southern chivalry*. It does not do to grumble, as these are war times, and the order of things seems to be reversed; but I could scarcely keep from it, as the car I was in was next to the baggage-car, where I had the *felicity* of seeing General B[eauregard] and his *staff* come, every now and then, and arrange their toilets. The sight of them ought to have consoled me; but alas! for poor, weak *humanity*, I could not help envying them their comfortable seats. I did not mind so much for myself, as men now-a-days seem to think that we women have no right to leave our homes, and that the railroads and rail-cars are for their exclusive benefit. I could not but feel for the sick and

[1] " During the whole war I never spent a more uncomfortable time . . ." Cumming, *Gleanings from Southland*, 73.

wounded men who were so crowded, and many of them lying on the floor. If General B[eauregard] was sick, he should have had a nice seat, but not a whole car; and why should his staff, more than other well soldiers, have so much room? [2]

I heard many remarks about it, but said nothing, as I think it wrong to encourage grumbling at this time. We must expect *little* annoyances, and, as we are all struggling in one common cause, must not mind them.

My Missouri friends were very kind and attentive, and it gave me great pleasure to listen to them talk over their campaigns.

The country through which we passed was one immense field of corn. We came nearly two hundred and fifty miles, and I scarcely saw an acre of cotton.

On my arrival at home I learned that Mobile had lost fearfully by the late battles near Richmond. Among the wounded and slain are friends whom I have known a lifetime. I called on one lady, who had just received a letter from her son, then in the Virginia army, telling her that his father had been mortally wounded, and is now a prisoner, and his uncle in the same position. The battle of Seven Pines, near the Chickahominy River, was fought on the 31st of May. On the morning of the 1st of June, a part of our army was drawn into an ambuscade and had to retire, thereby leaving our wounded in the hands of the enemy. In the first day's battle General J. E. Johnston, who was in command, was severely wounded. We were victorious, and had it not been for one of our general's failing to come up at the right time, we would have captured the whole Federal army, which was under the command of General Keys [Keyes].

The Eighth Alabama Regiment * lost many. It is said that it covered itself with glory in the last battle, and also in that of Williamsburg.

Among the killed are Lieutenant Henry Ellis, and Captain L. F. Summers, an eminent lawyer of this place. Lieutenant Mordicai

---

[2] Here Miss Cumming identified General P. G. T. Beauregard only by the initial " B " in the original edition of her journal, but in *Gleanings from Southland* she used his full name. The General was travelling to Bladon Springs, Alabama, to recruit his health. It was on his arrival at Mobile on this trip that he learned he had been relieved of his command and succeeded by General Bragg. T. Harry Williams, *P. G. T. Beauregard, Napoleon in Gray* (Baton Rouge, 1955), 157-59. In *Gleanings from Southland* Miss Cumming adds: " I caught a glimpse of General Beauregard several times, and was not a little surprised at the boyish appearance of the hero of Fort Sumter and Manassas. I expected to find something of the ' venerable ' in the man who had distinguished himself in Mexico and in our own war by his daring and bravery. I also expected to see more of the recklessness and dash peculiar to the Louisiana soldier " (73-74) .

* But a remnant of this gallant regiment is now living. It was with General Lee at the time of the surrender. While expecting to be ordered in line of battle they were told to throw down their arms. They took their flag, which they had borne triumphantly through many a battle, and tore it into shreds. Each man, while the tears ran down his cheeks, took a piece to keep as a sacred memento of the past.

[Mordecai], son of Dr. Mordecai, is mortally wounded. Lieutenant Josh. Kennedy is believed killed by all but his devoted wife. Captain Laughrey [Loughrey] and his brother are wounded and prisoners. Lieutenant Branigan [Brannegan] is badly wounded, and is also a prisoner. The fate of Captain Loughrey is uncertain; but, from what we can learn of him from men coming from the army, there is little doubt but that he is killed, as the last seen of him was when he had been wounded for the third time, and fell, it was supposed, dead.

The company of which Captain Loughrey was a member, the Emerald Guards, was one of the first which left here for Virginia. It was composed of the members of a fire company. The men in it were principally natives of the " Green Isle of the Ocean "; they who have come forward, like Brian of old, at every call in this eventful struggle, and who, having adopted this land as their own, are determined to maintain her rights at all hazards.

I was at the depot the morning the company left for Virginia. It numbered one hundred and fifteen men. They were dressed in dark green, the emblematic color of Ireland, and carried a very beautiful flag, presented to them by some ladies. It was a Confederate flag on one side, in the center of which was the full-length figure of Washington; on the other side was the harp, encircled with a wreath of shamrocks and the words " Erin-go-Bragh." Below that again was the Irish war-cry, " Faugh-a-ballagh! " which means " clear the way." They were escorted by all of the fire companies, with a very fine band of music.

At that time I thought, like many others, that they were going more on a frolic than any thing else, as we could not think it possible that the North really meant to try and subjugate us, and as soon as she saw we were in earnest would let us alone, as we asked nothing from her but that. Alas, how fearfully have our hopes fallen, one after the other! We are not to gain our independence but through the blood of our bravest and best. God grant it has not been spilled in vain!

July 3.—I have just had a visit from my friend, Dr. Wm. Hughes. He is on his way to Virginia, accompanied by Judge Thornton. Judge Thornton's son was more severely wounded than was at first thought, and has not been able to reach his home. Dr. Hughes brought me word of Mr. Oliver's death. Poor fellow! I left him apparently doing well, but the weather is so very warm that wounded men suffer. I believe he was an only son. May God comfort his poor mother, who is far away in Missouri!

July 4.—The day that a few years ago by us was commemorated with so much pride as a nation's anniversary for liberty won, now how changed! Part of that nation seeking to enslave the other! A gloomy, rainy day, such as last year. Nature's horizon, as the nation's, " in woe, like Rachel, weeps."

At the present moment our cause looks bright. In Virginia a star has arisen: his name ("Stonewall") the haughty foe has found, to his cost, has been given prophetically, as he has proved a wall of granite to them. For four weeks he has kept at bay more than one of their boasted armies.

News has just been received that our brave Virginia army under General Lee has been fighting for days, and has driven the enemy back step by step, placing thousands of them *hors du combat,* taking many prisoners, and spoils of all kinds. These battles have raged with an intensity and ferocity on both sides that have never been equaled. They commenced on the 26th of June, and the battle of Malvern Hill, which was fought on the 1st instant, as far as we can learn, has closed the slaughter. The enemy were under their young Napoleon, General McClellan, and had it not been for blundering again on the part of one of our generals, there would not have been one man left of the foe to tell the tale.

It would be invidious to say who on our side won the most laurels, as the valor shown by men from every state has proved that the same spirit lives in every one. All have been conspicuous for bravery in this eventful struggle. Lee, Jackson, Longstreet, Hill, and a host of others of our leading men, have won fresh laurels. The brave dead and wounded—alas! how the thought of them comes up, like a specter, to mar our triumphs.

July 11.—I have just come from the funeral of Mrs. B——, an old and valued friend. She was an old lady. It is remarked by all that we have had more deaths among our old citizens since the war than we ever had before. They seem to suffer much more mentally from it than do the young.

This has been one of the hottest days I have ever felt.

In the afternoon, a friend and myself paid a visit with Mrs. F. (a lady who visits there daily) to the General Hospital. In going through it I could not but contrast it with those I had seen in Mississippi. Every thing was in perfect order, and as cleanly as any private house. I was very much pleased to see that our men had such nice comfortable quarters to go to in case of their needing them. This was the first time my friend had ever been in a hospital, and she felt quite sad at the sight of so many young men being so far away from their homes. There were few very sick. We met some very nice young Texans, who were delighted to see us. To one, Frank Epperson, of the Eighteenth Texas Regiment, we promised to send some books. The hospital is in charge of Dr. Miller, who is said to be an excellent surgeon.

The ladies of the place have a society, and arrange so that there are some of them in the hospital every day, to attend to the wants of the patients. They prepare the delicacies, and take charge of all things sent as donations, and see that the persons they are meant for receive them.

54

The patriotism of the ladies of Mobile, I suppose, has not been outdone by any in the Confederacy. As soon as the war commenced, they formed themselves into a body, called the "Military Aid Society," for the benefit, not only of the soldiers, but their families. They have clothes made for the soldiers, and their families, who need employment, make them. In that way the war has not been felt as much by them as it would otherwise have been. I have been told by one of the clergymen that he has had fewer calls on him for aid than he had before the war. Soldiers coming, strangers, to this place, can have their wants supplied by this society. I believe it is supported by private donations, and money paid by the government for the work done.

July 16.—We have just received news of the death of Milton Boull-mett [Boullemet], eldest son of a particular friend. He was wounded at the battle of Malvern Hill, and died soon after.

The late battles around Richmond have caused Alabama to sit down in sackcloth and ashes, to mourn, like King David, for the loss of many a gallant son. She had at least seven regiments in the field— Third, Fourth, Sixth, Eighth, Ninth, Eleventh, and Twelfth. The men of the Third, Eighth, and Twelfth were nearly all from Mobile. I have mentioned the Eighth at the battle of Seven Pines, and how severely it suffered there. It has lost nearly all its remnant in their recent engagement.

The Third was in both, and I see, from a letter in this morning's paper, from Colonel Battle, that at Seven Pines General Longstreet ordered the name of that battle to be inscribed on its colors, for the bravery which the regiment exhibited there. Colonel Lomax, who was in command at that time, was killed. Six color-bearers were shot down, one after another.

Among the fallen are the flower of the youth of Mobile. William Treat, the colorbearer, fell clasping the colors. Charles Keeler is killed; he is one of two brothers who have already died in the service. Tyler Redwood is mortally wounded; one of three in one family who have died in the service. G. T. Summersill is another of a trio of brothers who have shared the same fate. Wm. Stewart, Barklow, H. S. Lockwood, W. N. Caufield [Caulfield], Wm. Jones, W. I. Led-yard, T. Leuseine, O. Cuthbert, and many, many others.

This gallant regiment was composed of nearly all our volunteer companies, and many times, have we all assembled, in the happy days of yore, when camping and soldiering were looked on as a grand frolic, and danced, and partaken of their generous hospitality. The fathers of many of the young men who now compose these companies had been members of them for years. I believe they were the first Alabamians who tendered their services to the Confederate government.

Milton Boullemet, but a few years ago, was an officer, along with my brother, in a boy's company, the "Mobile Blues." I think I see his handsome face yet, at a party we gave them on a Fourth of July. All of the volunteer military companies had left the city on excursions. A young lady tried to quiz them; she told them the ladies of Mobile tendered them their heartfelt thanks for remaining to protect them in case of the city being attacked by an enemy. One of them answered her, that he thought if the ladies depended on *them* for protection, they would fare badly. She told him he did not compliment his company. He answered, that "truth was before compliment." We little thought then that the life of nearly every boy in that company would be offered up in our defense.

Nearly every state in the Confederacy has to mourn, as Alabama does, over the loss of their bravest and best. The banks of the Chickahominy are now sacred, washed by the blood of martyrs. May their blood prove a talisman to keep back the foe from ever desecrating it with their unhallowed tread!

> " O, thy soft-rolling flood, Chickahominy River,
>   In thy flowing disturbeth my inmost soul;
> All unlike is thy gliding, so calm, to the horrors
>   Of carnage and bloodshed that round thee did roll.
>
> If thy tale could be told, Chickahominy River;
>   Of the heart-rending pangs of the young and the brave;
> Of the husband and father, whose soul, in departing,
>   Wrung with agony, prayed for a home in the grave.
>
> And yet this is not all, Chickahominy River;
>   The sad hearts that are breaking are far from thy shore;
> But their slain they have left thee, in trust, to thy keeping—
>   Chickahominy River, take care of thy store.
>
> Let thy banks guard them well, Chickahominy River;
>   Let the dust of the hero lie calmly at rest,
> Till the trump of the dead shall awake them to glory,
>   Immortal to live in the realms of the blest." [3]

Mrs. Judge Hopkins of this place is attending to the wounded. We hear much about the good she is doing; for which she has the blessings of all.

The state of Alabama has appropriated thirty thousand dollars for the benefit of her wounded; out of it ten thousand dollars have been given to Mrs. Hopkins. Mr. Titcomb and others have gone from here with supplies of all kinds, and we are told that the people in dear old Virginia are doing all in their power to benefit the sufferers.

It is rumored that Bragg's army is leaving Mississippi and going to East Tennessee. There is also a report that General Hindman has gained a victory in Arkansas, and has captured Curtis's whole army.

July 27.—Captain Curtis has just called to see me. He is *en route* for the army. He informed me that General Price has gone to Richmond to try to get an independent command, with which to free

---

[3] This poem is identified by Miss Cumming as by her mother in *Gleanings from Southland*, 75.

Missouri. Captain Curtis was very hopeful as to his receiving it, and drew a glowing picture of the army's triumphal entry into St. Louis, with General Price at its head. I do hope and pray he will not be disappointed.

I have been told by many that if the president will not accede to General Price's proposal he intends resigning; but I trust he is more of a patriot than that. If we can not have faith in President Davis, and fully trust that what he is doing is for the good of the cause, it is no reason why we should not do our duty.

August 4.—Paid a visit with Mrs. G. to the General Hospital; she took the patients some buttermilk, and nice wheat and corn bread. We offered our services, but there were enough ladies in attendance already, and we were not needed. We walked around and saw the patients; one man was dying, but the others seemed to be doing well.

We then went down town; there we met Mr. Candelish and Mr. Goddard, members of the Twenty-first Alabama Regiment. It has come from Tupelo to recruit. They informed us the army had left for Tennessee.

August 8.—Rev. Dr. Pierce, Mrs. S., and myself paid a visit to the Garner Hospital, which is near the depot. Every thing in it is in perfect order, and much credit is due to the surgeon in charge. It was a perfect treat to go through the dining-room and kitchen; they were so clean and neat; in fact, the whole place was the same. There was quite a number of ladies attending the patients, as I believe there is in all hospitals in the place. We took some books with us, which the men seem glad to receive. Dr. Pierce visits this hospital three days in the week.

August 9.—Went to Mr. Norton's funeral. He was a member of the Eighth Alabama Regiment, and had been with it from the time it went into the service. He arrived at home a few days before his death, having his last wants administered to by the hands of relatives and friends. He has a brother, a member of the same regiment, who is wounded and a prisoner.

I have just received a letter from my brother, written at Tuscaloosa, Ala., his company having marched through the interior. He speaks in glowing terms of the manner in which they were received all through the country, and says that in Tuscaloosa the ladies and old men met them in the streets with baskets full of all kinds of *good things* to eat.

Our city is crowded every day with troops passing through, on their way to Tennessee. They do not stay any time here, so we have no chance of seeing them.

August 14.—The weather is oppressively warm, and we have no ice. When we go walking in the evening, instead of going to the ice-cream saloon as in former days, we visit the *pumps*, as the water in them is much cooler than that from the hydrants. This resort has become quite a fashionable one, and indeed every thing is fashionable which we choose to do for comfort. War has cast aside all conventionalities, as it should. But with all the heat, the health of the city is excellent.

Provisions are very high, and there is a prospect of their getting higher. Dry goods have not increased much in price. I bought a very pretty chally dress for fifty cents per yard. A few weeks ago the city was full of silks, and cheaper than I have ever known them. At present there is scarcely a yard to be had. On going to buy some, we were told the government had bought it all to make *balloons* with.[4]

General Forney is now in command of this city, and is having it put in a complete state of defense; so I trust, if the vandals should come here, they will find some *little* work before them.

---

[4] Miss Cumming repeatedly remarks on Confederate shortages. For a full historical discussion see Mary Elizabeth Massey's *Ersatz in the Confederacy* (Columbia, S. C., 1952). Specific substitutes are detailed in Dr. Francis Peyre Porcher's *Resources of the Southern Fields and Forests* . . . (Charleston, 1863). An interesting group of home concoctions is described in the *Confederate Receipt Book* (Richmond, 1863). The use of balloons in the War is reported in considerable detail in F. Stansbury Haydon's *Aeronautics in the Union and Confederate Armies* (Baltimore, 1941).

IV: RINGGOLD, DALTON, CHATTANOOGA

August 31, 1862.—Yesterday I arrived at Ringgold, Ga., in company with Mrs. May and Mrs. Williamson. We came here for the purpose of entering one of the hospitals at this post. We left Mobile on the 28th inst.; Dr. Pierce and many others came to see us off. Dr. Pierce introduced us to a Mr. Fogle from New Orleans. We crossed the Bay in the steamer *Mary Wilson,* which took us about three hours. We arrived at Tensas Landing in Baldwin County, and then took the cars for Montgomery. Mr. Fogle was very attentive, as was also a friend of his, a fine-looking old gentleman, who was a little crusty; but, as I said before, men seem to think that women have no business traveling now-a-days; so we did not mind him.

The country through which we passed was not very fertile. It is famous for manufacturing turpentine.

There was a very sick soldier on the cars, who seemed to suffer much from pain in his head, and groaned a great deal, which irritated our friend, the old gentleman. We did what we could to relieve him, for which he seemed grateful.

On the 29th we arrived at Montgomery about 6 o'clock A. M. We went to a very fine hotel, the " Exchange," and got a nice breakfast, for which we paid one dollar each. Mr. Fogle and his friend found they had important business to detain them in Montgomery; so we were deprived of their pleasant company for the rest of the journey. They very kindly procured a carriage for us, and sent us to the depot, with instructions to the driver to put us in charge of the conductor, which he did. As we were on our way to the depot, Mrs. Williamson *naively* remarked, that she supposed the gentlemen had taken fright at the number of packages she had, and caused them to have such important business.

We left Montgomery about 8 A. M. on the West Point Railroad, and at 1 P. M. reached West Point, a post-village of Troup County, Ga., and is on the state line which divides Alabama and Georgia; is eighty-seven miles south-west of Atlanta, and forty miles from Columbus, Ga. The Chattahooche[e] River runs through it.

There was a lady from Mobile on the cars, who was going with her negroes to settle at some point on the road, as it is expected that that city will soon be in the hands of the Federals. Mrs. General McCoy of Mobile was in the car, on her way to join her invalid husband in Virginia; he having gone there to visit a young son, a member of the Third Alabama Regiment, who has recently died from wounds received at one of the late battles around Richmond.

There was a broken car on the road, and the conductor was afraid he would miss the connection at West Point—the passengers did not like the idea of having to remain a day at *West Point*—so he did his best to hurry us on.

I think we gained by having no gentleman with us, as the conductor, Mr. Phillips, paid us special attention, which he seemed to do to all the ladies who had no escort. We changed cars at West Point, and received the same kind attention from the next conductor; and when we reached Atlanta, which was about dark, he accompanied us to the Chattanooga train, secured seats for us, and then checked our baggage. I shall never forget his kindness. I could not but contrast this trip with my last, the one on the Mobile and Ohio Railroad. But I must remember that we had no *general and his staff* with us this time.

We arrived at Chattanooga on the 30th, at 6 A. M., tired and covered with dust, as we had come a distance of six hundred miles in about thirty-six hours. When within about thirty miles of Chattanooga, a special guard came around and examined our passes, which caused quite a commotion, as none of us had the right kind. We had procured them from the provost marshal in Mobile, but they did not amount to any thing, as an order had just been received from headquarters at Chattanooga prohibiting any one going in there without a special permit. The men were very angry; but they, along with some ladies, had to get out at one of the stopping-places. We told the guard our mission, and showed our order for transportation, and were allowed to go on, as it proved we were friends to the government. There was a Mrs. Hanly on the cars, whose husband is chief of General Hardee's artillery. She had a pass from General Hardee to go to any part of the Confederacy; it, however, proved of no avail; the guard told her she must get out; but she said firmly she "*would not go.*" When he saw her so determined, he gave up talking to her, and permitted her to go on. This lady had just come from Kentucky, and while there she had been taken for a spy, and very harshly treated by the Federals. She had succeeded in eluding the vigilance of the officers at Memphis, and had brought out contraband goods from that place, which she showed us when we reached Chattanooga. She gave us some nutmegs, which were very acceptable, as every thing of that kind is scarce, and we need them in seasoning food for the soldiers.

On arriving at Chattanooga, we went to the Crutchfield House, and then were told we could not get a room without a special pass from the provost marshal, and we could not get one from him, as we

Chattanooga From the North Bank of the Tennessee

Lookout Mountain and Vicinity

were not allowed to walk a square on the street without one. We were in a dilemma now, as we could not possibly eat without at least washing our hands. The clerk told us he would send water to the parlor for us to do that, and permit us to eat breakfast. If we could not get a pass after that, we must leave Chattanooga the way we came. After waiting in vain for water, I ventured to ask a white girl, who was sweeping the hall, for it. She quietly told us we could not have any till the next morning. I suppose this *femme de chambre* thought we were not dusty enough; for she walked into the parlor where we were and commenced sweeping away. In despair I went in search of Mrs. Hanly, who, more fortunate than we this time, had procured a room on General Hardee's pass, of which she very kindly gave us the use. After breakfast, a gentleman told Mrs. May and Mrs. Williamson he would take them to the post surgeon's office by a road where there were no guards.

After they left, I was sitting in the parlor, thinking how strange every thing was, when in walked my old friend from Kentucky—Major Proctor. I was never more glad to see any one. He was indeed a friend, as he came in need. I told him how we were situated. He said he would arrange matters for us. I went with him to Dr. Young of Kentucky, medical purveyor of Hardee's corps, who procured us passes. I found Mrs. May and Mrs. Williamson already there. Major Proctor gave his word for our being loyal Confederates, and " no spies."

The passes gave us permission to pass on the streets in the environs of Chattanooga until further orders. On our way back to the hotel, we had to show them to the guards, who did not seem to like the idea of asking us for them; but we did not mind it. Indeed, I am rather pleased that our authorities are so vigilant, as I think the southern people are too credulous, and apt to be imposed upon.

The army has gone into Kentucky. General Bragg has every hope that the Kentuckians will be glad to rid themselves of the hated Yankee yoke, and will rise *en masse* to join him.

Mrs. May and I called on the assistant medical director, Dr. Flewellen.[1] He informed us that Dr. Thornton, whom Mrs. May came to see, was here; so we concluded to leave on the evening train. We paid Dr. Young a visit before leaving, and he kindly procured transportation for us to this place; this was quite unexpected; Dr. Young is a whole-souled southerner.

We are stopping at a very nice hotel, the " Catoosa House," a palace compared with the Hotel de Crutchfield. This very nice little

---

[1] Dr. Ed. Archelaus Flewellen was one of the principal medical men of the Army of Tennessee. He was appointed surgeon to rank from May 16, 1861, became Assistant Medical Director June 28, 1862, Medical Director of Department No. 2 December 23, 1863, and Medical Director, with his office in Richmond, February 29, 1864. In March of 1864 he was reassigned to the Army of Tennessee under Dr. A. J. Foard, as Medical Director of Hospitals. Jones, " Roster . . . ," *loc. cit.,* 199; *Confederate States Medical and Surgical Journal,* I (1864) , 152.

village, on the Western and Atlantic Railroad, is twenty-nine miles south of Chattanooga. When we arrived, last evening, Dr. Griffin and Mrs. Crocker, whom I had known in Corinth, called on us, and informed us that Mrs. Glassburn was here. I went to see her; she had three of the ladies with her—the others had all gone home. Poor Mrs. Noland died shortly after leaving Corinth; I have no doubt, from disease contracted at that miserable place.

Mrs. Williamson and myself went to the Methodist Church this morning; in the afternoon we took a walk, and visited a saltpeter cave. The government is using the saltpeter for making gunpowder.[2] I am told this portion of the country abounds in such caves.

September 1.—We have changed our boarding-house, and are now stopping with a very nice lady by the name of Evans, who keeps an excellent table, has an abundance of milk, butter, and eggs, and only charges us one dollar per day. We paid two at the hotel.

Mrs. May called on Dr. Thornton, post surgeon here. He informed her that he had given her place in the hospital to some one else, as she was so long in coming.

September 4.—Mrs. May and myself went up to Chattanooga to-day; Mr. Miller accompanied us. We visited two of the hospitals there— one in a church on the top of a hill. We saw few very sick men; they looked to me as if all they needed was plenty of good food. They complained bitterly of their poor diet, and the scarcity of it. I was much pleased to hear them speak highly of their treatment by the ladies of the Mobile hospitals.

Within sight of this hospital flowed the Tennessee River. We sat down on its banks and ate our lunch. I was struck with the beauty of the scene around us. The river rolled at our feet. . . . This is truly the " Land of the mountain and the flood." I was enraptured with all I saw. . . .

Chattanooga, the terminus of the Nashville and Chattanooga Railroad and of the Western and Atlantic Railroad, is two hundred and fifty miles from Knoxville by water, and one hundred and forty miles

[2] The shortage of nitre was a considerable impediment in the manufacture of gunpowder. Of great concern to the government were problems of increasing its supply. One source was the saltpeter caves such as are found in northwest Georgia. The Executive Council of South Carolina sponsored the publication of Dr. Joseph LeConte's *Instructions for the Manufacture of Saltpetre* (Columbia, 1862), which gives directions for creating nitre beds. A less accustomed source (chamberlye from private homes) is celebrated in the ribald poem of Thomas Badger Wetmore, a distinguished Alabama lawyer, which is presumed to have been published in the Selma *Sentinel* of October 1, 1862. No copy of the paper survives, but one example of a Confederate broadside printing of it as " A New Sources of Niter " is extant. The poem has been reprinted many times, most recently as a souvenir of the Chicago Civil War Round Table's Second Annual Battlefield Tour in 1952. The background of this bit of Confederate bawdiness is set forth in Bell I. Wiley's *The Life of Johnny Reb* (Indianapolis, 1943), 304-305.

south-east of Nashville. The river runs north-west of it. It is famed for its stone-coal and iron ore. The town is in a valley; the houses are in a dilapidated condition; and, in fact, the whole place ill accords with the beautiful scenery by which it is surrounded. . . .

In the afternoon we paid a visit to another hospital in town, where Mrs. May met an old friend in the surgeon, Dr. Hunter. He was glad to see her, and asked her to come into his hospital; he was going to have it enlarged, and would like to have Mrs. Williamson and myself, besides Mrs. May, but as Dr. Stout,[3] the post surgeon, did not approve of more than one lady in a hospital, he could not take us without asking him. He took us all through his hospital. It was the upper part of a long row of warehouses, with windows east and west. The partitions between were taken away, making large wards, where a current of air could blow right through. There were some four or five of these rooms opening into each other. The whole was well white-washed. I thought the smell of the lime was better as a disinfectant than all the camphor or cologne in the world. The name of this hospital is the "Newsom"; so called in honor of the lady I met and admired so much in Corinth.[4]

This place was shelled some few months ago. This morning we took our lunch on a hill opposite to one across the river, where the Federals had planted their guns. They fired into the town without giving any notice. I am told it was a terrible sight to see the women and children

[3] Dr. Samuel Hollingsworth Stout would have achieved considerable fame as a medical innovator and administrator in any but a defeated country. He was born at Nashville in 1822 and commenced his medical practice in middle Tennessee in 1848, having rejected a commission in the United States navy. In May 1861 he became a surgeon in the Provisional Army of Tennessee. After a few months of field service with the Third Tennessee Regiment he undertook the administration of Gordon Hospital in Nashville. At the fall of Nashville he moved to Chattanooga. His remarkable administrative ability brought a rapid rise in his career and in July 1862 he was made Superintendent of Hospitals of the Army of Tennessee. In early 1863 he was made Medical Director of hospitals. In addition to his unusual ability demonstrated in his handling of the unprecedented number of sick and wounded, he exhibited special qualities in his advanced designs for well ventilated and easily serviced wards and in his effective establishment of the hospitals of the Army of Tennessee as mobile units on much the same pattern later made familiar in World War II. After the War Dr. Stout taught briefly in the Atlanta Medical College and practiced in Georgia and Texas. From the mass of official and unofficial records that he preserved during the War he published an interesting, but insufficiently detailed, narrative of his wartime service in the *St. Louis Medical and Surgical Journal*, LXIV (1893) and the *Southern Practitioner*, XXII-XXV (1900–1903) .

[4] " This hospital was named in honor of Mrs. Ella Newsom, a young, handsome, and wealthy widow, whose home was in Arkansas. She served as nurse and matron in the hospitals at Corinth, Miss., after the battle of Shiloh, and with great accepta- bility to the sick and wounded and their surgeons. Her fame preceded her arrival at Chattanooga, where she found the Newsom hospital named in her honor. After coming to that post she was assigned as chief matron of the Academy Hospital, in which she served until debility caused by long and laborious services forced her to seek a rest." Stout, " Some Facts . . . ," *Southern Practitioner*, XXV (1903) , 522.

running, and the balls flying around them. The Federals took possession of the town, but afterward gave it up. General Leadbetter had command of our forces at that time.

September 6.—Yesterday I went with a party, fishing; as usual at such parties, we caught no fish. We fished at the Chickamauga Creek, or river. It is a stream that takes its rise in Walker County, flows north-easterly, and enters the Tennessee River at Chattanooga. The scenery around it is wild and picturesque. There is an Indian legend connected with it, from which the river takes its name. The tale is that many years ago two Indian tribes met here and had a desperate battle, with great slaughter on both sides; hence, the name " Chickamauga, or River of Death."

Sunday, September 7.—Went to the Methodist Church this morning; heard a very good sermon.

There are two hospitals here, called the Buckner and the Bragg, in honor of those generals. Mrs. Williamson and I visited them in the afternoon. The Buckner is in a large brick building. Every thing about it is in perfect order. The surgeon in charge, Dr. McAllister, is from Alabama. The matron, Mrs. Beers,[5] is from Louisiana. We saw some very sick men there. One poor fellow the nurses were forcing to eat some very thick arrow-root mixed with wine, but he could not be induced to take it. I fixed some for him, as I had done before in Corinth, which he drank and said was delightful. We then visited the Bragg, which is being fixed up. Dr. Redwood of Alabama is surgeon; Mrs. Glassburn is matron of it. She and the ladies with her are doing much for the benefit of the soldiers.

September 8.—A very warm day. Mrs. Williamson and myself went out to try to get some sweet potatoes for some of the men in the Buckner Hospital. They are very scarce here at present, as the season is a dry one. We got some from a lady who would not take up any for her own use, but as soon as we told her who they were for she gave them to us, and would take no money for them. This lady had two young daughters, who were busy weaving and spinning. They had on dresses spun and woven by themselves. This ancient work is all the fashion now, as we are blockaded and can get no other kind of goods.

We are much pleased with our kind hostess, Mrs. Evans. Some few days ago one of her sons, a Methodist preacher, came to see her, and the first thing he asked us about was Miss Augusta Evans, the authoress, of Mobile,[6] saying he admired her and her works so much

[5] Mrs. Fannie A. Beers wrote of her experiences as a Confederate hospital matron in *Memories*.

[6] Augusta Jane Evans (later Wilson) of Mobile. Already well known for her *Inez* and *Beulah* this author would publish during the course of the War the literary sensation of the Confederacy, *Macaria* (Richmond, 1864). She achieved postwar fame with *St. Elmo*, an all-time bestseller. Her services as a wartime nurse in the Mobile area are discussed in W. P. Fidler's biography of her which has already been cited.

64

that he had named one of his daughters for her. We had a good prayer-meeting while he was here.

When I left Mobile Mr. McVoy gave me some money for his young son, a member of an Alabama regiment, who he had heard was sick up this way. On arriving here I found he was at Wither's [Withers's] Division Hospital, which was at Tyner's Station, Tenn. I wrote there, and received an answer from Mr. Colson of the same regiment, telling me that he was dead.

Judge Thornton of Mississippi is now at Dalton, with his wounded son. He brought him from Virginia, and has been unable to proceed further on the way with him. I intend going down to visit him.

There is a good deal of trouble about the ladies in some of the hospitals of this department. Our friends here have advised us to go home, as they say it is not considered respectable to go into one. I must confess, from all I had heard and seen, for awhile I wavered about the propriety of it; but when I remembered the suffering I had witnessed, and the relief I had given, my mind was made up to go into one if allowed to do so. Mrs. Williamson and Mrs. May have come to the same conclusion on the subject as myself. God has said, "Who can harm you if you be followers of that which is good?" I thought of this, and believed it, and gained strength from it. Christians should not mind what the world says, so that they are conscious of striving to do their duty to their God.

It seems strange that the aristocratic women of Great Britain have done with honor what is a disgrace for their sisters on this side of the Atlantic to do. This is not the first time I have heard these remarks. Not respectable! And who has made it so? If the Christian, high-toned, and educated women of our land shirk their duty, why others have to do it for them. It is useless to say the surgeons will not allow us; we have our rights, and if asserted properly will get them. This is our right, and ours alone.

In a book called the "Sunny South," written by the lamented Rev. J. H. Ingraham,[7] are the following words: "Soldiers fight the battles of our country, and the least we can do is to cherish them in their helplessness, and bind up their wounds, and all *true* women will do it, who love their country." Who among us does not echo his sentiments? Women of the South, let us remember that our fathers, husbands, brothers, and sons are giving up all that mortals can for us; that they are exposed hourly to the deadly missiles of the enemy; the fatigues of hard marching, through burning suns, frost, and sleet; pressed by hunger and thirst; subject to diseases of all kinds from exposure; and last, though by no means least, the evil influences that are common in a large army. Are we aware of all this, and unwilling to nurse these brave heroes who are sacrificing so much for us? What, in the name of common sense, are we to do? Sit calmly down, knowing

[7] Joseph Holt Ingraham, *The Sunny South* . . . (Philadelphia, 1860).

that there is many a parched lip which would bless us for a drop of water, and many a wound to be bound up? These things are not to be done, because it is not considered respectable! Heaven help the future of our country, for nothing but God's special aid can save any country where such doctrines are inculcated.

Women of the South, let us remember we have a foe as relentless as Tamerlane or Atilla, who, if we are to believe his own threats, has resolved to lay our towns in ashes, lay waste our fields, and make our fair land a blackened mass of ruins if we will not submit to his domination; and, unless every man and woman in the South do their duty, he will succeed, even though we had a president gifted with the wisdom of Solomon, and generals endowed with the genius of Frederick or Napoleon. I know there are hundreds of our women who look on this subject in the proper light, having household duties to attend to, which they can not leave; but have we not thousands who, at this moment, do not know what to do to pass the time that is hanging heavily on their hands? I mean the young: the old are not able for the work. If it will hurt a young girl to do what, in all ages, has been the special duty of woman—to relieve the suffering—it is high time the youth of our land were kept from the camp and field. If one is a disgrace, so is the other.

September 10.—I arrived at Dalton, Ga., to-day. Left Ringgold at 6 o'clock this morning; took a very nice breakfast a few miles below, for which we paid one dollar each. When I reached here, I found Judge Thornton and his son delighted to see me; the latter I had never seen before. Poor fellow! he had suffered terribly with his wound; was wasted almost to a skeleton. His father found him in a field hospital in Virginia—no one but a negro man nursing him. Mrs. Thornton is expected here in a few days, and I intend remaining until she comes. They are living with a very nice family by the name of Davis, who have kindly invited me to stay with them while I remain in this place.

Sunday, September 14.—A very warm day. I went to the Baptist Church, this morning, with Mr. Davis; it was in a very romantic spot. This is a most beautiful place, in a valley, with mountains each side of it. It is one hundred miles northwest of Atlanta, and is the county-seat of Whitfield [Whitefield], and the terminus of the East Tennessee and Knoxville Railroad. It is south of Ringgold; it has some manufactories, and a number of hospitals, with but few patients in them; a large number are daily expected. The ladies of the place are preparing to take care of them when they come.

I have made the aquaintance of quite a number of the residents here, and am much pleased with them. There is a great deal of simplicity and good-heartedness among them; many of them have a very peculiar accent, such as we read of in the " Georgia Scenes "; indeed,

66

I think the author must have lived in the place, as I have seen more than one of his characters here in real life.[8]

September 16.—I arrived at Chattanooga this morning, about 5 o'clock, having left Dalton on the 15th. Mrs. Thornton arrived there before I left. Her son was much overcome at the sight of her. Mr. and Mrs. Davis were very kind to me, as was also their niece, an interesting young girl, who had just lost a brother in the service. Mr. Davis has two sons in the army. I stopped at Ringgold on the way up. Mrs. May and Mrs. Williamson had preceded me, and we are now in the Newsom Hospital. It is a very large one, having been enlarged to double the size it was when we visited it before. The part we occupy is opposite to the wards we formerly visited. We have each a ward assigned us. The house our room is in was a large hotel; Mrs. May takes charge of it. On the south side is another ward—Mrs. Williamson in charge—formed of two two-story brick stores; on the north corner is a large brick house three stories high—was a private boarding-house—which is to be under my especial care. It is quite a handsome building. I am much pleased with my portion.

We have a good many patients. One man, by the name of Hughes, died in my ward this morning. He was a member of the Sixteenth Louisiana Regiment. I hope this is not ominous.

We have nothing to cook on but one small stove, and that a smoky one. It cooks for the whole of this side of the hospital. We have nothing to give the men to eat but wheat-bread (very nicely made at the government bakery), fresh beef, rice, tea, and coffee.

We have had no reliable news from the army since it went into Kentucky. A report came a week or two ago that it had reached Covington, and was about to shell Cincinnati. This good news we are almost afraid to believe.

September 19.—I have been kept quite busy ever since I came here; in fact, we all have been. We have a good deal to try us, but our minds were made up to expect that before we came. The stove smokes badly, and we find it almost impossible to do any thing with it; besides it is so small that we scarcely have room to cook on it what little we have. The surgeon, Dr. Hunter, like many other men, is totally ignorant of domestic arrangements, and also, like many others, wholly unaware of his ignorance. The only consolation we get from him is a fabulous tale about a woman (a " Mrs. Harris ") who cooked for five hundred people on the same kind of a stove.

One of our greatest trials is want of proper diet for sick men. We

[8] Augustus Baldwin Longstreet's *Georgia Scenes*, a classic of nineteenth-century American humor, was first published in 1835. It had been widely read by the sixties. At the time it was written this part of Georgia was still Indian country. The book's characters were sketched from the people of eastern Georgia, but sketched when that part of the state was still virtually frontier.

do the best we can with what we have—toast the bread and make beef-tea; and we have a little butter—bad at that.

There are no changes of clothing for the men; but we have cloth, and after our day's work is done, we each make a shirt, which is a great help. The last, though by no means the least, of our troubles is the steward, who has taken a dislike to us, and annoys us in every little petty way possible. His wife has charge of the wards across the street from us. The assistant surgeon complains of her inattention to her duties in waiting on the sick.

A man, by the name of Watt Jones, died in my ward to-day; another, by the name of Allen Jones, yesterday—both members of the Fourth Florida Regiment.

Our room is in the third story, facing the west; the view from it is really grand, and when worn out physically and mentally, I derive great pleasure from looking out. On the north of us runs the Tennessee River; opposite there is a range of hills—one rising above the other—dotted with beautiful residences, surrounded by prettily laid out gardens. On the southwest, is Lookout Mountain, its peak frowning down on the river which winds around its base—looking like a lion couchant, ready to spring on its prey.

Sunday, September 28.—Have been very busy all the week, too much so to write in my journal. Three men died in the course of the week. On the 26th, John Wilkinson, a member of the Fifth Mississippi Regiment, from Neshobo County, Miss.; on the 27th, D. W. Jarvis, from Coffeeville, Alabama, a member of the Thirty-second Alabama Regiment; same date, John Cotton, member of Sixteenth Louisiana Regiment, of Rappee [Rapides] Parish, La. These men were in a very low state when first brought in from the camps.

Diarrhea is the prevailing disease among the patients.[9] I have been so busy that I have not taken time to visit Mrs. May's ward. She has many sick men, as has also Mrs. Williamson. They both have a great deal of trouble. The stove smokes as badly as ever. I have the use of one that belongs to the surgeons. (They all mess together; their kitchen and dining-room are near my ward.) It answers for what little I have to cook—beef-tea, toast, sago, and arrow-root. I have a nice little distributing room in the ward, which the head nurse, George Bean, has fixed up very neatly.

The great cry of our sick is for milk. We could buy plenty, but have no money. We get a little every day for the worst cases, at our own expense. I intend letting the folks at home know how many are suffering for want of nourishment, for I feel confident that if they knew of it they would send us means.

[9] Wiley concludes that "dysentery and diarrhea were the most prevalent of all camp diseases." The formidable statistics he quotes are reinforced by the comment of one Confederate soldier in a letter to his wife: "It is a very rare thing to find a man in this army who has not got the diorreah." Wiley, *The Life of Johnny Reb*, 251-52.

Last week, in despair, I went to Dr. Young, the medical purveyor, and begged him to give me some wine; in fact, any little thing, I told him, would be acceptable. I did not come away empty-handed. He gave me arrow-root, sago, wine, and several kinds of spices, and many things in the way of clothing.

In every hospital there is invariably a fund; there is none at present in this. The reason, we have been told, is because the hospitals at this post are in debt to the government, by drawing more money from it than their due, and until it is paid we will get no more. The fund consists of money drawn instead of the soldiers rations, as the sick men are unable to eat the rations.[10]

Mrs. Williamson and myself went to the Episcopal Church this morning. There were very few present, and those were mostly soldiers. The pastor's, Rev. Mr. Denniston, sermon was a political one.

I went to give my sick men their dinners, and found that the food I had cooked for them was spoiled. I asked Huldah, the negro woman who cooks for the surgeons, who had ruined every thing. She told me the steward's wife had been over there and put handfuls of salt into the beef-tea and other things. She had done the same before, but I did not know who did it. My poor men had to go that day dinnerless. I do not know when I have felt so badly about any thing. I am afraid the next thing she does will be to attempt my life. We had made up our minds, if Dr. Hunter did not put an end to these persecutions, it would be impossible for us to remain here. One of the assistant surgeons came to me, and told me that if Dr. Hunter did not put a stop to them, he and the other assistant surgeons would do so. But I have been informed that Dr. Hunter has told the steward, that if his wife comes over to this side of the hospital he will turn her out altogether. It seems we will never get rid of troubles of this sort.

When we first came here Dr. Hunter told us there was another lady coming to assist us; we found out who she was, and concluded if she came we would not remain. We told Dr. Hunter what we knew of her, and he said that was strange, as she had certificates from our first surgeons. I told him there were some of them whose certificates I did not value as much as the paper they were written on. He said on no account would he have her come.

Had a visit a few days ago from Dr. Flewellen; he congratulated us

[10] The hospital fund was a commutation of rations which was paid out by the Commissary on requisitions from the hospitals according to the number of soldiers present in the hospitals as patients. C. S. Statutes, 1st Cong., Sess. II, Ch. 17, 1862. Dr. Stout wrote: " Under my directorship the surgeons utilized the hospital funds in every necessary way for the comfort of their patients. Not only were chickens, butter, eggs, milk, molasses, fruits and other edibles purchased, but leather to cobble shoes, dental material and cordials (home made) and vegetables purchased when needed and could be had. When Confederate currency would not purchase delicacies from the farmers, wagon-loads of spun cotton were purchased from the Roswell and other factories and foragers sent out with it to barter for delicacies." " Some Facts . . . ," Southern Practitioner, XXV (1903) , 280.

on our admission to the hospitals. He is one of the surgeons who approves of ladies being in hospitals. We went to see him when visiting this place, and he told us the ladies did good in many ways; the principle good was, that where they were the surgeons and nurses were more apt to attend to the patients than they would otherwise be.

We have a good deal of trouble about servants; the soldiers do the cooking, and in fact all the domestic work. We have a few free negroes, and they give no little trouble. For this reason the slaves here are not near so respectful as they are with us; although they seem to have great contempt for the free negroes. The other day I heard the doctor's servant indignantly say that some one had spoken to her as if she was free, and had no master to care for her.

There are quite a number of soldiers in the place who can not get on to their commands, as the country is filled with bush-whackers, and it is dangerous for them to go through it unless in very large bodies.

I am a good deal worried about my brother, as I have not heard from him since the army went into Kentucky.

September 30.—Orders have come to send off all the men who can be moved, as we are expecting a large number from General Breckinridge's command.

We had a visit this evening from a Kentuckian; his hopes are high about soon getting to his home, as the good news is confirmed about the success of Bragg's army in Kentucky.

This evening a great many patients came in. They are the returned prisoners of Fort Donelson.

We are very nicely fixed now. A Kentucky friend made us a present of a carpet, with the proviso that we would keep it for our own comfort; also some nice articles of bedding. Mrs. Bryant, the owner of the house we are in, is living in it; the family is a very pleasant one. They have had their sorrows, in the loss of a little child, since we have been here. We buy our milk from Mrs. Bryant. Their being here makes it pleasanter for us than it otherwise would be.

October 1.—One of Mrs. May's patients died a few days ago. His name was Huntley; was a lieutenant in the Twenty-seventh Mississippi Regiment. He was sick for some time, and died perfectly resigned, in the full hope of a blessed resurrection. He spoke a good deal about his family, and would like to have seen them before his departure from this world. Mrs. Williamson conversed and prayed with him, and was much gratified at the frame of mind in which he died. His father came to see him, but too late, as he was dead and buried. A few days before his death he told me that my friend, Lieutenant Booth, a member of the same regiment, was here sick. Dr. Hunter has sent a messenger around to all the hospitals in search of him, but he is not to be found.

In a letter received a few days ago from home, was a notice of the death of Charles Farrow, a member of the Twenty-first Alabama Regiment, the same who was taken prisoner at Shiloh. He was confined

70

at Camp Douglas;[11] was taken sick while on the transport, coming down; and, having no attention paid him, sank under his disease, and died on the 21st or 22d of September. Poor fellow! It seems but yesterday since I saw him, a boy. He was one of my brother's school-mates. They are dropping off, one by one. I little know what at this moment may be my brother's fate.

The relatives of Charles Farrow had the consolation of closing his eyes and ministering to his last wants, as he reached his home a few hours ere he breathed his last. He was a member of the Episcopal Church, and, I believe, a sincere and devout Christian. I feel for his poor mother and sisters who mourn for him.

October 2.—We are very busy, trying to get clothes made for the exchanged prisoners. They are in a dreadful state for want of them; many of them have not changed their clothes for more than a month. Some of the ladies of the place promised to help us, but we have as yet seen nothing of them; they do not assist us in any way. This is not a wealthy place, and our army has been here for some time, which has impoverished it still more.

The prisoners complain bitterly of their treatment while in Jackson, Miss. Some of them told me that if they had been convicts they could not have been worse treated. This is something I can not under-stand. Who could forget Fort Donelson, and the hardships our poor men endured there! Every time I think of it a cold shudder runs through me; and then, to think what these poor fellows have endured since, during nearly one long year, in a cold northern prison! I hope that the patriotic state of Mississippi "has not tired of well-doing."

October 4.—Last night one of the returned prisoners died, very suddenly, of congestive chills. His name was Thomas Goff, member of the First Border Rangers of Virginia; he has left a wife and four children to mourn their loss. His brother was with him, and has taken his death very hard. Dr. Hopping, who attended him, was very kind. He did not leave him from the time he was taken sick until he died.

Sunday, October 5.—A very warm day. I spent it in reading and talking to the patients. One died, named James Murray, member of the Thirty-second Alabama Regiment. We have a number of that regiment in the hospital—it either is or was stationed here.

October 6.—My patients are all doing well; but I feel much de-pressed on account of news that has just reached us from Kentucky. Buell has outwitted Bragg, and got to Louisville before him. Many are fearful that the latter will come out badly.

October 8.—The weather still continues warm.

More bad news. On the 20th ult. General Price had a battle in Iuka, Miss., and was defeated. It is said his men fought valiantly, but were overpowered by numbers.

[11] The Federal prison camp at Chicago.

71

On the 3d and 4th inst., another was fought at Corinth—said to be the most desperate of the war. General Van Dorn was in command. After a severe struggle for the place, and the loss of many men, we had to retire, as the place was so strongly fortified. I know what General Price's men will say; that, had he been in command,

> " Another sight had seen that morn—
> From Fate's dark book a leaf been torn."

Missouri, Texas, Arkansas, and Louisiana, no doubt, will be the losers in this sad affair, as those states were well represented in that army. I do sincerely hope that the wounded from it are well cared for. Mississippi is destined to be sacred ground, bathed with the blood of martyrs.

It is raining very hard. We still have our trials. Lately I have had a little kitchen to myself; and as every chimney seems to have been planned by the same architect, mine has the failing of others—is smoky.

Mrs. May is sick; and it is not much to be wondered at, as she has been so sorely tried in many ways. She is going home. I regret her leaving, as she has been so faithful to the sick. Mrs. Williamson is also complaining.

While in the midst of my troubles this morning, I received a letter from one of my Corinth patients, who had been badly wounded there, thanking me for what little attention I had paid him. He seemed so grateful that I felt I could bear more trials than I have to receive such gratitude in return. He is an officer in a Tennessee regiment, and is very hopeful about our cause; thinks that Buell is " whipped."

Sunday, October 12.—We have good news from Kentucky. A battle was fought on the 8th inst. at Perryville, and we won. I can scarcely rejoice, for I know we have lost many valuable lives.

I do hope some one prayed for me today, as I have been too cross to do so myself; have had one of the most trying days of my life. I wonder if Miss Nightingale had any of the hardships to endure that we have.

I have another kitchen, and the chimney of it smokes as badly as the others. I spent the whole day in it; did not even visit my patients. To add to all, it has poured down rain all day, and the wood was so wet that it was almost impossible to make it burn. I thought of home and home comforts not a few times.

We have men for cooks; but, as they are taken from the convalescent patients, they are scarcely fitted for the work. I have had some two or three, but as soon as they are initiated into the mysteries of the culinary art they take sick; so we have a good deal of it to do ourselves.

Dr. Hunter is doing all he can to help us, but he has but little power to do so, as servants are not to be had; and, although he is a disciple of Esculapius, can not cure smoky chimneys.

October 15.—The day has cleared off beautifully. Good news continues to come in from Kentucky. I have just received a note from a Kentuckian, with a vest, requesting me to enlarge it, as the hope of soon seeing his wife and children, whom he has been separated from for some time, has so inflated him that it needs altering.

J. Tew, a member of the Thirty-second Alabama Regiment, died to-day; is from Red Creek, Ala.; was a married man.

The colonel of that regiment (McKinstry) is from Mobile. He has visited his men in the hospital, and seemed much interested in them. He was post commandant of this place.

Two of our men died to-day: Robert Arnold, member of the Tenth South Carolina Regiment, and Mr. Schoff, member of the Sixteenth Louisiana Regiment.

We are in despair for diet for the men, as our money is all gone. I have written to our friends in Mobile to send us some. If they do not, I do not know what we will do, as we have nothing but beef, bread, and coffee; many of the men can not taste either of these things. I believe that many a man dies for want of proper nourishment. When they have money themselves, they give it to us to buy things with; but money is an article of which they have very little at this time. I hope there will be a change for the better soon, and that we will be able to get plenty of money, as Dr. Stout (who is said to be an excellent manager) is now medical director of the hospital department, from Atlanta to this post.

Sunday, October 19.—While visiting the men this afternoon, I found four who had not eaten any thing for some time. I sent a nurse to one of the citizens—Mrs. Moore; told him to tell her to send us some milk, for charity's sake, which she did, and the poor fellows drank it as if it really did them good. I could not help thinking, if I was only near some of my Mobile friends, how gladly they would give me as much as I wanted.

Went to the Episcopal Church this morning, but found it closed. Mrs. Williamson and I went, this evening, to the Presbyterian Church, accompanied by Rev. Mr. Williams, whom I knew in Okolona. He is a colporteur in this department. We heard an excellent sermon, preached by a chaplain. We were warned, as we have often been before, to try and live in obedience to God's commands, so that we might get his blessing instead of his curse. The ministers of the gospel seem to have done their part in this respect; so, if we go astray, it will be willful blindness.

October 21.—Mr. H. C. Jole of the Thirty-seventh Mississippi Regiment died to-day. The hospital is filled with men from Knoxville; they come in by the hundred, and all who are able are sent off again to other points. Many of them I never see.

News has just come that Bragg has had to abandon Kentucky, as

73

he did not get the aid he expected from the people. This is a sad blow to us.

October 24.—J. T. Barber of the Thirty-second Alabama Regiment, from Choctaw County, Ala., and Mr. Jones of the Twenty-second Mississippi Regiment, died to-day. I have little or no time to talk to the men on the subject of death; but they all seem religiously inclined, and ready to cast themselves at the feet of Him who is all-powerful to save. I have not yet met one scoffer.

Mrs. Williamson is very sick, and as I have the three wards to attend, I have no time to take care of her. Some days I leave her in the morning, and do not see her again till night.

Sunday, October 26.—On looking out of the window this morning, I saw that snow had fallen heavily through the night. The first thing I thought of was a few lines of an old Scotch song:

> " A' the hills are covered wi' snaw;
> It's surely winter fairly."

Lookout, and the adjoining hills and valleys, arrayed in their snowy attire, looked really beautiful. I should have enjoyed the scene but for the knowledge of what our men were suffering—our half-clad soldiers. . . .

It is said the army is very much demoralized by the retreat from Kentucky; but, I trust, when they get rested, all will be right again.

Dr. Hunter has written to one of the ladies of the Military Aid Society in Mobile, to see if she can not send us some bedding, as we have scarcely any.

Last night one of my patients died. His sufferings were so great it was a relief to see him go; he was entirely covered with erysipelas. He seemed well prepared for the change. His name was Newbern—was a member of the Thirty-second Alabama Regiment, and was from Citronelle, Miss.

October 27.—Patients from Bragg's army are coming in daily; the hospital is full of them. I never saw such exhausted and worn-out men; they are in rags, and many of them barefooted. It is said the whole army suffered much; that many a time they had nothing to eat but parched corn.

Mrs. Williamson is much worse; has typhoid fever. There is a negro girl waiting on her, which to me is a relief.

I thought I had found a treasure in a white woman whom I have made my head cook; but, on going into the kitchen this morning, found her in such a state of intoxication I had to dismiss her, and fall back on the convalescent men as cooks.[12] They do pretty well,

---

[12] Phoebe Yates Pember, who served as a matron in Chimborazo Hospital, Richmond, relates an amusing parallel story. She hired as an assistant a high-nosed Englishwoman with seven trunks and strong recommendations. Despite the excess baggage, Miss Pember expected much of her new helper, for the stealing of the

74

but it seems hard to make them understand the importance of cooking properly.

There are many things, if not correctly prepared, are very injurious to the sick. Even mush, simple as it is, is seldom properly made. It should be boiled at least an hour, otherwise it is very unwholesome.

October 29.—I have had more to do today than ever, and am completely worn out. I have a very nice lady to take charge of the kitchen, whose husband is a patient and able to help her, which will be pleasant for both, and a relief to me.

Mrs. Williamson has typhoid fever in its worst form, and is out of her mind. An apathy comes over those who have it. I have noticed the men with it; they seem perfectly indifferent as to what becomes of them. In this state they seldom speak of home. I sometimes think this is a blessing, as they would worry about it.

A lady has just arrived who came to see her husband, and found him dead. The shock nearly made her lose her reason. Poor thing! my heart aches for her. If Lincoln and his followers could see a few scenes like this, they would surely desist from this unholy strife. This incident is of daily occurrence.

October 31.—Halloween, or All Saints' Eve. . . . I can not help contrasting to-night with what it has been in days gone by, before "wild war's deadly blast" had come, when for the sake of "Auld Scotia" we held it in commemoration.

I received a telegram from home to-day, to know if I had heard from my brother. I wonder if he is in the land of the living.

November 1.—Had one man die to-day, named Robbins, from Pontotoc, Miss. Had quite a treat for the patients sent to us from Dr. Young—a large box of sweet oranges, and a quantity of nice clothes.

Sunday, November 2.—Went down to the depot this morning, as I heard General Withers's division was passing through on their way west, and I was in hopes I would hear something of my brother; was

---

liquor in her charge was the plague of her hospital life and the English matron expressed an aversion to even its odor. " 'It turned her witals.' " "The next day," wrote Miss Pember, "walking through one of the wards . . . I found a part of the building about eight to ten feet square, partitioned off, a roughly improvised plank partition dividing this temporary room from the rest of the ward. Seated comfortably therein was the new matron, entrenched among her trunks. A neat table and comfortable chair, abstracted from my few kitchen appurtenances, added to her comfort. Choice pieces of crockery . . . that had at one time adorned my shelves, were disposed tastefully around, and the drinks issued by me for the patients were conveniently placed at her elbow. She explained that she kept them there to prevent thefts. Perhaps the nausea communicated from their neighborhood tinted [tilted] the nose higher, and there was a defiant look about her, as if she sniffed the battle afar." A battle ensued, and Miss Pember was the victor—but not until the makeshift partition had been stormed and a very drunk matron carted away in an ambulance. Pember, *A Southern Woman's Story,* 48-54.

not disappointed, as I met Colonel Buck and Captain Muldon of the Twenty-fourth Alabama Regiment. They told me he was well. His company has gone another route. The army is *en route* for Murfreesboro, the western portion of this state. It is thirty miles south-east of Nashville.

Went to the Episcopal Church this morning; heard a very good sermon. Mr. Denniston introduced me to some very nice ladies belonging to the place. He is post chaplain here. He called to see us yesterday.

November 4.—Had a man die to-day by the name of Thomas Ford, of the Second Kentucky—"Morgan's Squardon." He was from Glasgow, Ky.

Our hospital is filled with men from Cheatham's command. I am told it suffered most at Perryville. We have few wounded, as they were left in Kentucky.

They say that the Kentuckians, on leaving their state, many of them old men, cried like children. They think it is gone from them forever, but I trust not.

November 7.—Our hospital is much enlarged; it now holds about seven hundred patients. We are getting a little more milk. Had a man die yesterday, named John Renfruit, from Barbour County, Ala.

Rev. Mr. Williams visits the patients often, and seems to be doing much good. Yesterday he brought an old friend of mine to see me, Lieutenant Hudson of Mobile, now with General Withers. I was much pleased to see him.

In the news from Virginia there is another "On to Richmond" in prospect.[13] General Burnside is to try it this time.

Sunday, November 9.—Mrs. Williamson is recovering.

Had a visit a few evenings ago from Mrs. Newsom. She has charge of a new hospital that is opened in the Crutchfield House; it is called the "Foard," in honor of the medical director of this army.

I had a letter yesterday from a Mrs. Young, in Charleston. She is going to send me a box of tracts and other reading matter for the men, which is much needed. She writes very encouragingly of the safety of Charleston. General Beauregard is in command there. I know the enemy dread to meet him.

November 10.—I went with a party horseback riding to-day. General Hardee was our "*pilot*," and an excellent one he was. He took us to the top of a very steep ridge; there was one of the finest views from

[13] "On to Richmond" was ridiculed as the watchword of the Federal army in a long comic poem, "Richmond Is a Hard Road to Travel," by John Reuben Thompson which was published (New Orleans, Augusta, [c. 1863]) to the tune of Dan Emmett's "Jordan Is a Hard Road To Travel." It was "dedicated" to General Ambrose E. Burnside and recounts the succession of Yankee generals and their "famous 'on to Richmond' double trouble." Richard B. Harwell, *Confederate Music* (Chapel Hill, N. C., 1950), 83, 138.

it I have ever beheld; every now and again we could see the river, as if peeping out from its many islands. Although we have had frost and snow, the trees had not shed their foliage, and were beautiful with the gorgeous hues of autumn. When we reached the summit, there was naught there save the "silent worshipers"; there was a solemnity which seemed like the "felt presence of the Deity"....

The author of the "Tactics"[14] is truly a military-looking man, and combines the *fortiter in re* with the *suaviter in modo*. At the commencement of the war, while a colonel, he had command of Fort Morgan. He is held in high esteem by his men. Major Roy, who I believe is his adjutant-general, was with him. He is a handsome man, and has a fine address. He spoke of the general most affectionately.

On reaching home, I found that one of my patients had died in my absence. His name was Thompson, a lieutenant in the Twenty-seventh Mississippi Regiment. He was brought into the hospital, a day or two ago, in a dying state. His captain was with him, and left me his sister's address. I have a lock of his hair, which I will send her when I write.

November 11.—Each corps of the army has hospitals assigned it; ours belongs to General Hardee's.[15] He visited it to day, and was much pleased with its order and its cleanliness. We are getting along much better in every way; have dried fruit, a few eggs and potatoes, and better cooks.

I went out shopping with Mrs. Newsom, and was quite amused at a bargain she was trying to make with a woman who had potatoes to sell. She tried to get them on credit; but the woman was inexorable, and would not give them; even with all the tales that Mrs. Newsom

[14] General William Joseph Hardee's *Rifle and Light Infantry Tactics* was probably the best known book in the Confederacy. It was reprinted in a dozen different issues in Mobile 1861 to 1863 and in at least ten other Confederate editions. In addition, large portions of it were incorporated into other similar manuals. Marjorie Lyle Crandall, *Confederate Imprints* (Boston, 1955), II, 416-21, 425-26.

Because of his *Tactics* General Hardee was one of the most widely famed officers in the Confederate armies. *The Southern Field and Fireside* quoted P. W. Alexander, correspondent of the Savannah *Republican*, in its issue of January 9, 1864: "In 1853, Lieut. Col. Hardee was assigned by Mr. [Jefferson] Davis, the then Federal Secretary of War, to the duty of arranging a system of Tactics for the use of the army and militia of the United States, and produced the work which has since become a household word. 'Hardee's Tactics,' by order of the War Department, superseded Scott's, and the Federal army is now using it, and has always used since the publication, the unaltered editions of 'Hardee's Tactics,' except that his name is no longer inserted as the author, wishing, no doubt, not to appear as having a 'rebel' as their military teacher."

[15] "At the very outset of my administration of the hospital department, I was embarrassed by the persistent demand of Lieutenant Generals Polk and Hardee that separate hospitals should be provided for the treatment of members of their commands, and the recognition of hospitals under State patronage, officered by State authority." Stout, "Some Facts . . . ," *Southern Practitioner* XXV (1903), 159-60.

told of the sick men needing them. The woman said she had no faith in hospitals paying; so Mrs. Newsom had to come away without them, and wait till she got the money. She is expecting some—the proceeds of a concert given by the ladies of the place.

November 15.—Mr. Rally, husband of the lady who had charge of the kitchen, died this morning. He had been all through the Kentucky campaign, and had been a good and brave soldier. His poor wife is almost heart-broken. I tried to get her to stay with me, but as everything here was connected with her sorrows, I could not prevail on her to remain. She had the consolation of being with him in his last moments—one that many a woman would give worlds to have.

Lost another patient—J. P. Allen of Hilliard's Legion, from Coosa County, Ala. He was a long and patient sufferer. His death was one of those we can think on with pleasure; it was that of a soldier of the cross. He met our great enemy with his armor on, and ready for the conflict. When I told him his moments were numbered, he said he was perfectly happy, and desired me to write to his wife, and tell her he hoped to meet her and his child in heaven. He made me a present of his Bible, which I shall treasure as long as I live.

All our men seem to die resigned; but it is difficult to judge of their frame of mind, as they are too far gone with disease when they come here to talk to them on the subject of death, which is another proof of the necessity of preparing, while in health, for that long journey from which no traveler returns. Nearly all of the men who have died here were in a dying state when brought from the camps.

Yesterday we had a visit from Dr. [Young] of Kentucky. He was on General Bragg's staff through the Kentucky campaign. He and some others went to the house of an old acquaintance and asked for food for themselves and horses, but the man was so afraid of the Federal authorities that he refused to give them any thing. This gentleman's daughters acted in defiance of all restraint, and gave them a cordial welcome, and entertained them by singing southern songs. Dr. [Young] blamed the people of Kentucky for the failure of the campaign, and says that General Bragg did not receive the aid he expected from them.

Sunday, November 16.—I called on Mrs. Newsom this morning, and found her cooking dinner, for about fifty men, on a small grate; she had to cook one article at a time. Mrs. Newsom was in distress on account of news she had just received from her home, in Arkansas. Her father, a Baptist minister, had been imprisoned and otherwise harshly treated, because he would not take the oath of allegiance to the United States government. I met a lady there, who had come to see her brother, and found him dead; she was in mourning for her husband, who died recently. Mr. Williams was holding service in the dining-room; it was filled with soldiers.

78

November 17.—Mr. W. James, a member of the Twenty-seventh Mississippi Regiment, died to-day.

I find I have more than I can possibly attend to. Dr. Hunter has written to Mrs. Ogden, requesting her to take the hospital in charge. I do hope she will come.

November 21.—Another death occurred to-day—J. B. Little of the Eighth Mississippi Regiment.

The steward's wife has gone; Mrs. Snow from Mobile has taken her place.

November 23.—Lieutenant Chamberlain of the Twenty-fourth Alabama Regiment brought us a box of clothing, a donation from the Mobile Military Aid Society.

The day has been very beautiful. I went to the Presbyterian Church in the morning; the Episcopal Church is still closed. I regret this, as the town is full of soldiers, and churches are much needed.

November 24.—The small-pox is in town. We are all ordered to be vaccinated.

Have just received a letter from Mr. McLean, he says provisions are so high in Mobile that it is almost impossible to live, and that speculators are making *piles* of money out of the misfortunes of their country. It will be a curse to them and their posterity after them, for it is the very blood of their fellow-mortals they are making it out of. I little thought, when we set out, that there was one man in the whole South who could be guilty of such a base act. How can they expect men to fight for them when they are taking the lives of their wives and children? They may shudder at the accusation, but in the eyes of God they are murderers. But there is a day of reckoning for them, and then may God have mercy on them! for if they only suffer one half the pangs of which they have been the cause, their case will be sad indeed.

This is a land flowing with milk and honey; enough of food in it to supply us if the blockade should last forever, and be much more effectual than it is. I trust, that good men—for we have many of them—will rise in their might, and drive these wretches from among us.

November 27.—W. H. Williams, one of Hardee's body-guard, died on the 25th. Had one case of small-pox, which has been sent to the pest-house. I am told the disease is of a mild type, and very few die of it.

The enemy are preparing to give battle to the Tennessee army; Rosecrans, their ablest general, is in command. News of a battle is daily expected.

Two ladies of this place, Mrs. Brooks and Mrs. Brewer, called on us to-day. I was much pleased with them.

Sunday, November 30.—Called on Mrs. Newsom this afternoon; had a long talk over our hospital trials. She related some of the hospital scenes at Bowling Green, which were truly awful—Corinth was heaven

79

in comparison. I met Major Richmond there, one of General Polk's aids. He is a fine-looking man, and very intelligent, with all the *suavity* of manner characteristic of the southern gentleman. He has traveled much, and related a number of anecdotes of scenes on the continent of Europe; told some few of England and Englishmen, and seemed to judge the whole, as many others have done, both in this country and the old, by the little he had seen, a mistake we are all liable to fall into. On the whole, his conversation was very interesting.

Dr. Hunter has gone on a visit to Mississippi; Dr. Abernethy [Abernathy] of Tennessee has taken his place. We have a nice old negro man belonging to the latter, who cooks for us. We get a good deal of money now, as the hospitals are out of debt. Some days we have as many as seven hundred patients; not more than one half of them are confined to bed.

December 3.—Mrs. Brewer sent me a beautiful cactus. She must have known how fond I was of flowers; it was a great treat.

I had a good laugh to-day at something I saw in one of our papers; it was a hit at my present employment. It is too good to be lost, and worthy of record:

Scene in hospital. *Lady* (at bedside of a sick soldier). How do you do? Is there any thing you want?

Soldier (curtly). No; I believe not.

Lady. Is there nothing I can do for you?

Soldier (with anxiety). No; I think not.

Lady. O, I do want to do something for you! Can't I wash your hands and face?

Soldier (resignedly). Well, if you want to, right bad, I reckon you can; but if you do you will be the fourteenth lady who has done so this morning! [16]

None of the men in Chattanooga will be distressed as this poor fellow was, as the ladies here are not at all lavish with their favors.

Have had a good deal of rain lately, and the weather is very cold. We are having clothes made for the hospital by women whose husbands are in the army. They are very poor, and have to support their children and selves as best they can.

December 5.—General Joseph E. Johnston is now in command of this department. With the change all seem pleased.

We have a patient, who is a prisoner in the guard-house, Captain Thatcher of St. Louis, Mo. He is to be tried as a traitor. As yet I have not seen him, but send him what is ordered. He sent me a Confederate star and a note of thanks for what little I had done for him. I sincerely trust he is not guilty.

Dr. Abernathy has been appointed house surgeon; Dr. P. Thornton

[16] A different version of this anecdote is related in James Morris Morgan's *Recollections of a Rebel Reefer* (Boston, New York, 1917). In Morgan's account the sick soldier was his friend Captain Francis Warrington Dawson. The story is doubtless apocryphal.

is now in charge. He is a nephew of Judge Thornton of Mississippi, and seems very much of a gentleman.

December 8.–More smoke. We have a grate in our room, but the chimney smokes so badly we find it impossible to have fire in it, and the weather is so cold I am fearful Mrs. Williamson will take sick again, and that I will share her fate. In despair, I went to see if Mrs. Brooks could not furnish me with a stove. She had none. There I met Mrs. General J. E. Johnston, who is stopping at Mrs. Brooks'. She is a noble-looking woman, and has fine conversational powers. The general has gone to the front, and I am told is much pleased with the state of the army. He intends making his head-quarters here.

I then called on Mrs. Brewer, who gave me a very nice stove, for which she would take no money. Mrs. Brewer said, to give it was a pleasure, as it was for the hospital.

December 9.–Received a box of bitter oranges from Mobile. I think they are a very good substitute for lemons.

The home folks are very despondent, and seem to think we are going to starve. I trust not; but it is wonderful how we manage to get along, hemmed in as we are, and the whole world arrayed against us; but were it not for the foes at home, the speculators, we would not be in want.

Have just received a lot of clothing, in the way of shirts and drawers, and some spices, from Dr. Young. They were sent to him by the ladies of Wetumpka, Alabama, for troops from that state; he also sent a number of Bibles, which are much needed.

December 30.–Have just recovered from a severe spell of sickness. I received much kindness from one and all, for which I am sincerely grateful. I suffered much, and thought often about the sick men, and my admiration rose more and more for their fortitude and patience.

Have received a number of letters from home, telling me about Christmas, and how unlike what it was before the war; but my folks say that all in Mobile are very thankful they are permitted to remain in peace, for they fully expected that by this time the enemy would be thundering at their ports. They also say that many there are making fortunes, and living as if there was no war. I am told it is the same in all large cities. There is no use worrying about these things. I expect all will come out right, and that there are enough self-sacrificing people in the land to save it.

The haughty foe has had another " On to Richmond," and been repulsed; Virginia has been again drenched with the blood of martyrs –Fredericksburg, another of her fair cities, laid in ruins. North Carolina has also suffered. Williamston and Hamilton have been completely sacked. Women and children are driven out without shelter, while their homes are laid in ruins. Well, these things will not always last. There is a day of retribution for the northern people.

ember 31.—The last day of 1862—how teeming with wonderful
has been the past year! . . .

he South has suffered, O, how terribly! Thousands and tens of
thousands of precious lives have been sacrificed to the god of war. In
every state of our beloved land there has been a temple erected to the
insatiate Moloch. This is not all: women and children have been left
homeless, and driven out into the pitiless storm, and even the bitterest
frowns of nature have had more kindness in them than the hearts of
our ruthless invaders. . . .

How hard it is to think of all this, knowing that the above is an
" owre true tale," without feeling hate, bitter hate, toward those who
are the cause of it! We were more than mortal were it otherwise, but
I trust that with it all we will leave vengeance to Him to whom it
belongs.

Amid all this suffering the star of hope for our cause shines brighter
and brighter, although in the West we have lost much territory.
Our armies are improving every way. They are better clad and better
fed than they were. We have much sickness, but nothing to what we
have had.

Life in camp has improved, physically and morally. The medical
department has also improved. Surgeons have to be thoroughly examined before receiving commissions. Congress has passed a law,
making provision for ladies (where they can be had) to take charge
of the domestic arrangements in hospitals.[17]

Manufactories have arisen where before the war they were not
known. Women, who thought such things impossible, are making
shoes and knitting socks. In every farm-house the spinning-wheel
and loom is heard. Fields are teeming with grain, where once grew
cotton and tobacco. We have enough vessels running the blockade
to keep us in tea and coffee, and cattle from Texas to keep us in beef.
In fact, if the war lasts much longer, we will be the most independent
people in the world.

Although we have lost many great and good men, numbers have
risen to take their place. The foe have work yet before them; they
have to conquer Lee, Jackson, Longstreet, Hill, and a host of others
in Virginia, with their invincible armies. Beauregard at Charleston;
Hindman and Price in the far west; the ubiquitous Morgan; and last,
though by no means least, the army of Tennessee, and its veteran

[17] An act entitled " An Act to better provide for the sick and wounded of the
army in hospitals " passed by the Confederate Congress September 27, 1862, did
much to improve the hospital service. A section of it provides for the employment
of matrons at a salary not to exceed forty dollars per month each, assistant matrons
at thirty-five dollars, and ward-matrons at thirty dollars. This law authorized the
employment of female nurses and acknowledged them as preferable in certain
areas of service. It restricted the detailing of soldiers as nurses to situations in
which the possibility of employing civilians had been exhausted and wisely
included the provision that such details should be permanent except in cases of
neglect of duty. *C. S. Statutes*, 1st Cong., Sess. II, Ch. 17, 1862.

commanders, Johnston and Bragg. I have not forgotten noble little Vicksburg and her heroic defenders; with these and God's blessing, I trust that the time is not far distant, when dove-eyed peace will hover o'er our now distracted land.

Mr. Burgess, a member of the battery my brother is in, called this evening and left some money for Mrs. Williamson, a Christmas donation from Mrs. Otis of Mobile. It is rumored a battle has commenced at Murfreesboro. May God give us the victory!

V: CHATTANOOGA, MOBILE

January 2, 1863.—Another year has commenced, alas! with bloodshed. When will it cease? I ask that question with nothing but echo for my answer. The North is putting forth all its energies to try and subjugate us, and seems determined to do its worst. May the God of hosts be with us!

A battle was fought at Murfreesboro on the 31st ultimo. We have come out of it victorious. Thousands of the enemy have been slain and wounded. We have taken upward of four thousand prisoners, and spoils of all kinds; but I can scarcely rejoice, for our wounded are coming in by the hundreds, and we have to witness the same sad spectacle as ever on such occasions. The weather is very cold, and I shudder to think what our men have had to suffer on the battle-field.

Our hospital is filled with wounded. Mrs. Williamson and myself are not able to do any thing for them. Dr. Thornton is sick. Dr. Hopping fills his place. I am anxious about my brother.

January 3.—The wounded kept coming in last night, till 12 o'clock. Every corner of the hospital is filled with patients, and the attendants had to give up their beds for them. None but slightly wounded are brought here, but they are bad enough. Many have to be carried from the ambulances, as they are unable to walk. We have sent off a great many to-day, to make room for others who will be in to-night. All that I or Mrs. Williamson have been able to do for them is to see that they get enough to eat. Bread, beef, and coffee are all we have to give them; they are thankful for that. Our cooks have been up for two or three nights in succession; the surgeons and nurses the same. I would not be surprised if they were all sick; they have so much to do.

I am told that the ladies of the place go down to the train every night with hot coffee and all kinds of refreshments for the wounded.

January 4.—We have had another battle—fought on Friday, the 2d. I believe we made the attack, and were repulsed with heavy loss. It is reported that our army is falling back. I hope this is not true, although we can scarcely expect to cope successfully with the enemy, as, comparatively speaking, our army is small, and we have the very flower of the northern army and one of their best generals to contend with. From what I have heard judges say, we ought to be satisfied if we can only hold our own.

We have about five hundred wounded prisoners in the hospital. They have their own surgeons with them. I saw some of the latter dressing their wounded, and was not a little shocked at the roughness with which they did it. Neither Mrs. Williamson or myself have visited any of them, as we are totally unable to go into the wards. They receive exactly the same food and attention that our men do. I have spoken to some who were walking about. They were Germans, and I am told the majority of them here are.

January 7.—Mrs. Brewer called to-day, and gave me one hundred dollars for the benefit of the wounded. Dr. Thornton received a contribution from the ladies of the place, and fifty dollars from the Hebrew M. A. S. of Mobile. He receives hundreds of dollars per day from the government. He makes the best possible use of it under the circumstances. He is right in that respect, as the government has provided it for the benefit of the men, and they ought to have it; but it is difficult to buy any thing in the way of delicacies. Eggs are not to be had at any price. He has sent foragers down into Georgia and Alabama, and I expect they will come back with plenty.

Our army has fallen back to Tullahoma. It is seventy miles southeast of Nashville. Many of our wounded are left in the hands of the enemy. I am told that the carnage on the last battle-field was dreadful.

I have heard from my brother, and he has escaped unhurt. The company of which he is a member—Garrety's [Garrity's] battery—has lost in killed three, and in wounded twenty-four—many of them severely.

Lieutenant Keith of the Thirty-second Alabama Regiment is killed. I pity his wife and family. His death will be a sad blow to them. I am told he was a good and brave officer.

The gallant General Hanson of Kentucky is among the slain. Of the young statesmen of Kentucky, he was one of the most gifted. He repeatedly represented it in the United States Congress, of which body he was a prominent member.

Sunday, January 11.—The hospital is filled with badly wounded, from almost every state. Many are getting furloughs to go home.

Instead of going to church I spent the day talking to the men. We have a badly wounded captain, named De Graffenread [De Graffenreid] —a member of the 151st Tennessee Regiment. He is said to be one of the richest men in the state. One of his men is with him, and very much devoted to him. He generally has two negro servants who go to the army with him. At present he has one waiting on him, who is attentive, and an excellent nurse, and he dotes on his master.

We do not have many of the wounded die, comparatively speaking. A few days ago I saw two handsome lads breathe their last. I do not know their names. The fact is, Mrs. Williamson and myself have so many to attend that we find it impossible to devote our time to them separately; and we are far from being well.

Mrs. Gilmer, whom I met in Corinth, is in the hospital. She has been for some time in the service in Mississippi.

January 12.—There are a large number of prisoners in camp near us. I saw some twenty-five hundred marched through the town. They tell the people that they will soon be here as conquerors.

All seem to have much more confidence in General Bragg than they had, and are much pleased at the prospect of affairs in Tennessee; for many thought it impossible for our small army to keep the enemy even at bay.

Captain Thatcher is now in the hospital. I went to see him. He related his story to me. I feel sorry for him, and sincerely trust that he will get justice. He was a member of the Missouri State Guard, and came out with General Price.

January 14.—We have received a box of oranges from Mobile, and some money from my friend, Mr. McLean.

Had a very nice ride to-day with Mrs. Newsom. We went on a foraging expedition, in search of milk, and found a woman who would sell us a quantity of buttermilk—a treat for the patients. We went round by the river part of the road. It was the wildest scenery I ever beheld. In one moment we were in a ravine so deep as almost to exclude from view the blue of heaven (a nice haunt for bogles and witches) , and at another time I trembled lest my horse might stumble and cast me into the ravine below.

Mrs. Newsom rode on as fearlessly as any knight of old, or one of our own cavalry. I believe the latter are the best horsemen in the world, the Indians not excepted.

In a letter received from my father and my friend Mr. McLean, both are much elated that the state of Alabama has been able to pay off the interest of her state debt in gold. The British war steamer *Vesuvius* came and took it away. My father was indignant at a telegram which Lord Lyons had dispatched from Washington, ordering the captain not to take the money, as it would be a breach of international law.[1] The dispatch did not arrive until the steamer had left. I wonder if they are as particular in regard to their dealings with the Federals? From what we hear on the subject I think not.

January 16.—I have just returned from another horseback ride with Mrs. Newsom; we visited the small-pox hospital, but were not allowed to go in; about six of Mrs. Newsom's nurses were there as patients. She inquired how they were, and if they needed any thing. They have

[1] This diplomatic incident is related in detail in a letter of Secretary of State Judah P. Benjamin to James M. Mason written at Richmond June 11, 1863. U. S. Navy Department, *Official Records of the Union and Confederate Navies in the War of the Rebellion* . . . (Washington, 1894–1927) , Ser. II, III, 796–802. Cited hereinafter as *Official Records* (Navy) .

very nice quarters, and one of our ablest army surgeons—Dr. Kratz—to attend them. The mortality from this loathsome disease is little or nothing.

I am as much pleased as ever with the wild and romantic scenery here; it is so varied. . . . Mrs. Newsom told me much about the scenery in Virginia, and said if I were to see that I would not be so enthusiastic about the views in Tennessee. I am not so sure about that, although Virginia has one advantage over Tennessee—the Atlantic Ocean—which to me would be a great one. This place is about three hundred and fifty miles inland from the gulf, or the ocean.

As I rode along side of this angelic woman, and listened to her conversation, I discovered a combination of admirable traits in her character, such as I never met in any woman before. She is

"A perfect woman, nobly planned,
To warn, to comfort, and command." [2]

January 18.—I arrived in Atlanta, in company with Mr. and Mrs. Brewer, at 3 o'clock A. M., too late to make the connection with the West Point train. As my health did not improve in the hospital, I was advised to try a change, and accordingly left Chattanooga yesterday for home.

We are at the Atlanta House, kept by a Mr. Thompson, quite a jolly landlord, and our fare is very good, considering the times.

This is a very cold and bleak day. I went out shopping with Mr. and Mrs. Brewer. They bought a handsome velvet mantle, for which they paid one hundred and fifty dollars. Mr. Brewer had a very fine shawl stolen from him; it was taken out of the parlor at the hotel; they say this city is a den of thieves. Mr. Brewer insisted on paying my hotel bill, which was five dollars, for two meals and two hours' sleep. We expect to leave on the cars by 6 o'clock, P. M.

Atlanta is in DeKalb County, Georgia; [3] is seven miles south-east of the Chattahooche River; one hundred miles west north-west of Macon; one hundred and seventy-one miles west of Augusta; one hundred and thirty miles from Chattanooga; seventy-five miles from West Point. It is the terminus of four railroads: the Augusta, the Macon and Western, the Atlantic and Western [Western and Atlantic], and the West Point. It is elevated, and quite a healthy place. I have been told that the wounded improve more rapidly here than at any other point.

January 20.—Arrived in Mobile last evening, about 10 o'clock P. M.; left Mr. and Mrs. Brewer in Montgomery; I left the latter place on the cars, in company with a friend of theirs, Mr. Weaver of Chattanooga. We took a very nice breakfast at Evergreen, a station on the road, and

[2] William Wordsworth, "She Was a Phantom of Delight," stanza 3.

[3] Atlanta is in Fulton County, which was laid out from DeKalb in 1854. In 1860 the city claimed a population of twelve thousand. Adiel Sherwood, *A Gazetteer of Georgia* . . . (4th ed., Macon, etc., 1860), 69.

had a delightful cup of coffee, for which we paid two dollars and fifty cents each.

Arrived at home quite unexpectedly to the home folks. Mr. Brewer telegraphed from Montgomery that I was coming, but, as usual with that *well-conducted* department, the dispatch did not reach here until to-day.

Home is such a contrast to that I have just left, and when I think of the men in camp I can not keep from feeling sad. I have met some soldiers here, members of Fowler's battery, from Tuscaloosa, Alabama. One Mr. Crochell played the violin beautifully, and I have no doubt with it serves to beguile many a weary hour in camp.

February 3.—Mobile has quite a number of troops in it; General Buckner is in command, and is doing his utmost to have the city placed in a state of defense.

I paid a visit, twelve miles across the bay, to the eastern shore, in Baldwin County, returning in a sail-boat, and came very near being capsized, from the tiles with which the bay is obstructed.

I have been to a fair, given for the benefit of the Protestant orphans; the ladies were all dressed very handsomely; the affair was one of the most splendid of the kind I ever attended, and it did not look much like war times.

Provisions are higher still. I have been not a little amused at the novel lights we have; instead of oil and candles, nature has bountifully supplied us with illuminators in our pitch pine knots. We have a little oil which we keep for special occasions. We put some pieces of pine in the grate, which gives light enough to see each other; all we can do is to converse, as it is impossible to sew or read by this light. We are compelled to retire in the dark, or else run the risk of having our complexion and every thing else ruined by the smoke of the pine torches. These are things which every body laughs at, saying it is war times, and they will soon be over.

Although there is a good deal of speculating, and people growing wealthy, still it seems a much greater boast to be poor than rich. Every one has his story of how hard it is for him to live. This seems to be the fashionable topic of the day. All are hopeful that this state of affairs will not last long, and feel that the cause is worth a struggle.

I have been trying to get some servants to go back with me, and also a few ladies. I have succeeded in getting one of the latter. We expect to leave in a few days. I have been presented with a number of books, from some of the bookstores, to take on with me.

February 10.—Arrived at Chattanooga at 7 A. M. Left Mobile on the 5th, by steamer to Montgomery. Captain Finnegan was very kind to myself and Miss Groom, who was with me. He did not charge us for our passage. We had transportation tickets for the cars, which only pays for half on the boat.

The Alabama River is formed of the Coosa and Tallapoosa rivers, which unite some ten miles north of Montgomery. It then flows west to Selma, below which point it is very tortuous, flowing south-west until it unites with the Tombigbee, forty-five miles north of Mobile. The river formed by this confluence is the Mobile, which empties into the Mobile Bay. It is three hundred miles in extent, and is navigable for large boats. Along its banks are immense cotton plantations. In peace times hundreds of thousands of bales of cotton pass down this river yearly, to be transported from thence to all parts of the world.

Had quite a pleasant trip. Duke Goodman, one of our wealthy planters, and his wife were on board. The latter showed us some very pretty homespun dresses. The material was grown, spun, and woven on her own plantation. The colors were very pretty, dyed from the bark of trees and wild roots.

We reached Selma early on the morning of the 7th. It is situated on a high bluff on the west bank of the river, seventy miles below Montgomery. It is in Dallas County, and is the terminus of the Alabama and Tennessee Railroad. The Central Railroad of Alabama extends west from it. We arrived too late to see a fine gunboat launched. There are one or two others being built; they are to be used for the protection of Mobile Bay.[4] Quantities of government work of all kinds are done here. There are some two or three large founderies [foundries].[5]

Miss Groom and myself paid a visit to Mrs. D[odgson], in the city, who gave us a delightful cup of tea, which is rather a delicacy these times.

On the way from Selma to Montgomery we made the acquaintance of a very nice lady, Mrs. Turner, and her brother, Mr. Davis. He is on his way to the army, and the lady to visit her husband, who is surgeon of the Seventh Arkansas Regiment.

We arrived at Montgomery on Sunday, the 8th, an hour too late for the West Point train, and put up at the Exchange Hotel, which is a very fine house. We paid three dollars each for our dinner, and a splendid one it was. Every thing was there, the same as in peace times. The house was filled with refugees, fashionably dressed, and evidently making the best of their condition.

At the table I met some old friends from Mobile. Miss Groom and I went to St. John's Church, and before service had a talk with Rev. Mr. Mitchell. He gave me some prayer-books, which were very acceptable. One of my old friends, Dr. Scott, a refugee from Pensacola, preached an excellent sermon.

We left Montgomery at 4 o'clock P. M.; arrived in Atlanta on the morning of the 9th, too late to make the connection for Chattanooga.

[4] The Confederate gunboats *Gaines* and *Selma* were built in Selma at about this time. *Official Records* (Navy), Ser. II, I, 253, 260.

[5] " Selma was a very important military depot of the Confederate States. A powder mill, nitre works, arsenal, shot and shell foundry, &c., &c., were operated here." Brewer, *Alabama*, 209.

We put up at the Trout House, a very fine hotel, but I do not like it as well as the Exchange in Montgomery. The weather was very cold, and there had just been a heavy fall of snow.

I went out shopping with Mrs. Turner. She bought a very neat straw bonnet, for which I think she paid fifty dollars. We paid five dollars each hotel bill. Left in the afternoon for this place. Our friend, Mr. Davis, in attending to our baggage, forgot his overcoat and blanket-shawl at the Trout House, which is a serious loss in this cold weather, and he on his way to camp. When within a few miles of this place the cars ran off the track, and we came up to town on a wood-car.

There is a great drawback in traveling in this country; the railroad is single, and if the returning train happens to be behindhand the other has to wait at the switches for it. We have been detained a good deal on this account; and another annoyance is the scarcity of wood; for miles the locomotive has gone at a snail's pace.

There were a number of ladies on the train with us, on their way to visit their husbands in the army.

It is remarked that there never were so many women and children traveling as there are now. Numbers of ladies, whose husbands are in the army, have been compelled to give up their homes for economy and protection, and seek others among their relatives. I know of many, with their children, who have been compelled to seek shelter under the parental roof. We have a large floating population—the people who have been driven from their homes by the invader.

Our friends left us to go to Shelbyville. Mrs. Thornton has a brother-in-law, wounded, in this hospital. He was much disappointed in not seeing her.

When I arrived at the hospital I found Mrs. Williamson well, and very busy. All were pleased to see me; but my heart sank within me when I looked around and saw the state of things. I had been away long enough to become *demoralized*. It had been snowing for some days, and the snow was melting, which made every thing damp and comfortless. A hospital is the most cheerless place in the world, and the last place I would remain in from choice. If it were not for the sake of the wounded and sick men, I do not think I could possibly stand it.

I found few of the patients whom I had left here; some have died, and others have gone to other hospitals. Mr. Noland and Mr. Kelly, two of our best nurses, are not expected to live. They were both here when we first came. Mr. Noland is too low to speak. I am much grieved to find him in this state. He was very kind to me when I was sick; and when buttermilk was ordered, searched the whole town to get it for me.

We have a patient—James Scott—who has been here ever since the army went into Kentucky. He accidentally broke his thigh while on the march. He has lain on his back for nearly four long weary months, and has never been known to murmur. I never saw such patient endurance. He is not eighteen years of age. I brought him a little present from home, which he prizes very highly.

We have a new ward near the river. It holds about fifty patients, and is set apart for cases of erysipelas. I visited it to-day, and found it nearly full. Mr. Kelly is there, with erysipelas all over his face and head; and Captain De Graffenreid, who also has it in his arm.

Sunday, February 15.—A very gloomy, rainy day; spent it very satis-factorily, going around visiting the patients. Have felt that I would not exchange places with any one. I hope I shall not grumble again at trifles; I scarcely see how I can when our men have to endure so much.

I came across two men who could not read, and spent some time reading to them. One was from Florida, and the other from North Carolina.

I have brought a can of oysters with me from home, a present from Mr. Hodge of Mobile. Captain De Graffenreid is very fond of them. As his case is a bad one, we give him the best we have. He told me he had been badly treated since I left. He is very peevish, and would say that any way; but he is a great sufferer.

We have a number of wounded prisoners—one, a very nice young man, by the name of Snyder. He says that nothing in the world would ever make him fight against the South again. He sees how he has wronged us. They all seem to wonder how we can be so kind to them. I asked Mr. Snyder what he would do when he went back North; he will then be compelled to join the army. He said he was going to Canada as soon as he could get there. One of them is a very large Irishman, by the name of McLean. He is severely wounded in the arm; it is supposed he will lose it.

February 21.—Mr. Noland and Mr. Kelly are dead; one died on the 16th and the other on the 17th. They were members of the Eleventh or Sixteenth Louisiana Regiment. Both were unmarried.

We have had heavy rains ever since I returned, which is the cause of a great deal of sickness. The hospital is filled with patients who come in every day; many die, whom neither Mrs. Williamson nor myself ever see.

Our room is a front one, and a hall some ten feet wide divides quite a large ward from us, which is filled with typhoid and pneumonia cases. I counted seven men in the ward, blistered severely. Though the room is so near ours, we have no time to spend in it. Many a time through the night we hear the men cough and groan, but we can not even allow our minds to dwell on these things, as it would unfit us for our duties. We visit the wards at least twice a day; but many of the patients are brought in at night, and are dead before morning.

A staircase leading to the floor above is near our room. On going up it, I am often met by men carrying a litter, with a white sheet over it. I know its contents without asking. Often the bearers have not the least idea of the inmate's name.

Had a man die in Dr. Hopping's ward; his name was Brittle Jones. He was a fine-looking man, and a patient sufferer. He talked a great deal of his wife, and asked me to write to her; said they had only been married a week when he left home. She lives in Jacksonville, Ala.

We have three white girls, who have come from Mobile, as laundresses. I can not but wonder at some persons, these war times. We gave these girls a very nice room. The beds in them were new, but hospital style, like what we have ourselves. They told me if they could not get better they would not stay. I begged them to give it a trial, and I would endeavor to improve matters. It is so difficult to get servants, that we are thankful to do any thing for them. We have men as *laundresses,* as well as in other capacities; [6] but their help is very uncertain, as not a day passes without an order from General Bragg " to send all the men to the front."

The girls brought me a present of a very large prayer-book, from Rev. Dr. Massey, in Mobile, which is very acceptable.

February 23.—A bright, beautiful day. Had a visit from Mrs. Dr. Hopping and Mrs. Moore; also Mr. Weaver; the latter brought me a letter from home.

A few days ago we received our first *pay.* I received one hundred and twenty dollars, for three months; Mrs. Williamson one hundred and five.[7] Our first feeling was not to take it, but then we remembered we could make good use of the money. Mine is nearly all gone already. I bought a common cotton delaine dress, for which I paid three dollars per yard; in good times it would have been twenty-five cents. I also bought a common calico, at two dollars and a quarter a yard, and a common pair of leather boots for sixteen dollars. These articles would have been higher in Mobile.

A day or two ago I received a letter from Lieutenant Goodman of the Ninth Mississippi Regiment—one of my old patients. I met him while in Mobile, and he kindly brought a parcel from there for me, and through mistake took it to the army. They sent it back by express; and, on receiving it from that office, the agents would accept no money when they knew it was for me, because I am in the hospital.

Sunday, March 1.—I have been very busy all day, too much so to go to church. Mrs. Williamson is quite well again. She is a member of the Methodist Church, a devout Christian, and is the means of doing much good; I think, as much as any chaplain possibly could. She is

[6] Dr. B. M. Wible wrote Dr. Stout on March 21, 1863: " It is impossible to procure laundresses at 12 dollars per month, and I am obliged to require nurses to perform laundry duty—that is negro women who aid in cleaning the wards are also required to wash." ALs dated at Tunnel Hill, Georgia, Stout Papers (Emory).

[7] These amounts clearly establish Miss Cumming as a Matron and Mrs. Williamson as an Assistant Matron.

greatly beloved by all; the patients look up to her as they would to a kind, sympathizing mother.

Miss Groom is helping Mrs. Snow; she has been quite sick.

Rev. Mr. Denniston visited the sick to-day.

March 9.—Yesterday was a very warm day. Just before sunset we had one of the most terrific hail-storms I have ever seen; some of the hail-stones were the size of a hen's egg. It broke nearly all of our windows on the west side of the house. It only lasted a few minutes. Had it been of much longer duration, I think the house would have fallen, as the rain poured through the windows in torrents, and would have swept all with it. We had a number of very sick men, and did what we could to have them cared for. Mrs. Williamson went up-stairs to see after the men there, and found Mr. Murray, a nurse, trying to hold in one of the window-sashes; all the glass being broken, the rain and hail poured right down on him. One of the patients, who we thought was dying, was lying so that he had the full benefit of the storm. Mrs. Williamson, in her haste to save him from being drowned on *dry land*, gave his bunk a pull, and down came bunk, man, and all on the floor. Poor Mrs. Williamson thought she had killed him, and it gave her such a fright that she ran and left him. Much to the surprise of all, he has taken a turn for the better. None of the men are any the worse.

They get plenty of fresh air now; Dr. Hunter is a great believer in that any way. He says that when men have been living in the field as ours have, without even a tent to cover them at night, when brought into a close room, especially when wounded, they get worse right away. I have seen the truth of this exemplified.

When we first came here, there was a very sick man, whose wife was nursing him; he was in a small room, which the wife would not permit a breath of fresh air to enter, thinking it would kill him, as he had a very bad cough; we all thought he would die. One day Dr. Hunter ordered him to be put into a large ward, where there were about twenty patients; but it was well ventilated. The wife was in a terrible state, and said the moving would kill her husband, and asked me to beg Dr. Hunter to have him moved back. I did so, but he would not grant my request; he said fresh air was the only thing that would save the man, and he did not care to have his murder on his conscience. I found him inexorable, and thought him very hard-hearted. From that time the man commenced to improve, and in a week or two received a furlough, and went home with his wife.

The doctors do not like the wives of the men to come and nurse them; they say they invariably kill them with kindness. There are some ladies who come to take care of their relatives, who seem to understand nursing, and are a great help, not only to their own folks, but to others around them; these the doctors do not object to.

March 10.—We have just received a box full of good things, from the Hebrew Military Aid Society in Mobile; preserves, sardines, wines, oysters, spices, and also twenty-four pairs of socks; we also received five hundred dollars, sent by Daniel Wheeler, Esq., from the Richmond fund in Mobile, all of which is most acceptable.

I received a letter a few days ago from Mr. Ellman, president of the Hebrew Military Aid Society, with a list of the articles in the box, informing me of its having been sent. I had told some of the patients what they might expect, and they have been anxiously looking for the arrival of the box.

I have an invitation to a grand ball, to be given in honor of General Johnston, our commander-in-chief; of course I have no idea of accepting.

Mrs. Williamson and I live like Sisters of Charity; we get up in the morning about 4 o'clock, and breakfast by candle-light, which meal consists of real coffee without milk, but sugar, hash, and bread; we eat it in our room. Unless we get up early, we find it impossible to get through with our duties. Mrs. Williamson prepares toddies and egg-nogs; I see that the delicacies for the sick are properly prepared. After the duties of the day are over, we then write letters for the men, telling their relations they are here, or informing them of their decease; other times mending some little articles for them. Mrs. Williamson is up many a night till 12 o'clock, working for her " dear boys," as she calls them.

We have a very nice set of men as cooks, who will not let us do any thing for ourselves, if they can help it. They make our fires, and bring us wood and water; in fact, we want for nothing they can procure for us. In the language of Mrs. Williamson, I say, " God bless them all." Our head cook is a young man about nineteen, by the name of Gordon Halford; he was very sick when he first came here; we paid him some little attention, and he is so grateful that he seems to think he can never repay us; he is a perfect treasure. We have another one, who is now quite sick, whose name is Allen; he is one of John Morgan's squadron, and the best of men. I can scarcely keep from laughing when I see him standing by the stove, turning battercakes; he is so tall. There is also a Mr. Drew, who came here sick; these men are serving their country as effectually as if they were in the field, and much better, for they could not stand field service; they get many a sneer for being here, but people who do what they feel to be their duty need not mind that.

The great trouble about hospitals is the sameness of the diet,[8] in the morning we have batter-cakes made of the mush left from the previous meal, rice, and stale bread, (I do not mean what the men

[8] " Medical officers were required to prescribe what was theoretically supposed to be appropriate diet for each patient. There was ' Full Diet,' ' Half Diet,' and ' Low Diet,' but victualing range was so limited that there was more of a distinction than a difference between them." Ferdinand E. Daniel, *Recollections of a Rebel Surgeon* . . . (Austin, Texas, 1899), 150.

leave, as nothing is used which has been in the wards,) hash made out of the soup-meat, toast, mush, milk, tea, coffee, and beefsteak. Our batter-cakes never have eggs in them; they have a little flour and soda, and are very nice. For dinner, we have beef and chicken soup, potatoes, rice, dried fruit, and for dessert a *luxurious* baked pudding, made of the same materials as the battercakes, with molasses for sweetening, with the addition of spices. For each meal we have what is called special diet, for the worst cases sometimes, as is specially ordered by the surgeons, and others whatever we can get the patient to eat; it generally consists of light diet, such as chicken and beef-tea, arrow-root, sago, boiled milk thickened with flour, milk, tea, and toast. We get a good deal of milk and eggs now. For supper we have dried fruit, toast, tea, and coffee.

Our kitchen is a nice one; it has a distributing room next to it. Our quartermaster, Captain Gribble, is very kind in supplying us with as many dishes as we want.

There is a large kitchen and convalescent dining-room down-stairs, and an officer's table, in a room by itself. The diet of the latter is the same as that of privates; the diet is far from being what it ought to be, but it is the best that can be had. We have trouble in keeping table-ware, no matter how closely it is watched; soldiers will carry it off; they seem to think that government property is theirs, and they have a right to take it whenever they please. We lose dozens of spoons, cups, plates, knives, and forks in this way. On the tables for the con-valescents we have table covers, although I prefer a well-scoured bare table; but the surgeons wish to make the hospital as much like home as possible.

There is one department in which I think there could be a great improvement—the laundry. When the men come in, their clothes are taken off and clean ones put on; their dirty ones are put in their haversacks, just as they are when taken off. When the men leave to go to another hospital, their soiled ones are put on again. I told Dr. Hunter I did not think it was right; he replied, it could not be avoided, as hundreds are coming and going daily. The fact is, it is almost impossible to get people to do washing.

March 16.—Our hospital has been divided; one division is called the Gilmer Hospital, in honor of Mrs. Gilmer, who is matron.[9] There are now four hospitals in this place: the Academy, of which Dr. Haw-thorne [Hawthorn] is chief surgeon,[10] and Mrs. Newsom matron; the

[9] " A[n] . . . important hospital first organized under my direction was the Gilmer Hospital, named in honor of Mrs. Gilmer of Pulaski, Tennessee, who performed noble service as matron and nurse, serving chiefly at Camps Cheatham and Trous-dale in Tennessee, and at Bowling Green, Ky., with Brown's 3d Tennessee Regi-ment, of which I was then the surgeon." Stout, " Some Facts . . . ," *Southern Practitioner*, XXV (1903) , 522.

[10] Dr. Hawthorn later became one of the famous surgeons of the South. How he became an Assistant Surgeon in the Confederate army is related by Dr. Daniel:

Foard, of which Mrs. Crocker of Mobile is matron, and Dr. Thornton surgeon; the Gilmer, of which Dr. Michelle [Michel] is surgeon and Mrs. Gorman matron; and our own, the Newsom.

Dr. Hunter has divided the money he received from Mobile between those hospitals, giving each one hundred dollars, keeping two for the Newsom, which is twice the size of the others; we have accommodations for five hundred patients.

March 20.–General Johnston has gone to Mississippi to take command of that department. I believe General Bragg is commander-in-chief of the department in Tennessee. I have been informed that the morning before the ball given to General Johnston he had *important* business in Atlanta. I have also been told he does not approve of such things at this time.

I paid a visit a day or two ago to Mrs. Newsom, accompanied by Dr. William Hughes; on our way there we met Major Morgan, a brother of the general. He had just returned from visiting his mother in Kentucky, and was on his way to join his brother-in-law, General Hill, in Virginia. He is not unlike his brother, J. Morgan. I told him I was afraid the latter would carry his daring too far. He replied, he had no fears on that score, and especially now since he is married, as on his wife's account he would likely be more cautious.

We found Mrs. Newsom, for a wonder, at leisure; her hospital is a very fine one; it is on top of a very high hill, commanding a view of the whole town. After we left her I went in search of milk, as that is the cry I hear from morning till night among the patients. I believe, if we could get plently of it, we would scarcely need any thing else. I have the promise of a little every day.

March 21.–In a package of letters I have just received from a friend in England, she says they have still great hopes of our success, and that the people sympathize a great deal with us. I wish they would show it differently from what they do. But we are told that the people are very anxious to recognize us, but the government seems determined not to do it. I trust we shall get along without the aid of any foreign power, though I think the colonies would have done very little without it. She also says she envies me the opportunity I have in administering to the wants of the suffering of our army.

" Hawthorn went out as a private soldier in the 10th Alabama infantry when he was a fresh graduate of medicine. . . . One of his company got shot through the foot, and all the surgeons were absent fishing, it was said. Some one said: ' Hawthorn in this man's company is a doctor—get him!' They got him. He cut down and tied the posterior tibial artery—the correct thing to do—and when the surgeon returned—it was Dr. Ford [Foard] . . . he asked who had done that operation; saying it was a neat operation and a creditable job. He was told the operator was Private Hawthorn . . . Dr. Ford [Foard] immediately appointed him assistant surgeon, and a little later he passed examination and was made surgeon, and soon became known throughout the army as one of the ablest surgeons we had." Daniel, *Recollections of a Rebel Surgeon*, 254-55.

March 24.—James Tucker died yesterday; he was a member of the Fourth Kentucky Regiment.

Doctors Foard and Stout paid a visit to the hospital this afternoon, and highly commended all the arrangements, and the order and cleanliness of every thing.[11]

Late in the afternoon we had a very severe storm, which carried away a part of our roof, and otherwise did a great deal of damage.

March 26.—Moses Compton has just died; he was a member of the First Alabama Regiment. I have written to his father, in Blount County, Alabama, and sent a lock of his son's hair, which I always do when I can.

I have only put the names down here of those to whom I have paid the most attention. I take no note of those whom Mrs. Williamson attends, nor of any who have special friends here.

March 31.—James Scott, the young man of whom I spoke some time ago, has just breathed his last. After lying on his back four months, he was able to walk about; he was then taken with pneumonia; recovered from that; was taken with diphtheria; from that he also recovered; and died from the effects of erysipelas. Poor child! what a happy release from woe and suffering! His young life had been one of sorrow, but he trusted in Him who trod this vale of tears before him. . . .

May God bless his poor widowed and childless mother! I believe this is the third son she has lost in this fratricidal conflict. I did not know any of the others, but trust they died with the same hope and faith this one has; if so, she will weep more in joy than sorrow, for they have only passed the portals of death a little while before her, that it may not be so dark and drear to her, since her loved ones have passed through.

Dr. Hopping took as much care of him as though he had been his own brother, and he had procured his discharge from the army. The nurses were also kind; they could not have been otherwise, for it was

[11] " Miss Cumming and her lady associates served a long time in the Newsom Hospital, and until it was removed from Chattanooga. They were the first ladies that took up their residence in any of the hospitals under my direction, serving therein night and day. Their advent to Chattanooga, championed by Rev. Mr. Miller, an Episcopal clergyman, and under the patronage of an association of ladies of Mobile, was at first a source of embarrassment. The meager supply of hospital buildings, and the crowded condition of the wards forbade the attempt to find accommodations for refined females who proposed to reside therein. I, therefore, discouraged them from remaining in Chattanooga. But Surgeon Hunter, who thought he could provide them with apartments in the buildings already occupied or in close vicinity to them, was permitted to enroll them as matrons in the Newsom Hospital." Stout, " Some Facts . . . ," *Southern Practitioner*, XXV (1903), 522.

" With his well-disciplined corps of male nurses, and Miss Cumming's corps of self-denying matrons, Surgeon Hunter soon converted [Newsom Hospital] into a model military hospital." *Ibid.*, 524.

a great pleasure to wait on him; he was so meek and uncomplaining. He was a member of the Forty-first Alabama Regiment, and from Fayette County, Alabama.

April 1.—William York died yesterday; he was from Williamson County, Tennessee.

A few days ago we had a man die, by the name of George Speaker; he was one of John Morgan's squadron. He died from a wound received at Shelbyville, in this state. His captain (Goldston) was with him and had him buried with full honors.

Easter Sunday, April 5.—A very beautiful day. I went to the Episcopal Church in the morning; Mr. Denniston preached an excellent sermon on the text, "The Lord has arisen indeed."

Spent the rest of the day, as usual, visiting the patients.

April 6.—Have met with a serious accident; I had the "blues" (that is what being discontented is called), and wished I had a book (Longfellow's Poems) ; I went to Mrs. Henderson's to try to procure it; while there one of the largest dogs I have ever seen jumped at me, and caught the elbow of my left arm in his mouth; I made sure from the crunch he made that the bone was broken. I was very much frightened, and believe, if a negro woman and Mrs. R.'s little girl had not been there, I should have been torn to pieces. What I most regret is that I shall not be able to visit the wards for some weeks, as we have so much erysipelas about, and it flies to wounds immediately. I have known nurses to take it from a scratch.

In the evening Mrs. Henderson (she was out when I received the bite) and a Mrs. Major Higgins called. They sympathized with me a great deal.

April 12.—My arm is fast getting better; I have put nothing on it but cold water, I believe that is a cure for almost every thing.

Mrs. Williamson is very busy, and goes about all the time in the wards.

Dr. Hunter has left for his home, in Mississippi, to bring his wife here. Dr. Patterson of Tennessee is now in charge. He is a perfect gentleman, and we are all much pleased with him.

I have been looking at some men working. I do not think that any of our negroes ever worked as hard. Our firewood is brought in in large logs. We have no saws, so the men have to cut it. There is one man now chopping away, who I am told is worth his thousands. He is dressed in grey homespun, and seems as much at home as if he had always been accustomed to that life. War is a great leveler, and makes philosophers of us, when nothing else will. It astonishes me to see how the men adapt themselves to circumstances. The men in the kitchen act as if that was their place, and always had been. I saw one of them receive a letter, this morning, from his wife, and as he read

98

about her and his little ones the tears trickled down his cheeks. They were manly ones, and will never disgrace the bravest and best.

April 13.—There has been a skirmish at the front, and a battle is expected there daily. I have just been looking at loads of wounded coming in.

There are numbers dying in our hospital every day, and scarcely any note is taken of them.

At home, when a member of a family is about to go to his last resting-place, loving friends are around the couch of the sufferer, and by kind words and acts rob King Death of half his terrors, and smooth the pathway to the valley and shadow of death. But here a man near dissolution is usually in a ward with perhaps twenty more. To wait on that number a single nurse keeps vigil. He knows the man will likely die during the night, but he can not spend time by his bedside, as others need his care. The ward is dimly lighted, as candles are scarce; the patient is perhaps in a dark corner; the death-rattle is heard; when that ceases the nurse knows that all is over. He then wakes some of the other nurses up, and in the silent hour of night these men prepare their comrade for the tomb, and bear him to the dead-house. The surgeon, when going his rounds the next morning, is not at all startled when he finds an empty bunk where the evening before was one occupied. He knows without asking what has become of the inmate, and that " somebody's darling " [12] has gone to his long home. It is sad to see so many dying with no kindred near them to sooth their last moments and close their eyes. What a sacred duty is here left undone by our women! I do not say that all are guilty of this neglect, for I know there are many good women who have their home duties to attend to, and others who have not strength physically; but how many are there, at this moment, who do not know how to pass their time— rich, refined, intellectual, and will I say Christian? They are so called, and I have no doubt would be much shocked were they called any thing else, and yet they not only neglect this Christian and sacred duty, but look on it as beneath them. How can we expect to succeed when there is such a gross disregard of our Savior's own words, " In that ye did it unto the least of these, ye did it unto me? "

And what an opportunity this is to exercise the greatest of all Christian virtues—charity? Yet it is not charity in the sense in which it is commonly used, but a sacred duty we owe to our own people and country; practicing which has made the most uncouth seem lovely, and the beauteous more beautiful. . . .

O, that the women of the South may wake from their dream ere it is too late. . . .

April 16.—We have had trouble in the wash-house; some one told

[12] This popular phrase of the day refers to the sentimental poem of that title by Miss Marie Ravenel LaCoste of Savannah. It was set to music by John Hill Hewitt and published in Macon and Savannah in 1864. Harwell, *Confederate Music,* 143.

Dr. Patterson that the three girls who came from Mobile had been dancing with some negroes, and that last Sunday they walked to the graveyard with one.

The first I have been told is positively a falsehood; the second, I had heard before. When told of it, I laughed, and said I expected it was another case of " Dame Blaize," " whom the king himself did follow as she walked on before." I suppose the girls were walking, and the negro happened to be going the same road; as I feel confident, from what I have seen of them, they would not knowingly do a wrong of that kind. Dr. Patterson had dismissed them. When I told him I did not believe any of the stories, he said he sent them off out of respect to the ladies in the hospital, and if we wished he would countermand the order. The girls were sent back, but in a little while came and told me that one of the non-commissioned officers in the hospital had gone into the wash-house, and spoken insultingly to them on the subject. I sent for Dr. Patterson and told him the circumstance; he was very angry, and said he would dismiss the man, as he would have no one in the hospital who did not behave properly. These are a few of the trials of hospital life, and I think they are serious ones; but I feel sure we shall have no more trouble on that score, as Dr. Patterson will not permit it.

Miss Groom's health has been so feeble that she has been compelled to leave for home; she left yesterday; I went as far as Atlanta with her. Dr. O'Neal, an assistant surgeon of the Gilmer Hospital, accompanied us. He gave me an account of the death of Captain De Graffenreid, the Tennesseean. He had been moved to the Gilmer Hospital, as it belongs to Polk's corps; he died very suddenly; a blood-vessel ruptured, and alarmed him so much that Dr. O'Neal thinks he died from fright. He was about fifty years of age. From all I have been told, I do not expect we had a braver man in the army; his men fairly idolized him, and the negro servant who nursed him cried like a child when he informed me of his death. His sister and brother-in-law came to see him; but too late, as he was dead and buried before they reached here. I have been told that they were indignant at his treatment in our hospital. They said: " To think that a man of his means should have been kept in a ward like any *other soldier*! " If they had come to me about him, I should have informed them, I was certain he was too good a soldier to have wished to be any place else. His own people could not have taken better care of him than he had from every one here. He had the best of medical attention, and as his case was a bad one, I prepared his food myself. He got the very best of what we had in the hospital—which was a good deal, as at that time we had the box of things sent from Mobile. Poor fellow! all these things do not trouble him now. He was not religious. " Leaving his sins to his Savior," let us think of him only as the hero he was. . . .

Dr. O'Neal met with a lady and gentleman going to Mobile, who kindly consented to take charge of Miss Groom. We put up at a hotel; I do not know its name. We remained there about two hours, for which we paid one dollar each.

In the cars, on my way back, I met a Mr. Pritchard from New Orleans. He related some of his trials before being sent out of that city. He also told me about a dinner given in Montreal, Canada, and that at it President Davis, Generals Lee and Jackson, had been highly complimented. I wonder the people there are not afraid to commit such a *breach of international law!*

Mrs. Dr. Turner was on the train, going to pay her husband another visit. She had just come from Alabama. She told me her brother had never got his coat and shawl from the Trout House. We met Colonel McNair of the Fourth Mississippi Cavalry. He had just come from Mississippi.

The cars were loaded with troops from Mobile, going to reinforce Bragg; among them were some Georgia regiments; their relatives were at the different depots to meet and take a look at them before they went up to the army. The banks all the way along were lined with ladies, waving their handkerchiefs, and throwing bouquets to the soldiers, greeting them with much enthusiasm, which the soldiers seemed to appreciate by cheering the ladies in return.

I was informed that the Thirty-sixth and Thirty-eighth Alabama Regiments were on the train; as I had some friends in them, I tried to see them, but failed; the train they were on stopped a half mile from the depot, so I was unable to see them at that time.

I noticed the country through which we passed was barren and poor-looking, and the people had a sickly appearance.

April 23.—There is a report that there is fighting at the front.

We have numbers of the Thirty-sixth and Thirty-eighth Alabama Regiments very sick. I suppose the sickness is caused by the change in coming so far south. Lieutenant Robinson, of Mobile, has been to call on some of his men.

I have received a letter from a friend in Mobile, requesting me to buy some dry goods and children's shoes for her. There is not a pair of the latter in the whole place. Calico is three dollars and fifty cents per yard, and white domestic four.

April 28.—One of my patients, by the name of Lee, has just died; was a member of the Thirty-third Alabama Regiment. His wife lives in Butler County, Alabama. He was out of his mind previous to his death.

A number of wounded Federals were brought in a few days ago.

May 4.—Mr. A. W. Davis died yesterday. He was a member of the Twenty-fifth Alabama Regiment; was sick a long time, and died perfectly happy.

Mr. McCullough also died yesterday of consumption. He was here a long time, and bore his sufferings with a great deal of fortitude. He died a Christian—he has no relations except a brother and sister, who live in Hardin County, Kentucky. He requested me to see that his captain got his silver watch and money, and have them sent to his brother and sister. He was a member of the Sixth Kentucky Regiment. Some time ago I sent a message to some of the officers from that regiment about him, and they immediately called and kindly offered to assist him in any way.

We are still very busy. We have almost every thing to buy ourselves. We pay two dollars per gallon for sweet milk; one dollar for buttermilk; eggs, one dollar per dozen; butter, one fifty per pound; coffee, five dollars.

May 5.—I had quite a treat to-day—have been with a party, horseback riding, to the top of Lookout Mountain. I do not know how many feet its elevation is, but the road we took was four miles from the base. It is a made one, and many parts of it is cut out of solid rock; some portions are very narrow, and it made me quite nervous and giddy to look back. . . .

When we reached the summit, the view from it was really entrancing.

We sat on the Point of Rocks, which is the furtherest point of the mountain, under the shade of some magnificent trees. The scene presented below was one of the most beautiful pictures I ever beheld. The Tennessee River, with its various windings, made the plain beneath look like many islands. . . .

We sat for some time in perfect silence; I was completely awed; I thought of our Savior when he preached his memorable " sermon on the mount." I am afraid we have not profited much by it, or we would not be as we are now.

I am told that on a clear day, with a good glass, seven states can be seen from the top of this mountain.

As we came down, a Mr. Chandler, who was with us, took us to a natural stone bridge, which was about a hundred feet high. A very fine spring of water gushed from the side of the rocks forming this bridge, making a perfect waterfall. The whole scene was like fairy land. I do not think that Switzerland or Scotland has any finer scenes than we have here. Had this country only poets to sing her beauties, I have no doubt they would be as famous as any in the old world.

May 9.—We are in daily expectation of a battle; and we are completely out of rags—a very necessary article at this time. We have just received two boxes, both from Mobile. The good people of that place could not have sent us any thing more acceptable. We also received a dispatch from there requesting transportation for some laundresses, who are coming on. We are much in need of them. There are numbers of poor people here, but many seem to be unfit for any thing. They are the most miserable looking beings I have ever met. Reading or writing with them is out of the question. I expect, if I were to ask them about education, they would scarcely know what I meant. I hope the people we see here are not a fair specimen of the poorer class of country people in Tennessee. I also received a letter from a relative, informing me that the military aid society had some medicines they would send us, if we needed them. I asked Dr. Patterson, and he replied that nothing would be more acceptable, as many of our men have died for want of them.

Strange to say that although the government does not provide near enough of medicines, it will not permit us to spend our hospital fund for them, and we find it impossible to spend what we have on edibles, as they are not to be bought.

May 10.—A member of the Thirty-sixth Tennessee Regiment, Mr. Pike, has just died. He left a message with me for his wife, who lives in Smith County, Virginia. He told me to tell her he was perfectly happy. The nurses have informed me he was a most patient sufferer, and prayed nearly all the time.

We have a number of returned prisoners; I believe they are General Churchill's men, who were taken at Arkansas Post. Some of them have told me that the ladies in the North treated them with a great deal of kindness, for which they have my blessing. Among our patients we have a colonel, who seems to be much of a gentleman, and is a Christian; he tells me that General Bragg, the best-abused man in the world, has a personal dislike for him, and tries to annoy him in every possible way. I regret hearing any thing like this about one so high in command, as I think it shows a littleness of mind, and makes us lose confidence in him.

May 11.—I note this as being one of the gloomiest days since the war. News has just been received that one of our brightest stars has left us; he has gone to shine in a more glorious sphere than this. The good and great General Stonewall Jackson has fallen; he was wounded at the battle of Chancellorsville, and lived a few days afterward. When I first heard of it I was speechless, and thought, with the apostle, "how unsearchable are His judgments, and His ways are past finding out. For who hath known the mind of the Lord." Dark and mysterious indeed, are his ways. Who dare attempt to fathom them, when such men as Jackson are cut down in the zenith of their glory, and at the very hour of their country's need?

The honor of taking this great man's life was not reserved for the foe, but for his own men, as if it were a sacrifice they offered to the Lord, as Jephtha gave up his daughter. . . .

May 18.—Dr. Hunter has come back, and brought his wife with him.

News has come that there has been a destructive raid in Mississippi, and that the raiders have destroyed Jackson. Mrs. Hunter's home is near there, so she is miserable accordingly. The papers are filled with accounts of raids which have taken place all over the Confederacy. Mississippi and North Alabama have suffered from these horrible scourges. The raiders burn houses and destroy provisions of all kinds, and I am told they have positive orders to destroy all farming implements. This is the way they think they will make us submit—ruin the country, and starve us. I have no fear of their succeeding by such fiendish means. There is an overruling Providence who will not permit this long. There is no doubt but we will have great suffering, but it will be of short duration. General Forrest has lately captured four times his own number of these marauders, at Rome, Georgia.

I received a letter from Dr. Davis, father of the young man who died a short time since. Poor man! he had just heard of the death of another son, who was wounded and a prisoner (he was captured at the battle of Murfreesboro), and of two others, who are very sick at Wartrace, where part of our army is at present.

I am told that Breckinridge's command is now on its way to Mississippi, to join the army at Vicksburg, which is closely besieged. I can not see how it is possible that we are ever going to hold it against the immense power which the enemy are bringing against it.

We have more trials with our domestic arrangements. It seems that the laundresses, for whom transportation was provided, have husbands in the army, and have taken this method of getting to see them without expense. The transportation agent here found out they were at the depot, and what they intended doing. He sent word to Dr. Stout, and Dr. Hunter sent down three of our surgeons to see after them. They brought up two of them to our room; I could scarcely keep from laughing, as they looked like real *prisoners of war*, and the doctors like their captors. They were very nice looking women; one of them said she had never washed her own clothes, and didn't see how she was going to wash for any one else. I felt provoked at them for being so dishonest. Dr. Stout has sent orders that they must be kept till they work out the price of their transportation tickets.

Joseph Morton died to-day; he was a member of the Second Arkansas Regiment, and was from Sylvia County, Arkansas.

May 20.—Last evening a friend sent me word that my brother was in the Gilmer Hospital. (It is now on the same hill as the Academy). I went there immediately, and was glad to find that he had not much the matter with him. He has a carbuncle on his arm, caused by bad food. A change of air and diet would, I feel certain, benefit him more than any thing else.

I staid all night with Mrs. Gorman, the matron of the hospital; it is a perfect treat to visit there. The hospital buildings are newly put up; they are composed of four or five two-story wards, each large enough for about fifty patients. Each ward has a small room attached to it, used as a distributing-room and pantry, and another, used as a bath-room. I went through Dr. Cannon's ward. (Dr. Cannon is the same whom I met in Corinth.) Every thing about it was in perfect order. The bunks had on white comforts, not the least soiled, although they had been in use some time. The view from the upper part of these wards is perfectly entrancing; the trees are magnificent. I called Dr. Cannon's attention to the scene, and asked him if there was any thing in England to equal it (he is an Englishman). He said he had seen nothing to surpass it, and that he considered the view from his window one of the finest in the world.

This morning, before leaving, I paid a visit to the Academy Hospital, which is but a short distance from the other. They both belong to General Polk's corps. Both have been put up since we came to Chattanooga. The Academy has been finished some time. It is perfect in every department. The wards are but one story high, each holding about twenty-five patients. They have a small distributing room for every two of these wards. The food is brought from the kitchen to them, and distributed by a ward matron.

They have very few patients at present. The wards are fixed up very nicely, having been newly whitewashed, and Mrs. Newsom has them very tastefully dressed with evergreens. The attendants sleep in tents, some of which are fixed up as nicely as any house. I visited one belonging to the druggist's wife, who is one of the matrons. There was a place dug in the ground about three feet deep, the sides bricked around, and floored with planks, on which was a carpet. It had a chimney and fire-place; the tent-cloth was put overall, and gutters around, to keep out the rain. A very nice lady has charge of the linen room. In this hospital the patients have their clothes washed as soon as they come in. The wash-house is a little ways from the rest of the hospital; in it are large boilers, built on brick, and an ironing-room, and a shed for drying the clothes in wet weather.

There is one great drawback which we all have: the water used has to be carried from the river in barrels. The wards are at least twenty yards apart. Mrs. Newsom tells me that Dr. Hawthorn, the surgeon, is one of the best managers she has ever been with; but I have been told one thing about him, that proves that he is not a humane man; I refer to his method of punishing the men by bucking and gagging; sometimes he puts a bayonet in their mouth instead of a stick, and ties it so tightly that the blood gushes out. Many a time he has made the men stay in this position twenty-four hours, giving them neither food nor water. I do not think there is any necessity for going to such extremes.[13] We have as good discipline in our hospital as there is any need for, and nothing of that kind is ever resorted to.

On my way back this morning, I called on Mrs. Brewer, and had an

[13] Bucking and gagging was a common display of discipline in the Confederate armies. It and comparable punishments are discussed in detail in the chapter " Kicking Over the Traces " in Wiley, *The Life of Johnny Reb*, 217-43. Dr. Stout wrote of Dr. Hawthorn: " Though a rigid disciplinarian, he was a humane officer." " Some Facts . . . ," *Southern Practitioner*, XXV (1903), 566.

introduction to Major-General McCown, who is now under arrest for disobedience of orders, or, as a lady the other day told me, *for giving his men coffee!* I found him very pleasant in conversation; he told us he had experienced nothing here in comparison with what he had endured in other campaigns. I think he had been in the regular army, and had been at Salt Lake, or on some expedition against the Indians.

May 22.—All kinds of bad news is floating about; viz: Jackson, Mississippi, burnt to the ground; Vicksburg fallen, etc. The fall of Vicksburg has cast a gloom over all, but it is not the Confederacy, and the enemy will have to do some hard fighting before they take that. Many are calling General Pemberton, who was in command, a traitor.

Sunday, May 24.—Charles Maguire died to-day of typhoid fever; he was a member of the Eighteenth Alabama Regiment. His wife lives in Sinclair County, Alabama.

A few days ago James Barstow, one of my patients, died. He had been here for some time. He was from Yorkshire, England. He was very sad when he spoke of his home, and was grieved to think he could not let his people know where he was. He was much relieved when I informed him I knew of a way of sending letters through the blockade, and would write to his friends. The morning after this conversation, being very busy, I did not visit the wards, when, to my surprise, one of the nurses came and told me he was dead. I had no chance of asking him what part of Yorkshire he was from, so I wrote to Lieutenant Robinson, Company E, Seventh Arkansas Regiment, of which Mr. Barstow had been a member, to see if he could give me any information concerning his people, and also about a cousin who had come to this country with him, and had died in the service. Lieutenant Robinson could give me little or no satisfaction on the subject, but referred me to Mr. Tunstall, in Jackson Fort, Arkansas. He spoke very highly of Mr. Barstow, and said he had been a good and brave soldier. The latter left over one hundred dollars, which he gave to Mr. Andrews, his nurse, who had been very kind to him. I have taken part of it, and had a nice head-board put to his grave, the best I could get in this place. On it was inscribed: " To the memory of James Barstow, Seventh Arkansas Regiment. Born in Yorkshire, England; died in Chattanooga, Tennessee, May 19, 1863, of typhoid fever, aged twenty-two years. He sacrificed his life for his adopted country, and fell a martyr for liberty. . . .

May 28.—Vicksburg has not yet fallen, but all think it is a matter of time, and it would not surprise us to hear of its capture at any moment, as the enemy have surrounded it with an overwhelming force; but our troops are holding it manfully. Every attack on it is repulsed with great loss to the enemy. It is said that lately the enemy attacked it with bravery and determination; advancing right on our breastworks, and were mowed down by thousands. The people in the place are suffering terribly.

106

I went with a party to visit a very large cave, called Nick-o'-Jack [Nickajack]; it is some sixty miles from here, on the Nashville road, and about half a mile from the railroad. It was well worth going to see. The entrance has a magnificent arch. There is a lake running through it, which reminded me of a picture I had seen of the valley of the shadow of death. We went a great distance through it, and crept through many a small crevice, and came out with a few shades of the Ethiopian on us. Having no soap with which to remove it, we made use of clay, which we found a very good substitute. The party was a very pleasant one. We had a nice collation set on some boards for tables, and more good things than I thought were in the Confederacy.

We have received two boxes from Mobile, one filled with medicines from the military aid society; the other with cans of oysters bought with money given by Mr. Sibley.

I have just paid a visit to the Foard Hospital. It is the receiving one, and is now in a nice new building. On going in I was stopped by a guard, and had to wait till Dr. Thornton came to my rescue. The latter kindly gave me a pass to go and come whenever I please. We have many strange things to do in these war times.

May 31.—There is a great deal of excitement in town in regard to the death of Dr. Thornton. He was killed last night by two Irishmen from our hospital. One was a man who took charge of the dining-room; the other, one of our best nurses. It seems they were both intoxicated, and went to Dr. Thornton's house, near the hospital, and insisted on him giving them whisky. He ordered them off. On their going out the gate, he followed them, when one stabbed him with a knife, and he died half an hour afterward.

The men have been arrested. If they had not been under the influence of liquor I am certain they would not have committed the deed.

June 1.—Have been to Dr. Thornton's funeral. He was buried from the Presbyterian Church. A large concourse was in attendance.

There has been a desperate battle at Port Hudson. It is said that our forces were attacked by negro troops, and the slaughter of the latter was terrible.

I have a young cousin, Edwin Lessel, there in our army, who I am anxious to hear from. He is a native of Nova Scotia, and when the war broke out, as he had only been a short time in this country, I told him he had better go home, as he could not have the same feeling toward the enemy as the southerners. He answered me, that was all a mistake; that from the time he was a little boy his highest ambition was to have a shot at them; and now the chance had come, he had no idea of throwing it away. He enlisted as a private in the " Scotch Guards," which is now in the Second Alabama Regiment.

107

June 6.—All kinds of rumors are coming in daily from the army. A battle is expected momentarily.

We have had a great deal of rain lately, which makes it sickly and otherwise disagreeable.

Vallandigham passed through here a few days ago. He had little or no notice taken of him, as he is not a southerner; but still clings to the delusion that the Union can again be restored. What madness in any sane man! That can never be until the terrible past is wiped out, and sinks into oblivion; or until the many thousands who have been slain shall be brought to life, and the outrages which have been committed on our people undone. I can not but admire him for his independence of character in defying Lincoln and his minions. Would that we had many more like him in the North, then our hopes of peace would be bright indeed. Many think if we can only hold out a little longer, that the peace party there will rise in its might, and demand of the black republicans to desist from this unholy strife.[14]

Sunday, June 7.—Have had quite a number of men die to-day. I have not been very well for some days, and hence have not visited the sick. Mrs. Williamson has been paying them all attention. She has told me about two, whom she has been attending in the room near ours. One was a Mr. Allison from Louisiana, between sixty and seventy years of age. He was a substitute; and has left eight children, the most of whom are in the service. The other one, Mr. Johnson, in the next bunk to him, was in his seventeenth year. About the same time the spirits of the aged pilgrim and youthful martyr were wafted to realms on high, where I trust they are now at rest in the " balm-breathing presence of God."

We have a very nice lady, Mrs. Ellis, wife of one of the officers, in the hospital, who takes charge of the linen department, and is of great assistance.

A chaplain preached this afternoon in one of our wards; his text was, " Seek ye first the kingdom of heaven." The sermon was a very impressive one. The men listened to it with the most profound attention. I have observed that soldiers generally are very attentive listeners during divine service. I should have enjoyed the sermon much better

[14] Clement L. Vallandigham was exiled from the North because of his campaign against prevailing policies for the prosecution of the War. The perceptive British officer, Lt. Col. Sir Arthur James Lyon Fremantle met him at General Hardee's headquarters near Wartrace, Tennessee, May 29, 1863, and recorded his impression: " [Mr. Vallandigham] (called the Apostle of Liberty) is a good-looking man, apparently not much over forty, and had been turned out of the North three days before. Rosecrans had wished to hand him over to Bragg by flag of truce; but as the latter declined to receive him in that manner, he was, as General Hardee expressed it, ' *dumped down* ' in the neutral ground between the lines, and left there. He then received hospitality from the Confederates in the capacity of a destitute stranger. They do not in any way receive him officially, and it does not suit the policy of either party to be identified with one another." *Three Months in the Southern States, April–June 1863* (Edinburgh, London, 1863), 138.

if my attention had not been drawn to the extravagant dress of the speaker. I could not but think, if he had worn a gown to hide it, that it would have been much more in keeping with his priestly office. His uniform was one of the most showy I have ever seen worn by any of our officers since the war; it was of the finest black broadcloth, cut " *a la militaire*," with the usual amount of gilt buttons. . . .

I am told he is much beloved in the army, and has been the means of doing a great deal of good. His clothes were presented to him by his brigade, for his kindness to the men; but I do wish he would not wear them, especially at this time, when such clothes are certain to be the subject of remark, worn by any one, but much more by an embassador of the lowly Jesus. I often wish I was not quite so prejudiced against these things. Affectation in dress I dislike, as much as in manners. . . .

June 9.—Yesterday my friend, Mrs. Brewer, invited me to accompany her on a visit to Lookout Mountain. There was quite a large party, and a very delightful one. It was given in honor of General McCown, who was of the number. We stopped at a very pretty house on the summit, and had an addition to our party of two very pretty girls—the Misses Cox—who are the nymphs and reign sole queens of this enchanting spot. One of them I thought perfectly beautiful. The day was cool and pleasant, and the scenery even more beautiful than when I was last there; the foliage was in its maturity, and the wind, sighing through the trees, filled me with a pleasurable sadness which I can never describe. . . .

As we looked down at the plain beneath, I asked one of the gentlemen if he thought a cannon-ball fired from there could reach us. He said no; he did not think it possible. After partaking of a very fine lunch, we started to pay a visit to Rock City,[15] some two miles distant from the Point of Rocks; but found it was too late, as it would be impossible to descend the mountain after dark. I was disappointed, as I had heard much of this natural curiosity. I have been told it has trees, castles, and mountains of solid rock, cut by Nature's masonry.

We stopped a few hours at a very large house, built for a hotel, but then empty. It is owned by Mrs. Colonel Whitesides [Whiteside], who was of the party.[16] We procured some very delicious water from a spring on the brow of the mountain, which abounds in

" Story-telling glens, and founts, and brooks."

June 19.—One of our patients, by the name of Miller, died yesterday. He was a member of the Thirty-third Alabama Regiment. He came

[15] Rock City has been a tourist attraction for more than a hundred years. Robert Sparks Walker, *Lookout, the Story of a Mountain* (Kingsport, Tenn., 1941), 23-24.
[16] Mrs. Whiteside was the widow of Col. James A. Whiteside who had owned most of the north end of Lookout Mountain and had initiated the residential and tourist development of it. Walker, *ibid.*, 193-96.

here a few weeks ago with typhoid fever; then took erysipelas, from the effects of which he died. He was perfectly resigned to his death, and left a message for his wife and children, who live in Dale County, Alabama.

The erysipelas, which is infectious, is spreading. Two of the girls in the washhouse had their ears bored, and have it very badly, taken from washing the clothes, though they are never touched by them until they are put into a large boiler and well boiled. One of the girls is a perfect sight; her face is so swollen that her eyes are closed, and part of her hair has had to be cut off.

June 23.—The hospital is again filled with very sick, sent from the army, in prospect of a battle. News has come that we gained a victory last week in Virginia.

A Federal negro has just died in the hospital; he came in very sick.

June 25.—Yesterday we sent many of our sick off. To-day the hospital is again filled with wounded.

Yesterday, being St. John the Baptist's day, the Mason's anniversary, there was a grand picnic given by the country people to the soldiers. While in the midst of it, the enemy came upon them, and I am told we have sustained a severe loss. Our army was taken by surprise. The fight was at Hoover's Gap. Mrs. Dr. Turner has just come from there; her husband hurried her off at 12 o'clock last night.

We are still sending the wounded away who are able to be moved, to make room for more, as the battle is still progressing.

June 27.—I was congratulating myself that my brother, who had received a furlough and gone home, would miss this battle. To my surprise he arrived this morning. I asked him why he came. He replied, he could not think of being absent from the expected battle. I tried to persuade him to remain here, as from all accounts our army is retreating, but failed in doing so, and he has gone to the front. He is much improved in health. He enjoyed himself very much while in Mobile, but thought the people too *gay* for these war times. Mrs. May came back with him; she could not have come at a time when her services were more required; she will assist Mrs. Snow who has a great deal to do.

We have a great many wounded; the same old story—men mutilated in every possible way. In one place there are three men lying along side of each other; each has lost a leg. One has just died. I am sick at heart at these scenes, and there seems to be little prospect of a change.

Last week we had a German die, named Massinger. He left over two hundred dollars with me, to give to a friend, Robert Bolt, a member of the Twenty-fourth Texas Regiment. He gave his watch to his nurse, Mr. Byrne, who had been very kind to him.

We have been busy lately making blackberry cordial and blackberry preserves. I have made about twenty-five gallons of the cordial. I never was any place where there were such quantities of blackberries. The country people bring them in by the bushel.

June 29.—Another rainy day. We all feel very miserable. It is now 9 o'clock P. M., and the train from the army has not come in; many are afraid it has been captured. This anxiety is enough to kill any one. We do not know the moment that we may hear of a disaster to our army. It is supposed that Rosecrans is trying to outflank it. I do pity General Bragg from my heart. Every body now is against him. He has always had to fight under great disadvantages. He has to confront one of the best generals the Federals have, and at the present time part of his army is in Mississippi. General Morgan has gone on another raiding expedition into Kentucky. I do not like these raids; they do not seem right.

Yesterday a man died, by the name of Murphy, belonging to the Thirty-sixth Alabama Regiment; he was from Jackson County, Mississippi.

July 1.—Great excitement in town. News has come that the enemy is across the river, and intends shelling the place. We are having hospital flags put up, but I do not see that they will do any good, as it is said the enemy pay no respect to them. We are packing up in a hurry to move. Our hospital being near the river, we will be *honored* by the first shot. The house we are now in is marked by last year's shelling. I believe the delay of the cars the other evening was owing to moving the wounded, as our army is hastily retreating.

July 3.—We have just received news that Bragg and his whole army will be here in a day or two, and that there is a race between him and Rosecrans as to who will get here first.

We had an Englishman die to-day, by the name of Read, in Dr. Hopping's ward. He was fully seventy years of age; was a prisoner, and said to be a bushwhacker. He denied it to the last. I did feel so sorry to see so old a man die in such a place.

Mrs. Williamson talked a great deal to him, and is confident he was innocent. He seemed to be religious, and prayed to the last; he was a large, fine-looking man; lived in Tennessee at the time of his arrest. He had been ten years in this country.

We have had a room filled with that class of men. One who had killed his captain looked as if he was crazy, and was manacled, hands and feet. It was heart-breaking to look at him when he died. Poor fellow! perhaps his captain provoked him to commit the deed.

We have another (I think he is a Frenchman), who was General Bragg's orderly. They say he stole the general's uniform. The poor fellow is deranged, or acts as if he was.

There is a Mr. Bears, who is under arrest for desertion, who seems to be one of the nicest kind of men, and a good Christian. He says

111

when he left his regiment he had no idea of deserting—only went to see his wife. I do not think that is any excuse for his crime; still, we can not help feeling sorry for him. It is bad enough to see men suffer who are under no ban, but when they are here as those men are, it is distressing indeed.

Mrs. McFarland, a very nice lady from Mobile, has come to assist us. She will take charge of the convalescents, and see that their diet is properly prepared. This is a very important department in a hospital, but few persons seem to think so. All that this class of men require is good diet and a change from camp life. We get plenty of all kinds of vegetables, much more than we are able to cook in the utensils we have.

One day I called on the quartermaster, and asked him to give me a very nice stove he had. He refused, saying we had stoves enough. The next time I saw Dr. Stout I told him, so he gave me an order to get it right away.

Dr. Stout says he wishes the hospitals under his care to be better supplied than any hotel in the Confederacy, and every dollar we receive from the government spent.[17] Dr. Hunter has one great fault; he is loth to spend the money, and seems to think he is saving for the government. I do not think so, as the men are sent here from the army to recruit, and a change of diet is the main thing they need.

The assistant surgeons do all in their power to have the men well cared for, and they could not be more attentive than they are. There is not a day passes that I do not hear the patients speak in their praise. We have six; Dr. Hopping, a Georgian, is one of the kindest and best of men; he is a gentleman in the full sense of the term, and is much beloved by all.

Dr. Soles is one of those men who have no enemies. He takes the world easy; and, as the old saying, like master like man, all of his nurses take after him. We have more *scolding* to do in his ward than any of the others. When we tell the nurses about keeping their ward clean, they seem to think it is nonsense. But Dr. Soles's patients are all well cared for.

Dr. Burt is always in a good humor, and leads one to believe that there is such a thing in the world as constant sunshine. His patients have many a time told me, that the sight of him almost makes them well. His ward is his hobby; I call him " my ward; " it is always in

[17] Dr. Stout's success as a hospital administrator stemmed in a measure from his wise and liberal use of the hospital fund. This particular idea seems to have been well impressed on the medical personnel. Miss Cumming refers to it again in her entry for August 13. On March 25, Dr. Flewellen, in a letter recommending the purchase of cows and the planting of gardens by the individual hospitals, wrote: " I do think any efficient officer in charge of a hospital ought to be able to feed our sick better than can be done at our best hotels. It is to me always a source of annoyance and mortification to hear of any shortcoming in this particular." ALs, Stout Papers (Emory) .

perfect order. His ward has two bath-rooms, in which is a bathing-tub and shower-bath.

The other three surgeons I do not know much about, as the largest part of their wards are across the street; but I know they are most attentive to the patients. One of them, Dr. Nichol, is Dr. Burt's rival in the " ward " line, but there is a good deal of rivalry between all in that respect. Dr. Nichol was very cross one day, and found fault with Mrs. Williamson and myself, and said we did not visit his ward enough. We both make it a rule not to visit the wards when the surgeons are in them, and Dr. Nichol took it for granted we did not visit his at all, and told me one day he thought his patients would fare badly if he did not have good nurses, as Mrs. Williamson and myself did not attend them. I answered him, that I thought they would, if they waited for us to nurse them, as it is as much as we can do to see that the nurses do their duty. It is too bad to accuse Mrs. Williamson of neglect, when she has actually starved herself many a time to give food to the soldiers. There is no doctor who need feel at all flattered if we pay more attention to his sick than the others, as we have made a compact that where we see the surgeon at all neglectful we will devote the most care on that ward.

I have already mentioned Dr. Hunter very frequently. His hobby is, that he was the first to solve a problem, which was finding out that ladies are of service in the hospitals; this he prides himself on.

I see by a Mobile paper that General Pemberton has issued an order to his men, telling them that he has heard that he is called a traitor, and that he is determined to die in the trenches rather than surrender Vicksburg. It is also said that the garrison is well supplied with provisions, and can hold out many a day yet. The enemy seem to have put forth all their energy to take it. God grant that they never may.

July 4.—What a glorious day this was once. Alas! how changed. It is now one of universal sorrow and gloom. If we could only visit the homes of many North and South, what a picture of desolation would be presented! . . .

The hospital is filled with sick and wounded men, and men worn out with hunger and fatigue. The wounded are chiefly from Lidell's [Liddell's] Arkansas Brigade.

Mr. Bears, the prisoner, died to-day; his death was one of the happiest I have yet witnessed.

Sunday, July 5.—Went to church this afternoon, and for the first time, I saw Rev. Dr. Quintard; knew him immediately, from a description I had read of him, written by Rev. Dr. Cross.[18] I was intro-

---

[18] Chaplain Charles Todd Quintard was a man of medical training and " about the last of February, 1863, in consideration of his great faithfulness and efficiency, and in compliance with a request of his fellow chaplains, he was assigned by General Bragg to the charge of the hospitals of Polk's corps, as a sort of general missionary, to look after the spiritual interests of the sick and wounded . . ."

duced to him by Mr. E. Stickney. He inquired all about the hospitals; had heard of the time when Rev. Mr. Miller and the Mobile ladies had started on their mission; said he thought the reason it had proved a failure was because the ladies had not been educated in nursing, as are the Sisters of Charity, and he hoped some day we would have a sisterhood in the church as was in the day of the apostles, and is now in many parts of the old country.

He had been a surgeon in the army, and at one time had charge of a hospital, and had experienced a good deal of trouble with ladies in it.

He was much shocked at the state in which he found the church. The seats, floors, and every place else was covered with dust. He asked me if that was its usual condition. I answered, that I did not know, but the fact is, it is scarcely ever open, Mr. Denniston having duties to call him elsewhere.

Before preaching, Dr. Quintard appointed a committee of men to raise funds, for the purpose of having the church cleaned and seats put in it, as at present the seats are rough planks.

Our army is coming in as fast as it can; we are near the river, and many of the men pass our hospital. Poor fellows, they look completely worn out, but very unlike what they were retreating from Corinth; camp life and hardships have improved them so much.

July 6.—I have just had a visit from our old surgeon, Dr. P. Thornton. He is in Wharton's cavalry, which is under Wheeler. They covered the retreat. He says they fought day and night for a week, and that our men have had a trying time, as every thing had to be brought off in a hurry, and we had so many mountains to cross. He also says they have left the enemy far behind.

We have just received orders to send every man away. Those who are not able to leave this place are to be sent to other hospitals, as we are so near the river, and would get, in case of an attack, the full benefit of the firing.

This place already begins to look like Corinth. Troops are passing and repassing constantly; the noise from the wagons is deafening. We used to have guards to stop wagons and horsemen galloping past; but those things are not heeded now.

It is thought, if this place should be well fortified, and we chose to hold it, it would stand a siege of years, as it has the strongest natural defenses in the Confederacy.

All are in the dark as to what is going to be done. Some feel satis-

Joseph Cross, *Camp and Field: Papers from the Portfolio of an Army Chaplain* (vols. I & II Macon, Ga., 1864; vols. III & IV in one, Columbia, S. C., 1864), III & IV, 250-51.

In the passage to which Miss Cumming refers, Dr. Cross tells how he met " a gentleman in a deep-blue overcoat, with military boots encasing his pantaloons . . . . His eyes, one of them defective, were ' black as sloes,' and his hair, beard, and mustache, dark as the raven's plumage. His complexion and features were manifestly Gallic, and no one could have mistaken him for other than a Frenchman." III & IV, 247.

fied that General Bragg could not have made any other move than the one he has, as the Federals were aiming to flank him, and he had not men enough to force them to fight. If he had enemies before, they can be numbered now by the score. He seems to have no friends except the Alabamians; they have not lost confidence in him. He has certainly had much to contend with. I do not feel competent to judge of his abilities as a commander, but I do wish, for his own sake and that of the country, he would leave this department, as the confidence of men in a commander is every thing.

I am told that many of the Tennesseeans have deserted. I think we are well rid of all who are base enough to live under the Lincoln government after the outrages it has committed on us. . . .

With this retreat, as with every other I have seen, the men are so worn out that they tell all kind of stories about the army's being demoralized. I have got used to this, and do not put faith in it. After they are well rested they will forget it.

July 7.—My brother came to see me to-day, and I could scarcely repress the tears. He looked so badly, I could hardly believe he was the same I had seen ten days ago. He met the army near Tullahoma, and has been on the move ever since. He had a horse, and was much better off than many others. He says the retreat from Kentucky was nothing to this one, and said, " If Bragg had only let us fight, I would not grumble, as I know we would have whipped them." I have been told the same by many others of the men; all seemed eager for the fight; but General Bragg knows best what to do.

It is again rumored that Vicksburg has fallen; but I will wait for more proof before believing it. I observe, at a time like this, that our people always get low-spirited, and are ready to believe all the bad news they hear.

I had a visit from Captain Goldston of Morgan's squadron. He had just come from Kentucky and had seen Mr. Speaker's mother and sisters. Mrs. Williamson had given Captain Goldston a lock of Mr. Speaker's hair; he had given it to them, and they sent us their thanks for our attention to him.

July 9.—Vicksburg has really gone. I suppose we were compelled to surrender it. I wish our people would not tell so many untruths as they have about this place. Only a few days ago we heard there were provisions enough in it to last six months, and now it is said our troops were dying of starvation. All looks gloomy; there is scarcely one bright spot to be seen.

General Lee went into Pennsylvania, and had a desperate battle at Gettysburg. After losing many of our best men, he was compelled to retreat. It is said he has brought out a vast amount of spoils. All these disasters only serve to prolong the war; for I am certain that, happen what will, we will never be slaves to the foe. . . .

115

There is an old Scotch proverb which says "It is a lang road that has na a turnin." The Federals have been having every thing their own way lately. Our day will soon come. . . .

July 13.—Went out shopping to-day, and met John Hazzard [Hazard] of Mobile, captain of the Confederate Guards, which is in the Twenty-fourth Alabama Regiment. Camp life had improved him so much I scarcely knew him. He is a noble-looking young man, and one that Mobile may well be proud of. I had a visit a few days ago from Captain O'Brien of the same regiment.

General Bragg visited our hospital and complimented it highly. It is a pity we have to move, but there is too much noise here. We have been compelled to have the street barricaded to prevent wagons passing.

July 18.—I went to the church this afternoon to practice for the choir, and there I found Dr. Quintard and Dr. Cannon enveloped in a cloud of dust. They were both sweeping, trying to make the church look as clean as possible. Mr. Stickney and I went and procured covering for the communion table; after every thing was fixed we scarcely knew the place. Dr. Quintard is a man of great energy. He has already collected twenty-five hundred dollars, and contracted for seats for the church.

Dr. Quintard introduced me to Colonel Palmer of the Eighteenth Tennessee Regiment. He is a fine-looking man, and I am told brave to a fault. He was wounded at the battle of Murfreesboro.

Our hospital has been divided; Dr. Hunter and the Newsom Hospital have gone to Cleveland in this state. Three of the ladies have gone with it. Mrs. Williamson, Miss Ellis, and myself are going to Kingston, Georgia; Dr. Hopping is going there too. Drs. Burt and Soles are going to a new hospital in this place, called Camp Direction Hospital. I regret leaving Dr. Hunter, as he has been very kind to us, and I also regret leaving his wife, who is a very lovely woman.

I had a visit from Rev. Mr. Williams. We shall miss him very much, as he has been most attentive to our patients, praying and talking to them in season and out of season.

I have spent the best part of the week visiting. I spent one evening at Mr. Corbin's, Mrs. Dr. Fry's father; had music, and a very delightful evening.

I spent another with Mrs. Whiteside. There I met quite a pleasant party, and among them some ladies from Kentucky; Dr. Quintard, and Dr. Cannon, and Mr. Stickney. I had heard much of the vocal powers of one of the Kentucky ladies, but must own I have been sadly disappointed. She had a very remarkable voice, but has put the science of music at defiance; sings to suit her fancy. She sang the "*Gloria in Excelsis*," the most solemn and beautiful anthem we have, with as many operatic touches as the "*Casta Diva*." Mrs. Whiteside is a refined and highly intelligent lady, and has the faculty of making

116

every one at ease in her house. Her young daughter, who played for us, is a sweet young lady. I shall ever remember the family with pleasure.

My friends, Mr. and Mrs. Brewer, are packing up to leave. The last time I saw them, Mr. Brewer said he put no faith in General Bragg erecting fortifications, and that he would not be surprised to wake up some morning and find the army gone.

Sunday, July 19.—This morning Dr. Quintard preached to a crowded house. Almost every general in the army was present. I saw General Polk; he is really a noble-looking man. One of his daughters was with him. She is very pretty.

Dr. Quintard preached a very fine sermon. His text was, " For we are journeying unto the place of which the Lord hath said, I will give it you." In the afternoon Dr. Cannon preached a sequel to it; an excellent one.

The first was reminding us that, whether in peace or war, there was a journey we were all taking, that sooner or later would come to an end; and warning us to prepare to enter into that land which the Lord has prepared for those who keep his commandments. The last was telling us about the blessed rest which God had prepared for his people. How many such teachings do we despise!

" It is written, As I live, saith the Lord, every knee shall bow to me, and every tongue shall confess to God."

We fall down and worship, but certainly not the Maker and Ruler of all things. There are few who would like being called the enemies of God, and yet has he not said, He that is not with me is against me? And are we not commanded to worship him with our whole heart? I know of many, apparently good men, who do not seem to think that they have any right to confess Christ before men; and these men know in their hearts that the Bible is no fable, and yet they reject its teachings every hour of their lives. When I ask these men why they live so, the answer often is that there are so many wicked men in the church. I sometimes ask them if that is the answer they intend giving the Judge of all on that great day when we shall have to give an account, not of what our neighbors have done, but what we ourselves have? I scarcely think the excuse will avail, that we went astray because our neighbor did . . .

We do not reason thus about our worldly affairs. Why should we not use common sense regarding our spiritual ones? " To him that knoweth to do good, and doeth it not, to him *it* is sin." There is no more sublime sight than the man of intellect and great mind, bowing in adoration to his Maker.

A good moral man without religion is like a mariner trying to find his way through the seas without a compass. . . .

July 21.—We intend leaving to-morrow, and are now at Dr. Taylor's house; he is a surgeon in the army, and for some time was one of our

117

patients. Mrs. Hodges, who is keeping house for him, has very kindly invited us to remain with her until we leave, as all our household things have been sent to the train.

I rode out this afternoon, in company with Dr. Burt, and paid a visit to the Twenty-fourth Alabama Regiment. There I saw Lieutenant Chamberlain, now captain, and Captain Fowler, whom I met in Okolona. The regiment was encamped in a grove of trees; it had a few tents for the officers and commissary stores. The only protection the men have from inclement weather is their blankets put on sticks about three feet high.

The men were busy preparing supper, and I did not think looked altogether pleased at my visiting them, as their attire and employment is not such as they would wish them to be. But there is more true glory in their dress than all the gilt lace, brass buttons, and holiday attire usually worn by fireside soldiers, and in their work, than if they had scores of attendants to do it for them.

I could not help contrasting this camp with the one I last visited. It was when the war first commenced, and our house had been emptied of furniture to put in the tents, as we thought it impossible for men to do without certain things which they had been accustomed to at home. Since then they have learned a few lessons, in this respect, as we all have.

I saw this regiment when it first went into active service, not more than a year ago; it was then a large regiment, and now a mere fragment answers to the roll-call.

Yesterday Mrs. Williamson and I visited the soldiers' grave-yard. That hallowed spot! There reposes the dust of men from every state in the South. There is naught to mark the places where these heroes sleep, save slight mounds of earth; at the head of each is a small piece of wood, numbered. But it matters little that no marble monument is there, for

"What hallows ground where heroes sleep?
'T is not the sculptured piles you heap!"

No; it is a nation's tears and grateful benedictions which make their last resting-place a sacred spot. By their grateful country they shall ever be remembered. . . .

The head-board I had put at Mr. Barstow's grave was quite conspicuous. The inscription had been put on so strangely, that I could scarcely make sense out of it. I feel confident that no one will take the artist for a pupil of Lindley Murray's.

There were two others: one erected by some kind friend; the other I had put at the head of Mr. Davis's grave, at his father's request.

We returned by way of the river. The scenery on its banks is really enchanting.

"Not Katrine, in her mirror blue,
Gives back the shaggy banks more true," [19]

than does the Tennessee the lofty and rugged hills that look down upon its placid waters.

We saw many of our men at work on the fortifications; they looked well, and were cheerful. They seemed to have little faith that their work would amount to any thing, and said they would not be at all surprised if by to-morrow they were ordered to evacuate Chattanooga, and that they were only given the work to do for fear they might forget how it was done. We intend taking two girls from here with us. They are orphans; neither of them can read. The eldest is nineteen years of age, the other sixteen. They begged so very hard for us to take them along. I am in hopes we can be of some service to them by teaching them.

I regret leaving Chattanooga as the army is here, but its movements are very uncertain; perhaps before many days we may be much nearer it than we cared for, although Dr. Stout does not seem to think so, as he is having another new hospital erected at Camp Direction. I do not know why, but few persons think that General Bragg intends holding this place.

[19] Sir Walter Scott, *The Lady of the Lake*, canto first, stanza 19, ll. 375-76.

VI: KINGSTON, CHEROKEE SPRINGS

✝✝

July 23, 1863.—We arrived in Kingston, Georgia, last evening, and put up at one of the hotels; we paid three dollars each for breakfast and a night's lodging; paying it out of the donation money, of which we have still some on hand. Dr. A[vent] called early this morning; he is post surgeon, a fine-looking old gentleman, and a man highly respected for his surgical abilities. He was left in charge of our wounded at Murfreesboro, and, I am told, has written a valuable book on surgery, from his experience at that place. He is a man of sterling principle, but a little eccentric. The first information we received from him was, that he did not approve of ladies in hospitals; that was nothing new from a doctor, but we were a little taken aback to hear it said so bluntly. He then told us his principal objection was, that the accommodations in hospitals were not fit for ladies. We assured him he need give himself no uneasiness on that score, as we were all good *soldiers*, and had been accustomed to hardships.

He then said the two girls we brought from Chattanooga could not remain as servants, as he intended having a number of negroes on the place, and that would be putting them on equality; and if we could not retain them in some other capacity, they would have to be dismissed. There is always plenty of sewing to be done in the hospital, and we knew we could give them employment in that department.

He also told us that he wished us all to eat at the officers' table, with himself and the assistant surgeon, as he thought a table was not fit to eat at where there were no ladies. We did not object to that plan till we had given it a trial.

We were escorted to the house which we now occupy. It consists of two small rooms on the ground floor. We are about a square and a half from the dining-room and kitchen; so when Drs. A[vent] and Hopping called to take us to dinner, we made quite a procession. On the way, Dr. A[vent] informed me that he was a strict disciplinarian, and as I had charge of every thing in the domestic line, if there was not a good dinner that day, he would call me to account. I laughed

---

[1] Because of her critical remarks Miss Cumming referred to Dr. Avent only by his initial. Dr. Benjamin W. Avent had been commissioned in the Confederate service July 19, 1861. Jones, " Roster . . . ," *loc. cit.*, 168. Early in the War he had been Surgeon General of the Provisional Army of Tennessee and, as such, had been Dr. Stout's superior officer.

and told him, if he talked in that way, I should think him a real Pharaoh, as I had not even had time to look around me.

We had an excellent dinner—a much better one than we had eaten in many a day. The two girls looked as if they felt themselves sadly out of place, but we are in the *army*, and must *obey* orders.

This is quite a small place, and there does not seem to be a large building in it, with the exception of the churches and hotels. Of the latter there are no less than four. It is in Cass County; is on the Western and Atlantic Railroad, sixty-two miles north-west of Atlanta, and at the junction of the Rome branch railroad; it is not quite twenty miles from the latter city.

Dr. A[vent] has been here for some time, and has converted some old stores into very nice wards, which will do very well for winter, but are entirely too close for summer.

July 27.—We are getting along pretty well; we have moved into the building in which is the kitchen and dining-room. The house is a very small one, and although this part of Georgia abounds in lime, it seems to be little used in the houses; the walls are generally boarded. This house has the addition of paper on its walls, which we have been compelled to take down, owing to its being in tatters.

All our cooks are negroes, and I find I have much more to do than when we had our soldiers in that capacity. A negro is a negro at best, and nothing more. They have to be told the same thing every day, and watched to see if they do it then.

I see by the Mobile papers that General Buckner, who is in command of that post, is making great preparations for a siege, as there is an attack expected there soon. I hope the city will be able to stand as nobly as Charleston is doing, and that we will have no more Vicksburg disasters.

Many of the returned prisoners are blaming Pemberton alone for the fall of Vicksburg, saying that the place was not properly provisioned, and that that was the cause of its surrender. The suffering of our men, both there and at Port Hudson, was terrible. Poor fellows! it does seem hard to have had to endure so much from the incompetency of their commander.

If the people have to leave Mobile, I do not see what is to become of them. I have seen enough of *refugeeing* to prove that it is not the best thing in the world. But Mobilians will have to do as others have done before them—the best they can under the circumstances—knowing it is the fortune of war, and all for the cause.

July 30.—Yesterday Miss Ellis and myself visited Rome, for the purpose of doing some shopping for the hospitals and ourselves.

I was very much pleased with the appearance of Rome. Like the renowned city, the name of which it bears, it is built on several hills. It has some very handsome buildings; the principal streets are broad and clean. It resembles ancient Rome in another respect, that of having had a conquering hero march into it in triumph; although not a Cæsar in name, yet equal to any of them in bravery.

I am told that when Forrest entered Rome with his prisoners, he was met by the ladies and presented with a wreath of flowers, and the pathway of his gallant army was strewn with them. They were the heartfelt offerings of a truly grateful people to their deliverers for freeing them from the ruthless invader. The people at present are in daily expectation of another raid; and, as there are very few troops there to defend the place, they expect to be left to the mercy of the foe.

Many persons think that a military necessity may force General Bragg down here, and that Kingston will be his head-quarters. No movement astonishes me now, and, like a true soldier, I obey orders, and *try* to *ask* no questions.

There are many handsome store buildings, and they were pretty well supplied with goods, and cheaper than I have seen any place in the Confederacy. I bought a very pretty calico dress for three dollars per yard, and a pretty gray homespun for one dollar and seventy-five cents per yard.

I searched the whole place for a white-wash brush, but failed in getting one.

I have heard much of the kindness of the people here to strangers, and that the society is of the very best.

We took dinner, and were kindly entertained at the house of a very nice lady, a relative of Miss Ellis. There we met an old lady who had been in the Quintard Hospital, in this place, and to judge from her conversation I should think that the ladies and surgeons did not get along very well together. From what I have experienced and seen, I expect there are faults on both sides.

There are a number of hospitals in Rome, which are being broken up. As they seem to be very fine ones, and it is a healthy locality, I am always suspicious of some new movement taking place in the army when I hear of such things.

Rome is in Floyd County, Georgia, at the confluence of the Etowah and Ostenaola [Oostanaula] rivers, which forms the Coosa River. Steamboats of moderate size navigate the Coosa River, and can ascend as far as this place. Thousands of bales of cotton are annually exported from this point.

August 1.—We have a number of patients very sick, and we are kept very busy, as the two girls we brought with us from Chattanooga are both ill, and I suppose will have to leave. Two of our cooks are also down. I asked Dr. A[vent] to let some of the men come and assist in the kitchen, but he refused, saying that such work was *degrading* to them.

The surgeons have been compelled to find boarding-houses outside of the hospital. Dr. A[vent] found it was against the regulations for them to board in the hospitals; so we have gone back to the plan of having our own table.

August 3.—I am beginning to think that we shall not be able to remain here, as Dr. A[vent] has proved himself a real *Pharaoh*—expecting brick without straw. We have many sick, and much to do. Our servants are still sick, and when we ask Dr. A[vent] for more, he tells us the government will not allow him to grant the request.

The poor government is blamed for every thing. I have many a time heard it charged with faults which I thought were owing to subordinate officers. Dr. Hunter was constantly telling us about orders he had received from head-quarters: allowing us so much soap and no more, and even regulating how many pieces each person must have washed. I have never been able to ascertain whether head-quarters meant General Bragg, the surgeon-general, or President Davis. I think sometimes it is only a mythical term, merely used to frighten us. If not, I think it is a pity that those worthies have not something of more importance on which to spend their time. I have often thought that they are surely not aware of the price of paper, or they would be a little more sparing of their dispatches. I wish they would send me a few blank sheets, as I find it difficult to get enough for my private use.

We have no wash-house. When I asked Dr. A[vent] for one, he told me that his grandmother and mother never had any but the canopy of heaven for theirs, and he did not intend having any other in the hospital. I argued the case with him as best I could; I told him that a hospital was not a private house, and it was our duty to do all in our power to promote the health of the attendants as well as the patients; and that whoever washed ought to have a covering of some kind; and the clothing, whether dirty or clean, needed to be covered in case of rain. I found him inexorable.

I feel confident that the doctor has never had charge of a hospital before, and it is useless to try and teach any one who has such un-bounded faith in his progenitors. I have made up my mind to let things take their course, and if I find I can not get along, will leave.

Numbers of troops are being transported down the road. No one can tell where they are going to.

August 7.—I intend leaving to-day for Chattanooga.

This morning I sent for Dr. A[vent], and told him that it was impossible for us to get along without more servants; and I told him further that I knew of some who could be hired, and asked his consent; but he would not give it. So I then told him that Mrs. Williamson and myself would leave. At this he became quite angry, and said he could not compel us to remain, but since he had *hired* us ladies, he would pay us for the time we had been there. The latter part he said with emphasis, and then left me. Had he remained longer, I should have informed him that when we " hired " ourselves, we were not aware it was to him, but to the same government which had " hired " him.

I am beginning to think that we were spoiled in the Newsom Hospital; but I should hope that there are not many surgeons in the department such as Dr. A[vent]. If there are, it is not much wonder that so few ladies of refinement enter them.

I ask but one thing from any surgeon, and that is, to be treated with the same respect due to men in their own sphere of life. I waive all claim for that due me as a lady, but think I have a right to expect the other. I scarcely think that Dr. A[vent] would dared to have spoken to one of his assistant surgeons as he did to me.

All this has made me feel more for our proud-spirited men, who I know have to endure insults from the petty officers over them. Well, these trials must be endured for a little while; they will soon, I trust, be over with; and then, it is for the cause we have to put up with them.

August 8.—Arrived in Chattanooga last evening, and am now at the Gilmer Hospital.

On the cars coming from Kingston, a gentleman and lady came in at one of the depots. The gentleman had to stand, as the car was very much crowded. I offered him part of my seat, which he accepted. He then told me he was a chaplain in a hospital near Ringgold, and that they were in want of some ladies in it. I have called on Dr. Stout, and he has sent down there to make inquiries concerning it.

Last evening I went to the Episcopal Church, and a chaplain preached a most excellent sermon. His text was, " The wind bloweth where it listeth," etc. He reminded us of how much more frequently the wind blew soft than in a storm, and so with the " still small voice: " it spoke oftener to us in the calm than in the tempest. The church was filled with soldiers. I spent part of to-day at Camp Direction Hospital, where are many of the folks from the Newsom Hospital.

The hospital is an excellent one; every thing about it is entirely new; but I can not look on those things with the same pleasure which I have heretofore, as it is impossible to feel that any thing connected with our army is permanent. The whole place is surrounded with breastworks, some of which are within a stone's throw of the hospital.

I spent the evening at Mrs. Whiteside[']s, and had a very pleasant time, practicing for the church. Mr. E. Stickney escorted me, to whom I am much indebted for his kindness ever since I have been here. He is from Alabama, and is much of a gentleman.

This afternoon I sent Mr. Massinger's money by express to Mr. Bolt, in care of Captain Cupples.

August 10.—This morning Mrs. Crocker and myself called on Dr. Stout. He informed me that he could not hear of any hospital that would suit Mrs. Williamson and myself, with the exception of one, where there was a lady already. She would be head matron, and he did not think we would be willing to go on that account. I told him we did not go into the hospital for position, and if we were only doing something for the cause, cared for little else. We were willing to make the trial.

Dr. Stout complimented the women for what they were doing in the hospitals. So we told him that we had always heard that he was opposed to them in that capacity. He replied, he knew how he had received that name. When surgeon of a hospital in Nashville, the ladies had interfered with him so much that he was compelled to forbid them coming to it,[2] but when he saw them having but one aim—that of doing good, and doing it in the right way—no man could think more of them than he did; furthermore, there was no end to the good they could do. I have heard many surgeons remark the same thing.

August 12.—We arrived at Cherokee Springs, near Ringgold, Ga., this evening. We are both much fatigued and out of sorts. We are here among strangers and feel very lonely. I can not help looking back with regret on the days we spent at the Newsom Hospital. It seems to me that there was not a person in it, from the lowest to the highest, but greeted us with a smile of pleasure, and they were ready at any moment to do us a favor.

Well, when I went back to Kingston from Chattanooga, I found that Dr. A[vent] had quarreled with Mrs. Williamson; so I felt I was justified in the step I had taken, as any one who could quarrel with good, patient Mrs. Williamson would quarrel with any one.

We regretted leaving Dr. Hopping, as a brother could not have been kinder than he has been, and every one of his nurses were as kind as himself.

On the cars coming here we met Dr. Quintard, Dr. P. Thornton, and General Hindman; the latter was on his way to rejoin the Tennessee army. He has not been with it in some time, having been in Mississippi, attending the trial of one of our generals. He saw some of the men of his old command at the different stations which we passed, who seemed much pleased at seeing him. He commented a good deal on the state of the country; I could not but think it a pity that a man who could arrange every thing so nicely, should not be at the *head of affairs*; but then our people are so *blind*!

He told me he was proud to say he was of Scotch descent; his forefathers had fought at the battle of Culloden, with the ill-fated Prince Charlie, and had been exiled to this country. His name is Thomas Culloden.[3]

Dr. Quintard adverted to our having an order of sisterhood in the church; this he seems to have very much at heart. We had our sunbonnets with us, and he wished to know if they were our uniform; we have never worn any, as we can not afford any clothes but what we may

[2] In Dr. Stout's own copy of Miss Cumming's book (now in the collection of the editor) he marked this passage and added the marginal note: "Not true. Never forbade ladies coming into the [Gordon] hospital at Nashville. Did say I was much annoyed by indiscreet interference on the part of certain ladies at N. with the discipline of the hospital. S. H. Stout."

[3] Perhaps the General was teasing. His middle name was Carmichael.

chance to have. We have always made a rule of wearing the simplest kind of dress, as we think any other kind sadly out of place in a hospital; calico or homespun is the only dress fit to wear, but to get the former is a rare treat.

We got out at Ringgold; Dr. Gamble, the post surgeon, and Dr. Gore, were at the depot to receive us; Dr. Quintard, being an old acquaintance of Dr. Gore, he introduced us.

Dr. Gore took us to the Bragg Hospital, of which he is surgeon, and introduced us to two very nice ladies—the matrons, Mrs. Byrom and Miss Burford—who received us very kindly.

We left there in a wagon, in company with Colonel Gaither, from Kentucky, a cousin of Dr. Bemiss, the surgeon of the hospital in which we now are.[4]

From what little we have seen of Dr. Bemiss we think we will like him; we have a room in a house set apart for the officers; our stay here is temporary, as there is a house now being erected for our accommodation. Dr. Bemiss told us we could either have our meals brought to our room or eat at the officers' table.

A very polite young man came and asked us what we would have for supper, just as they do in hotels. I am afraid I have given him offense, as I could not keep from laughing at such a question, and told him I did not know there was any choice in a hospital. He said he meant whether we would have tea or coffee, as supper was over, and it would have to be prepared; he brought us some tea, without milk, very good bread and butter, and eggs, the latter boiled as hard as a stone.

August 13.—This morning the same young man came and asked us if we were going to the table, or would we have our meals brought to us. We concluded to try the table, as it would save trouble; it was set in a small room, and around it were seated officers of all ranks; they were convalescent.

I have met our old Corinth friend among the patients, Dr. Devine [Divine]; he was very much pleased to see me, and said, as we were strangers here, if there was any thing he could do for us, not to hesitate one moment in asking him, for it would give him great pleasure to assist us in any way.

[4] Dr. B. M. Wible had known Dr. S. M. Bemiss in Kentucky. On October 10, 1862, he had written to Dr. Stout: " I commend Dr. S. M. Bemiss of Louisville to your kind consideration. He is a refugee from Lincoln tyranny. Please guide him so as to enable him to enter the medical department of the army. His industry, medical ability and administrative talent, would make him an important addition to our department of the Army." ALs, Stout Papers (Emory).

Dr. Bemiss first served as a contract surgeon with Dr. Wible. Appointed Assistant Surgeon by Dr. Stout in December 1863, he soon became his chief's most trusted lieutenant. Just before the close of the War (April 6, 1865) he was ordered by Surgeon General S. P. Moore to succeed Dr. Stout as Medical Director. Jones, " Roster . . . ," *loc. cit.,* 172; Stout, " Some Facts . . . ," *Southern Practitioner,* XXV (1903), 453.

The house we are in is a frame building, such as is usually put up for summer use, at watering-places. It has a hall through the center, and rooms each side.

Dr. Bemiss called early in the morning and took us through the hospital. It is situated in a valley, and is one of the most lovely spots I ever beheld; I told Dr. Bemiss it put me in mind of a picture I had seen of the "Dream of Arcadia." All around it had an air of perfect tranquility; it seems to me if the men get well any place they will here.

The hospital covers about thirty acres of ground, abounding in mineral springs, and in nice shady nooks.

We visited the wards; there are only three, although there are accommodations for five hundred patients; they are composed of tents, which are very tastefully arranged. Each ward is separate, having a wide street in the center, shaded by magnificent trees.

At present the hospital is filled with patients, a few of whom are sick enough to be confined to their beds; they are mostly chronic cases, sent here for the benefit of the water.

As we have never been in a hospital for chronic cases, we do not know how we shall like it; it always seemed to me that, do what we will for them, they would not get well. No one, unless those who have been waiting on sick men, can have the least idea how depressing it is not to see them recover; it has many a time made me quite melancholy, and I have known it to have the same effect on the surgeons.

Mrs. Williamson and I are going to do what is best suited to our taste—see that the men receive the food prepared for them. We will now have plenty of time to read and talk to them.

We were much pleased at the kind manner which Dr. Bemiss exhibited for all; he spoke to the men with as much feeling as a kind father would to his children.

We came to one man who had been very sick, and Dr. Bemiss told us that he scarcely ate any thing, but there was a kind of corn-cake which he wished, and no one could make out what kind it was. On his explaining, we understood that he wished corn meal batter-cakes; we had them made for him, and he ate them with a great relish. Dr. Bemiss was delighted, and said that after all there was no one like a woman to take care of the sick.

As this has been a watering-place, there are quite a number of small wooden houses on it, which are set apart for various purposes. Each ward has one connected with it, where are put the lowest patients. One is a linen and ironing-room, of which a man has charge; besides, there is a woman who does the mending and part of the ironing.

The patients and attendants have their washing and ironing done in the hospital. I wonder what "head-quarters" would say if this were known. It seems strange that in one hospital can be done what is unlawful in another.

127

We visited the wash-house; as yet it has nothing but the "canopy of heaven" for a covering, if I except some very fine shade-trees, and tents in which to put the clothes in case of rain. Water is supplied from a "branch." Mr. Love, a soldier, and his wife have charge, and are responsible to the man in the linen-room for the clothes. Near the wash-house is a bathing-house; the water for it is supplied from the same branch.

There is also a place for dyeing comforts, as the latter are made out of cotton in its pure state, which soils very easily. Then there is a quilting-room, where these comforts are made, after being dyed. All of this is under the superintendence of the man who has charge of the linen-room.

There is also a fine bakery, and a convalescent kitchen, in which are large boilers for cooking. The convalescent dining-room, which is new, is covered and open at the sides. A horn calls the patients to their meals, which has quite a romantic sound, like old feudal times.

We next visited the kitchen, where the diet for the very sick is prepared; in which are four stoves and as many cooks, besides a head one, who takes charge of every thing. There are no less than two hundred and fifty patients fed every day from this kitchen. From it the convalescent officers' table is supplied—a thing that in Chattanooga (not head-quarters this time) Dr. Stout would on no account permit. Although the officers had a separate table and separate rooms, their diet was the same as the convalescent privates.

Dr. Bemiss has come up to Dr. Stout's standard of having the hospital as well supplied as any hotel in the South. There is a profusion of all kinds of good things—fowls, vegetables, and fruits of all kinds; but there is one thing lacking, and an important one—milk. The doctor says he intends getting some cows.

The head cook sees that each nurse is provided with what is prescribed on the diet-list for the patients. The surgeons put down on their books what kind of diet they want, and the head nurse copies it, and hands it to the steward, who makes a register of the number of men. The head cook has a list of the articles which come under the different classes of diet, and distributes them accordingly.[5]

We were introduced to the chief matron. She does not visit the wards, but attends to seeing the delicacies prepared for the sick.

We thought we had seen all of this excellent hospital, but found we were mistaken; for it has a reading-room, in which are books and

[5] The Special Orders issued at the neighboring hospital at Tunnel Hill by Surgeon Wible on January 23, 1863, required the medical officers to "enter their prescriptions of medicines and diets in Prescription Books, with the name and number of bed of each patient. Full Diet will be designated by the letters F. D. Half diet by the letters H. D. Low diet by the letters L. D.

"The Diet Table ordinarily will be as follows: Full Diet: Bacon, Beef, Soup, Vegetables, Bread, &c. Half Diet: Soup, Rice, Bread, Milk, &c. Low Diet: Beef Tea; Coffee; Chicken Soup; Milk, &c. Special Articles of Diet ordered will be noted on the prescriptions." ADs, Stout Papers (Thomas).

papers. The chaplain, Mr. Green (the one I met on the cars) , intends having a chapel put up, and I think the place will then be complete.

Take the hospital altogether, I do not see how it could be more perfect; but Dr. Bemiss tells me that there is a much better one at Catoosa Springs, some few miles distant,[6] Dr. Foster is the surgeon, and his wife and niece matrons.

General Bragg is in this hospital sick. He has his head-quarters at Dr. Gamble's house, which is near here. Mrs. Bragg is with the general.

Sunday, August 16.—To-day Dr. Quintard preached twice. As our chapel is not yet up, he had service under a large oak-tree. In the morning his text was one I had heard him preach from in Chatta-nooga: " We are journeying on to the place of which the Lord hath said, I will give it you." He asked me before preaching if I would object hearing it again. I told him, on the contrary, that I would be much pleased. . . .

Mr. Green, our chaplain, sat with Dr. Quintard, and I observed he did not assist him with the service. This caused me to reflect on the diversity of the Christian religion, and I thought what a pity it is that there should be any difference about it. . . .

Dr. Quintard gave out that he would have service after dark; I did not see how he could, as we had no lights of any kind, but I was not long in finding out. He omitted the most part of the service in which the congregation joins, and read out the lines of the psalm and hymn, like a good Methodist, and preached a very fine extempore sermon.

I can now understand how it is that he is so popular and does so much good in the army. He suits himself and all he does to the times.

We had a call from Dr. Sizemore and his wife; he is now assistant surgeon in the Foard Hospital, in Ringgold; Mrs. Sizemore is matron. We had a long talk about Corinth, and the terrible times we had seen there.

This morning Mrs. Dr. Gamble, Mrs. Bragg, and myself raised the tunes, but in the evening Dr. Quintard did not give us the chance, as he raised them himself. General Bragg attended service. His health is very bad, which is no wonder, as he is so much harassed. He is a member of the church, and, I am told, a sincere Christian. He has done his utmost to have Christianity diffused in the army.

Mrs. Bragg has the appearance of being a very modest, lady-like person, as I am told she is. She is also in bad health. It is said she

---

[6] Catoosa Springs, a resort similar to Miss Cumming's Cherokee Springs, had been promoted as a Southern watering-place, a " Saratoga of the Confederate States " complete with " Brass and String Band of superior Musicians." A circular issued in 1861 noted: " The medicinal virtues of these many and varied Mineral Waters are now too well known to require an extensive description. In addition to the Red, White and Black Sulphur Springs—many of them combined with Iron and Magnesia—is an inexhaustible well of the purest Freestone.

" Our accomodations are very extensive. We have many pleasant cottages separate from the main hotel . . ." *Catoosa Springs, The Saratoga of the Confederate States* . . . (Savannah, 1861) , [3].

worries a good deal whenever she hears of the necessity of shooting any of the men, and pleads for them when she can.

August 18.—We are still quite pleased with every thing; have a few very sick; all is a great contrast from Chattanooga, where we had so many die.

Mr. Green is very attentive; is constantly visiting the men; and he also does all of their writing, which is another great help to us. The fact is, Mrs. Williamson and myself will be spoiled if we have no more to do than we have now.

We have three assistant surgeons—Drs. Bateman, Ray [Rhea] and Divine—who all seem to be perfect gentlemen, and kind, attentive physicians. Dr. Rhea is a member of the Presbyterian Church, and Dr. Divine of the Episcopal.

The young soldier who was so attentive the first evening we came here is named Frank Laws. He is an excellent young man, and a member of the Episcopal Church. He has charge of the officers' department.

We have a patient, Lieutenant Griffin of Texas, who lost his foot at the battle of Murfreesboro; he is a very handsome young man, and is as cheerful as if he had met with no loss; his wound is not yet healed. He was in the same hospital in Chattanooga in which Mrs. Newsom was, and is unbounded in her praise.

All the men who are able are busy erecting the chapel out of the branches of trees.

Fast-Day, August 21.—Our chapel is finished. Mr. Green preached in it, and an excellent sermon he gave us; it was quite stirring and encouraging. . . .

Mr. Green's text was, " Rend your heart, and not your garments." As General Bragg was leaving the church, a dispatch was handed to him, seemingly an important one. I hope nothing is the matter.

The morning services were pretty well attended by the privates; some of the officers instead of going played checkers. I had a conversation with one of them on the subject, and told him that the war would not close until men gave God the homage which he demanded. He did not agree with me; I asked him if he believed the Bible. He answered yes. I then asked him if he and the others had obeyed the commands in it, in seemingly grudging to give God that one day. I said nothing more, but was gratified to see him attend the afternoon service.

We have had but two meals, and none of the men have found any fault.

I had an introduction to Major Clark of Kentucky, and Major Austin of Texas; the latter one of Morgan's men; he was not with him on his late disastrous campaign. I was making eggnog when I received the introduction, and they jestingly asked me for some. I told them they must first get an order from the surgeon under whose care they were, as General Bragg, being so near, might put me *under arrest* for disobedience of orders.

August 22.—The enemy are shelling Chattanooga; all the hospitals are leaving there. I can not help, from looking round and thinking, that perhaps ere many days we may be compelled to leave here.

August 28.—Our surgeons mess together; to-day they had a dinner party; we were at it. Mr. and Mrs. Green were there, and we had quite a pleasant time. Rev. Mr. Bryson has presented the hospital with a number of interesting books, which have just run the blockade from England. Mr. Bryson is a Presbyterian minister, and a co-laborer with Dr. Quintard in the responsible work of supervising and promoting the spiritual interest of the army. I am not personally acquainted with him, but I have often heard him spoken of in terms of the highest commendation, as a zealous worker in the cause.

Mrs. Green is a very pleasant lady; is from Columbia, South Carolina; a sister-in-law to Rev. Dr. Palmer from New Orleans. The doctor was here a few days ago, and looked the worse for wear. He had just come from Chattanooga, and I have been told was holding divine service when that place was shelled, and went on with it as if nothing was the matter.

Troops are daily passing, they say from Mississippi, to reinforce our army. We are expecting a battle every day. General Bragg left here several days ago. If General Rosecrans should try to outflank our army by Rome, it will be compelled to fall back. General Bragg has a trying time, as there seems to be so many points from which the enemy can march their army right down on us; and they have so many more men than we have, that they can make any movement they please.

After dinner Mrs. Green, Mrs. Collier (whose husband is here sick), Mrs. Williamson, and myself walked down to Catoosa depot, to see if we could hear of any news from Chattanooga, but the train did not come in. I hope nothing is the matter, and that it has not been captured by the enemy.

A number of men were at the depot, expecting to get off, and were much disappointed at not succeeding.

We have a very sick doctor here, who has been telling me he is greatly in favor of our having negroes in the army; somehow I do not like the idea; his arguments were, however, very plausible.

We have had a man desert, which has annoyed Dr. Bemiss not a little. He made pretense he was very sick, and the surgeons were very kind to him, and every thing that the hospital could afford was given him; his father came to see him, and because he could not get a furlough for him carried him off. The old man called himself a Baptist preacher, and wanted to hold service. I have very little patience with any one who could be guilty of leading his son to commit such a crime. Dr. Bemiss has sent after them.

131

Sunday, August 30.—During afternoon service the old man and his son who deserted were brought back; I do not think I ever saw a sadder sight; they will be sent to the army for trial.

September 1.—Our sick are all doing pretty well, with the exception of two, who I think will die; one of them is named E. Edney; he is from Tennessee.

I see by papers just received from home that they have adopted a system which I think will be productive of much good—giving sketches of history. I have often lamented the ignorance of our men in that respect; I think example is every thing; and when we know how others have suffered in defense of liberty, we shall know how to imitate them.

I see by the same paper that General Morgan, who is now a prisoner, has had his head shaved, and been treated with all kinds of indignities. These things seem almost incredible. Why, savages respect a brave man, and a man like General Morgan, one would think, would gain the admiration of any people who had any sense of chivalry; and we all know how kindly he has always treated whoever was in his power. But they can not degrade such a man; his spirit will soar above any insult they can heap upon him.

September 3.—I have just received a letter from Dr. Burt; he was in Chattanooga at the time it was bombarded. He says there was no warning given, and that the scene of the women and children running from the shells was distressing in the extreme, and when he left there, there were hundreds encamping in the woods, without shelter of any kind.

I have observed an article in the Mobile Advertiser and Register, of August 29th, from Virginia, signed A; I admire the spirit in which it is written, but am not a little astonished at what the writer says about the soldiers and people of the South-west; says he learns they are talking of submission.

I can tell him, from what I have seen, I have heard not a breath of such a thing. Chattanooga was called a Union place, but I saw nothing of it while there. To be sure, I did not mingle much with the people, but nearly all I knew, rich and poor, had their men folks in our army. I want no better sign of loyalty.

If he means the soldiers of this army, he has made a grand mistake. I have seen hundreds of them sick, ragged, hungry, and worn out with fatigue, and not one word of submission with it all; but the reverse: angry because they were not allowed to fight; and I am told that many of the Tennesseeans who deserted have come back and resolved

> " To prevail in the cause that is dearer than life,
> Or, crushed in its ruins, to die! "

I am proud of what this correspondent says about " Old Virginia " and her invincible armies: that they are determined to fight till the last. I certainly would have been much surprised could he have said any thing else.

He is right when he says we had grown arrogant and self-confident, and were punished with defeat, as we have been before, and shall ever be, when we forget the Giver of all victory. We profess to be Christians: do not let us make a mockery of the name, but give Him the glory and honor unto whom it is due.

In the same paper of the 30th, I see letters, the tone of which I am much pleased with, and I only hope the writers are acting up to the spirit of them, and leading others by their example to do the same.

One of the letters is from a lady in Mississippi, who signs herself "Sylvia;" the other signs herself an "Alabama Woman." The first is a call to the women of Mississippi to abstain from festivities, and, above all things, to give no countenance to "stay-at-homes," who wear gilt lace and buttons. She says that, upon the occasion of the last Grierson raid into that state, the "home chivalry," instead of protecting the ladies, took to the woods.

I thought, when this war broke out, that the women in every state had too high an appreciation of the truly noble to need such an appeal. But alas! not all the recitals of the sufferings and more than human endurance of our brave martyrs have been able to deter us from the festal hall. The sound of the viol is heard as much, and even more, than it was before dread war held high carnival in every state of our beloved land. We forget that every step we take

> "Gives back a coffin's hollow moan,"

and every strain of music

> "Wafts forth a dying soldier's groan."

As for paying respect to brass buttons, that is only the natural consequence of the first fault; for we all know that there could be no festivities among ladies by themselves; and as all our true patriots are in the field, why, none but the "gold-lace gentry" are left.

If every young girl, not only in Mississippi, but in every other state, were to treat the "home chivalry" with the scorn and contempt that this writer seems to have for them, I would be willing to stake almost any thing on the issue, that in one month there would not be one able-bodied man out of the field.

The Alabama woman's letter is headed with the late earnest appeal of our President, calling on the women of the South to do their duty at all hazards. It treats pretty much of the same subject as the Mississippi lady's, but also of a few other evils with which our land is cursed.

When she comes down on extortioners and speculators, I can echo her sentiments with all my heart; but when she says that none but native southerners must fill offices, I can tell her that if the native southerners, who, when the war was first inaugurated, used to wear

133

their blue badges, and cry " secession and war to the knife," had come forward as I know foreigners have done, we would not now be in need of the late earnest appeal for men, by our beloved President. And I not only think it bad taste, but unfeeling, in any of our people to draw distinctions at the present time, when we all know how nobly foreigners have poured out their blood in our defense.

The next whom this lady is roused against are the surgeons, nurses, and chaplains. From what I have seen of the first two, I think I have a right to be somewhat of a judge; and I do not think, taking them as a whole, that we have more patriotic and devoted men to the cause than our surgeons, though of course there are exceptions. And as for the nurses in the hospitals, how can I say enough in their praise (of course not all) ; patient, kind; as good nurses as it is in the power of men to be; for they were never designed to nurse. Not one where I have been is able for field service. This woman says they must all go to the front. When she talks thus, she does it as men say we women do, without reason.

What can we do with our sick and wounded men in the hospitals, if all the surgeons are sent to the front? And he must be a shrewd surgeon indeed who deceives the examining boards—the dread of all hospitals—that are constantly coming around and taking away our men after we have initiated them into the mysteries of nursing, etc.

Many a time have I felt indignant, when I have heard these brave men and patriots, who have lost health and been maimed in the service of their country, called by the ignominious name of " hospital rats."

The chaplains I can say but little about, having seen so few. But I say one thing, that I had thought our government very remiss in not providing them.

At one time the Newsom Hospital had accommodation for seven hundred patients, and the requisite number of attendants. Surely such an establishment ought to have had at least one chaplain, and work enough for him, without taking the " sword of Gideon," as this lady said they should.

I have wished for one many a time, when our poor dying soldiers have desired to hear about the Great Physician. And had it not been for good, kind Mrs. Williamson praying with them, we should have been badly off indeed. This is the first hospital I have been in where there was one, and he has not spent much idle time.

The first part of the letter, taken as a whole, I like; and I should think if any thing would arouse to a sense of duty those whom it is meant for, it would. But the conclusion does not appear rational. It has rather too much of the Mokanna spirit. I am always afraid, when I hear such ultra views on a subject, that there must be a reaction, and the very reverse spirit exhibited at last. She calls on the men, women, and children to come forward like Roman Curtius, willing to offer heart, soul, and body upon the shrine of liberty, and

134

to come, although we stumble over the dead bodies of those we love on earth, and vultures prey upon the blood-smeared faces in our path, and our streams offer only a crimson, surging flood to slake our thirst; she calls on us to rise, waving our battle-flag in triumph over these horrors, and the graves of the unknown dead, and says our enemy's offer is only submission. " Join me in this vow: Though I stand the last stricken child of the Confederacy, by the blood that cries out from our reeking sod, and the skeletons that fill each holy mound—the strong hand crossed in death—each darkened home and broken heart— each pang of hunger, throb of pain, and every dying sigh—in the name of the eternal God—never! "

Now, I do not think, even to save the country, that there are in it any men, women, or children who could stand to see vultures eating our slain, or touch the water colored with their blood. And if we only do our duty, as the president has admonished us, there will be no need of waving flags over the horrors that the writer has pictured.

And as for the oath, I must say I have a mortal antipathy to taking an oath I am not certain about keeping; and none of us in this transitory world can tell what a day may bring forth.

The foe with his numerous armies may prevail, and for those very sins the writer has enumerated the Lord may permit us to be subjugated. I am not for one moment saying that I have the least idea that such will be the case, but we can be certain of nothing that is in the future. Well, if such should be the case, and we feel that we have done our duty, and our whole duty, hard as it seems just now, we will have to bear it, knowing it will be the Lord's doing.

But, as I said before, I only hope these ladies are doing as well as talking, remembering that " action is sublime," and that " the rhythm of a well-spent life is sweeter far than song."

There is one very important item which I have left out in this " Alabama woman's " letter. She says, let the women go into the hospitals. Now she comes to what is woman's true sphere: in war, the men to fight, and the women to nurse the wounded and sick, are words I have already quoted. I have no patience with women whom I hear telling what wonders they would do if they were only men, when I see so much of their own legitimate work left undone. Ladies can be of service in the hospitals, and of great service. I have heard more than one surgeon say, if he could get the right kind, he would have them in almost every department. I could name many things they could do, without ever once going into a ward.

All have not the gift of nursing, but they can do the housekeeping, and there is much of that in a hospital.

I know many will say the surgeons will not have them, nor can I blame the surgeons if the stories are true which I have heard about the ladies interfering with them. I have been nearly two years in the hospital service, and I have never spent one day without seeing women's work left undone, and I have had no time to do the surgeons'.

The sick in a hospital are as much under the care of the surgeon and assistant surgeons as men in the field are under the control of their officers. And would we not think a woman out of her senses were she to say that because she had made the clothes the soldiers wore, and attended to their wants otherwise, she had a right to command them; or that she would do nothing for them because that right was not given her, even if she had a better knowledge of Hardee's tactics than some of our officers. The surgeons are alone responsible for the sick under their control, and have the right to direct what should be done for them.

Are the women of the South going into the hospitals? I am afraid candor will compel me to say they are not! It is not respectable, and requires too constant attention, and a hospital has none of the comforts of home! About the first excuse I have already said much; but will here add, from my experience since last writing on that subject, that a lady's respectability must be at a low ebb when it can be endangered by going into a hospital.

I have attended to the soldiers of our army in hospitals and out of them, and in all sincerity I can say that, so far as their bearing toward ladies is concerned, I have never heard one word spoken or seen one act at which the most fastidious and refined woman could take exception.

This was more than I looked for; I knew that our army was composed of the lowest as well as the highest, and I did expect to find some among them void of delicacy.

I can not tell whether our army is an exception to the rule or not; but about it I can say that, as regards real native refinement, that which all the Chesterfields in the world can not give, a more perfect army of gentlemen could not be than they are. I do not know what they are in camp, but speak of what I have seen in other places.

To the next two excuses—that is, to constant work, and hospitals not being like home—I wonder if soldier's work is just such as they wish, and if the camp is any thing like home?—I think there is no need of giving the answers; they are obvious.

Last evening Mrs. General Patton Anderson came here; she has a little boy who is very sick, and she thinks the water will benefit him. She is stopping in the same house with us.

I have just heard that the Newsom Hospital has left Cleveland, Tennessee. The enemy must be near there, or we are going to fall back. I usually judge the movements of the army by those of the hospitals.

How I would dislike to have to leave this beautiful place; but perhaps we shall, and about it there is no use worrying.

Mrs. Dr. Gamble and Mrs. Bragg have left, which looks ominous, as we think the general intends making an important move, and has given them time to get out of the way.

Sunday, August [i. e., September] 6.—Since writing in this journal a sad change has come over the spirit of my dreams. What but a few hours ago was a scene of order and comfort, has disappeared, and in its place vacancy.

When the afternoon service was over, starting to visit the sick, I met Dr. Rhea going to give orders to pack up immediately, as a raid was momentarily expected, and we would have to leave. The first thing done was to send off the sick, and to see that they were properly cared for; and then it seemed like magic the way every tent was leveled with the ground.

It is not more than a few hours since the order came, and we are nearly all packed, and many of the hospital things sent to the depot, which is some two miles distant. I suppose the cooks will be up all night, preparing rations. We will have to spread comforts on the floor to rest on for the night, as our bedding has been carried off. We do not expect to leave before morning. If the enemy do not capture us I shall be thankful.

We have three very sick men—Lieutenant Payne, Dr. Mitchell, and a Mr. Green. The last we shall be compelled to leave, as he is in a dying state. The nurse who has had him in charge is very much alarmed that he will be compelled to remain with him. He does not like the idea of being captured, having been a prisoner before, and has had as much as he cares for of prison life. Dr. Bemiss thinks he will be able to get some one in the place to take care of the sick man.

August [i. e., September] 7.—We arrived at Dalton about 6 P. M., and expect to be detained here all night. I must say this last move has not made me the better Christian, for I certainly love my enemies less than ever.

I can not count the trains that are with us; they are so many. On them are all the hospitals which were in Ringgold—sick, attendants, and much of the furniture. We have left all our bunks. We are in a box-car, and in it are not less than twenty-five persons, besides bedding, trunks, tables, chairs, etc.

Our journey from the Springs to Ringgold was a laughable one. We had two wagons, one filled far above its sides with baggage of all kinds; on top of all was seated Mrs. Anderson, her children, servant, and Mrs. Williamson. I took my seat with them, but it was a higher position than I had been accustomed to, and I was fearful of having a downfall, in the way of a bath, as we had some of the worst kind of roads to go on, and a few streams to cross. Accordingly I made a trial of the other wagon; it contained Miss S. and two sick officers, Lieutenant Payne and Dr. Mitchell. They were on mattresses. I managed to get a seat, and did very well. On leaving that beautiful spot, I could not help thinking of *her* who was the primitive cause of all our woe leaving the garden of Eden; I do not presume to think that the

137

place was like that garden where sin had never entered to blight its beauties, which Milton has portrayed so beautifully; a place

> " Where gods might dwell,
> Or wander with delight." [7]

But it was a lovely spot, and I have no doubt came as near it as any other in this sin-stricken world. I had not, like Eve, " hoped to spend the respite of my days " there, but I did think we would be permitted to remain a little longer, and could not " patiently resign what so *unjustly* we had lost."

Lieutenant Green asked to be raised up, to " cast one long lingering look behind," and he exclaimed, " O, how beautiful! Is it not hard to be driven from it? "

August [i. e., September] 8.—We have been detained at Dalton all night, and as there was an uncertainty as to when the train would leave, we could not get off to go to any place.

Mrs. Williamson, who is not very well, managed to get on some of the baggage and rest for the night. Some of the other ladies did the same. Mrs. Dr. Cross (whose husband is one of the surgeons) and her two daughters sat up on chairs; I do not recollect of seeing them lay their heads down once.

Mrs. General Anderson, her three children, and myself had a space about four feet square on the floor. Mrs Anderson spread a comfort, on which she placed her children, and seated herself along side of them.

I managed to get my head on my valise, with my mouth in the direction of the door, where Drs. Gore and Bemiss were seated on chairs. I was so much pleased that I had procured a place where I could get some fresh air, that I exclaimed, " O, this is so nice! " Dr. Gore laughed, and said he was glad I was so much pleased. I can not tell what became of my feet, but think I managed after awhile to get them under a table. Every time I moved, Mrs. Anderson said I was taking part of her children's bed. We had many a good laugh through the night at our novel positions.

I could not but admire the ease with which Mrs. Anderson took this trip, as she had three young children, and one quite sick. They seemed to be no trouble to herself or any one else. She is a fine-looking woman, refined, intellectual, and a Christian, a fit companion for her brave husband. If we are to judge of him by what his men say about him, he is one on whose " brow shame is ashamed to sit." My brother has been for some time in his command, and is one of his many admirers.

At Tunnel Hill we saw a number of new hospital buildings; there were so many that they looked like a village. It does seem too bad that we are compelled to leave all of our hard work for the enemy to destroy.

[7] John Milton, *Paradise Lost*, Book 7, ll. 329-30.

The hospitals at the different stations which we passed were packing up to move. We think this bodes a very important move of General Bragg's. Some are hopeful and certain it will be a good one, while others are prophesying all kinds of evil.

Mrs. Anderson, who is well acquainted with General Bragg, says her husband has every confidence in him, and thinks he is one of our greatest generals.

She has related some very amusing anecdotes in regard to " private opinion publicly expressed," which she has heard about our generals. At one time she had to sit quietly and hear two ladies discuss the merits of her husband. They spoke so highly in his praise, that each wished to claim him as being a native of their own state. One saying he was a Mississippian, the other a Floridian. They had quite a quarrel on the subject. He is neither, but is a Kentuckian. His command is from Mississippi, and he has been living some time in Florida.

Mrs. Anderson was more fortunate in hearing good of her husband than I think most of our generals' wives would have been, for the characters of our generals, both military and civil, do not receive what St. Paul says is the greatest of all Christian graces, and the best-abused man we have is our commander-in-chief; so his subordinate generals need not mind.

I have heard many say that General Bragg has shown more patriotism by holding his position and braving all slander than any thing else he has done.

This is a free country, and people can say what they please, and at this time, when we are not at liberty to act as we please, it seems a kind of revenge to use that unruly member which we are told to keep in restraint.

The men are all busy out doors getting coffee made for the sick; some of whom have suffered no little in their journey. Lieutenant Payne has been very ill; we have sent him some cordial, which seems to do him a great deal of good.

VII: ATLANTA, NEWNAN

✠✠

September 9, 1863.—Arrived at Newnan, Georgia, this morning about 8 o'clock.

We left Dalton yesterday morning, reaching Atlanta at 6 o'clock P. M. On our arrival we saw numbers of families around the depot, in tents and old cars—refugees, who had been driven from their homes by the enemy. Some of them had left home on the advance of our army, as wherever it is there is a scarcity of provisions.

We put up at the Atlanta Hotel. Dr. Young, whom the shells at Chattanooga had put under the necessity of changing his abode, and Major Proctor, spent the evening with us. Major Proctor was very low-spirited, as he thought his chance of getting to his home in Kentucky less than ever. General Bragg, as a rule, is not a favorite with Kentuckians, as they think he had no good reason for leaving Kentucky when he did; but he was little spoken about that evening.

Dr. Young's indignation was so great against the extortioners and speculators, that he had none left for any one else. He was bitter in the extreme, which it is not much to be wondered at, when we think of how he and others have given up homes, friends, and every thing dear to them for the cause, and find such Shylocks preying on the very heart-blood of our country; and it is enough to make even the " stones cry out." Dr. Young told us that our money was more depreciated in Atlanta than in any place in the Confederacy. He said that for himself, " if the Confederacy fell, he would think it an honor to sink with it and its money in his pocket, rather than to have made his thousands."

We found Atlanta full of the " gilt-lace gentry; " a sure sign, they say, " there will be a battle soon." If General Bragg is a strict disciplinarian, why is it that nearly every place we go to is filled with officers; apparently in good health, and doing nothing?

We left our sick at different posts on the road.

Newnan seems to be a very nice little town; it is the capital of Coweta County, and is forty miles south-west of Atlanta, on the West Point road.[1] We are at the Coweta Hotel, a very pleasant one, kept by

[1] Newnan had been selected as the site for a hospital on the recommendation of Dr. F. E. Daniel who wrote Dr. Stout November 1, 1862: " I am requested by Dr. Logan [at Atlanta] to suggest further, that, at Noonan [Newnan] & Lagrange, two points on the West Pt R R, and designated in his district, 500 or 600 sick can be accomodated. It is a section of the country where the people have as

Colonel Colyer [Colyar] of Tennessee, a member of congress. He has been driven from his home, and, for want of something better to do, has turned hotel-keeper. The fare is very good, but we had no wheat-bread for breakfast, and I am not *southern enough* to like corn-bread.

The first thing we were told on our arrival was, that the citizens did not like the idea of the hospitals coming here. This seems strange; it can not be that these people have no relatives in the army, as we know how nobly Georgia has come forward at every call for troops; and have we not heard of their bravery on every battle-field in Virginia?

Well, if they have relatives in the army, do they not expect they stand a chance of being sick or wounded, and that, unless hospitals are provided for them, these same relatives would be in a terrible state, and denounce the government and every body connected with it?

I do not doubt but that they would be very much displeased if they were to hear that the people in some of the towns in Virginia, where most of the Georgia troops are, were opposed to having hospitals among them for the benefit of those troops. True, a hospital is not the most pleasant place in the world, where we have stern war, stripped of all its glory, and nothing but the sad realities presented—fell disease, with all its noxious vapors, and the poor, emaciated frames—men who went forth to the army, flushed with health and strength, but now, by wounds and disease, made nearly as helpless as infants. But what are we to do? Let the men suffer?

I sincerely trust that it is mere idle talk we have heard, and that the people here have not forgotten, " Do unto others as you would have them do unto you."

The next thing we were told was, that there is great hostility shown to the refugees in this place. Can this really be the case? But if the former is true, then the latter may be. If the enemy are culpable, who have driven these people from their homes, and forced them to seek others among strangers, how much more so are those persons who are now living, surrounded with all the comforts of home. True, in a measure, all are suffering now; but sympathy costs nothing . . .

If these people would only think of what may be their own fate; for if we are to judge from the signs of the times, the war is far from being over, and if for no other reason than that they may need the same kindness shown to themselves, they ought to show all they can to the strangers. . . .

Dr. Gamble and his surgeons have been out all day in search of hospital accommodations, and have succeeded in getting room for one thousand patients. They have taken nearly all the large buildings and stores. It astonishes me to see how cheerfully our men go to work again to fix up more hospitals.

---

yet but remotely felt the effects of the war, and he intimates that the country is still rich in such articles as the sick would need,—such as poultry, eggs, butter, milk, etc; articles which could not well be shipped to Chattanooga." ALs, Stout Papers (Emory) .

I observed the people on the cars coming down, and that every body seemed to take their trials as a matter of course. Suffering has made them strong. It is said, the only grumblers we have are those who stay at home and have had no reason to feel the war.

September 13.—Went to the Methodist Church; heard an excellent sermon.

All are on the tiptoe of expectation, watching the development of General Bragg's movements. He is marching his army into Georgia, having abandoned Chattanooga and Cumberland Gap; the latter place has been given up without firing a gun. Tennessee is now wholly at the mercy of the enemy.

Hundreds of troops are daily passing from Virginia to reinforce Bragg, of whom many are now predicting great things, saying that all he needed was plenty of men, which he has never had, and that the general he has had to contend against here outwitted General Lee in Western Virginia. Besides, the troops our men have to fight against are the Western ones, in bravery much superior to those that are opposed to the Virginia army.

But I am satisfied that both armies are brave enough for our good, as our losses have proved, and opened our eyes to the disagreeable fact, that one of our men is not equal to five of the enemy, as we at first thought. No one for a moment will say that our troops have not fought with a determination and bravery that have never been sur-passed perhaps in any army, and that they have not always been opposed to at least double their numbers. Still, "honor to whom honor is due." I have never spoken to any of our men on the subject, who have not told me that the enemy have exhibited a bravery and determination worthy of a better cause.

I have wondered at this, as I thought the race to which we all belong—the Anglo-Saxon one—never could make good soldiers without they were fighting for principle; or, in other words, had good con-sciences, and felt that their honor was at stake. We all know that the enemy have nothing of that kind to fight for. We have never wished to subjugate them or to take away their liberties, but have begged like suppliants, to be left to ourselves, with the sin of slavery (?) on our own shoulders.

Mrs. Williamson and myself have determined, that no matter how fine our hospital may be, or nice the place, not to fix our hearts on it; for if we do, we shall certainly have to run; although I can not see how we are to move further south, for, as the saying is, we are almost at the "jumping-off place." If we should make a move north, we would gladly leave a palace, no matter what trouble it would give; as then we should know our cause was succeeding.

It is rumored that Forrest has had a fight near Ringgold. We are quite anxious about some of our attendants and hospital stores, which were left behind.

Dr. Bemiss is very much annoyed about two of his men having deserted. One of them, from Tennessee, was an excellent man. I asked Dr. Bemiss how he thought such a man could desert. He answered, nothing would have made him except an earnest appeal from his wife, and that the women were the cause of nearly all the desertions. This is certainly not very complimentary to us, nor to the women of '76 and Sparta, to whom our men are constantly comparing us.

September 17.—We have nothing arranged in the hospital, but it is filled with sick; many of them are on the floors. Mrs. Williamson and myself have two small rooms. One is used as a dining-room, sitting-room, and for making toddies, eggnogs, etc. A number of the officers we had at the Springs have followed us here, and they eat at our table for the present. They are to have a hospital set apart for them, as it is thought a better plan than having distinctions made where the privates are in the matter of rooms, and eating at separate tables. The doctors all seem to dislike having the care of them.

Dr. McAllister has been persuaded to accept the honor by the promise of some valuable piece of furniture from the other hospitals. Dr. McAllister is a strict disciplinarian, and I am told the officers do not like him on that account. The doctors object to officers because, they say, they are apt to dictate, and expect much more attention than the privates. I have heard surgeons say they would rather attend five privates than one officer. For my own part, I have never known any difference; have treated them the same as privates, and received kind treatment in return.

Mrs. Johnston, one of the ladies of the place, called on us. She told me of a lady from whom she thought I could procure some milk. Her little boy went with me to show me where the lady lived; he is a pretty little fellow, and very talkative. He related quite a number of stories in his childish way; among other things, he told me a story about some, to use his own words, "mean old refugees." I asked him if he did not like refugees. He looked at me in astonishment, and said, "No; who would like refugees?" I tried to get him to tell me why they were not to be liked; this he could not do, but seemed to think I ought to know what every body else did.

September 19.—We have received news that a battle has commenced. A number of surgeons from this post have been ordered to the front. Drs. Rhea and Bateman will go from our hospital. We regret losing them, as we have so many sick.

On hearing of the commencement of a battle it sends a thrill of horror through me, and especially such a one as it is said this will be. Both armies have been collecting all the forces they could muster, intending to put their strength in the conflict. It will send many a gallant spirit away to that land "from whence no traveler returns."

I must try and dismiss this gloomy subject, as we have much to do.

I feel it is a great blessing, and keeps our thoughts from wandering to the bloody drama.

We had numbers of sick come in last night. As it is impossible to attend to them all, immediately after they come in, I go around to visit them, and from having seen so many, can nearly always tell at a glance who are most in need of special care.

Mrs. Johnston went round with me this morning. I passed a fine, healthy-looking man, and I thought he was one who was out of place there, and ought to be back with the army. I had passed him without speaking, and saw a tear in his eye; so curiosity made me go back to find out who he was. He had been three years in the service, and this was his first visit to a hospital. He had been injured by the upsetting of a train. So much for judging from appearances.

September 20.—Mrs. Williamson and myself went to the Presbyterian Church this morning; heard a very good sermon from the pastor. He gave a glowing description of the glories of heaven, but spoiled it by saying, with bitterness, that there would be no taking churches there for hospitals. It was rather too much rancor to be used in such a place, and in a scene like the one he was describing.

All the churches here have been taken for hospital purposes, and this is the last Sunday service will be held in that one. When I looked around and saw how neat every thing was in it, and thought of the ruin which would be wrought in making it ready for patients, I could not wonder that he was annoyed, and more so as I do not think there is any necessity for taking them at present, as I know there are more buildings which we could get; for instance, a young ladies' college, and I have no doubt others; so at present they are not really needed; and, without that, I think we should not take them. We act as if churches were built rather for our amusement than the worship of the living God. He has told us he is a jealous God, and will visit every sin against him; not only visit it on us, but on the third and fourth generation. If this ignoring his sacred temple will not bring retribution, I think nothing will. How can we expect a blessing, or any thing but curses, such as were pronounced many times on the children of Israel, when they were guilty of the same offense of forgetting their Maker. We have their example, and deserve a worse downfall.

September 26.—A great battle was fought on the 19th and 20th at Chickamauga River—a victory for us. Alas! what scenes of horror does not even the word victory bring up before us!

Major Jewitt of the Thirty-eighth or Thirty-sixth Alabama Regiment is among the killed. He was an eminent lawyer of Alabama. Captain O'Brien of the Twenty-fourth Alabama Regiment is also among the killed. He was from Mobile, and a better or braver man we have not lost. He was by profession a lawyer. When the war broke out, he enlisted as a private in the Third Alabama Regiment. After serving with it in Virginia for some time, was elected Captain of the "Emmet Guards," a company composed of men from the "Emerald Isle."

God pity his heart-broken and desolate mother. I am told the Twenty-fourth Alabama Regiment suffered severely. General Helm of Kentucky and General Preston Smith are killed; General Hood lost a leg (the second time he has been wounded); General Adams is wounded and a prisoner. We have many men here who knew General Helm personally. They deeply mourn his death, and say the country has lost one of its bravest—a true patriot and soldier.

Major Richmond was killed while carrying dispatches for General Polk. Thus has passed away a Christian, a soldier, and accomplished gentleman. He was one of the noblest of men. . . .

Captain Hammond, a brother of Mrs. Johnston, was killed. He was in one of the Georgia regiments.

Generals Polk and Hindman are both suspended for disobedience of orders. General Hindman is in this place, and is slightly wounded.

I have been a good deal worried about my brother. I went down to the train one evening to ascertain something about him; Miss C. D. and Miss M. C. accompanied me. There were quite a number of ladies at the depot.

Sunday, September 27.—The weather has turned quite cool. I am glad, as it will be much better for the wounded.

I took a ride this afternoon with Mrs. Johnston; we visited her brother's grave. I am quite pleased with this place. It is not so hilly nor thickly wooded as North Georgia, but it is quite pretty.

September 28.—Last evening, Rev. Dr. Husten made a speech at the depot, calling on the people to send up provisions and nurses to Chickamauga, for the purpose of feeding and nursing the wounded, as General Bragg has gone with his whole army to take Chattanooga, and requires the services of every man who is able to travel, and there are not enough left to take care of the sufferers. Our cooks have been up all night long, cooking food to send up. The same has been done in all the other hospitals.

This morning Mrs. Johnston called, and I went with her to a meeting, which was held in town, about the wounded.

Dr. Heustis addressed us, and presented a picture of suffering that would have wrung the heart of the most hardened, and said he had only told us about our own men; that if they were in such distress we could guess in what state the prisoners were.

He told us the principal thing needed was something to eat, and he believed that in one place where the men were lying, that if a basket full of biscuits was put down in the midst of them, they would let out a shout of joy that would rend the air. He had worked day and night while there, dressing wounds and giving the men water to drink,

145

and said he believed many persons could be kept busy doing nothing but the latter. He urged all the men to go that could possibly do so; said that ladies could not go yet, as there is no place for them to stay. The enemy had destroyed a portion of the railroad, and the wounded had to be taken to a place called the "Burnt Shed," some twenty miles distant from the battle-field, there to await transportation on the cars.

Colonel Colyar of Tennessee made a very stirring speech, and was ready himself to go. A collection was then taken up, and many hundreds of dollars given. Mrs. Johnston introduced me to Dr. Heustis. I told him I was very anxious to go; I knew I could get some place to stay, as I was well acquainted in that neighborhood; the Burnt Shed being only a short distance from Cherokee Springs. He tried to persuade me not to think of it. On my way home I met our chaplain, Mr. Green, who told me he was going, and that if I wished I could go with him, and stay with a very nice lady, a friend of his. I intend leaving this afternoon, and am busy collecting what I can to take with me. Dr. Divine has just received a box full of delicacies from Mississippi, for troops from that state. It is impossible to send any thing to the army at present. He has given me some nice wine and other things.

Some of the ladies of the place intend going up in a few days, but none are ready to go at present. Mrs. Colonel Griffin gave me a black man for a servant.

October 6.—Left here on the 28th ult., about 3 o'clock A. M. The cars were densely crowded with soldiers returning to their commands. When we arrived at the Burnt Shed, found that the rail track had been finished to Ringgold; so we passed on to that place. As I was familiar with it, I went to the nearest building, which had been the Bragg Hospital.

There was no light to be seen any place, excepting that which came from a fire outside, around which stood a crowd of shivering soldiers.

Wounded men, wrapped in their blankets, were lying on the balcony. I went into a room which was filled with others in the same state; some of whom were suffering for want of water. They all seemed perfectly resigned; the more so as we had been victorious. How they seemed to glory in it!

After finding a vacant room to put my baggage in, I went to our old friend, Mrs. Evans. She was delighted to see me, said she had often wondered what had become of Mrs. Williamson and myself.

She had passed through the fearful ordeal of having been under the fire of the enemy; and she was obliged to live in the woods for some days.

I remained there until after breakfast; then I went down to the main hospital, where I was introduced to the surgeon in charge, Dr. Ushery [Ussery]. He gave me bandages to roll; I was assisted by a young man by the name of Dearing [Deering], from Kentucky, who was disabled by being wounded in one of his arms.[2] Mr. Green and the colored man were kept busy all day dressing wounds.

Mr. Deering and myself sat on the up-stairs gallery, where we could see the wagon trains come in with their precious burdens. As many as fifty came in at one time. We rolled bandages until the afternoon, and could scarcely supply the demand. The surgeons were getting the wounded men ready to send off on the train. I was rejoiced when we were told we had rolled enough for that day. This work had been quite a trial for me, as I had been compelled to see our poor fellows brought in as they were taken from the field hospital, and I had no chance of doing any thing for them.

There had been no rain for some time, and the wagons raised the dust in clouds, and when the men were taken out of them they were almost as black as negroes.

I took the blackberry wine which Dr. Divine had given me and put it in a bucket of water, which made a nice drink. With it and something to eat, Mr. Deering and I went down and waited on the men; I never saw any thing relished as much as it was. When we came to Mississippians, and told them it was from Mississippi, they relished it still more. I wondered if the ladies of Mississippi who made it had the least idea by whom and where it would be used.

While in one of the rooms a gentleman came up to me and said he was rejoiced to see me, and that I was the first lady he had seen there. He told me these men were Kentuckians, and that he was leaving on the train with some wounded. He said any attention I paid to these sufferers he would take as a personal favor.

After he left I asked one of the men who he was, and was informed he was Professor Pickett, a Baptist minister, and chaplain of a Kentucky brigade, and that he was a true Christian and zealous patriot, and had done much good in the cause.

We went into the cars which were filled with the wounded. Mr. Deering, while waiting on the patients, ran the risk of having his arm again broken, as he had the use of but one hand.

About dark I took some cloth for bandages and went to Mrs. Evans's to remain all night. On reaching there I met a widow lady, Mrs. ———. I asked Mrs. Evans what the ladies of the place were doing, as not one of them had visited the hospital that day; and I said, if they would all roll bandages, that would be all I would ask of them.

[2] The following is from a flier issued to advertise Miss Cumming's *Gleanings from Southland:* "*Dear Old-Time Friend*—Do you recall a wounded boy soldier, who at Ringgold, Ga., in 1864 [1863], assisted you to roll bandages, give the wounded men toddy, food, etc., after the battle of Chickamauga? Well, I was that boy. . . . I now write to thank you for your devotion to our soldiers. Your crown surely awaits you. When the monument to our Southern women is built, I want your name to be one of those at the top, in letters large enough to be read from every corner of the Confederacy.—*John R. Deering, Chaplain 4th Brigade, Kentucky Division* [United Confederate Veterans]."

Mrs. —— did not seem to like my remarks, and said the surgeons had never asked them, and that the Federals had taken all the cloth they had to make bandages with. I answered her that I supposed the surgeons thought the ladies did not need asking, and that there was plenty of cloth at the hospitals. She said she would work at them tomorrow. She then assisted me with what I had.

Colonels Walter and Hays, who were stopping at Mrs. Evans's, came in. Colonel Walter said, word for word, what I had about the ladies; only added that such neglect pained him very much. To this Mrs. —— said nothing.

I think these two gentlemen were there for the purpose of seeing that the wounded were properly cared for. I believe they are on General Bragg's staff. Colonel Walter was very talkative. He spoke highly of the Mobile ladies and their beauty; said it was a dangerous place for any one who was at all susceptible of the tender passion, and that, fortified as he was by age and a wife, he nearly lost his heart. Both of these men seemed high-toned gentlemen; such as most all our educated southerners are.

Next morning, the 30th, I arose early, and took a hurried breakfast, and when leaving asked Mrs. —— if she intended coming for the bandages. She answered, with emphasis, " I never go to hospitals, but will send for them."

On reaching the hospital, to my joy and surprise, I found that Dr. Stout had arrived early in the morning, and with him a hospital corps of surgeons and nurses; among them my kind friends, Dr. Burt and Mrs. Ellis. I knew that now the wounded would be well cared for.

Dr. Stout and his corps had been at the " Burnt Shed " for some days. He told me that when he went there, he found quite a number of regimental surgeons, and, to his sorrow, nearly all were intoxicated.[3] He had done what he could to have every thing put in as good order as the place would admit of. He also said that no words could tell the amount of good which had been done by the Georgia Relief Committees; that had it not been for them, many of our men would have died of starvation. Part of the Atlanta Committee (I think it was) was then with him. He introduced me to some of the members; among

[3] Wiley declares that it was the reiterated complaint of the soldiers that the surgeons drank the whiskey intended for patients. He quotes from William H. Taylor's De Quibus (Richmond, 1908), 320, that the surgeons were accustomed to going on a spree the night following each receipt of spirits and they they succeeded usually, in Taylor's words, in " drinking up every drop . . . before morning." Wiley, The Life of Johnny Reb, 260. Miss Pember recounts at length her trials in controlling the rations of whiskey. She tells of one patient with a crushed ankle for whom a drunken surgeon had " set " the well leg, pp. 159-60. Dr. Stout penciled this note in his copy of the Journal: " Not true. Only found one regimental surgeon & he a contract physician drunk. S. H. Stout." H. H. Cunningham discusses drinking on the part of medical officers in Doctors in Gray, pp. 259-60. " The reports of drunkenness," he summarizes, " seem to have been exaggerated; the number was probably not excessive."

them was Neal Brown, ex-governor of Tennessee, who was a Unionist when the war broke out; but after seeing how badly the Federal government acted, joined our side.

I had made up my mind, on seeing so many there to take care of the wounded, that I would go right back to Newnan, as I had left Mrs. Williamson quite sick, and much work to do.

I have always had a great desire to go on a battle-field. I can not call it idle curiosity; but a wish to see and know the most of every thing, so that I might judge for myself, and know how I may be of service.

There was a Mrs. Weir, from Griffin, Georgia, who had come to nurse her son. He had lost a leg, and was at a private house near the battle-field. This lady told me she had a young friend, whose corpse she had heard was still on the battle-field unburied. She kindly asked me to go with her.

The field was some fifteen miles distant; so we had to watch our chances of getting a conveyance. There were wagons coming in all the time with the wounded, but none going back that day; so an opportunity for getting out seemed slender. Mr. Deering was on the watch for us. A very nice-looking covered private wagon came, and after depositing its load, Dr. Deering requested the owner to take us; but he stoutly refused, saying his horses were completely worn out. Mr. Deering then told him that there was one of the ladies who had nursed at least one thousand Confederates, and was very anxious to go out to the field. He immediately drew up and invited us all in, Mr. Deering going with us.

We found our kind driver quite intelligent and very talkative. He related to us many anecdotes of the late battle. His name was Tedford. The first line of battle was formed on his farm, but I believe was moved before there was any fighting. His wife's pantry had suffered from our own men. She was ordered out of the house, and took shelter in the woods. After the battle, when the men found the house deserted, they went in and took every thing they could get; even taking some preserves which Mrs. Tedford had hid away in an attic. They also took her clothes and tore them up; the latter might have been done for the benefit of the wounded, which Mr. Tedford seemed to think. He did not grumble, for he was too happy about our having gained the victory for that.

The battle was partly fought at Tedford's Ford, on his brother's farm, and he said that the havoc made there was very great.

He related an incident to us about his brother, or one of his neighbor's sons, who had been in the service during the war. He had been on duty at a post far south, and had been sent to Bragg's army when it was reinforced. He was killed on or near his father's farm.

We traveled over the roughest roads I ever was on. I thought, if this was the road our wounded had to come, they must indeed suffer; and, sure enough, we met what seemed to me hundreds of wagons, with their loads, going to Ringgold. We also saw many wounded men wending their way on foot, looking wearied enough. We stopped and spoke to them; all were cheerful.

On arriving at Mr. Strickland's house, where Mrs. Weir's son was, Mr. Tedford begged me to go on to Mr. Hunt's, where part of Hindman's Division Hospital was. He told me that there was a nice young lady there, Miss Hunt, who was doing a great deal for the wounded, and he was certain she would be delighted to have my help. The temptation was a great one. I was anxious to see what a field hospital was like, and to know if I could be of any service; and another thing, I had heard nothing certain regarding my brother. He was in Hindman's division; so I thought by going there I might hear from him.

On our way we met Dr. Rhea, who had just heard of a brother being badly wounded, and was on his way to see him. He and the other surgeons had had a hard time since leaving us. They had wandered two days on foot in search of head-quarters, or any one who could tell them where to go. They had been all that time without food, but had come across a pig, which they had *pressed*. They had quite a number of nurses with them. I think he said they were at Claiborne's [Cleburne's] Division Hospital, and if I recollect the number rightly, he told me the first day they went there, there were no less than twelve hundred men to attend. This seems almost incredible, but we have had many more wounded than killed. He also told me that at first they had neither food to give the men or cloth to dress their wounds, and that at present rags were very scarce. I promised to send them some, and go and see them.

Mr. Hunt's house was a small cottage, surrounded by a garden. In the latter were tents, flies, and sheds, which were filled with wounded.

I went to the house with Mr. Tedford, who introduced me to one of the surgeons. He informed me that this was Managault's [Manigault's] Brigade Hospital, and also that Captain Chamberlain and Lieutenant Cooper of the Twenty-fourth Alabama Regiment were lying badly wounded in the house. I went in to see them; found them lying on the floor, but on mattresses. They were old friends, and glad to see me. Captain Chamberlain looked very badly, as besides his being wounded his health was delicate.

I was introduced to Miss Hunt, a very nice-looking young girl, and as I had already heard much of her kindness to the soldiers, knew she was a true southern woman.

My wounded friends informed me that Lieutenant Bond of the company of which my brother is a member had been to see them, and but one man had been killed in the company.

Captain Chamberlain introduced me to the surgeons—Drs. Cochran of the Twenty-fourth Alabama Regiment, Gibbs, and Gourie [Gourrier], who had charge of the hospital; the latter I had met before in Chattanooga. Dr. Cochran took me around to see the Mobilians—an old man by the name of Chillion, Mr. New, and Mr. Brown—neither of whom I had seen before. Mr. Chillion is a brother of Mr. Chillion, a well-known Roman Catholic priest. He is now in his seventieth year, and has been in the service since the commencement of the war. He went through the Kentucky campaign, and every other in which the Twenty-fourth Alabama Regiment has been, and kept up as well as the youngest man. The poor old man actually cried when he found out who I was. He is a Frenchman, and I could scarcely make him understand me. He requested me to write to Mrs. Chaudron and Mrs. Percy Walker of Mobile, and let them know where he was. The men were lying on bunks made out of branches of trees.

I visited the room where Mr. Hunt and his family were. They had been driven from every corner of their house, which was filled with wounded, and had taken shelter in a small kitchen. I don't know how many there were, but this room was sleeping-room, dining-room, kitchen, and every thing else for the whole family. In it were two bedsteads, and some of the family were then lying sick. I heard no grumbling or complaint from any of them, with the exception of the old man, who sat by the fire, and it is not much to be wondered that he murmured a little.

Before the battle his farm was stocked and his barn filled with grain, and now he has nothing left but the house over his head. Winter is coming on, and with it want and starvation for him and his family; as all the neighbors for miles around had shared the same fate, he could expect no aid from them.

Before the battle the enemy had full possession of that country, and helped themselves to what they wanted. After the battle our troops took what was left, the houses being empty, as the inmates were forced to fly from the bullets. There had been fighting in Mr. Hunt's yard, and many killed there.

It was in this house that Captain O'Brien had breathed his last. He lived two days after he was wounded.

When Miss Hunt and I retired for the night, we went up into a loft in the house, which had no flooring. We had to be careful for fear of falling through the plastering. It was filled with furniture, which had been taken out of the rooms. We had a mattress, with which we made a comfortable bed.

The next morning when Miss Hunt got up, as there were no windows, it was as dark as night. The ceiling was so low we could not stand upright. On coming down-stairs we found it raining in torrents, and as there were so many persons crowded together, it was any thing else but comfortable. The surgeons ate in the hall, and very kindly asked me to take breakfast with them, but I declined; I felt as if I never should eat again. The scenes with which I was surrounded had

151

taken away all my appetite. They sent me a cup of pure coffee, which did me more good than any thing I ever took in my life. I think if Cowper had drank coffee instead of tea, he would have found it a still more cheering beverage.

I found my two friends much better than they were the evening previous. I had a small basket with me, into which I had put a few articles on leaving Ringgold, thinking I might meet some one on the road who would need them. I had no idea when leaving Ringgold of visiting any of the hospitals, as I had been told I could be of no service in them, or I should have taken plenty of every thing with me. I had a few biscuits and a box of sardines; the latter I received from the Mobile Hebrew Military Aid Society while I was in Chattanooga. I divided them around, and they seemed to be relished.

The Georgia Aid Society had as yet done nothing for this hospital. There seemed to be no food of any kind, excepting cornbread and bacon, provided by the government; any thing else was private property. What cooking was done for the patients was done outside in the rain.

I found I could be of little service there, and became very anxious to get back to where I had left Mrs. Weir, as I knew I could very readily get a conveyance from there to Ringgold. Mr. Deering tried everywhere to get some kind of a wagon, but his efforts were of no avail. He went to Mr. Tedford's to ask him for his, but our men had broken into his barn the evening before, and taken what little corn he had left to feed his mules, and he had gone in search of provender.

It rained so hard that I found it impossible to visit the patients. I was gratified to see how much solicitude the surgeons exhibited for them. They were out in the rain nearly all the morning, trying to make the patients as comfortable as possible. They said that the rain was pouring down on some of them, but it could not be avoided. They informed me that from what they had heard of many of the other brigade hospitals, the men were in a much worse plight than theirs. They blamed Dr. Foard for not attending to their wants, or appointing a deputy. They had a number of patients who were ready for transportation, but there were no wagons.

I asked what Drs. Foard and Flewellen were doing, and said that I thought these hospitals their especial care. Was answered, "They were watching General Bragg look at the army."

There was a man there who had had his arm cut off on the late battle-field, and he was not only walking about, but nursing the others, and apparently quite well.

I assisted Miss Hunt in making some arrow-root, and showed how she could prepare it without milk, as that article was scarce. Captain Chamberlain had a little wine, which made it very nice. There were no chickens or eggs to be had for miles around.

152

I have always found eggnog the best thing ever given to wounded men. It is not only nourishing, but a stimulant.

Miss Hunt is very pleasant, well educated, and intelligent. She was assiduous in her attention to the suffering.

Captain Chamberlain was expecting his wife, and Lieutenant Cooper his mother. I should like to have remained until these ladies came, but I could not.

Deus's [Deas's] Brigade Hospital I wished to visit, but the rain prevented me. I heard there were some Mobilians wounded there, among them Mr. Murray, adjutant Thirty-sixth Alabama Regiment.

As we found it impossible to get a wagon, Drs. Gourrier and Gibbs kindly offered the use of their horses, which was gratefully accepted. Miss Hunt loaned me her saddle and skirt.

I took leave of my two Mobile friends with many regrets. I had seen numbers die from such wounds as theirs, and did not know but this might be the last time we would meet on earth.

As we rode out of the yard I tried to look neither to the right or left, for I knew there were many pairs of eyes looking sadly at us from the sheds and tents. I could do nothing for them, and when that is the case I try to steel my heart against their sorrows.

I saw men cooking out in the rain; it seemed like hard work keeping the fire up; a perfect war between the two elements; all around had a most cheerless aspect.

As we rode out the tents of the different field hospitals came in view; when we thought of the inmates and their sufferings, it only served to add to the gloom.

I looked in the direction of the battle-field, and thought of the nameless dead who were there. A nation weeps for them, and that day nature, like Rachel, was shedding tears for her children, because they were not.

I thought of the awful conflict which had so recently raged between brother and brother. " O, what a field of fratricide was there! " it makes one cry out in anguish, as did brave Faulkland of old. " Peace! peace! when will it come? Alas! who can tell?"

We were near that fatal stream—the Chickamauga—the " River of Death! " How prophetic its name! I could think of nothing but that terrible strife, and our gallant patriots that fell there. . . .

When I arrived at Mrs. Strickland's I was pretty well soaked. Mrs. Strickland gave me a change of garments, and seated by a nice fire, I forgot that I had ever been out in the rain.

Like her neighbors, Mrs. Strickland has suffered in the way of provisions, and is now drawing rations from our government.

Mrs. Weir found her son improved in health. There were more wounded men there, but the house is not so crowded as Mr. Hunt's. There were some few tents in the yard.

On the next day, October 2d, the sun shone out brightly, casting a joyous glow over all nature. Two days before Mrs. Weir had visited a hospital, and had promised to take the men clothes. She and I went to the Georgia Relief Society, and procured some, and took them to the men, but we found their bunks empty. Since Mrs. Weir visited them they had gone the way of all the earth. The hospital belonged to General Brown's brigade. As there was no one else in it needing clothes, we went to Cheatham's Division Hospital, which was near. Dr. Rice, the chief surgeon, very kindly offered to take us through the hospital. He spoke very highly in praise of the Georgia Relief Society, and of the good which it had done.

Dr. Rice introduced us to one of his surgeons, who took us into a " fly " about one hundred feet long, and every man in it had a limb amputated. It was a sad sight, and I could scarcely refrain from tears.

I told them they had the consolation of having suffered for the right and in self-defense. Compared with them how pitiable were the hundreds of wounded prisoners, whose hospital was in sight of them, for they had no such consolation.

We had a basket full of eatables, but scarcely any wanted them; all had plenty, given by the societies; we found it the same with the clothes.

We went into another place, where we were told the worst wounded were. As soon as I went in my name was pronounced; I found it was by a man who had been one of our cooks in the Newsom Hospital. Poor fellow! he was so over-joyed to see me he could scarcely speak. He said while there he had thought of Mrs. Williamson and myself a thousand times, and wished he was with us. Every thing was done for him that could possibly be in that place, but it was very far from being the Newsom Hospital. His wound was a very painful one, and he said he suffered mostly for want of soft rags. I gave him some few which I had with me, and Mrs. Weir promised to send him more. (She has come well provided with every thing for the wounded.) I have been told by surgeons that many a time they have had nothing but old tent cloth to bind up wounds.

I reluctantly left my friend, and almost wished I had not seen him, as it was impossible for me to remain with him.

The surgeon who went around with us wished to know if we wanted to see any more. I told him no; I had seen enough. He kindly offered to go with us to where the prisoners were; but, knowing we could do nothing for them, we refused. I had seen enough harrowing scenes among our own men to make me miserable. The surgeon informed us that the prisoners were as well cared for as was possible under the circumstances.

As Mrs. Weir and I walked back I thought I never had been out in a more beautiful day; the sun was glimmering through the trees, arraying them with brilliant tints. The woods were changing their summer garb, and decking themselves in gorgeous autumn costume ere stern winter came to dismantle them. . . .

154

As we walked along, Mrs. Weir and I said what a pity it was the enemy would not let us enjoy our country by ourselves; and we had not the least objection to have them come and live peacefully with us. There was certainly room enough for all. But why talk of these things now? The day for them seems to have passed forever.

I remarked to Mrs. Weir that I would like to have a relic from the battle-field of Chickamauga. As I said this, two young soldiers come out of the woods; one stepped up to me and remarked, he had a book that he had taken out of the pocket of a dead Federal, and that, if I would accept it, I could have it with pleasure.

On receiving it, I asked the soldier his name and regiment. The former I have forgotten; he was a member of the Fourth Arkansas Regiment. Both of the young men walked on whistling, as if they had not a care in the world.

The book was a small one, with a red cover, and was stained with blood. It is an allegory called the "Journey Home," by Rev. E. A. Monro.[4] It had likely been given to the poor fellow out of whose pocket it had been taken by a mother or sister, ere his departure from his home, with a prayer that it might help to prepare him for the journey which he had now taken. The fly-leaf was torn out, and there was no name, no mark of any kind on the book.

Early in the morning of that day I made eggnog for Mrs. Weir's son and the rest of the wounded. On going out to the tents, I met a gentleman taking care of a wounded man. When he spoke, I recognized him as a son of the "land of brown heath." I asked him what part of Scotland he was from. At the question he seemed astonished, and wanted to know how I knew he was Scotch. I do not think he liked my knowing it by his accent—a weakness I have noticed many Scotch people have on this side of the water. I do not see why, as I think it is the sweetest accent in the world. He had been a number of years in this country. He and his friends were recently from Augusta, Georgia.

There had been a number of Georgia troops wounded and killed in this last battle. I had concluded not to visit the battle-field, as much time had elapsed since the battle. I am told that the effluvia arising from the carnage makes it almost impossible to go within a mile of it.

There was no conveyance to get to town with, excepting the ambulances filled with wounded. I left Mrs. Strickland with many regrets. She had treated me with a great deal of kindness, and seemed to be an excellent, good-hearted lady. It was with difficulty I got her to take money for the time I had been in her house. I should not have offered her any, only I was fully aware of her destitute condition.

The ambulance drove up, and bidding Mrs. Weir and her son good-by, I took my seat by the driver, a soldier. Mr. Deering went

[4] Edward Monro's *The Journey Home: An Allegory* (London, 1854).

155

into the next ambulance. We were to lead one of those long dreary looking trains, of which I had seen so many.

There were two men with us; one was wounded in the jaw, and had the erysipelas very badly; the other had one of his legs broken, which was nicely fixed in a splint. The latter I expected to suffer very much from the jolting, but he seemed to suffer little compared with the other.

I thought I had seen the worst our men had to endure, but this ride proved I was mistaken. I never saw such roads in my life; the rain had been heavy and made deep ruts in it. We had to pass two or three fords, in which the water was so high that it nearly came into our wagon. We came to one which had a wagon stuck fast in it, and blocking up the way; our driver and some others had to unharness their mules and get it out of the mire before we could proceed. All this was very trying to the wounded, and the wonder to me is how they could live after such a ride, for it was really harrowing.

On arriving at the hospital I found a number of ladies there from Newnan; also our post surgeon, Dr. Gamble, and Dr. Gore of Bragg Hospital. I was delighted to see them all. The ladies had brought quantities of good things, which they were giving to the men as they were brought in. The wounded, to save them another move, were taken to the cars instead of the hospital.

There were also some gentlemen from Newnan; among them was Colonel Colyar, who seems to be an excellent man. He has suffered much by the war, having been driven from his state and home; but he bears it like a hero, and is always pleasant and never grumbling.

The ladies were Mrs. Dr. Reese, Miss Julia Lowe, Miss Barber, and others whose names I have forgotten.

There was a Mrs. Welsh of St. Louis; she had gone up with the Lagrange Relief Society. She told me she had been imprisoned in St. Louis for attending to our wounded, and as she would not take the oath was exiled.

I sent out a quantity of rags and other things, given me by the Newnan ladies, to my friends at Manigault Hospital, and to Dr. Rhea at Cleburne's Division Hospital.

Numbers of persons were there looking for their relatives. I met a lady who was in Dr. Capers's hospital in Corinth. Two of her sons were badly wounded, and she was on her way to see them.

On the train coming up was a fine-looking lady, Mrs. Birch, who seemed to be in great distress about her son, who she had heard was badly wounded. She had found him and was taking him home. She was dressed in black, for a son who I think died in the Virginia army.

I saw thousands of small arms at the depot, which had been captured on the battle-field, and many prisoners.

At Ringgold I met Rev. Mr. Owen P. Thackery, an Episcopal clergyman from Florida. He was there with supplies for the Florida troops. He had stopped at many of the hospitals on his way up, and

156

was much pleased with the manner with which they were conducted, and he said what gave him more pleasure than that was the religious feeling expressed by the men. A lady has come with him to enter the hospitals. She was then at Marietta, and Dr. Gamble requested me to stop on my way to Newnan and take her with me.

Drs. Bateman and Sizemore came to see me, and gave me a history of all their troubles since leaving Newnan. They said they had been in want of every thing for the wounded, and that they fully believed many a man had died for the want of nourishment, and that when they did get any thing they had nothing to cook it in, and no one that knew how to cook.

From what they said, and from my own observations, I feel confident that ladies could be of much service in field hospitals. And if I only had the means, there is where I should go. I could get some one to assist me, who would go for the pure love of doing good. We could have an independent conveyance, and as we should be non-combatants and sisters of charity (they have always been respected by the enemy), we could do what I have often wished: go through the lines and take care of our badly wounded who are prisoners.

Dr. Burt is in charge of the hospital, and is busy getting it fixed. As I was detained in Ringgold a day longer than I expected, I went to try and get some furniture for the hospital, and fortunately met with Dr. Stickney, medical purveyor of Polk's corps. He kindly supplied me with many things, and gave a promise of more.

I also met my friend, Dr. Young, who gave me some relics which he had picked off the battle-field; among them some letters. One of them was from a young girl in Illinois to her cousin.

In reading it I could not but wonder how she could sit down and encourage her friends to come here as murderers and robbers, for they are nothing else. She raves about the Union as I have heard the men do. I think they must all be demented to even talk of such a thing now. They speak of us as if we did not have common sense, and had to be dictated to by them. She calls herself a " real sucker." [5] That has certainly a lady-like sound.

She then goes on to tell her cousin that she and all the others thought that as they had had a great many victories lately the *rebels* were completely whipped; but she had evidently just heard of the repulse at Charleston, and she is afraid the war is not over yet. Poor thing, what will she say when she hears of the repulse the " dear Union soldiers " have had up here? She says they must expect the bitter with the sweet; I think she will have a good deal of bitter yet before the *rebels* are whipped.

She then says she knows it is the Lord's doing, and ere long the fetters will be broken and the negro set free. I should like to know

[5] " Sucker " was the nickname for inhabitants of Illinois. Mitford M. Mathews, *A Dictionary of Americanisms on Historical Principles* (Chicago, 1951), II, 1672.

what kind of freedom she means; if it is the hatred and contempt which is generally shown the negro by these dear lovers of the race, excepting when they wish to use them in politics, and then, if they could, I think they would raise a certain old gentleman from the lower regions to aid them to get office.

If the negro should be set free by this war, which I believe he will be, whether we gain or not, it will be the Lord's doing. The time has come when his mission has ended as a slave, and while he has been benefited by slavery the white race has suffered from its influence.

We all know what the negro is free and as a slave. In the latter capacity he is better, morally and physically, than in the former, and he is much more respected in his place. Who is it that can not relate story after story of the degradation of the negro in the North and in the West India Islands? Why, slavery is heaven to it in comparison. That the South has not fully done her duty by them I do not believe any good southerner will deny; but who does his whole duty, and whose fault is it that she has not done so in this respect? None but the abolitionists'; for instead of our statesmen spending their time in legislating for the good of their country and all in it, they have been spending it in combating the evil influences which have been engendered by these fanatics and base politicians.

Captain Marryatt, whose opinion, notwithstanding all his prejudices, I think ought to go for something, in his diary,[6] said, with a prophetic ken, which has been but too truly fulfilled, that, from his observations of the abolitionists, unless the wise people of the North would rise in their might and put that party down, they would be the cause of the Union being dissolved, and of one of the most horrible civil wars this world has ever seen. This book was written over thirty years ago, and we all know that the author did not favor the system of slavery.

This girl goes on to tell how the copperheads in her state were trying to have peace meetings, and that the ladies of the section in which she lived sang "Union songs" and broke up the meetings. What a laudable enterprise that!

I can not but admire her spirit in the conclusion of the letter, and I only hope that a similar one is in all of our southern women, for our very existence is at stake; but not so with our enemies.

She says she would rather know that the dearest friend she had was wounded on the battle-field than hear of his deserting. She also tells the recipient that, if he wishes to please her, he must do his duty as a soldier. He has taken her advice, and gone where he will be judged according to the light given him in this world. May the Lord have mercy on his soul!

I left Ringgold on the afternoon of the 3d. Mr. McHenry, one of

[6] Frederick Marryatt, *A Diary in America* . . . (3 vols., London, 1839).

Dr. Burt's nurses, went to Marietta with me. We arrived there about daylight Sunday morning, the 4th. I went to the Gilmer Hospital, where my friends, Dr. Cannon and Mrs. Crocker, are staying.

Marietta is one of the prettiest towns in Georgia, and is quite an aristocratic place. At present it is filled with refugees from all parts of the Confederate States. It is the capital of Cobb County, Georgia; is situated on the Western and Atlantic Railroad, and is twenty miles north-west of Atlanta. Kenesaw Mountain, which is a very high one, is some few miles distant. The town itself is higher than any other on the railroad; I went to church with Dr. Cannon; the church was a very neat little building. I heard an excellent sermon preached by the rector, Mr. Benedict, on the subject of Esau selling his birthright. I could not but think how many of us are equally guilty. After service, Dr. Cannon introduced me to Mr. Benedict, who kindly invited me to go and stay at his house, which invitation I accepted.

I met my friend, Mr. E. Stickney, and he assisted me in finding Mrs. Harrison, the lady from Florida, with whom I made arrangements to come to Newnan. She has a large quantity of wines and delicacies brought from Florida for the benefit of the wounded.

We then paid a visit to Mrs. Newsom, who is in the Academy Hospital. She did not look well. We had a long talk about the late battle. By it she has lost many friends. I told her how agreeably surprised I was at finding our wounded at the field hospital as well cared for as they were; she thought as I did, she having been there to see her brother.

I think that Dr. Heustis has done a vast deal of good by the pictures he drew of the suffering and horrors which he had seen; but had he ever been at Corinth, I do not think he would have been quite so shocked.

Before the afternoon service, I went round with Dr. Cannon and visited the patients in the Gilmer Hospital. One of them presented a sad sight. He was a young lad, with both eyes shot out. Mrs. Crocker told me he had never been heard to murmur. I took a note of his name, as I intended inquiring about him again. His name is T. C. Wyatt, from Jasper County, Mississippi, and a member of the Eighth Mississippi Regiment.

Dr. Cannon took me to visit a Scotchman, who seemed pleased to see me. The hospital is a very fine one, and every thing in it is in perfect order.

At the afternoon service Dr. Cannon played the organ. A lady and myself assisted in the singing. After service we all went to Mr. Benedict's house, and spent a pleasant evening. I heard a conversation between two gentlemen about our late battle. One made some very harsh remarks about General Bragg; the other wished to know why he made them, and said, was it because he had gained the most brilliant victory of the war, or because he had *dared* to arrest General Polk?

159

and said, if the latter, he could not but applaud him, as it showed, no matter how high the offender, he would be brought to justice.

I was admiring Mr. Benedict's church, and he informed me that it was the first Sunday he had had service for some time, as the church had been stripped, as every other church in the place, for a hospital; but that the post surgeon had found out he could do without them. Mr. Benedict has a lovely wife and six children. I left them the next morning with many regrets, and shall ever feel grateful for their kindness.

I had a letter of introduction from Dr. Gamble to Mrs. Major Fairbanks, but did not have time to deliver it. Mr. Benedict procured her carriage for me to go and see Mrs. General Anderson, who was living in the country. There I was introduced to Mrs. Bibia, a fine old lady, the General's mother, who was going to Atlanta on the same train with me.

Mrs. Crocker and I went shopping. I bought a very common dress and paid three dollars per yard. In good times it would have cost ten cents. At the Gilmer Hospital I met Captain Prendagrast [Prendergast]. He had been in the British army, and is now a member of the Tenth Tennessee Regiment, and was wounded in the late battle.

While at Marietta I was told that the refugees in that place had behaved very badly, especially those from New Orleans. They had come there and treated the citizens as if they were far beneath them, and had done little else but give balls and parties. I suppose the refugees are as much to blame as the people for the treatment they have received. I left Marietta about 3 P. M. At the train I met Mr. Benedict, who was going to Augusta, and Mrs. Bibia. We were detained some time at the depot.

While there we heard a soldier on top of the train make a speech. We, however, could not make out what he said, but knew it must be something amusing from the mirth it caused, and the hearty applause with which it was received. A young man came in and told Mrs. Bibia that the soldier was pretending that he was one of " Joe Brown's Pets," as the Georgia militia are called.[7] He was telling a piteous story about the manner in which he had been treated; said he had been the whole of two weeks in the army, and as yet had *nary* a furlough, and also said the Georgia militia were nobly defending the rear of Bragg's army. The poor militia have many taunts to stand.

While on the train I conversed with a very intelligent lady, who had just come through the lines. She was in Shelbyville when our army had to retreat from there, and in the hurry broke her arm, and had been compelled to remain. She went I think to Winchester, where General Rosecrans had his head-quarters. There she saw how the

[7] General Richard Taylor referred to these soldiers as " Governor Brown's ' army,' composed of men that he had refused to the Confederate service." *Destruction and Reconstruction* (New York, 1955) , 259.

"dear Union army" treated the people. She said the soldiers went into any place they pleased, took every thing they wanted, and she had observed that when the officers were appealed to they made a fuss and talked a great deal, but did not pretend to have the thing restored. General Rosecrans tried to be very attentive to her, but she refused to accept any of his kindness. He very *gentlemanly* entertained her by telling her how bad off we were, and taunting her with it. He seemed to be well posted about every thing that was being done in the Confederacy. She thinks that we must have many spies among us.

I have always thought the southern people were too confiding, and put faith where they ought not to. I should not like to see them with the cunning of the Yankee, but I think they ought to act with more caution and discretion, as that is nothing but wisdom.

Every second man in the North might be a spy, and it would make little matter, as we are not going there to take any thing from them; but the case is very different with us. One spy in any of our cities might be its ruin.

On reaching Atlanta Mr. Benedict went shopping with me. I bought a net for the hair, and for it I paid fifteen dollars. In good times it would have been fifty cents. Mr. Benedict ordered one hundred pamphlet prayer-books for me, which will be very acceptable to the men.[8]

On reaching here I found Mrs. Williamson much improved in health, and the hospital filled with sick.

We would much prefer being nearer the front, and if our army is successful our hospital will return to Ringgold. I found some letters awaiting me. In one from my father, he is quite desponding. He thinks the late victory will amount to nothing, as Bragg is too long making a move. "Why stands Scotland idly now?"

October 12.—The hospital is filled with wounded—the very worst which were on the battle-field. There was a raid expected, and they had to be taken off in a hurry. They were put on the train about three or four days ago, and have had little to eat; and many of them have not had their wounds dressed during that time. One of our nurses told me he had never seen wounded in such a state before, and says that many will be certain to die.

A man, Mr. Groover, is wounded through both knees, and his back is full of bed-sores, caused from lying on a hard bunk made of branches of trees. He lay in one position on his back, from the time he was put on the train until he was taken off. The train was filled with slop and dirt of all kinds, and he had to lie in the midst of it. He is only one of many others who had to do likewise. On going into the ward the same sad spectacle greets us. One of our southern poets has drawn a picture only too faithfully of the scene in nearly all. Its vividness struck me so forcibly that I insert it:

[8] Probably the Protestant Episcopal Church's *The Order for Daily Morning and Evening Prayer* . . . (Atlanta, Ga., 1863).

A CALL TO THE HOSPITAL.

Fold away all your bright-tinted dresses,
  Turn the key on your jewels to-day,
And the wealth of your tendril-like tresses
  Braid back in a serious way.
No more delicate gloves, no more laces,
  No more trifling in boudoir or bower;
But come, with your souls in your faces,
  To meet the stern wants of the hour!

Look around by the torch-light unsteady—
  The dead and the dying seem one;
What! trembling and paling already,
  Before your dear mission's begun?
These wounds are more precious than ghastly—
  Time presses her lips to each scar;
While she chants of that glory which vastly
  Transcends all the horrors of war.

Pause here by the bedside; how mellow
  The light showers down on that brow!
Such a brave, brawny visage! Poor fellow!
  Some homestead is missing him now;
Some wife shades her eyes in the clearing;
  Some mother sits moaning, distress'd;
While the loved one lies faint, but unfearing,
  With the enemy's ball in his breast. . . .

Pass on; it is useless to linger
  While others are claiming your care;
There is need for your delicate finger,
  For your womanly sympathy there.
There are sick ones athirst for caressing,
  There are dying ones raving of home,
There are wounds to be bound with a blessing,
  And shrouds to make ready for some.

They have gathered about you the harvest
  Of death in its ghastliest view;
The nearest as well as the farthest
  Is here with the traitor and true.
And crowned with your beautiful patience,
  Made sunny with the love at the heart,
You must balsam the wounds of a nation,
  Nor falter nor shrink from your part.

Up and down through the wards, where the fever
  Stalks noisome, and gaunt, and impure
You must go with your steadfast endeavor
  To comfort, to counsel, to cure.
I grant you the task's superhuman,
  But strength will be given to you
To do for these dear ones what woman
  Alone in her pity can do.

162

And the lips of the mothers will bless you
    As angels sweet-visaged and pale!
And the little ones run to caress you,
    And the wives and sisters cry " Hail! "
But e'en if you drop down unheeded,
    What matter? God's ways are the best;
You have poured out your life where 't was needed,
    And he will take care of the rest.[9]

I have just received a letter from my brother, dated the 8th inst. He says the army has been in line of battle ever since the late battle, and are waiting for the enemy to make the attack.

We had two deaths this past week—one named Roberts, who was wounded at the late battle; his wife lives in Macon County, Georgia; the other is named Jesse Ferrell, from Thomas County, Georgia. He has been here since we first came.

Sunday, October 18.—Nearly all the wounded are doing well. We shall not lose near as many as we thought. We have a room with seven men in it, who have lost a limb each. It is a perfect treat to go into it, as the men seem to do little else but laugh. They are young men, and say to me, and I must tell all the young ladies to come and see them, and that they will make excellent husbands, as they will be sure never to run away.

We have a wounded captain, named Desha, related to the family in Mobile of that name. He is from Kentucky, and a cousin of Professor Pickett, whom I met at Ringgold. I have been told he is one of the bravest and best men in our army. I was conversing with him one day relative to the ignorance of our men. He said there was no doubt it was very great, but not greater than that of the northerners. He had seen hundreds of letters from the people in the North, and they were not only illiterate, but vulgar. This I have often heard said before.

Dr. Bemiss is as kind as ever to the patients. He is constantly going around inquiring if they get enough to eat, and is using every means to get plenty for them. We get quantities of buttermilk, which is a great treat.

Dr. Bemiss tells me he has over fifty relatives in the army, and he has not heard from them since the battle.

The president has just paid a visit to the Tennessee army; it is said for the purpose of making inquiries as to the dissatisfaction against General Bragg among his officers.

It seems that all his generals, excepting General Breckinridge, sent a petition to the president to have him removed. General Bragg has

[9] Four stanzas of this poem which appear in the original edition of Miss Cumming's journal are omitted here. With two stanzas omitted, it is printed in William Gilmore Simms's *War Poetry of the South* (New York, 1867), 218-20, with its source indicated as the Charleston *Courier*.

heard of it, and begged to be relieved, but the president refuses, as he says he does not know who to put in his place.

Sunday, October 26.—Mrs. Harrison, the lady from Florida, has taken charge of the ward at the Springs. She had a pretty hard time at the beginning. The first day the rain poured into her room in torrents. She told me this as a joke, as she has determined not to complain. I think, like myself, she has something of the Mark Tapley spirit, and thinks, unless she has drawbacks, there will be no credit in staying in a hospital. A number of our patients have been sent down to the Springs, and Mrs. Harrison is paying them the most devoted attention.

To-day is Sunday, but we are too busy to think of going to church. Mrs. Williamson and myself are up at 4 o'clock every morning, preparing eggnog and toddies for the wounded; they are compelled to have them before eating. One of our patients, by the name of Davis, has had his arm amputated, and is doing well.

October 28.—On my way to the wards this morning I was annoyed at something which happened. I had made up my mind to leave the hospital, but on entering the wards all of this feeling vanished. When I saw the smile with which I was greeted on every side, and the poor sufferers so glad to see me, I made up my mind, I hope for the last time, that, happen what may, nothing will ever make me leave the hospital as long as I can be of any service to the suffering.

The surgeons have told me it is impossible for Mr. Groover to live. I have written to his wife, and told her of his condition. Poor man! he cried like a child when spoken to about his wife, and begged me not to let her know how badly he was wounded.

We have a badly wounded man, named Robbins; he has always a smile on his face and a joke for every one. He sings hymns all the time, and I am told on the battle-field he was as cheerful as he is now.

We have two lads severely wounded; one named Moore, from North Carolina, wounded in the lungs. He is as patient as if he were an old man. The other, named Seborn Horton, from Alabama; he is not more than sixteen years of age. He is a great sufferer. Nothing pleases him better than to have ladies come to see him, and I beg all the girls, little and big, to come. One day I took some ladies to see him, and there was a crowd of little girls standing around him. I remarked that he would be pleased now. He answered that he was, but he was afraid the girls would not come back again. They had brought him a bouquet, which he prized very highly. Our men all seem fond of flowers.

We have numbers of Texas soldiers, members of Hood's division. They are a fine-looking lot of men, and seem brave enough to face any danger. I have had not a little quarreling with them. They will have it that this army is not to be compared with the one in Virginia for bravery. I do not agree with them, for I have always heard it said that up here we have the flower of the North with which to contend. But these things do for something to talk about. It is amusing to hear the men abusing the different states. Of course it is all in jest, but sometimes they wax quite warm on the subject.

When our army was in Mississippi, had I believed one half the stories told of the people, I should have thought it the meanest state in the Confederacy.

While in Tennessee the same story was told; and now that we are in Georgia, it is honored by the same cognomen. I have come to the conclusion that where our army is that by it the country is injured, and that makes the people do things they otherwise would not. This the soldiers do not think about.

It is reported that General Thomas has superseded General Rosecrans, and that at Chattanooga we have the enemy completely hemmed in.

Our army is on Missionary Ridge and Lookout Mountain, and we have possession of the Nashville Railroad. The enemy have to haul their supplies from a great distance. On this account it is rumored that they are starving in Chattanooga. But I have heard some say that, with all their drawbacks, they are not only not starving, but are being heavily reinforced. It seems like folly to listen to any thing. I hope and pray that General Bragg will not feel too secure, and that he will be on the alert. Nearly all the defeats we have ever had have been from our want of caution.

November 1.—A mild beautiful day. Mrs. Dr. Reese called with her carriage, and took me down to visit our patients at the Springs. They are all doing well. Mrs. Harrison seems perfectly happy in her new vocation.

After leaving there we visited Major Brewster's, where our old patient, Lieutenant Payne, is lying very sick. We left him in Atlanta, and from there he went to Dr. Collier's, near Atlanta, followed us here, and since then has been growing worse. He is now in good hands, and is receiving every attention.

On the 29th ult., Mr. G. Cross died. He was wounded at the battle of Chickamauga. When he was first brought here, we did not think he could live but a few days. He was a member of the Twenty-seventh Tennessee Regiment. He has a sister in Atlanta, to whom I have written.

We have an addition of two surgeons, Dr. Wellford from Virginia and Dr. Glenn from New Orleans. Dr. Glenn came out of New Orleans a registered enemy to the United States. Dr. Wellford is from that heroic but unfortunate city, Fredericksburg, where the enemy robbed him, and destroyed every thing he possessed.

In letters received from home I see that the president has visited Mobile. All are perfectly delighted with him. He made a speech

165

which my father thinks a very fine one. He reviewed the troops, and the folks say he has a fine commanding military appearance.

November 3.—A very warm day, and our patients are suffering very much. If the weather was cool it would be better for them. One of the wards, called the carriage ward (as it had been a carriage house), has about fifty patients, and it is heart-breaking to hear them groan. I think it is even worse than Corinth, as the men here seem to suffer much more. There they either died or were taken to another hospital. Fresh wounds are scarcely ever as painful as old ones.

This ward is a large, low-roofed, white-washed room, roughly boarded, so that there are not a few openings where the daylight peeps through.

On entering, the first man to the right is Mr. Robbins, about fifty years of age. The doctors say he is one of the worst wounded men we have. His appearance is weak and languid, and there is very little hope of his recovery. Near him is Mr. McVay, an Irishman, much emaciated. One of his legs has been amputated above the knee, and the bone is protruding about an inch, which is very painful.

To the left is Mr. Groover, wounded in both knees. While marching, a cannon-ball took off the cap of one, and the under part of the other, and his back is one solid bed-sore. We have tried to relieve his suffering in every way. The very sight of his face is distressing, and makes me feel as if I would sacrifice almost any thing to palliate his pain. The effluvia from his wounds is sickening.

Further on are a dozen or so badly wounded: one without a leg; another without an arm, and some with wounds which are awful to look at, but their faces denote all they need is plenty to eat. I passed on, telling them that they are *beneath* my notice.

At the head of this group is Mr. Conda, an Irishman, with his leg in a sling. His wound, though not a bad looking one, is very painful, and he sleeps but little day or night. The clammy sweat constantly on his forehead tells how acutely he suffers; so that there is no need of asking him how he is.

Opposite him is Mr. Horton, another great sufferer. Just beyond is a man who has about two inches of his shin-bone cut out, and it is growing up.

Along side of him is Mr. Sparks, who came here with apparently a slight wound in the leg. It is now so painful that he not only groans day and night, but many a time his plaint can be heard in the street. His nose is pinched, and all his features have the appearance of a great sufferer. A little ways from him is Mr. Robinson, a lad about seventeen. The calf of his leg is a solid sore. He wails most dolefully, and we find it impossible to assuage his pain.

He and many of the others might have their limbs amputated, but the doctors say that their systems are not in a fit state, and that they would not stand the shock. There are many other badly wounded men in the ward, but they do not seem to suffer so acutely.

In looking over letters received from a friend in Mobile, I was a little astonished at an assertion in one about the planters. It seems they will not sell produce unless at an exorbitant price, and many will take nothing in return but gold and silver. If this is really the case, which I have no reason to doubt, I am at a loss to understand how they can be so blinded. Are they not aware that we are blockaded, and can only procure food from them; and do they not also know, if the enemy succeed—which they assuredly will, if the planters and others act as they are now doing—that they will be ruined, as well as every body else? Heaven help the country! I am getting sick at heart with seeing men from whom we expected so much acting as they are now doing. I wonder if they expect men to fight for them and their property, if they leave their wives and children to starve? The men will be more than mortal if they do it.

It is too bad that President Davis can not devise some way of making these Esaus, who would not only sell their own birthright, but ours, for a mess of pottage, give up their stores. They are ours by right. God did not shower his blessing on the land, as he has done this summer, for them alone.

It is said the planters were to blame for the fall of Vicksburg, and that after its fall the enemy came and took all their cotton, corn, and every thing else they had. If this report be true, it is a just judgment on them. And will they not all suffer the same?

> " Men of the South! look up, behold
>   The deep and sullen gloom
> Which darkens o'er your sunny land,
>   With thunder in its womb!
>
> Are ye so blind ye can not see
>   The omens in the sky?
> Are ye so deaf ye can not hear
>   The tramp of foemen nigh?
>
> Look north, look west, the ominous sky
>   Is moonless, starless, black,
> And from the east comes hurrying up
>   A sweeping thunder rack! "

When I think of these wretches, and of the men who are lying here, having suffered so much to save them and their wealth, I can scarcely keep from crying out on them. What is every bushel of corn and acre of land these planters have compared with the sacrifice these men have made? A mere cipher. Why, such comparisons are odious!

I noticed a very good article in a Mobile paper, signed " Gray Hairs." The writer is calling on the people to try and improve the currency, and denouncing the grand jury for not doing something about the matter.

167

The papers are filled with good advice, if the people would only take it, and be warned before it is too late.

Many are placing their hopes of peace on the peace party in the North. I do think we have had enough of that. The North always seems to get as many men as they want in spite of "peace parties" and every thing else.

Sunday, November 8.—I am kept quite busy; I do not have time to talk or read to the men. Mrs. Williamson's health being bad, she was advised a change of air, and has gone to Mobile.

Captain Smith, one of my Corinth patients, called to see me. He has never wholly recovered from his wound. He was appointed major of his regiment, and had to resign on account of his health. He is now chaplain of the regiment. He is hopeful about our cause, as indeed all our soldiers are.

I have received a letter from a Kentucky friend, and with it a trophy found on the late battle-field. It is a kind of book, called " The Holy Comforter," in which are appropriate selections from Scripture. It is for the use of a sick-room.

My friend says he can not see what such people as the enemy have to do with any thing of that kind, and wishes they would only profit by such teachings. He forgot that wicked people would not put on a cloak of any thing that is wicked wherewith to cover evil, as then it would be no mask.

When we look at the history of the world, and the persecutions, called religious ones, how little the calm and holy spirit of religion has had to do with it all!

Christianity breathes nothing but peace and good-will toward men; but if men, in their blindness and evil hearts, pervert it, it loses none of its sanctity or truthfulness, but only adds tenfold to the condemnation of those who abuse it. The devil quoted Scripture, why may not his followers?

I am not one of those who say there are no Christians in the North, because of the terrible blasphemy which is now raging there. If we are to believe their own papers, the birthday of Tom Paine is kept as a grand festival; and men wearing the garb of the sanctuary cry, Down with the Holy Bible because it upholds slavery . . .

I think . . . that there are many good and true Christians in the North—men who have not let the wicked one take possession of them altogether. And it is with the hope that we have many such that I look forward to that happy day when they will rise in their might, and with one voice demand that the demagogues and fanatics who are now having full sway desist from this unholy strife, and treat us as they should. They seem to have forgotten that we are God's creatures as well as they, with at least as much power of reasoning.

My Kentucky friend says he has just heard from his home, and that his wife is dying, and he is not permitted to go and see her. It is not much wonder that he is so bitter.

November 13.—Dr. Bemiss left to-day. He is going to assist Dr. Stout. We all regret his leaving. To use the phrase of a friend, " he is a gentleman and scholar, with his heart in the right place." A more devoted patriot we have not in the cause.

Dr. J. N. Hughes of Kentucky is his successor, and I am told is a true patriot and a high-toned southern gentleman.

Our wounded are doing badly; gangrene in its worst form has broken out among them. Those whom we thought were almost well are now suffering severely. A wound which a few days ago was not the size of a silver dime is now eight or ten inches in diameter.

The surgeons are doing all in their power to stop its progress. Nearly every man in the room where they were so full of jokes has taken it; there is very little laughing among them now. It is a most painful disease, and plays sad havoc with the men every way. We can not tempt them to eat, and we have very little sweet milk, and that is the cry with them all. Many a day I have felt as if I would walk any distance to get it for them. It is distressing to go into the wards for I hear but the one cry—milk!

I have told every body that I have met about it, but with no effect. If all would give a very little, there is no end to the amount of good of which it would be productive.

The people say that they use it for their negroes and children, as they have no fresh meat; but I expect they could spare a little for these wounded patriots.

Mrs. Johnston's little boy, my talkative friend, comes every day with milk. His mother tells me that she can not get him to taste it himself, for he desires to bring his share to the soldiers.

We have had a number of ladies from the country visiting the wounded; many of them have come twenty miles. They bring baskets full of all kinds of eatables. It does me good to see them come, as the very best we can give wounded men is not enough. And another thing: the diet is a change; they bring ham, biscuits, chickens, pies, cakes, etc.

November 16.—The weather is delightful, and our wounded doing a little better.

We had two men die to-day—the first in three weeks. When they were brought in we did not think they would live but a day or two. One, named Patrick Conda, was a member of the Tenth Tennessee Regiment, and was wounded at the late battle. His sufferings were great, and he bore them with much fortitude. He blessed me every time I did any little thing for him. He was a member of the Roman Catholic Church, and died trusting in the atoning blood of his blessed Savior. He was a native of Ireland, but all his relatives live in New York.

The other patient who died is named William G. Elliott; he was a member of the Forty-third or Forty-eighth Alabama Regiment. He died from fever. At the time he was brought in he was deranged, and died in that state.

The youth, Seborn Horton, has just breathed his last. Poor child! I trust he is now at rest in the bosom of his God, secure from woe and sin. He was like many other badly wounded men whom I have seen, deranged a short time before his death. I have written to his mother, who lives in Marshall County, Alabama.

November 17.—Poor Mr. Groover is at last released from all his sufferings. Last night at 9 o'clock his spirit took its flight. He died at peace with his God. His wife has been with him about a week, and is much consoled that she has had the privilege of ministering to his last wants. She has two children, and has lost two brothers, two brothers-in-law, and now her husband, in this unholy conflict.

Dr. Hughes, who is very kind to the patients, and doing all in his power to alleviate their sufferings, has had Mr. Groover moved into a room by himself, and every thing about him as comfortable as possible. Mrs. and Miss Lowe, ladies of the place, were with Mrs. Groover at the time of her husband's death.

I have made the acquaintance of some very nice people here. Among them Mr. Dougherty's family; he keeps a hotel near us. He has three married daughters, highly educated and refined ladies. He is what is called an Irish-Scotchman, and two of his daughters are named respectively, Caledonia and Hibernia. He is a native of that town of historic fame, Londonderry.

John Munroe, a member of the Second Alabama Regiment, died to-day. He was a member of the Presbyterian Church, and he died perfectly happy. Mr. Neligen, the head nurse of the ward in which he was, has written to his wife. She lives in Coosa County, Alabama.

November 19.—With the exception of a few, the wounded are doing pretty well.

We have one man, Captain Thompson, who lost a leg at Chickamauga, and while in the field hospital took gangrene and pneumonia besides. No words can ever express the suffering which this man has endured, and I have never seen him without a smile on his countenance, nor heard a murmur from his lips. One of his men is nursing him, and is very devoted to him.

Mr. Green, our chaplain, has gone on a visit somewhere; so I got one of the ladies of the place to send for Mr. Smith, the Methodist presiding elder, who came and prayed with the captain and many of the others. Captain Thompson's cousin, Miss Womack, a very nice young lady, has come to see him. She is with me, assisting.

November 21.—I have received a letter from Dr. Hopping. He has now charge of the Kingston Hospital, and is anxious to have Mrs. Williamson and myself there again. His wife is with him, and is one of the matrons. I should like very much to go, so as to be near the army; and had fully made up my mind to go either there or to Ringgold, but Dr. Hughes and Dr. Gamble are both unwilling to have Mrs. Williamson and myself leave, and I think it best to wait until the next battle. Our army may be defeated, and in that case the hospitals brought further in the rear.

Some few days ago I received a letter from my brother. He says his battery is stationed on the top of Lookout Mountain, and that he never saw such accurate firing as that of the enemy from below. He says their balls come right to where they are. The enemy have taken our cavalry by surprise, and by it we have lost a very important place, called Racoon Mountain. The enemy now have sole possession of the Nashville Railroad, and are being heavily reinforced.

I am losing all confidence in General Bragg. He seems to make no use of his victories. I have been told by many of Longstreet's men that after the battle of Chickamauga, there were thousands of troops who had come from Virginia, who had never fired a gun in the battle, and with them he might have gone and taken Chattanooga.

I have observed that Wellington and Napoleon, especially the latter, gained nearly all of their great victories by the celerity of their movements. Indeed, it has been the case with the most of great generals. But we must not judge, as we can not tell with what General Bragg has to contend. We have so few men, compared with the enemy, that were it not for the feeling which animates ours we would never gain.

To-day, Miss Womack and myself took a walk, and visited some of of the patients, who are in tents, about two squares distant. They are some of the gangrene cases, all of which are either in tents or rooms by themselves. They are doing pretty well. Many of them are great sufferers from this terrible disease. It has to be burned out with nitric acid, which is a very painful operation. I sometimes look at the wounds while being dressed, and they are dreadful. My wonder is how they can ever be healed.

After visiting them, we went to Mrs. Hill's to see Captain Insey, one of the men who was sick at Judge Thornton's, in Okolona, Miss. He is now very ill. He is a member of the Ninth Alabama Batallion. I have a friend in it, James Kay, of whose welfare I was glad to hear, as his mother had written to me concerning him. Mr. Kay is one of our Mobile boys, and I was much gratified when Captain Insey informed me that he is a brave and good soldier.

Captain Thompson is very low, and there is no hope of his recovery. He is perfectly resigned to his fate, and talks as calmly on the subject as if he was going to pay a visit to his family.

November 23.—About 1 o'clock P. M., Captain Thompson breathed his last. The suffering patriot and the brave soldier has passed away from earth. . . .

He was a member of the Forty-fifth Mississippi Regiment. He has left a wife and, I believe, four children to mourn their loss.

Miss Womack, by great exertion, has been able to have his remains sent home to his wife. She lives in Summit, Mississippi. The man who nursed him has not had a furlough since entering the service; so Dr. Hughes has procured him one, and sent the corpse home by him.

Two men died yesterday in the court-house ward, by the name of Alexander. One, Wm. S., was wounded through the lungs. He suffered much and patiently. I talked and read to him a good deal, which he seemed glad to have me do. I think he was not sensible of his situation, but he seemed resigned. He was a member of the Sixty-third Tennessee Regiment. His mother lives in Knox County, Tennessee. This is the second son whom she has lost in the service. The other man was named W. B., from the same state as the first, and they were not related, nor had ever heard of each other before. He had been here for some months, and I think had consumption. I am told, after bidding all round him farewell, he breathed his last as calmly as if he were going asleep. He had passed through much tribulation; but had cast his care upon Him who had trod this vale of tears, and who is now seated in glorious majesty on high, waiting to receive the spirits of the righteous. He was a member of the Forty-first Tennessee Regiment. I have sent a letter to his mother, who lives in Marshall County, Tennessee. I sent it to his captain (Captain Osborne), who will forward it through the lines.

November 24.—The enemy have been heavily reinforced, and a battle is daily expected. Dr. Divine has been ordered to the front.

Dr. Hughes has received orders to have the hospital enlarged. A number of the wounded have been sent to the Springs so as to make room for more. A change of any kind is good for sick and wounded; to even move them from one hospital to the other is of benefit.

There has been desperate fighting round Charleston lately. Fort Sumter has been assaulted a number of times, and each time the enemy have been repulsed with great slaughter.

November 26.—A bright, beautiful day, but the sunshine is forgotten on account of the bad news. We have some wounded men just brought in, members of Walthal's [Walthall's] brigade. They say that on the afternoon of the 25th, the brigade being on Lookout Mountain, the enemy surrounded them before they had the least idea of their being anywhere near them.

The whole brigade has been nearly killed or captured. One man told me he never had such a run in his life. He believes there must have been at least a thousand shots fired at him at one time, not one of them hitting him.

The enemy came on them from all sides, many climbing the steepest part of the mountain.

Our people never will learn watchfulness. Nothing seems to be a lesson to them.

We have lost the mountain. The troops are concentrating on Missionary Ridge.

I expect my brother is captured this time, as he was on the mountain; and he, like many others, has as great an attachment for his gun as if it was a thing of life, and would either be captured with it, or die before giving it up.

November 28.—A gloomy day, but still gloomier news. I can not see one gleam of light either on nature's horizon or the nation's. Alas! for the fate of our brave army. It has had a battle; and, after fighting desperately, had to retreat leaving the wounded in the enemy's hands. It is bad enough to be wounded, and with friends; but wounded and a prisoner, how dreadful that must be! May God comfort them, and be their stay in affliction! For once, the sight of the wounded coming in makes me perfectly happy, for I know that they at least are not in the hands of the enemy. The hospital is again filled with the same sad spectacle—men mutilated in every possible way.

Last night Lieutenant Payne breathed his last. He was a member of the Twelfth Tennessee Regiment, and was in his twentieth year. The only regret he had when dying, was being unable to see his father and mother, who are in the enemy's lines. Major Payne, his brother, was with him, and his last wants were ministered to by the hands of loving friends. He suffered long and patiently. Mrs. Williamson had conversed with him on the subject of religion before he or any of us had the least idea of his being cut off so soon, and she found that he walked humbly with his God. . . .

Mr. Davis, the young man who had his arm amputated, is doing pretty well. His father is nursing him. He has lost a son and a son-in-law in this war, and has five more sons in the army, and he has not heard from either of them in some time. He is sixty-four years old—nurses this one as well as any young man could. I have not yet heard one murmur from him. The son has suffered a good deal, as he has had gangrene.

We have some dreadful cases of that awful disease. One man, by the name of Deal, a large, fine-looking Texan, who was wounded at Chickamauga. We thought it was impossible to cast a cloud o'er his spirits, as he formerly laughed and made fun of every thing and every body. Since he has had gangrene he is grave enough. He is wounded I think in three places; in his back, in one of his knees, and his chest. The doctors are fearful they will not be able to stop the gangrene on his back before it eats inwardly and reaches some vital part; nor on his knee at all, and that he will likely lose his leg.

We have more just such cases. A Texan, named Hempflin, wounded at the same battle. When he first came here he was able to walk about for some weeks, but has taken gangrene in his wound, and is now hovering between life and death. The disease has eaten into one of the main arteries. Continued compression of the vessel is necessary to

173

save him from instant death. A number of men are detailed for that purpose, who remain with him night and day. They relieve each other every twenty minutes.

A young man, who was slightly wounded on one of his legs, received a furlough, which elated him so much that he jumped around a good deal; the consequence was that he hit his wound against something, causing it to bleed. The surgeons, on examining, found one of the large arteries ruptured, and there was every likelihood of the man's bleeding to death. Men were detailed to keep up manual compression for three weeks. The man is now well, and has gone home.

The manner in which some of our men's lives are saved is a perfect miracle. I never expected to see this man get well. But our doctors never despair while there is life.

Sunday, November 29.—A very cold day. Mr. Moore, who is now our chaplain, had service in the court-house.

The news to-day from the army is a little more cheering, but it is almost impossible to hear any thing definite. We had a few wounded brought in last night.

I see by the papers that the Georgia legislature has appropriated a large sum of money for the relief of the soldiers' families in their state. I do hope that all the other states will imitate them. Men can not be expected to fight when their wives and children are starving.

I see by the same papers that Lincoln is out with another call for three hundred thousand more troops. Many are confident he will not get them, but that is one of the phantoms we have been chasing and placing our hopes upon ever since the war, and time after time it has vanished like the " baseless fabric of a dream," which it is. When Lincoln has failed to get men from his own land, he has used every means at his command to recruit in foreign countries. And, notwithstanding Lord Lyons's punctilio about international law, thousands of men have been recruited on British soil. They are men deluded in every possible way.

Lincoln may get men to fill his last call, and yet, if the South is only true to herself, she can never be conquered. "The battle is not always to the strong."

I look around me sometimes, and see so many good intelligent men, and think what a sad thing it would be were we subjugated. I believe such a thing is a moral impossibility, and can never happen.

I firmly believe there is not a state in the Confederacy that will not be scourged by the invader, for the sins we have committed in our prosperity, forgetting the Most High, who is the giver of all good. True, the enemy have sinned as well as we, which sins they will have to answer for, if not to-day, some other. . . .

Another of our phantoms—foreign intervention—I am in hopes has vanished forever from the minds of our people. I have often thought,

174

if we could have it, the war would cease; for, boastful as the Federals are, I do not think they would go to war with foreign powers.

Many have praised France for her goodwill toward us, but to save my life I can not see what she has done.

I believe now, more than ever, we ought to judge people by their acts and not their words. The latter cost nothing. They will not put money in our coffers, nor aid us in any way . . .

The consciousness of having done our duty will be better than all the flattery they could give us.

When the war commenced, my main hope for aid was from Great Britain, as I had always thought of her as the defender of the oppressed, but like many others of my hopes, this one has also fallen.

I have heard many say that she rejoices at this struggle, as she has always been jealous of the growing power of the United States, and she will wait until we wear each other out before giving us any aid. I have always rejected this cruel, heartless accusation with indignation, for I can not bring myself to think that the people whom I have loved to look up to for every thing that was magnanimous and great, could rejoice at the misery of any nation, much less that of its descendants. If such could be the case, I think, with nations as with individuals, that for every dishonest and unprincipled motive, no matter how seemingly clothed with justice the act may be, an account must be given; and if Great Britain is base enough to keep back from giving us aid, from the motive imputed to her, her day of reckoning will surely come. I have thought that she did not give us aid because she could not consistently be an abettor of slavery. But I have given up that notion, for I know that the Britons are endowed with judgment enough to see through the mask worn by the abolitionists, and to know that we, not they, are the true friend of the negro.

Mr. Lindsay, M. P., made a speech lately in Middlesex, England, in which he says he has conversed with Dr. Livingston on the condition of the negro in Africa, and Dr. Livingston had told him it was not possible to conceive any thing like the degradation of the race in that country.

If people would only think, they would see, even taking Mrs. Stowe's book for their standard, that there are no negroes on the face of the earth as happy as those who are slaves in this country.[10] Mrs. Stowe drew a true picture when she drew Uncle Tom, for we have many such among us; and from all we can learn such characters are rare in the North and other countries where the negro race is. As for Mr. Legree, few southerners deny having such among us. I

[10] More than a decade after its first publication, *Uncle Tom's Cabin* was still a powerful propaganda weapon for the North. " The stock of some tract dispensers included large quantities of *Uncle Tom's Cabin* . . . [T]he Protestant Episcopal Book Society in August 1864 sent 47,000 copies of Mrs. Stowe's book to the central office of the [United States Christian] Commission at Philadelphia " for army distribution. Wiley, *The Life of Billy Yank* (Indianapolis, New York, 1952) , 273.

know of one, a Scotchman. He whipped a negro child to death; was tried and put in the penitentiary. Hanging would have been too good for such a man, so all said. . . . I know of a few more Legrees. Two are New Englanders and one a Dutchman. They beat their negroes, but they are despised by all who know them. . . . But we all know that atrocities committed by wicked men are no standard by which to judge the nation to whom they belong.

I have often alleged as a reason for foreigners and northerners ill-treating negroes so much more than the southerners, that the negro, like his master, is not over-fond of work. The foreigner is accustomed to have white servants work from daylight till dark, and many of them after dark; they expect the same work from the negro, but all in vain, for the *darky* has no such ideas of life—eat, sleep, and no work, is his motto. These people, not understanding the character of the negro, lose patience with him, and try by whipping to get the same amount of work from them as they have been in the habit of getting from white servants. Many a time, while we have listened to the tales about the work done by white servants in Scotland, we have said, who could live in a country where such things are done, and where there was such slavery. The southern people do not respect any one who over-works his servants. That they have not done their whole duty by the slaves they do not deny. They should have laws protecting them from these monsters; but, as I have said before, they are not to blame. And as soon as we have peace, I am told that the first thing our people will do is to improve their condition.

But I have wandered from the subject of recognition. I feel confident that it is not on account of slavery that Britain has kept aloof from us. The why and the wherefore is yet to be known. She has borne insult after insult from the Federals . . .

This M. P., Mr. Lindsay, makes an acknowledgment in his speech, which proves that that *immaculate British* government has not only permitted recruiting, but he says that the very guns and ammunition now used in bombarding Charleston came from England. What is Lord Lyons about? Perhaps that is not a breach of the law, only *bending* it. Well, we have certainly enough to contend with—foes within and the whole world without. . . .

I hope that our people will not be deluded any longer, but look to themselves, having a full trust in God, and in the justice of our cause.

November 30.—One of the coldest days I have experienced in a long time. The water froze in the buckets and pitchers in our rooms. My heart sickens when I think of the sufferings of our men. I have been told that many of them have scarcely enough clothes to cover them, and neither shoes nor stockings. We have had many come here in this plight. This makes me feel perfectly miserable; I wish I could forget it.

The good news which we heard yesterday, to-day is confirmed. The

176

enemy pursued our people as far as Ringgold, when General Cleburne, with his gallant command, turned and fought them, driving them back, killing and capturing thousands. Gen. Cleburne, I am told, is a brave officer. He is a son of that isle which has produced one of the princes of generals, Wellington; and I am told he is not without some of the fire that glowed in his illustrious countryman.

Troops are passing daily to reinforce this army.

December 3.—Mrs. Williamson has returned from Mobile, and she brought us quite a number of rags. The Mobilians are as kind as ever. We expected her to bring coffee and tea, but they are too high. The former was fifteen dollars per pound; the latter sixteen dollars. She paid sixty-five dollars for a pair of boots; the most I have paid for the article is thirty dollars.

December 7.—I received a letter from my brother to-day. He is well, and has lost every thing except the clothes which he has on. I intend sending him some.

The weather is intensely cold, and our men must be suffering very much, for they are only half clad, and half shod. I often wonder how the enemy dare to taunt us about our rags and poverty. Are they really so blind to true principle as not to know that men who fight as ours do, and as they are kept, must have something high and holy to enable them to do it? There is more glory in their rags than all the glitter and gilt lace that the Federals have in their possession.

Our army is at Dalton, and I expect will remain there all winter. My brother blames the infantry for our defeat on Missionary Ridge; but I expect it is all for the best, and that we shall do better next time.

December 8.—A very gloomy, wet, cold day. I have not been able to go to see any of the patients on account of the weather.

We get along very nicely now. Mrs. Williamson has taken charge of the linen department, and keeps two girls busy sewing all the time. We have numbers of pads to make for the wounded. The fact is, there is always plenty to do in the way of sewing.

We have all the whiskey now in charge.[11] Miss Womack makes eggnog and toddies, and gives out the whiskey as the surgeons prescribe it. Besides that, we have all of the delicacies, such as coffee, tea, sugar, butter, eggs, etc. Miss Womack has not much idle time.

A very nice woman has charge of the distributing-room, and attends to preparing little extras for the sick. She has a kitchen in which is a stove, and all I have to do is to send her word what I want prepared for the patients.

We have a large kitchen in which are three stoves, where the diet

[11] In a similar situation Miss Pember wrote of the position of a matron: " Added now to the other difficulties was the dragonship of the Hesperides,—the guarding of the liquefied golden fruit to which access had been open to a certain extent before her reign." *A Southern Woman's Story,* 33.

is prepared for those who are on the diet-list. Many a time there are two hundred patients fed from it.

The kitchen itself does very well in good weather, but when it rains the cooks, stoves, and every thing else in it get a shower-bath.

It has no chimneys, and the stove pipes are put through the roof, without an elbow or any covering. Many a time the cooks are up all night, trying to keep the water out of the stoves. But no matter what happens, the breakfast is always ready at the right time.

There is a kitchen for the convalescents, which has a brick furnace with boilers and an oven in it. We have also a very fine bakery. All has been put up since we have been here, at government expense.

Our hospital, with the exception of the tents, which are by themselves, occupies a square of store buildings, and the courthouse. Many of the buildings are in a dilapidated condition, but they are all nicely whitewashed, and kept in perfect order.

Miss Womack received a letter from a cousin, a surgeon in the army, entreating her to leave the hospital, saying that it is no place for a refined, modest young lady. I have perhaps made a mistake as regards the meaning of the word modesty. As far as my judgment goes, a lady who feels that her modesty would be compromised by going into a hospital, and ministering to the wants of her suffering countrymen, who have braved all in her defense, could not rightly lay claim to a very large share of that excellent virtue—modesty—which the wise tell us is ever the companion of sense. . . .

I am thoroughly disgusted with this kind of talk. When will our people cease to look on the surface of things? At this rate, never! If the scenes we are daily witnessing will not serve to cure this miserable weakness, nothing will.

There is scarcely a day passes that I do not hear some derogatory remarks about the ladies who are in the hospitals, until I think, if there is any credit due them at all, it is for the moral courage they have in braving public opinion.

A very nice lady, a member of the Methodist Church, told me that she would go into the hospital if she had in it a brother, a surgeon. I wonder if the Sisters of Charity have brothers, surgeons, in the hospitals where they go? It seems strange that they can do with honor what is wrong for other Christian women to do.

Well, I can not but pity those people who have such false notions of propriety.

After getting tired of hearing what is said, I told a lady friend that she would oblige me by telling the good people of Newnan, that when I first went into the hospitals I was not aware of there being such a place in the world as Newnan, and they must excuse me for not asking their advice on the subject; and since without it I had taken the step I had, I could not say I had any thing to regret in the matter; far from that, I can truly say, that there is no position in the world that a woman can occupy, no matter how high or exalted it may be, for which I would exchange the one I have. And no happiness which any thing earthly could give, could compare with the pleasure I have experienced in receiving the blessings of the suffering and dying.

As for no " refined or modest " lady staying in them, from my own experience, and that of every surgeon whom I have heard speak on the subject, I have come to the conclusion that, in truth, none but the " refined and modest " have any business in hospitals. Our post surgeon called on me the other day, and told me he had determined to permit none but such to enter any of his hospitals; and he earnestly warned me to be careful whom I took to stay with me.

But I feel confident we shall always have the approval of the truly good. I have not asked Miss Womack to remain; her own sense of right has determined her to do so.

Mrs. Byrom and I took a walk to the graveyard last Sunday. We saw two of our men buried; one was named S. Brazelton, a member of the Fiftieth Alabama Regiment; the name of the other I did not learn; he came from some of the other hospitals. All the men of our hospital are now buried by the chaplain, Mr. Moore.

The graves have head-boards, on which is the occupant's name and regiment.

We had a man by the name of Vaughn die very suddenly on the 3d.

Sunday, December 13.—A gloomy, rainy day. We had service in the carriage ward. Rev. Mr. Ransom, a chaplain from Tennessee, preached an excellent sermon. He told us that the Lord was dealing with us as a surgeon would with sick and wounded men; that we were morally sick, and the Lord was giving us bitter medicines.

I looked about the ward, which is very large, and there were the halt, the lame, and the blind, all eagerly drinking in the words of comfort. Miss J. Lowe, a lady of the place, Miss Womack, Mrs. Williamson, and myself were there. We always made a rule of attending service when it is held in the wards, as we think it gives encouragement to the men.

The reason we have service there is because there are always numbers of wounded men anxious to hear the word of God, and are not able to leave their beds.

December 16.—A very disagreeable day; it is cold, windy, and rainy. I have managed to get round the wards once; nearly all are doing well.

I have spent a good portion of the day with one of our patients, who died to-night at 9 o'clock. Miss Womack and myself were with him when he breathed his last.

He was a young Texan, by the name of Thomas Watson, a member of the Fourth Texas Regiment—one of General Hood's men—and came here with some members of his company, who were wounded, to nurse them. A few days ago he was taken with double pneumonia and sore

179

throat. Dr. Wellford attended him, and did all that mortal could do, but in vain. It was God's will he should go.

He was a handsome lad, in his eighteenth year, and was a general favorite. He often told Miss Womack and myself about his mother, and how she had buckled on his armor, and told him to go and battle for his country.

When he was informed that all hope was over, he sent for me, and told me what he wished done. He wanted the money due him collected and sent to his mother. This I tried to have done, but there was no paymaster here, and we have been told that it will be impossible. He then asked me to write, and tell her he was dying happy, and hoped to meet her in heaven.

Toward night he became delirious, and raved about the battles in which he had participated. He spoke a good deal about some ladies in the place who had been very kind to him; and, more than any thing else, he raved about his mother—spoke to her as he had no doubt done when a child. Toward the last he grew calm, and recognized Miss Womack and myself, who were standing by, and thanked us for past kindness. I wiped the clammy sweat from his forehead, and brushed back the brown curls clustering on it. He muttered a prayer, and while it was on his lips his spirit took its flight to God, who gave it. Mr. Moore has attended him closely since he was first taken. He and another chaplain, Mr. Daniel, were with him this evening.

After our return, Miss Womack told me that she had experienced more real pleasure to-night than she had at all the places of amusement which she had ever attended. I observed the night as we came back, and I never saw such a sky in my life; it was dark in the extreme. . . .

December 17.—Miss Womack, Mrs. M., and myself went to Mr. Watson's grave. We got there in time to see the coffin lowered, and the sod cover his remains. I trust his spirit has gone " where the wicked cease from troubling, and the weary are at rest." He was laid with the true and the brave. No one could wish " couch more magnificent."

Sunday, December 20.—A very cold day. The patients are all doing pretty well.

Yesterday we lost another of our nurses, named Crittenden. He was about the same age as Mr. Watson. He was a member of the Fifth South Carolina Regiment. He was ill but a few days, and died from the effects of a sore throat. He was a sincere Christian, and leaves no relatives to mourn for him.

On the 15th, Mr. Robertson died from the effects of a wound in the calf of one of his legs. Gangrene had set in, which destroyed the muscles and integuments extensively. He suffered severely, and nothing could be done to relieve him. Some ladies of the place took great interest in him and were very kind. He was a member of the Sixtieth

North Carolina Regiment. His mother lives in Cherokee County, North Carolina, on the borders of Tennessee.

Another man died the same day, named Wm. Kirwin, a member of the Eighth Arkansas Regiment, who has a sister living in Issart County, Arkansas. He suffered a long time from consumption.

In a Mobile paper of the 14th inst. is a letter from Richmond, signed " Gamma." The writer says he knows of four commissaries and quartermasters there who have made fortunes since the war. One, when he entered the service, was not worth a dollar, but after being in office a year and a half bought a farm for fifty thousand dollars, and has now retired with as much more on which to live. The other three are, if any thing, worse.

Is the president powerless to remove this moral leprosy which is eating the very vitals of the Confederacy? I really think that honest men who wink at those things are nearly as bad as the culprits. I am acquainted with one instance where we all knew there was as plain a case of robbery as any could be, but nothing was done to the miscreant.

Is was reported that one of General Bragg's quartermasters was making thousands off the government.

General Bragg, on making inquiry, had proof enough against him to have him tried. He sent word to the president some two or three times before he could get him to have any thing done in the matter. At last this quartermaster underwent a trial. Fraud after fraud was proved on him; but as some of our most influential men had become his security to a large amount, they managed to get him off with the *penalty* of his losing his commission. I consider the bitterest foe we are fighting openly better than such a man.

Christmas-day, December 25.—We have had quite a pleasant one. Miss Womack and myself were up hours before daylight making eggnog. We wished to give some to all in the hospital, but could not procure eggs enough; so we gave it to the wounded who are convalescent, the cooks, and the nurses.

Just at peep of dawn the little gallery in front of our house was crowded with the wounded. The scene was worthy of a picture; many of them without a leg or an arm, and they were as cheerful and contented as if no harm had ever happened them. I constantly hear the unmarried ones wondering if the girls will marry them now. Dr. Hughes did his best to have a nice dinner for the convalescents and nurses. Turkeys, chickens, vegetables, and pies. I only wish the men in the army could have fared as well.

In the afternoon we had a call from all of our surgeons, and from one or two from the other hospitals. I had hard work to get Mrs. Williamson to spare a few hours from working for " her dear boys," and have a kind of holiday for once, as nearly all of our wounded are doing well. Mr. Deal is still suffering very much, but his surgeon, Dr. Wellford, thinks he will save his leg.

181

We have only lost one or two from gangrene. I am confident that nothing but the care and watchfulness bestowed on them by the surgeons has been the means of saving the lives of many. Their recovery has taken me by surprise, as I could not see how it was possible for such bad wounds to heal.

Many of the wounded are still in tents, with chimneys which smoke badly, and the whole tent has rather an uncomfortable appearance; still I like tents for wounded, as they seem to improve much more rapidly in them than in rooms.

The nurses, on windy nights, are compelled to sit up and hold on to the tent-poles to prevent their being blown down.

Drs. Divine, Reese, Wellford, and Burks are our assistant surgeons. Dr. Divine is one of the best of his profession; he is from Mississippi. Dr. Reese is an odd kind of a man; seems to be an excellent doctor, but I think is rather rough with the wounded, though he is very kind and attentive. He is from Alabama. Dr. Wellford is a perfect Virginia gentleman. He is one of the gentlest and most attentive surgeons that I have ever met. I think we owe the recovery of many of the wounded mainly to his great care. I have known him many a time work from daylight till dark attending to the wounds. Dr. Burks of Kentucky has been here but a short time; so I can say little about him. The men all like him very much, and they are generally good judges. He has taken Dr. Glenn's place, the latter having been transferred to some other post.

Dr. Wellford has a nurse from Arkansas. He came here with the wounded after the battle of Chickamauga. We called him "rough diamond," as he is so rough-looking, and seems to have such a kind heart. He thinks nothing a trouble which he has to do for the wounded.

Another is Mr. Harper. The wounded men have told me that it annoyed them to see him work as much as he does.

We are using a great deal of charcoal on the wounds, and the nurses have it to pulverize, which gives them constant work, besides the dirt which it causes in the wards.

I see by Mobile papers that Captain Hazard, of the Twenty-fourth Alabama Regiment, was captured at Missionary Ridge. Mr. C. Larbuzan [Labuzan] is badly wounded, and also a prisoner. Mobile has suffered not a little in this respect.

General Bragg has resigned. For his own sake and ours, I am heartily glad.

Sunday, December 27.—Mr. Moore had service in one of the wards, and preached a very good sermon. He is a great favorite with the men.

We had one man die yesterday; another is dying to-day. It is bitter cold, and pouring down rain.

December 30.—I have spent the whole day trying to get milk for the sick, and I think I have succeeded in securing a little. We have two cows, but the milk they give is but a mite, compared to what we need. Many of the convalescent soldiers go round to the citizens begging for milk, who think they can not make better use of it than giving it to them. I do not doubt but these soldiers are in want of it; still we have others to whom it is a necessity.

Lincoln has again refused to exchange prisoners. I do think this is the cruelest act of which he has been guilty, not only to us, but his own men. He is fully aware that we can scarcely get enough of the necessaries of life to feed our own men; and how can he expect us to feed his. Human lives are nothing to him; all the prisoners we have might die of starvation, and I do not expect they would cost him a thought, as all he has to do is to issue a call for so many more thousands to be offered up on his altars of sacrifice. How long will the people of the North submit to this Moloch. He knows that every one of our men is of value to us, for we have not the dregs of the earth to draw from; but our every man is a patriot, battling for all that is dear to him.[12]

December 31.—One of the stormiest and bleakest nights I have ever witnessed. I looked out and the darkness was fearful. The sky appeared as if God had shut out the light of his countenance from us forever. The elements are warring like our poor selves.

I never look on such a night without thinking of the soldier who may be at that moment doing sentinel duty. How dreary must be his walk as he paces along,

> " And thinks of the two on the low trundle-bed,
>   Far away in the cot on the mountain;
> His musket falls slack, his face, dark and grim,
>   Grows gentle with memories tender,
> As he mutters a prayer for the children asleep,
>   And their mother, may Heaven defend her." [13]

Another sun has run its yearly course, and to all appearances we arc no nearer the goal of liberty than we were this day last year. No

---

[12] " Whatever the feelings of resentment on the part of the Confederates may have been against those who were invading and desolating their native land . . . the desire for the speedy exchange and return of the great army of veterans, held captives in Northern prisons, was earnest and universal; and this desire for speedy and continuous exchange on the part of the government, as well as on the part of the people, sprang not merely from motives of compassion for their unfortunate kindred and fellow-soldiers, but also from the dictates of that policy, which would exchange on the part of a weak and struggling people, a large army of prisoners (consumers and non-combatants, requiring an army for their safe-keeping) , for an army of tried veterans." Jones, *Medical and Surgical Memoirs*, III, pt. 1, 405.

[13] This is a portion of the third stanza of " All Quiet Along the Potomac To-Night," a poem by Mrs. Ethel Lynn Eliot Beers set to music by John Hill Hewitt and published in four Confederate editions. The controversy concerning its authorship is discussed in Harwell, *Confederate Music*, 80-81. A facsimile of a Confederate music sheet of it appears in his *Songs of the Confederacy* (New York, 1951) , 88-89.

gleam of light comes to tell us that reason has returned to the darkened minds of our ruthless foe. We have to listen to tales of wrong committed on our people, enough to rouse the blood in the coldest heart, and make us in despair cry aloud for vengeance. . . .

In the past year we have suffered disaster after disaster, but nothing is worth having which does not cost a struggle; and, then, as our beloved president tells us, it is only for a little while. The enemy has brought army after army against Richmond, and have as often had to retire in dismay and confusion before the invincible Lee and his veteran army.

The enemy have the Mississippi River only in name. Louisiana is almost as free from them as it has been since the fall of New Orleans. Texas is ours. Mississippi is guarded by that king of cavalrymen, Forrest. Charleston,

> " Through coming years its name
> A talisman shall be."

Shell after shell has been hurled against its sacred walls. Column after column of the invader round it have found graves.

Ah! would I could say as much about Tennessee. How my heart sickens at the desecration of her sacred vales and mountains! Our dead are not permitted to lie in their resting-places; houses are fired, and their inmates cast out into the ruthless storm. . . .

On the water we have the gallant Captains Semmes and Maffitt, bringing dismay to the grasping Yankee, by destroying what to him is dearer than life.

We have many true and determined men yet, who will never yield as long as the life-blood streams through their veins. I have no fear for our cause; our martyrs have not offered up their lives in vain. . . .

184

VIII: NEWNAN, MOBILE

January 1, 1864.—A bitter cold day. The sun is shining as brilliantly as if there never had been a cloud to veil its glory. I trust it is ominous of the coming year, and that the clouds overhanging our national horizon may soon vanish forever. . . .

Mr. Sparks, who suffered so much from his wound after walking about, has had his leg amputated. He seems a great deal better, and does not now suffer so much.

Sunday, January 3.—Part of our hospital was destroyed by fire last night. It originated in the officers' quarters of the Buckner Hospital, through the negligence of a negro servant. I have been told that some of the officers who were wounded nearly lost their lives. We lost two buildings; they had few patients in them, and no one was hurt.[1] But a short time since they were filled with badly wounded, who, fortunately, had been removed.

We had stores and every thing else moved from our rooms. Among them were two barrels of whiskey, a box of coffee, the latter just received from Wilmington, and many other valuables.[2] We lost nothing except a quantity of hospital clothing.

[1] Dr. William T. McAllister reported to Dr. C. B. Gamble in a letter of January 3, 1864: "I have the honor to report that last night one of my wards, which was used for Commissioned Officers, was burned. It contained (38) thirty eight Bunks. The loss of Government property was very inconsiderable. The greater part of the building was saved. The principal loss being (2) two Small Cooking Stoves. I regret the misfortune, but it was one of those accidental occurrences which will sometimes occur in despite of the best precautions. The fire originated in an adjoining Cook Kitchen." To Dr. Stout in a letter of the same date Dr. Gamble reported the destruction of two wards by this fire. After an inspection trip only a few weeks before Dr. Bemiss had written the Medical Director on November 28, 1863: "I have to state in conclusion that surgeons in charge of hospitals that I have visited are not as a general rule as careful to guard against fire as they should be." Dr. Bemiss particularly noted the danger of placing stoves too near woodwork. Stout Papers (Emory).

[2] "I insisted that no sloppy substitutes for coffee should be served at the hospital tables—that the *bona fide* article should alone be used—that when the commissaries could not supply it, messengers be sent to the ports of Charleston and Wilmington to purchase it from blockade runners in car-load lots and distributed to the hospitals. The last car load of coffee purchased at Wilmington for the use of the hospitals cost twelve dollars in Confederate currency per pound." Stout, "Some Facts . . . ," *Southern Practitioner*, XXV (1903), 281.

Mr. Sparks is injured. He was not near the fire, but became very much alarmed, and is now suffering very much.

We have no fire-engines, and all did their part in arresting the flames. Dr. Hughes is an old gentleman, but worked harder than any one.

A number of parties have been given here lately. Miss Womack cried out: " O, if the people would only keep from dancing, we would not have this trouble." I believe I echoed her sentiments.

Mrs. Johnston visited the wards with me this afternoon. The men, with the exception of one or two, are doing well.

Mrs. Williamson always spends Sunday in the wards, and benefits the men much by talking to them.

After we had left Chattanooga, on a visit there, I met one of the nurses who was with us in the Newsom Hospital, and he was very low with typhoid fever. He inquired anxiously after Mrs. Williamson, and said that, since lying on his sick-bed, he had often thought of her, and all he had heard her say to the patients, and wished he had profited more by her counsels. He was removed from Chattanooga to Ringgold. Mrs. Williamson went to see him, and he told her he had resolved to lead a new life, and that her teaching had been the means of converting him. This is not an isolated case, by any means.

I am often afraid that Mrs. Williamson will injure herself with work. She never sees a man with ragged clothes but she mends them for him, and many a night 12 o'clock does not find her in bed.

I often think of how much good the ladies of this place could accomplish in this respect. Many a man goes back to the front as ragged as he came from it. I had determined to let this subject drop, but somehow I always get back to it. I can not help losing my temper when I see so many idle women unwilling to do any little thing for these heroes, who have suffered so much.

I hinted to some of the ladies about having tobacco bags made, as the tobacco gets scattered all over the beds, but none offered to make them; some were kind enough to give me the pieces to have them made. After the labors of the day are past, Miss Womack and myself make as many as we can.

January 4.—It has rained so hard to-day that I have been unable to visit the wards.

It is rumored that there will be a raid here soon, from Rome. No one seems to give the rumor credit. There is a direct road from here to that place.

Had a visit in the afternoon from Drs. Reese and Burks. Dr. Burks was in Columbus when Mrs. Ogden went there, and said he never regretted any thing more than her leaving that place. He said the Mobile ladies had done much good during their short stay there.

January 11.—The weather still bad. We had five of Scott's cavalry dine with us to-day. They are friends of Dr. Hughes and Miss

186

Womack, and are Louisianians. They are very hopeful of our cause, but we seldom meet a soldier down-hearted. It is only the home folks who grumble.

Miss Womack is one of the most enthusiastic southerners I have met. She is from Louisiana, and, like Governor Brown about Georgia, thinks the other states all very well in their way, but they are not Louisiana.

These gentlemen informed her of a friend in Louisiana who had married a Federal general. They were all a good deal annoyed that this lady had lowered herself in such a manner. I told Miss Womack that no Alabama girl would be guilty of such a disgraceful act. She replied, that the girl was so ugly that no Confederate would marry her.

Miss Womack is the daughter of a wealthy planter, and, like many of the rest of our ladies, is determined to be independent of foreign manufacture. She has three pretty homespun dresses of different colors, which she manufactured herself, out of the raw cotton. She has also knit a number of pairs of socks for the soldiers.

January 15.—The weather has cleared off, and all seem glad of the change.

Mr. Bradley has had his arm amputated; he came here with a slight wound on his elbow, made by an ax. Gangrene got into it, and could not be arrested. It eat so rapidly that the joint was nearly destroyed.

Sunday, January 17.—Went to the Methodist Church, now reopened for service. Mr. Holland, a young man, apparently not over eighteen years of age, from Kentucky, preached.[3] To all appearance his sermon was extempore. His language was most eloquent, and he spoke with great fluency. His subject was prayer, and he discoursed on the mysterious power of that great moral lever with all the clearness and force of an able and experienced divine. He is certainly a young man of extraordinary abilities.

In the evening Mr. Moore preached an excellent sermon in a ward filled with patients. We burn tallow-candles, and we always carry ours with us to light up the ward, as well as we can.

I often think of these meetings, and how strange every thing has turned. The ward is usually filled with men dressed in all kinds of uniforms, and some, unable to be up, are in their bunks. The ward is

[3] Once a private soldier in General Morgan's command, Robert Afton Holland was chaplain of Buford's Brigade at Perryville. He later came south and joined the Georgia Conference of the Methodist Episcopal Church, South. He is described as "not yet twenty" in 1864 in Dr. Cross's *Camp and Field.* Dr. Cross wrote of him: "Having ascertained that a chaplain could do comparatively little among the cavalry, he determined to connect himself with the infantry. Pending this transition, however, he attended the Georgia Conference at Macon, and was persuaded to cast in his lot with that noble brotherhood of Christian ministers. He was a perfect stranger . . . yet the Bishop readily assented to his transfer, and appointed him to Thomaston circuit. Having preached there for a year with great success, he is now doing a good work in Newnan, both for the Church and for the military hospitals." III & IV, 287.

dimly lighted, but not too dim to prevent us distinguishing the faces of the men, and see the eagerness with which they listen to the expounding of the word of God, and the words of comfort in the solemn prayers which are offered up in their behalf, and frequently in behalf of our cruel enemies.

January 20.—A beautiful day. I have received a letter from my brother. As usual, it is filled with bright hopes of the future—pictures of the enemy flying in dismay and confusion the next time they meet, and wiping out the disgrace of Missionary Ridge. He says they are in comfortable winter-quarters, having built log-cabins. He had a nice Christmas dinner sent from home.

In a letter from Mrs. Dr. Burt, who is now living with her father, in the upper part of Georgia, among the mountains, she says the people there are almost starving, and that our cavalry behave very badly, taking every thing they can lay their hands on; and that her mother and self are compelled to hide their jeans from them. I regret hearing of our own people doing such things.

Sunday, January 24.—The Coweta House is now a ward in the Bragg Hospital for the accommodation of Florida troops. Mrs. Harrison and a friend of hers, Mrs. Harris, from Florida, are its matrons.

This morning Dr. Adams, an assistant surgeon, who is a deacon in the Episcopal Church, had prayers in one of the rooms. The service was attended mainly by refugees, as there has never been an Episcopal Church in this place. There is a Methodist, Baptist, and Presbyterian Church here. Dr. Gamble, Mrs. Gamble, and Mrs. Harrison, are members of the Episcopal Church, and also some of the officers who are stationed at the post, and their families.

January 25.—I sat up last night until 12 o'clock, with the corpse of a young child, daughter of a Mrs. Shivers. Others were there, and they had quite a political discussion, a lady taking the lead. She denounced President Davis, and said Stephens should be in his place. I sometimes think it is such a pity, that women are not allowed to hold office, as they seem to know *exactly* how things should be managed.

Colonel I. T. Berry of the Sixty-sixth Georgia Regiment was there. He is lame from a wound received at one of the battles in Virginia. He had served under Jackson, and said he did not admire him as a commander, as he was entirely too reckless. Colonel Berry is a very handsome man, of a well-informed mind and fine conversational powers. He is a graduate of West Point.

January 29.—We are sadly in want of comforts, cotton to make mattresses, spoons, knives and forks, and in fact every thing. Many of our men have to eat their food with their fingers.

A few days ago I went up to Atlanta with the hope of getting some of these things from Dr. Blackie, our medical purveyor, but he had gone to Montgomery. I went into one of the stores to see at what price

I could buy them. The commonest kind of knives and forks were one hundred and fifty dollars per dozen; the same for common spoons, and cups and saucers.[4]

I see by the papers, that the people in Atlanta are raising large sums of money to equip General Morgan's cavalry.

General Morgan is at present in Richmond, and has had great honors showered on him. He has visited Libby Prison, and says the contrast of our treatment of prisoners with that of the northern people is very great, and he does not wish us to imitate the latter in their severity. There is not much fear of our doing so.

January 31.—Arrived in Mobile to-day about 12 o'clock P. M., having left Newnan on the 29th.

While crossing Mobile Bay on the steamer, we came near having a disaster. The boat ran against one of the forts with which the bay is filled. We got off without any damage. We were all very much alarmed. Captain Richmond, brother of the late Major Richmond, was on board, who kindly offered to assist me in case of an accident.

March 3.—I returned to Newnan some few days ago. I had quite a pleasant time in Mobile; I found it gayer than ever. The excuse is, that there are so many soldiers there away from their homes, and the ladies say they must do what they can to entertain them. Quite a plausible reason!

I noticed that the privates and officers mingled together at the festivities.

At one party which I attended (indeed the only one) the order of things was reversed; the ladies waited on the gentlemen, as they say it is an honor to wait on soldiers. The refreshments consisted of coffee mixed with rye, with sugar and milk, wheat-bread, and butter. These are luxuries now.

While visiting, the whole topic of conversation is, What can be procured to eat? This pervades all classes of society, and has ceased to be a vulgarism. The greatest treat that can be given is a cup of coffee or tea, with milk and sugar.

They have a very nice oil, distilled from pitch, called Confederate, which is a great improvement on the " pine-knot " lights.

I went shopping with a lady, who paid eight dollars per yard for a calico dress, ten for a gingham, twenty for a common delaine; children's boots fifty dollars; ladies', seventy-five.

Many of the ladies were dressed in homespun, which makes very pretty street dresses when trimmed, but they are not economical, as they do not wash as well as calico.

---

[4] " At Marietta, Georgia . . . a detailed soldier was found who was a potter by trade. This man, a German by birth, was ordered by the surgeon in charge to manufacture cups, saucers, dishes, plates, mugs, pitchers, bowls, bed pans and chamber pots. The output of the pottery was soon adequate for the supply of deficiencies in the hospitals." Stout, " Some Facts . . . ," *Southern Practitioner*, XXV (1903) , 281.

Provisions are higher than ever. The most influential men we have, that is, among the non-combatants, have formed themselves into a society called the Supply Association, for the benefit of those who are short of means. They send agents around the country who buy as they can, and the food is retailed by these gentlemen at cost; and I believe besides they see that soldiers' families who can not buy do not suffer for want of food.

They have what is called a free market; it is supported wholly by donations of money and provisions. Many of the planters send all kinds of vegetables to it.

I made the acquaintance of some members of the Twenty-ninth Alabama Regiment, with whom I was much pleased. I went to a review of the regiment; as it has never been in a battle, it was complete in every way. The men were a contrast with the war-worn veterans that I had been accustomed to see. As it was expected to be soon sent to the front, I could not help feeling sad when looking at the review. " For a field of the dead rushed red on my sight." *

I never will look again on a regiment of soldiers with pleasure.

This regiment is commanded by Colonel Connelly [Conoley]. It was with General Bragg's army at Pensacola, and when that army went to Mississippi, it was sent on duty to Mobile.

While I was in Mobile, the cry that " the enemy is coming " was raised two or three times. There was a report that an immense army was coming through Florida, another through Mississippi, and another by Pascagoola [Pascagoula], and at the same time the fleet was to attack the forts down the bay. For a little while poor Mobile seemed as if it was going to be gobbled up all at once, but the enemy have found a few stumbling-blocks in their way. " All their views have come to naught," and the Mobilians breathe free again; although I expect only for a little while, as I have no idea but what the enemy will honor it with a visit.

The mayor and General Maury had large bills posted, begging the people to leave, telling them they intended to defend the city at all hazards, but the people paid little heed to them, as the cry of wolf has been raised so often that this time they were determined to wait till he came. Many of them had gone, and, getting tired of waiting, had returned, and were not to be sent off so easily again.

I visited the fortifications, which seem to be very formidable. The city is all cut up, and many a beautiful garden and tree has been demolished.

I also visited a very fine gun-boat—the *Tennessee*—said to be one

* The records of nearly all our regiments have been lost, so that it is almost impossible to get a correct account of our losses. Captain Abernethy, who had command of this gallant regiment at the battle of Franklin, when but a remnant of it remained, told me that it went into that battle with twenty-three officers; after it was over, twenty of them and over two hundred privates lay prostrate on the field.

of the largest afloat. Lieutenant Jordan, one of the officers, kindly showed us all over. It is a ram, and has many a dark-looking corner, where the men are to be stowed away in case of a battle. All looked very mysterious. I certainly felt I should not like to be one of the crew. There were a few more gun-boats nearly completed, but we did not go on board of them.

My old friend, Rev. Mr. Miller, is now post chaplain of Mobile. I visited a library which he has for the use of the soldiers.

Since my last visit to Mobile many of her brave sons have been laid low in the dust, and many a once happy home left desolate.

Mrs. Otis's son, Mr. Bancroft, a member of the Third Alabama Regiment, was severely wounded at the battle of Chancellor[s]ville. His fate is still uncertain, as the tent he was in was set on fire by a shell, and many suppose he was burned up. What a terrible fate! How I do pity his poor mother; but her trust is in God.

Mrs. Wilson's son, Eugene, a member of the Eighth Alabama Regiment, was killed at Gettysburg. I had known him when a little boy. He was a member of the " Mobile Blues," and, like nearly all of that company, has offered up his young life on the altar of his country. His poor mother could not speak to me, her heart was so full. May God be with and strengthen all such!

On leaving Mobile, my friend, Mr. McLean, introduced me to his friend, Mr. Labuzan, who kindly offered to escort me as far as Montgomery. He was on his way to the interior of Alabama, in search of a home for his family, having decided to take them from the city. Mr. Labuzan is one of many who have suffered by the war. He has three sons in the army; one, Catesby, was badly wounded at Missionary Ridge; he is now a prisoner, and his father has no idea at this moment that he lives. When his family last heard from him, his life was almost despaired of. I am told, a nobler boy never fought for his country.

On the cars from Montgomery to West Point, I met a very nice lady, Mrs. Davis, from Marion, Alabama. When she left that place she said there was great excitement there, expecting the enemy. She was then on her way to Georgia, where her father lives.

On the cars from West Point I met Lieutenant Sewell, of the Twenty-fourth Alabama Regiment, who had been on furlough to Mobile. He said he thought the times looked very gloomy. I asked him how long he had been in Mobile. He replied, " Two weeks." I said, " Just long enough to be demoralized, as no one near or in the army ever spoke of gloomy times." He answered, that was a fact; that the further he got from the army the more demoralized the people were. He then paid the usual compliments to the ladies. I told him of this talk I really had become weary, and I thought they did not deserve all that was said in their praise, and if we were whipped they would be to blame. I also said a man did not deserve the name of man, if he did not fight for his country; nor a woman, the name of woman, if she did not do all in her power to aid the men. Even when

191

a woman does her best, it is a mite compared with what our men have to endure. He had the candor to acquiesce in all I said.

I found very few of my former patients here. Many of the very worst cases of gangrene are cured, and the subjects walking about. Some of the men have been furloughed, and gone home; others, whose homes are in the enemy's lines, have gone to stay with friends. Mr. Moore, the lad who was wounded through the lungs at the battle of Chickamauga, is still unable to move himself, and he has scarcely ever been heard to murmur. He is a great sufferer, as he has a bad cough. We call him our pet. He is from North Carolina, and his people have suffered much from the enemy.

A number of our nurses and cooks have been sent to the front. I regret this, as they were nearly all good men. We have to go to work now and teach others.

March 11.—We have very few patients at present. I have been very busy fixing up my old clothes. It takes much more time to make the old clothes look well than to make new ones. I often wonder what our Yankee sisters would say if they saw what shifts we are put to. I suppose they think it grieves us, but they are mistaken, for it is a subject of mirth, as we, like the men, have become philosophers.

Miss Womack's sister lately paid her a visit. She is a high-spirited Louisiana girl. She has just left school, and intends, after paying a visit to some relatives in East Georgia, to go with another lady and take charge of a hospital in West Point, Ga. Dr. Oslin, the surgeon in charge there, says he will have no ladies in his hospital excepting educated and refined ones. At present he has none. She is quite as enthusiastic as her sister on the subject of Louisiana, and quarreled with one of the nurses, a native of Georgia, but a member of a Louisiana regiment, because he called himself a Louisianian.

There has been a skirmish near Dalton. We drove the enemy back to their intrenchments.

March 22.—Our most Christian enemy, profiting by the teaching of such men as Beecher, not content to employ the scum of the earth to destroy us, have formed a plot foul enough to blacken the name of a Nero. They send a band of assassins into Virginia for the purpose of freeing the prisoners and setting them loose on the helpless inhabitants, with full power to do their worst and lay waste the whole country. Positive orders were given to give no quarter to President Davis and his cabinet. They were to be murdered. Richmond was to be left a mass of ruins. Colonel Dahlgren, one of the leaders in this dark conspiracy, has gone to his final account. Papers with the whole design and the names of his accomplices were found on his person. Some of the men in his command have been captured. Many of our people are insisting to have them hung as brigands, as they have forfeited all claim to be treated as prisoners of war; but our high-souled president is firm in his resolve not to have them punished. It is said that some of his cabinet have protested against this leniency, but to no effect.

We have had a very heavy fall of snow. All enjoyed it. Old and young were out snow-balling each other. Drs. Hughes and Burks got up a very fine equipage in the way of a sleigh. The runners were made by one of the men, and the carriage part was a packing-box. Instead of furs, blankets were used. The whole affair would have been a most *attractive* turnout in Broadway. After giving some of the Newnan ladies a drive, Dr. Hughes called and took Miss Womack. On her return she gave me a ludicrous description of her ride; said that the doctor had to get out and push her, the sleigh, and horse along. I did not venture in it, as it gave signs of dissolution, and I did not like the idea of being dumped into a bed of slush, or being forced to walk home through it.[5]

I have just received a letter from an officer who is in Longstreet's corps. He says our army has fallen back from Knoxville to a place called Lick Creek, on the Virginia road. This gentleman says that East Tennessee is completely sacked, and that he thinks many of the inhabitants will die of starvation. He also says there has been a religious revival in the army. The whole of that corps has re-enlisted for the war, no matter how long it may last. Our whole army has done the same.

I have been told that nearly all of East Tennessee is Union. One of the soldiers informed me that while passing through portions of it with prisoners, the ladies gave the best they had to the prisoners; and although our men were as much in want of food, they would not give them a mouthful.

March 24.—Numbers of soldiers are constantly passing to reinforce Johnston's army. They are mainly troops from Mobile. I have been told that the Seventeenth and Twenty-ninth Alabama Regiments are among them.

Good Friday, March 25.—It has poured down rain all day. Dr. Adams had prayers in the Coweta House.

I have bought a number of home-made socks and stockings. The socks cost two dollars per pair, and the stockings five dollars. Many of the poorer class of country people round here earn their living by knitting these articles and weaving cloth. There is no appearance of poverty among the people in this town. With the exception of tea,

[5] This was a famous snowfall in Georgia and provided the occasion for a long remembered snow battle between the divisions of Hardee's Corps encamped at Dalton. D. S. Heran wrote Mrs. S. E. D. Smith a detailed account of it on March 22. In full battle array, he declared, the battle continued all day. " Bugles were sounded, regiments formed, their colors proudly floating to the breeze, our field officer in command, the charge was sounded, and away we went with a yell . . . It was an exciting scene, and was engaged in by both officers and privates finely, and, I am happy to say, ended in the kindest feeling." Smith, *The Soldier's Friend*, 255-57.

coffee, and fresh beef, they seem to want for nothing. Nearly all have plantations a short distance from town, on which they raise stock of all kinds. I believe it is the same in all of the small towns in Georgia where the enemy has not been.

We have a great deal of trouble at present about our money. Bills above five dollars are heavily discounted. We are to have a new issue soon. It is said it will be a great improvement on the old.

Easter Sunday, March 27.—In the morning I went to the Coweta House to prayers. In the afternoon went to the Methodist Church, where the negroes had service. Mr. Holland preached a sermon suited to their understanding. After getting through he came down from the pulpit, and the negroes crowded around him, shaking his hands. They seemed perfectly happy; some of the older ones fairly dancing with joy. This excitement is in keeping with the excitable character of the negro—although we have an Episcopal Church in Mobile, which belongs to them, where they go through the service as solemnly as we do.

Sunday, April 3.—A very lovely day. Troops are still passing. In the morning Mrs. Williamson and myself took a walk to the depot to see if any of our friends were among the soldiers. Mrs. Williamson was expecting to see Mr. Tylman, from Mobile, a member of the Eighth Alabama Regiment, on his way to Virginia.

In the afternoon Miss Womack and I took a walk in the woods, in company with Mr. and Mrs. Bears [Beers] and Dr. Hughes. "The hoary worshipers of Deity" were budding forth with all the freshness and beauty of young spring. The woods were filled with wild flowers, and there was a soft, balmy spirit sighing through the trees, casting a soothing influence over all, making us forget for awhile the cares and strife with which we are surrounded. We sat for some time on the logs, and sang hymns, among them "Old Hundred," which brought memories of the past to us all. Dr. Hughes proved himself a very good singer. He is an enthusiastic southerner, over sixty years of age, and has left wife and home for the cause. He tells me that his daughters in Kentucky are indefatigable in working for the southern cause. They are very kind to our men who are in the northern prisons, as I am told that nearly all the women of that state are. They and many other ladies have made up thousands of suits of clothing for them, and taken them to the prisons in person. . . .

April 5.—We have just returned from a concert given by the ladies of this place for the benefit of the wounded at the expected battle. There was no attempt at any thing extra.

One young lady sang some simple, old-fashioned ballads with a great deal of taste.

A German, who has charge of the linen-room in the Buckner Hospital, played the violin and piano very well, but the crowning feature of the whole was the singing of Mrs. Dr. Gamble. Her voice is one of the finest amateur ones to which I have ever listened, and is highly cultivated. She sang one song, its name I have forgotten, that brought tears to all eyes. Another, " Ranch Desvache," was beautiful. She sang, with more taste than I have ever heard an American sing a Scotch song, the " Lass o' Gowrie," with which every one was so much pleased that many sent notes requesting her to repeat it, which she kindly did. Mrs. Beers, matron of the Buckner Hospital, sang " Home, Sweet Home," with a great deal of feeling. It scarcely does to sing such a song at present, as it touches the heart a little too deeply.[6]

Sunday, April 10.—A real April day, cloud and sunshine. This morning Dr. Adams preached a very interesting sermon. His text was, " Ye are my friends if ye do whatsoever I command you." I think it is a pity that he is not a chaplain instead of a surgeon. I told him so, but he says his health will not permit it.

There is a religious revival here in which the citizens take very little interest, but the soldiers a great deal.

Dr. McFerrin, a Methodist preacher, is holding it. He is a chaplain, and his very soul seems to be in the work. He is one of the most earnest preachers I ever heard.

The people are very gay. Nearly every night a party is given. The gentlemen who attend them are the *attachees* of the hospital and the officers of the post.

April 20.—When General Johnston took command of the army, he ordered that every tenth man should draw a two weeks' furlough, and then, if they chose, could transfer it to any of their comrades, which is often done by those whose homes are in the enemy's lines. There are many of the latter.

My brother has just called on his way to the army, having drawn a two weeks' furlough and been to Mobile. While there, he went to a party every night. He brought a number of tobacco bags with him, given him by the ladies, for, to use his own words, " some poor fellows whose mothers and sisters are in the enemy's lines." Miss Womack added to his stock, as the " poor fellows" are from Louisiana.

Lord John Russell has informed President Davis that he can not permit the building of rams for the " so-called " Confederate government, as that would be a breach of *that neutrality* which the British government has been so careful in keeping between the two nations.

[6] " Concerts, tableaux, plays, etc., were also given for the benefit of refugees or to raise money to send boxes to the front: at all these I assisted, but had no time for rehearsals, etc. I could only run over and sing my song or songs and then run back to my patients. Some money was realized, but the entertainments were never a great financial success, because all soldiers were invited guests. Still, some good was always accomplished. These amusements were greatly encouraged by physicians and others, as safety valves to relieve the high-pressure of excitement, uncertainty, and dread which were characteristic of the time." Beers, *Memories*, 114.

I think the less Lord Russell says on that subject the better; as, thanks to Smith O'Brien, and many others as good authority, we all know how that has been kept, and how Great Britain has aided the North in every possible way. If Britain feels that she can not consistently league with *barbarians* who have the *crime* of slavery dimming their national character, let her act honestly, and not cry neutrality with her voice while she is doing all in her power with her hands to aid our enemy: and to think how much stronger they are than we! I shall begin to think what I have often been told about Britain is true, that she is afraid of the North:

> " Is it England mocks us with her grief!
> Who hate but dare not chide the imperial thief! "

But from all we know, Lord Russell does not represent the feeling of the British people. Had they their way, we would have been recognized long ago.

President Davis's answer is worthy of the upright man, which he is. He tells Lord Russell that it is useless for him to try and blind us, when not a day passes without ships, laden with deluded people, leaving Britain to aid our enemies. I am certain that Davis would not be guilty of resorting to such a subterfuge as this lord has, even to save the country and cause, which we all know he has so much at heart.

April 25.—I have received a letter, of the 20th inst., from my brother. He says the enemy are reported in heavy force at Ringgold, and our army is anticipating an attack. He also says he has just got through washing his clothes, and is ready for them.

May 1.—I never saw a greater profusion of flowers than there is here, nor more beautiful ones. My kind friend, Mr. Dougherty, has given me full possession of his garden; so the soldiers get plenty, and they are very fond of them. We put them all over the wards.

May 4.—Yesterday we had quite a grand wedding in the place. Dr. Divine led to the altar Dr. Calhoun's eldest daughter. Dr. Quintard came from Atlanta to perform the ceremony, which took place in the Presbyterian Church, at 11 o'clock, A. M. The church was darkened, and lighted with lamps and candles, which did not burn very brightly. I thought the sunlight would have been in much better taste. There were nine bridesmaids, and the same number of groomsmen. Many of the latter came from the army for the occasion, as that number of young men, I do not expect, could be raised in the whole county. And, indeed, they were not all young men; I noticed one or two of our married surgeons among them. On looking at the ladies dresses, which were made of new Swiss muslin, I could not keep from wondering how much it had cost, and where such a quantity had come from. The article is very scarce at present; the last I heard of cost fifty dollars per yard. The whole scene at the wedding was quite pretty and impressive. I believe that this is the first time that an Episcopal clergyman in full canonicals has officiated in this place. I have been told that nearly all of the mules and carriage horses at the wedding were taken by an impressing officer. He kindly permitted the owners to ride home before taking them from them. It is said that he had heard of the affair, and laid in wait so the people could not hide them.

Dr. Quintard and Mrs. Harrison spent the previous evening with us. He has built a new church in Atlanta. Mrs. Harrison asked him how he procured the materials for it. He said that he paid a visit to a nail factory near it, preached once or twice, and baptized some children. He was then presented with as many nails as he needed. I believe he procured the lumber in the same manner. He told us that there had been a great religious revival throughout the whole army, many being converted and joining the church. Nearly all of our leading generals have joined. Bishop Lay, from Arkansas, is with the army, and is doing much good in winning souls to Christ.

Last evening Dr. Quintard preached to a large audience in the Methodist Church, from the text, " Be sure your sin will find you out." The sermon was very impressive. At its close Rev. Mr. Smith offered up an appropriate prayer.

Dr. Gamble has left his post. He has been appointed chief surgeon of General Anderson's division. The general is now in Florida. We all regret Dr. Gamble's leaving. Dr. Wible of Kentucky is his successor, and is very highly spoken of.

We have another hospital added to this post—the Gamble, so called in honor of Dr. Gamble. It is our old ward, the Springs. Dr. Divine is surgeon; Mrs. Dr. Wildman and a Miss Rigby are the matrons—both excellent ladies.

May 17.—There has been fighting near Dalton for some days. Our army has left that place, and is moving down, drawing the enemy with it. We are told that the enemy are suffering severe losses.

I went to Atlanta on the 15th instant, in company with some ladies and gentlemen of this place. We intended going to the scene of conflict, but, as the army is on the move, had to come back. We reached Atlanta on the morning of the 16th, about daylight. Mrs. Harris and myself went to the Gate City Hospital. It is the distributing one. There I met an old friend in Mr. Tucker, the head nurse. The hospital was filled with wounded, who had come in that morning from the front. Mr. Tucker told me that he had dressed the wounds of four hundred men since 4 o'clock the previous day. He had been up all that night at his work.

Mrs. Harrison was told that her son was wounded, and that he had been sent to Newnan.

That morning was one of the gloomiest I ever passed. It was damp and cheerless; and, look which way I would, the prospect was dreary. Hundreds of wounded men, dirty, bloody, and weary, were all around us. And when I thought of the many more which were expected, I was filled with despair, and felt like humbling myself in the dust, and praying more earnestly than ever before, that God would send us peace. . . .

We remained nearly all day in an old car, expecting to get on to the front. There was a relief committee, from Lagrange, in the same car with us. I observed that several such committees were in Atlanta, from every part of Georgia. The good people of Newnan had supplied us with quantities of every thing. In the afternoon, Mrs. Harris, Mrs. Barnes, Mrs. Auld and myself went to the cars, on their arrival from the front; and O, what a sight we there beheld! No less than three long trains filled, outside and in, with wounded. Nearly all seemed to be wounded in the head, face, and hands. I asked some one near me why this was. They replied, because our men had fought behind breastworks.

There were ladies at the depot with baskets filled with edibles of all kinds, and buckets of milk, coffee, and lemonade; and I noticed many had wines. I observed a number of old gentlemen assisting—the only manner in which they could serve their country. I noticed one in particular, an aristocratic-looking gentleman, who wore a white linen apron.

The ladies in Atlanta have been doing this work ever since the commencement of the war. They have had tables set at the depot for the benefit of the soldiers. Our party went to the distributing hospital; there we found plenty of work. A number of the Atlanta ladies were there before us, dressing wounds. I commenced to dress one man's hand, which was badly wounded. (Strange as it may seem, this was the first wound I had ever dressed. I had always had plenty of other work to do.) Just as I had got through, Dr. Jackson, who had gone with us from Newnan, requested me to come and assist him. We were in an immense hall, crowded with wounded; some walking about, others sitting on the floor—all waiting to have their wounds dressed. As soon as that was done, they were sent off to make room for others. Surgeons, ladies, and nurses were scattered all about, so intently employed that they did not seem to notice each other. I brought the patients to Dr. Jackson and unbound the stiff bandages from their wounds, making them ready for him to dress. These men were called by the surgeons slightly wounded. One poor fellow from Alabama had both hands disabled. From one he had lost all his fingers excepting the fourth and thumb; and on the other he was shot through the wrist. This man was perfectly helpless. There were many just such *slight* wounds. One or two had lost an eye. Dr. Wellford was near where we were, as busy as he could possibly be, one of the ladies assisting him as I was Dr. Jackson. After getting nearly through, I went into the rooms which were filled with badly wounded men in bed. I noticed many ladies bathing the men's faces and attending to their wants in other ways.

While in one of the rooms, a young man called me by name, and told me he had seen my brother the night before, and that he was well. This young man was named Laramar, from Mobile, a member of the Fortieth Alabama Regiment. There was another with him; his name, I think, was Reese, a member of the same regiment. There was also a Mr. Cox of Mobile, whom I knew, waiting on them. He is in the ordnance department in Atlanta.

Mr. Laramar informed me that the Seventeenth and Twenty-ninth Alabama regiments had suffered severely, and that Captain Haily [Hailey] of the Twenty-ninth was killed, and many of the others in that regiment.

It was a bright, moonlight night, and there were some folks who came into the hospital with provisions for the men. Dr. Wellford and a number of us took them and went all over, to see if we could find any in want, but nearly all had been supplied.

The men were lying all over the platform of the depot, preferring to remain there, so as to be ready for the train which would take them to other places.

I was informed that there were about seven or eight hundred wounded who had come in that evening.

Dr. Pursley is surgeon of the receiving hospital, and seemed to be doing all in his power for the sufferers. Every one in it looked wearied and worn out with the constant work which they had to do. The matron was very ill.

Dr. Bemiss, who is assistant medical director, was at the hospital, and going around in his usual kind manner, seeing that the men were attended to. About 10 o'clock he took Mrs. Harris and myself to Mrs. Lowenthall's, where he boarded, who received us very kindly.

There was a young man visiting her, who was dressed in the extreme of fashion, with the addition of a few diamonds. I could not help contrasting him with the men I had just seen, who had been fighting for every thing truly noble—wounded, covered with dust, and many of them in rags.

Foppish dress is bad taste in a man at any time; but if there is one time more than another when it is out of place, it is the present. And I can not see why men think of such things just now, as no woman whose opinion is of any value has respect for those who do.

I have heard soldiers (I mean the fighting kind) say, that nothing disheartens them so much as to see men so over-dressed.

I had promised Dr. Bemiss that I would remain to breakfast the next morning, forgetting I had promised Mr. Tucker to be at the hospital by daylight, as he expected hundreds of wounded.

I kept my first promise, and as Mrs. Harris did not feel very well, I went to the hospital by myself. While crossing the depot I met my friend, Mr. Gribble, and he accompanied me to it. On arriving there I found that no more wounded had come, but there were many there already, for whom I made toddies.

199

The scene which presented itself to me in the large room where we had been the night before was sickening.

There was pile after pile of rags, just as they had been taken from the wounds, covered with blood and the water used in bathing them. All of the attendants were too much exhausted to clean up.

These are things to which we have to shut our eyes, if we wish to do any good, as they can not be avoided.

I met Dr. Calvart [Calvert] of the Thirty-eighth Alabama Regiment, who requested me to get some rags for him, which I did, and assisted him as much as I could. He had some badly wounded men from his regiment.

Dr. Calvert told me he had not eaten any thing for some time. I gave him some coffee, bread, and meat; and when I recollect now the place in which he ate it, I think we can get used to any thing. It was in the room or hall which I have just described.

We had concluded to return to Newnan, and as the cars did not start till 9 A. M., I visited one of the other hospitals, Dr. Calvert going with me; I think the name of it was the Medical College. The building is a very handsome one, and had just been fitted up. Every thing about it was in perfect order. It is one of the nicest hospitals in which I have ever been. It was filled with badly wounded men, as I am told is the case with every hospital in Atlanta. I found men there from every state in the Confederacy.

We left Atlanta on the passenger-car, and when half-way down had to get out, as the freight train that had left some hours before had met with an accident, and blocked up the road.

We got into a freight-car in front; in it there was a very large man, who had been in the car on which the accident happened; he had got mashed between two beams; his collar-bone was broken and his chest very much bruised, so that it was with difficulty he could breathe. His face was so much bruised that his eyes were almost closed. There were a number of surgeons on the cars, who were very kind to him. He is in our hospital, under Dr. Wellford's care.

Major Davis of the Twentieth Alabama Regiment is at the Buckner Hospital, wounded in the head. On hearing he was from Mobile, I went to see him. He gave me a great deal of encouragement regarding this retreat of the army. Many can not understand why it is. He spoke very highly of General Johnston as a commander, and said he believed that in all his retreating he had not left as much as an old wheel for the enemy, and he never fought them unless he was certain of a victory. He also said that the men were better fed and better clad than they had ever been.

There is much talk at present about one of our cavalry officers, who is said to have killed six prisoners that he expected would be re-captured. It is reported that many of the men of the army have petitioned Gen. Johnston to send this officer to the enemy, and let them do what they please with him.

200

Major Davis approved of what the men had done, and regretted that their petition had not been granted, as no punishment could be too severe for any man guilty of such barbarity. He also told me the enemy had shot six of our innocent men in retaliation.

When will men cease to do what is unjustifiable in the eyes of both God and man?

Major Davis spoke highly of Ben Lane Poesy [Posey]; says he is one of the bravest men we have, although a little eccentric.

May 20.—I went up to Atlanta again, but as the army is still retreating I came right back. While there, I met Doctor and Mrs. Hopping, just from Kingston. They came away in a great hurry, leaving a large portion of the hospital stores behind. They did not receive orders to move until our army had entered Kingston. The enemy was expected in by Rome, so Johnston has had to fall back.

Mrs. Hopping represented the scene among the inhabitants at Kingston as harrowing, at the prospect of having the enemy come among them, as they carry ruin and desolation in their path.

While in search of Mrs. Harris I went into the Trout House, in the hall of which I saw a young man lying wounded. I learned he was from Mobile. His name is Leslie, and he is a member of the Seventeenth Alabama Regiment. His wound was not a bad one. He told me that his colonel was in the hotel severely wounded. I paid the latter a visit to see if I could be of any service to him, but found him doing much better than I had expected; his wife was with him.

The Seventeenth Regiment was in Mobile when I was there last; since then it has suffered very much.

I again visited the Gate City Hospital. There were not quite as many wounded as when I was last there. While standing on the gallery I heard a young man just come from a hospital in Cassville, grumbling very much at some doctor who had made him leave there in such a hurry that he had not time to get his clothes. He was giving it to officers in general, and spoke as if he was fighting to please them.

I listened awhile, and then asked him what he was fighting for. He replied, for his country. I then told him how he had been talking. He said he knew that it was wrong, but really the men had a great deal to endure from their officers.

I have heard many complaints of this kind; I think that often the men are to blame; they treat their officers with too much contempt.

Our officers should be the best of our men, and their rank respected if they are not.

Let the privates do their part, and if they have got petty officers over them who abuse the " little brief authority " with which they are clothed, take no notice of it, remembering that there are crosses which must be borne for the good of the cause, and that to " bear is to conquer."

I know that our men have a good deal to contend with in that respect, as our officers are elected as our civilians are, and whoever is the best electioneerer gets the office, and often not from any personal merit.[7] I am fearful that this same evil will be the means of doing much harm to our cause, if one half of the tales are true which we are constantly listening to, of the drunkenness and evil of all kinds of which these petty officers are guilty. I know of one instance, the truth of which I can vouch for.

The captain of a battery at one time was inebriated while the company was being drilled. He imagined that one of the men had treated him with contempt; so ordered him to be tied to one of the gun-carriages, and dragged behind for twenty miles. This was done by order of a man who, I am told, was never sober enough at the time of any of the battles to lead his men.

The man who had been thus badly treated was so indignant at the insult, that he immediately applied for an exchange into a company of sharp-shooters—many thought for the purpose of shooting the captain.

I asked a gentleman who had been telling me about some of these misdemeanors, why the culprits were not brought to justice, as drunkenness was a thing which our commanding generals seem very strict about. He answered, that there was a compact between the petty officers to defend each other at all hazards, so it was impossible for a private to have justice.

But we must expect the evil as well as the good. On the other hand, I know of officers so much beloved that their men would lay down their lives in their defense. And the terrible slaughter of our officers shows that there is no lack of bravery among them. It is said that in every battle we lose many more of them, in proportion, than we do privates.

I have seen enough of our men to know that they will do much better by good treatment than bad.

On the cars, coming back, I met Captain O'Rearin [O'Rear] of the Twenty-ninth Alabama Regiment; he was wounded slightly. He told me that he did not believe Captain Hailey was killed.

May 24.—We have good news from the Trans-Mississippi Department. General Taylor has gained a victory over General Banks in Louisiana.

---

[7] Company officers in the Confederate armies were generally elected by the soldiers. Such elections were not always conducive to the best discipline and were opposed by the leaders with military backgrounds, but Basil Duke wrote in defense of the system: " The officers elected by the regiments first raised were, generally, about the best men that could have been selected. The men, at that time, in good faith, chose those they believed best qualified for the duties of command, and elected individuals who had manifested, or were thought to possess, courage, energy, and good sense." Duke, *History of Morgan's Cavalry*, 79. For a concise discussion of the elective system see E. M. Coulter, *The Confederate States of America*, Vol. VII of " A History of the South " (Baton Rouge, 1950) , 229-30.

We have had more fighting in Virginia. General Longstreet is wounded. The enemy under Grant is trying to get Richmond by Petersburg. They are certainly very determined. If we hold Richmond against such odds as they bring against it, I think it will be a wonder.

I see by the Mobile papers that a relief corps is coming from there, but it will be useless to come while our army is on the move.

We have a number of the sick and wounded from the Twenty-ninth Alabama Regiment. One lad, in his sixteenth year, is very ill; he requested me to write to his father, and let him know where he is. I said why not write to your mother After hesitating awhile, tears filled his eyes, and with a quivering lip he told me she was deranged on account of her sons all leaving her for the army; he had run away two years ago. Dr. Hughes intends sending him home as soon as he is able to travel.

We get quantities of vegetables now. We have two nice gardens. Milk is still scarce.

Mrs. Brooks has taken charge of one of our large rooms. She sees that the worst cases in it are cared for, and provides them with milk and any other delicacies which they may require. This is of great assistance to me and great benefit to the patient.

We are kept very busy. Miss Womack takes charge of all the groceries, as I call them—whiskey, butter, etc.—and keeps a daily account of every thing that is received and issued, which is measured or weighed. The liquor of all kinds is given out on an order from the druggist, for each ward separately. I make a daily report to the steward of every article used in our kitchen, besides keeping a weekly and monthly account, not only of the articles consumed, but of all the cooking utensils, dishes, etc., which are used in the kitchen. In the care of the dishes I have the assistance of Mr. Bohannon, a nice young man, who is disabled by a wound.

I would not mind if we had more to do than we have; but I have found out that there is sly pilfering going on in the hospital. I have told Dr. Hughes, and he is trying to put a stop to the robbery. I do hope he will succeed in his efforts.

He turned off one man for dishonesty, but I believe he went to another hospital. To me all of this is a great grievance. I do not begin to get enough to feed the patients; it is with the strictest economy we can give them what we do; and here are men right before us, robbing them of what are bare necessities.

We daily see soldiers who have come from the front, ragged, bare-footed, and half-starved, while right along side of them men dressed in the best the land can afford, and eating the best of fare. To get all of this they are defrauding soldiers of the comforts provided for them by the government.

I have been told of one man who a year ago was not worth a cent; he was made commissary of a hospital post, and is now worth thousands.

We are badly off for dishes, spoons, and knives and forks; of the last we are much in need. The men have to eat with their fingers. A hospital is all very well when we can get what we want, but to live as we do—with just half enough of food and furniture—it is a very trying place.

A young man died to-day, by the name of Charles Rogers, a member of the Eleventh Alabama Regiment. He was sick a long time. His mother lives in Wilcox County, Alabama.

May 30.—We have had a great deal of excitement lately. Word was brought in by some one that five thousand Federal cavalry were twelve miles distant. We were ordered to pack, and the men were all sent to the woods. After preparing for the reception of the enemy we were told that it was some of our own cavalry who had been the cause of all this excitement.

There are many tales related of the Georgia militia. It seems that there was but one man in the whole place who could be prevailed on to go out as a scout. But the poor militia are constantly having some tale told on them. I think the governor is to blame for the contempt in which the Georgia militia are held. He holds to the doctrine of state rights with a greater tenacity than is at all needed at present.[8] According to his views, Georgia had not only a right to secede in the beginning, but she can secede from the Confederacy any time she pleases. Many of the Georgians fairly worship both him and Stephens. I think that both have done our cause a vast deal of harm, at home and abroad. They have denounced the administration time and again, because it has not done exactly as they thought right. Whatever may be their views on that subject, I think they had better, for the present, keep them to themselves, as they will be productive of nothing but harm. If the present administration can not guide our affairs, why no one else can, and it is the duty of every man to give it his hearty support. " My country right, my country wrong, but still my country."

I think one of the most dignified and manly papers which President Davis has issued, is one in answer to Stephens, who had asked him to propose for peace after every victory. Davis says that no southerner with true pride, could wish to do more in that respect than he has already done.[9]

[8] Governor Joseph E. Brown contended constantly with the Confederate government on every conceivable issue which he felt endangered his concept of state rights. The standard treatment of Brown is Louise B. Hill's *Joseph E. Brown and the Confederacy* (Chapel Hill, N. C., 1939) .

[9] For an illuminating discussion of the relationship between President Davis and Vice-President Stephens see James Z. Rabun's " Alexander H. Stephens and Jefferson Davis," *American Historical Review*, LVIII (1953) , 290-321. The same historian's editing of a letter from Stephens to his brother Linton as *A Letter for Posterity* (Atlanta, 1954) is a definitive statement of Stephens' intransigence and of the efforts for peace which derived from the situation here mentioned by Miss Cumming.

June 7.—Our brave army is still struggling to maintain her ground, against great odds. We have had some fearful battles. One was fought at New Hope Church, where the gallant Cleburne and Stewart drove the enemy back with great loss to them. I have been told by men who were there that the dead of the enemy lay in heaps.

I have just received a letter from one of my old patients, a chaplain, dated June 1, from Southside, Virginia. He is in a Tennessee regiment, in Longstreet's corps. He has been in all the late battles, and he says they were appalling. The Tennesseeans lost heavily. General Johnston's brigade lost three lieutenant-colonels, and many other officers and men. General Beauregard was in command. We drove the enemy back from every point. Will they ever see that we are in earnest, and let us alone?

My friend says his father is a prisoner in Tennessee.

June 10.—Lewis's Kentucky brigade has been lately in an engagement, and has lost heavily. Many of the men are killed and captured. In it were three brothers, named Laws, from Louisville, Kentucky; one of them, Frank, I knew well. He was an excellent young man. He and one of his brothers left here not very long ago to rejoin the army. We have been told that all three are prisoners. Frank was mortally wounded, and is supposed dead. The youngest is wounded, but not so badly. O, my heart aches when I see the very flower of our land snatched away as they are. A friend, in contemplating a battlefield, writes that his heart is almost broken; and it is not much wonder.

There is not a day passes but we hear of the death of some of the men we have had here as nurses or patients. I bid good-by to many a man, and the next thing we hear he is dead and gone.

A week or two ago I received from Dr. Quintard a package of books, " Balm for the Weary and Wounded." [10] It is a work prepared by himself for the soldiers. The little fellow of the Twenty-ninth Alabama has got one, which he seems to prize like gold.

June 18.—General Polk was killed on the 14th instant by a cannon-ball, while reconnoitering. Another of our brightest and best has left us; a star has gone from earth to shine in the " bright galaxy round God's throne." When we see such taken from our midst, at a time

[10] This little book had just come from the press of Evans & Cogswell in Columbia. Dr. Quintard noted that the first four copies were forwarded to General Leonidas Polk. C. T. Quintard, *Dr. Quintard* (Sewanee, Tenn., 1905), 97. The fate of these copies was revealed after the General's death on June 14: " In the left pocket of his coat was found his Book of Common-Prayer, and the right four copies of a little manual entitled ' Balm for the Weary and [the] Wounded.' Upon the fly-leaf of three of these had been written the names respectively of ' General Jos. E. Johnston,' ' Lieutenant-General Hardee,' ' Lieutenant-General Hood,' ' with the compliments of Lieutenant-General Leonidas Polk, June 12th, 1864.' Upon that of the fourth was inscribed his own name. All were saturated with his blood." Augusta, Georgia. Saint Paul's Church, *Funeral Services at the Burial of the Right Rev. Leonidas Polk . . .* (Columbia, S. C., 1864), 6.

when we have so much need of them, we think "how unsearchable are the ways of the Lord!" But, as Dr. Quintard sets forth in a sermon preached on the subject, these things are sent to remind us that we are not of this world, and that God makes it one of weariness; so we may lift our thoughts aloft and think of what is holy.

At the commencement of the war, when the northern people heaped insult after insult upon us, without any provocation, I felt it was the duty of all to fight till the last in defense of our rights. When General Polk laid aside his pastoral staff to take in its stead the sword of justice, I was proud of our having such a champion, and felt more confidence in the justice of our cause than ever. Since then I have seen that now, more than ever, we have need of our ablest and best to lead our armies against sin, the world, and the devil. And I have thought, with regret, of General Polk having taken the step which he did; but he did not cast aside his priestly robe without deliberating on it prayerfully; and, in the language of Dr. Quintard, "patriotism, inherited rights, a just cause, present good, the claims of posterity, all beckoned him on, and he clutched the sword of public justice and fought bravely for home, truth, and God." He never forgot, while fighting against his earthly foe, to set an example to all around him, that a man can be a soldier of his country and at the same time a soldier of the cross. I have ever heard his name coupled with every thing that is brave and noble. He won by his gentle and manly bearing the hearts of both officers and men, and as long as the life-blood streams through their veins he will never be forgotten. . . .

The enemy say our army is a rabble. Has the world ever seen such a rabble? I think not! General Polk is one of many such as we have in our rabble.

June 22.—Good news from all quarters. The gallant Forrest has gained a victory in North Mississippi, nearly capturing a whole command.

Morgan is again in the saddle, bringing dismay to the *loyal* Kentuckians.

We have gained a victory at Lynchburg, Virginia.

Grant has effected nothing at Petersburg.

The enemy have been defeated in Florida.

Johnston is teaching them a lesson up here, letting them know that they shall not pollute our soil with impunity.

June 24.—I have just witnessed the death of John Patterson, a member of the Third Florida Regiment. He had been in the hospital for some time, and not being very sick, I paid him little attention. A few days ago he was taken very ill, and all that could be done for him was of no avail. Mr. Moore, who is very attentive, had spoken to him on the subject of religion, and he had then made up his mind to live for God. This morning he begged me not to leave him, and I did not unless when compelled. Mr. Moore prayed and talked with him a good portion of the day. Colonel Mashburn and Lieutenant Sutton, of his regiment, were with him. He did not feel assured that he would be accepted at the last hour, as he had been so long in seeking the Lord. I read some hymns to him, two of which seemed to give him great consolation; they were "Just as I am without one plea," and "Jesus, savior of my soul." Mrs. Williamson and I were with him when he breathed his last, at nine o'clock to-night. The last words he uttered were, "Take me, Lord, 'tis all I have to give." He is one of five brothers who have died in the service. What a record and a tale is in these few words! Five of one circle offered up a sacrifice for freedom; they are

> "Martyrs in heroic story,
> Worth a hundred Agincourts!"

He requested me to write to his sister, who lives in Madison County, Florida. His colonel tried to get a detail to carry his body home, but was unsuccessful.

June 24.—My brother writes that the army is now south of Marietta, and as it passed through that beautiful city the people cheered them on, and seemed perfectly hopeful of success, expecting them back soon as conquerors. He also says that the army is in fine spirits, and that they get plenty to eat, and have coffee and sugar; but says they are all certain that it is General Bragg who is getting them so many good things.

Another of the brave youths of Mobile, Ben. Scattergood, has fallen a martyr for his country. He was a member of Garrity's battery, and was killed instantly, near Resaca.

All the churches, with the exception of one, have again had to be taken for hospitals, and the young ladies' college besides.[11] We have two very large sheds put up; one is on the court-house square. I like them very much for wounded, and the patients are all perfectly delighted with them. They have board roofs and tent-cloth sides, so as to be raised up or let down, as circumstances may require. They are twelve feet in width, and one hundred feet in length, with bunks arranged on each side, with an aisle in the center about five feet wide. I think this is the best arrangement that can be made for wounded in summer. They are well ventilated, and have none of the inconveniences of tents. Post Surgeon Wible has always been an advocate of them, and these have been put up at his suggestion.

A few weeks ago an article appeared in one of the papers of this place complimentary to the hospitals here. The editor said that, when the hospitals first came, there was great prejudice against them, on account of the sickness of which the people were afraid they might be the cause. But the reverse effect has been produced; that never, since

[11] The College Temple. M. P. Kellogg was president and proprietor. Mary G. Jones and Lily Reynolds, *Coweta County Chronicles* . . . (Atlanta, 1928), 142.

Newnan was a town, had it been more healthy, more quiet or pleasant as a place of residence. After complimenting all in them, he ends with a deserved one to the sick and wounded soldiers who from time to time filled them, saying that, by their quiet, unobtrusive conduct, urbane manners, and dignified bearing, they have convinced the most skeptical that southern soldiers and gentlemen are synonymous terms.

June 30.—We get very little in the way of chickens, eggs, etc. The fact is, the government gives us no money to buy any thing with, which is very annoying.

Mrs. Dr. Pierce has sent a bottle of lotion for the use of the patients in cases of inflammation. As usual, the surgeons paid little or no attention to it, as it had been made by a lady. I found one of the patients suffering very much from a carbuncle. Dr. Wellford had been doing his best to get it ready for lancing. The head nurse said that Dr. Wellford told him to try any thing he pleased, as he was tired of trying things himself. I got him to try the lotion, and by next morning the carbuncle was ready for lancing, and the man had a good night's sleep, the first he had had in a long time. This is a cause of triumph for us ladies. Dr. Wellford is much pleased with the lotion, and is anxious to get more.

A young man has died lately, who was wounded in the arm and in the head at the battle of Chickamauga. A minie-ball entered at the inner corner of one eye and made its exit at the temple of the opposite side. He was in a critical condition for several months. His wound in the arm healed, and that in the temple, near his eye, also healed; the other closed, with the exception of a slight aperture, from which a discharge kept up, the left side of the forehead being swollen all the time. The young man walked about for weeks, looking very well and cheerful, though he often complained of dull pain in his head. He was at length taken suddenly ill, and became insensible. The surgeons thought he was suffering under compression of the brain. A consultation was held, and it was decided that the only chance to save his life was to trephine. The operation was performed, I think, by Surgeon Pim, medical inspector. It proved unsuccessful, and the poor fellow never rallied—lived a day or two in a state of insensibility, and then breathed his last. The post-mortem examination proved that the inner skull was seriously fractured, so much as to make it evident that a fatal issue was inevitable. This young man lay for months in bed, with a bandage over both eyes, and seemed to suffer very little. I never saw him without a smile on his countenance.

July 12.—Our hospital is filled with sick and wounded. The army is now eight miles east of Atlanta. The enemy have driven it back step by step. General Johnston has given up every stronghold. All are now breathless with expectation, waiting to see what move he will make next. There is much conjecturing on the subject. Few seem to have lost confidence in General Johnston; they think he is acting as well as he can with his means.

We have had some desperately fought battles lately; our side does not lose nearly as many as the enemy.

We have a captain from Tennessee who lost a leg at the battle of New Hope Church. He was for some time a prisoner, and was sent through the lines. He says he saw the dead of the enemy at New Hope Church, and at some places they were piled six deep. They told him that in every battle fought lately they had lost at least five to our one.

As the army has moved east of us, this part of the country is left open, so the enemy can pay us a visit any time they please. It is a moral impossibility for our army to protect the whole country. The enemy have Rome, and they have hung some of the first citizens of the place. Not a day passes but we hear of some brutal outrage committed by these vandals. I have been told that when they reached Cassville the town was given up for them to sack. The whole place has been laid in ruins, and other outrages committed, all because some of the ladies thoughtlessly insulted the prisoners who passed through there about two years ago. We daily see droves of wagons passing, filled with people who have been driven from their homes by the ruthless invader.

We have a very nice old man—Mr. Yerby—who is forager and a little of every thing else; we call him our right-hand man. When we want any thing extra done, or any particular message carried, we call on him. He is friendly with all the country people, and if there is a possible chance of getting any thing from them he gets it. Many a bundle of nice rags he brings us, and a great treat they are. He entered the service at the commencement of the war, and he has two sons in it; one of whom is a prisoner, and he has not heard from him for many a day.

A day or two ago he heard of the death of a young brother, who had just received a commission.

Lately he received a letter from a sister, living in Athens, Georgia, informing him that her cousin, living near there, an old man, between seventy and eighty years of age, was riding in a wagon, when he was accosted by some Federal cavalry, who ordered him out of his wagon, and took all he had from him. They unharnessed his horse, and put a negro who was with him on it, and made the old man walk along side of the negro. He remonstrated, and the vandals beat him; then placed him on an old unsaddled mule, and carried him off. These valiant knights, who war so bravely on helpless old age, women, and children, have sent this old man to a prison in the North.

Our men are not all killed off yet; if these *heroes* wish to display their valor they will find a few who are ready to combat with them. How hard it is for us to know of these outrages, without the bitterest and most deadly hatred being aroused against these fiends in human shape.

209

If there was ever one spark of Union feeling in the breast of the Georgians, surely this will extinguish it.

We have a number of Louisianians, members of Point Coupee Battery. Like all from that state, they are very clannish. One, Mr. Dodart, ever since the war commenced, has fought side by side with his son. Poor man! he can scarcely restrain the tears when he talks about his wife and children, who are now in New Orleans. Another of them, Mr. Lambert, informed me that in coming through Alabama, I think near Demopolis, the battery encamped a few days near the house of a wealthy lady. She very kindly invited them to spend the evening at her house, and entertained them very handsomely. She told them that a few days previous an Alabama battery had been there, and by their misbehavior had frightened all who came in contact with them.

Among these Louisianians is a little boy; I am told he is as brave as any of them, and has done good service in the field.

July 15.—We have had an anxious time within the last few days. On the 13th instant a scout brought word that the Federal cavalry had captured a number of men guarding Moore's Bridge, some twelve miles distant, and that in large force they were advancing on the town.

The post commandant, Colonel Griffin, telegraphed to General Johnston, requesting him to send troops here. He then collected all the men from the hospitals who were able for duty, and sent them, under the command of a Kentucky captain, to meet the foe.

We all went to work to prepare for the enemy's reception. The first thing done was to send into the woods the negroes, poultry, cattle, convalescents, and all the nurses, excepting those actually needed to take care of the sick.

A wagon was loaded with all the valuables and sent to parts unknown. We had valises packed with a few clothes, and baskets filled with provisions, in case we should be compelled to take to the woods.

We have been told that the enemy burn every hospital building, and we had no idea that they would show us any mercy. We packed our trunks, and concluded to remain in the hospital, thinking it might be as safe a place as any.

We had a large quantity of whiskey, which we were afraid to keep, for fear if the enemy should get it they would act worse than without it, so it was sent to the woods.

All the surgeons left except Dr. Hughes, who remained at his post. The excitement in town was very great. I do not suppose there was an eye closed all night. On looking out we could see lights all over the place, the people moving every thing that was movable.

About 12 at midnight, Miss Womack concluded to go down to her aunt's, living near West Point. The train was expected from Atlanta at 2 A. M. She got ready, and some of the men carried her baggage to the depot. I started with her; on our way down we met a gentleman, who informed us that the train would not be down as the conductor was fearful of its being captured. We sat up all night long, and it was a night of dread. Every now and again some one came into town telling us that the enemy were but a few miles off. Every little noise we heard, we made sure they had come. A man came in and told us that they were on the outskirts of the town, waiting for daylight.

Next morning—the 14th—we waited in vain for the enemy; I thought I never had heard of cavalry taking so long to come a few miles. Our head cook did not leave, saying he was tired of running. We had to have something to eat; so, having no cooks, we all went to work and got breakfast ready, fully expecting the Yankees to eat it instead of our men.

After breakfast there was still no tidings of the foe. We went to work and prepared dinner; Miss Womack peeling potatoes and shelling peas, etc., all the time wondering if the Yankees would like their dinner, as we knew that they would not be backward in helping themselves; but by dinner-time the joyful tidings arrived that General Johnston had sent cavalry and driven them back.

We breathe free again, but only for a little while, as I do not see what is to prevent them coming in at any time. The men are coming back very much exhausted. The negro women are nearly all sick, and vowing they will never run again. One old woman, who, I am certain, the enemy could not be paid to take, is nearly dead. The women carried all their clothes with them, as they hear the Federals rob black as well as white. Many an amusing story is related about the hiding.

It is a blessing we can laugh, for this great anxiety is enough to kill any one. I can not help wishing that our *kind* northern *friends*, who *love* us so dearly that they will have us unite with them, whether we will or no, only had a little of it.

Sunday, July 17.—I went down to the train to see Miss Womack off. After she left we were informed that there was a raid near West Point, and that Miss Womack will reach there in time to meet it. It is useless to think of going any place and getting rid of the enemy, as they seem to have it in their power to overrun the whole country.

Miss Womack and I have agreed that, if either should lose our clothes, the one spared would share with the other. The enemy have a particular liking for ladies' wardrobes. I presume they send them to their *lady-loves* in the North. I wonder how they feel in their stolen finery!

I do not suppose that the men would rob us as they do if they were not incited by the importunities of their women. Many letters, taken from dead Federals on the battle-fields, contain petitions from the women to send them valuables from the South. One says she wants a silk dress; another, a watch; and one writer told her husband that now was the time to get a piano, as they could not afford to buy one.

211

"O shame, where is thy blush!" What a commentary on the society of "the best government the world ever saw!" Would we had the pen of a Thackeray to delineate the angelic and supereminent virtues of this *great* people!

On my return I met a friend from Mobile, Dr. Henderson, the surgeon of a hospital in that place. He brought me a letter from home, which was gladly received. He has been visiting the army, and intends remaining here till the expected great battle comes off. He is an Englishman, and came out from England last fall. On his arrival he received a commission in our army.

This afternoon we went to a funeral in the Methodist Church. Dr. Adams officiated, as the deceased was an Episcopalian—young Colston of Louisville. He was the color-bearer of a Kentucky regiment, and a gallant soldier. He was buried with the full honors of war. The day was very lovely. We walked round that sacred spot, the soldiers' grave-yard, and I saw many a familiar name on the head-boards of the graves —the occupants now calmly sleeping, heedless of the cannon's roar, and the peal of musketry. . . .

Though no towering monument is there to mark their last resting-place, it matters little, Nature shall adorn them with her choicest sweets. . . .

July 25.—Heavy fighting is reported at the front. Drs. Henderson, Divine, and Reese are on their way there. Dr. Henderson has spent the week at the Gamble Hospital with Dr. Wildman. Dr. Wildman is an Englishman. Last Monday our surgeons made up their minds that Dr. Henderson had been sent here by Dr. Foard to "spy out the nakedness of the land." It was in vain I protested that I believed such was not the case. In going into the wards I found the nurses all busy, getting ready for the great inspector, as they called him. I did not try to undeceive them, as I knew the wards could not be injured by a little extra cleanliness. The next day the nurses were sadly disappointed, as no inspector had been round to see how nicely they had put on their comforts and set their little bottles in military array.

July 27.—We had heavy fighting on the 22d. Lieutenant John Lyons, whom I visited in Corinth, was killed. His death will be a sad blow to his poor mother and wife. He had a brother wounded at the battle of Spottsylvania Court-house. He lived a short time after the battle, and his devoted mother was with him when he breathed his last.

A day or two ago we received a lot of badly wounded; some of them are shot near the spine, which paralyzes them so that they can neither use hands or feet. There is one very large man, named Brown, who is as helpless as an infant. Another, Captain Curran, is almost as bad. A fine-looking young man from Kentucky has lost a leg and arm; there is but little hope of his recovery. Mr. Pullet, a Georgian, is wounded through the lungs; the least movement causes the blood to run in streams from his wound; the doctors have little hope of saving him. Mr. Thomas is wounded through the head; his brain is oozing out, and at times he is delirious. Mr. Orr is injured in the spine, and is perfectly helpless. Mr. Summers of Mississippi is wounded in the right hand, and can not feed himself. Mr. Harper is badly wounded, and can scarcely eat any thing. Mr. Latta, his friend, has had his leg amputated. I have written to the chaplain of their regiments, the Twelfth and Forty-seventh Tennessee, informing him of their condition. Mr. Henderson from Tennessee is severely wounded. We have so many poor, helpless fellows, that it is heart-breaking to look at them. I went down to the train when they arrived, and they were a sad sight to behold. A handsome Texan died as soon as he was brought up to the hospital. A particular friend and one of his officers were with him. There were about fifty brought to our hospital. A number were sent to the Gamble.

The first thing we did was to get them something to eat. We had buttermilk, which they relished.

Mrs. Captain Nutt, a lady from Louisiana, brought us some nice rags, an article which we were entirely out of; and she also gave us her aid. Mr. Moore also assisted. At a time like this the nurses are all kept busy attending to the wants of the surgeons. We washed the men's hands and faces, and fed them.

Among these martyrs is a young man who, the surgeons are certain, shot himself intentionally. We have a case of that kind now and then. Some time ago, a man, rather than be returned to duty, cut three of his fingers off with an ax, and a bad job he made of it.[12]

[12] A less violent case of malingering is described in a letter of November 14, 1863, from Dr. Robert Battey, in charge of Polk Hospital at Rome, to Dr. W. L. Nichol, in charge of the Gamble Hospital:

" I beg leave to report as the result of my investigation of the complaints made by Private J. R. Maltbie, Co. C. 4 Tenn Regt—a patient in this hospital as follows

" Private Maltbie has been an inmate of the hospital since 27 August last under the care of Surgeon King. Dr. King informs me that during all this time he had been unable to find any satisfactory evidence of diseases in his case, notwithstanding his complaints are varied and often of an exaggerated character. Surgn King advised with me two weeks since as to the propriety of subjecting him to an energetic and painful course of treatment for the malady feigned to which I dissented, believing milder measures might accomplish the end desired. At the request of Dr. King he was carefully examined by the Examining Board (of which I am a member) who were fully of the opinion that the case was one of decided malingering.

" Maltbie some weeks ago made complaint to me of harsh usage in his confinement in barracks without cause. I found on enquiry that his confinement was due to a prolonged absence without leave in the country. He complained also that he desired to play cards at night and was denied candles to prosecute his game. The card playing at night did not meet my approval and our candle supply would not permit them to be issued to patients for even harmless amusement. He complains of the remedies used for his relief and refuses to submit to rational and proper treatment.

" Upon the point of Medical attention I can testify of my observation to the promptness, regularity and faithfulness of Surgn King, his attendant, as well as

As Miss Womack is gone, Mrs. Williamson takes her place; so we have many more duties now than we had. Many of the men are unable to feed themselves. I go over at mealtime and assist the nurses.

Mr. Rabbit, a member of Garrity's battery, is here badly wounded. He has suffered awfully from having gangrene in his wound. Dr. Wellford, his surgeon, thought at one time he would lose his leg.

There is an old lady here taking care of her sick son; she lives across the river, about fifteen miles distant. She says she has the *felicity* of having the Federal cavalry surrounding her place. They go into houses, and what they do not carry away they destroy. They have a dreadful antipathy to crockery, and break all the poor people's dishes.

I met a Mr. Miller visiting Mr. Dougherty's, who told me that these vandals had called on him, and after robbing him of every thing worth taking, took some dressed leather that he prized very highly, and before his eyes cut it into pieces. It seems to me that they are bent on creating a market for their own wares.

Sunday, July 31.—A most exciting day. The town is filled with troops. Last Thursday, the 28th, about dark, scouts brought in word that the enemy was crossing the river in large force. There was little heed paid to the report, as we had heard so many lately. About 9 o'clock the whole sky was illuminated by a glare of light, in the direction of Palmetto, a small town on the railroad. We knew then what we had to expect, and got ready as usual; whisky, and every thing of any consequence, was sent off; the men who were able taking to the woods.

Some of the negro women refused to go this time, as they had such a hard time of it before; but off they went, " truck " and all. The old woman who had suffered so much before we could not prevail upon to remain behind the others.

On the 29th scouts came in, and reported that the enemy had gone in the direction of Jonesboro, on the Macon road. We had respite again.

Yesterday morning, while I was in the yard of the court-house, attending to the patients, I saw a man ride in haste to town and a crowd collect around him. We were informed he was a courier, and had brought news that the enemy were within six miles of the place.

He was not through talking when the locomotive gave a most unearthly whistle, and immediately we heard the firing of musketry. I

his entire competency for his duties. I have met few Med Officers more conscientious in the discharge of duty.

" I am of the opinion that the Medical Board in declining to grant a furlough to Maltbie were actuated by motives entirely pure, earnestly desiring both the good of the soldier and the service, harboring towards him no resentment or malice, but pitying rather his weakness and want of patriotism in thus avoiding his duty and seeking to practice an imposition upon the service. . . ." Stout Papers (Emory).

asked Captain Curran, to whom I was talking, what that meant. He answered—fighting.

I never saw men run as all did. The crowd who had been around the courier dispersed in double-quick time. I hurried across the street to secure some money and little trinkets that the men had given me to take care of, thinking they would be more secure with me than themselves. On crossing, two or three shots whizzed past me, so I have been under fire for once.

After securing my valuables I went to look at the fighting. I had just got out when we heard cheering, and shouting that " the Yankees were running! " A lady and myself were looking at them, when a gentleman told us to hurry away, as the enemy was planting cannon on a hill near, intending to shell the town.

It seems that the night before General Roddy and his command were passing on their way to Atlanta. They were detained here all night; I do not know why. The engineer on the train saw a reconnoitering party of the enemy coming, and blew the whistle as an alarm. All the men near flew to arms. The enemy, not knowing there were any troops there, thought the train was running off, so rode up to demand a surrender, and received a volley of musketry—a thing they were not expecting. They retreated as speedily as possible.

General Roddy got his men into order (they were cavalry, but had no horses), and awaited the advance of the enemy. I saw General Roddy riding about in haste, without coat or saddle. A lady and myself tried to procure him a saddle, but were unsuccessful; the lady got him a blanket.

It was rumored that the enemy had surrounded the town and would likely fire upon it. We all suffered much from suspense, as we had many wounded; and if there was a battle in town, they would fare worse than any others. How I did hate to think about all the poor fellows lying so helpless, momentarily expecting a shell to be thrown in their midst.

We had them all moved into the strongest buildings; the court-house was crowded, although every one said a cannon-ball could easily penetrate its walls.

Roddy's men were drawn up in line of battle on one side of our hospital. The citizens sent baskets of provisions to the soldiers who were in battle array, and we sent them what we could.

At 12 A. M., Wheeler's cavalry was seen approaching the town. O, how joyfully we hailed them! They came galloping in by two different roads; the enemy, in the mean time hearing of their approach, were retreating. They were hotly pursued, and when four miles from town our men came up with them, where they made a stand, and had quite a battle.

We heard the booming of cannon, it seemed to me, about two hours. We eagerly listened to hear if it came nearer, as then we would know

215

whether we were successful or not; but it did not seem to move from one spot. We had no idea in what force the enemy were, so did not know what to expect.

About 4 P. M. word was brought that we had killed and captured the whole command. Then the wounded from both sides were brought in. I do not know how many there were in all, but not over nine or ten were brought to our hospital.

Hundreds of well prisoners marched in in a different manner from what they had expected.

Captain ——, a patient in one of the hospitals, went to the battle as a spectator; he took charge of a prisoner, promising to bring him to town. Instead of doing so, he took him into the woods and shot him. A gentleman who was with him did not see the deed, but heard the shot.

A friend has told me that when our soldiers were informed of the circumstance they were very indignant, and vowed, if they could lay hands on the captain, they would hang him.

Such men ought not to be permitted to bring dishonor on a brave people, and deserve punishment. I have never been an advocate of the black flag, but I think it would be mercy to an act of this kind. For then the enemy would know what they had to expect, and would fight valiantly before giving themselves up. This unfortunate man had surrendered in the faith that he would be treated as a prisoner of war.

There might be some excuse for a man in the heat of battle refusing to take prisoners, when he saw his comrades slain around him, but this captain had no such excuse. He has been guilty of murder, and of the most cowardly kind.

I have earnestly prayed that, when the history of this war is written, all the dark pages may be on the side of the enemy; but alas! for poor frail humanity, such is not to be the case.

When this captain was asked by a friend why he had committed the deed, he gave as a justification the barbarous treatment of his mother and sister by Federal soldiers.

It is much to be regretted that a young man who had won enviable laurels on many a battle-field, and is now suffering from his third wound, should have tarnished his former good name by such an act.

Dr. Hughes and other surgeons were for hours on the battle-field, attending to the wounded. Dr. Hughes says he never worked harder in his life.

Four fifths of the wounded were Federals, who appeared very grateful for what he did for them.

At the commencement of the battle, Dr. Hughes and others had sent word around to the citizens, telling them to prepare food for our soldiers by the time they would return.

Mrs. Williamson and myself were kept busy all the afternoon receiving the food. All—rich and poor—sent something. One crowd of very poor-looking women brought some corn-bread and beans, which, I am certain, they could ill afford. They said they would gladly do without themselves, so our brave defenders had them.

When the men came in, some of the nurses helped us to serve out the food, as we found it impossible to do so by ourselves.

We were very busy till about 10 o'clock, P. M., when an officer proposed that some of the commissary officers should take the things and divide them.

The men had remained in the yard while we handed them the food. They put me in mind of a lot of hungry wolves. Poor fellows! many of them had not eaten any thing in a long time. They were mainly Wheeler's men; Roddy's men had been fed by the citizens.

I heard many complaints against General Wheeler; the men say, if he had acted differently, not one of the raiders would have escaped. As it is, many hundreds have escaped, and their general, McCook, with them.

It seems that General Roddy had his men all ready to make a charge, and General Wheeler would not give the word of command. Many of the prisoners say, had the charge been made, all would have surrendered, as they were prepared for it. Our men speak very highly of the manner in which the people of Newnan have treated them.

To-day the town has been one scene of military display, as nearly all of the cavalry are here. I have seen many handsome flags—trophies. I sent and asked for a piece of one, which was given me.

The wounded prisoners have been taken to the Buckner Hospital. The cannon that we expected would shell Newnan is here. The firing we heard did not do any damage. It is said that there was so much consternation among the enemy that they did not know where they were firing.

Some of the negro men from the Gamble Hospital have been telling us that there was quite an exciting scene there yesterday morning when the raiders came in. All were at breakfast, and knew nothing of the enemy's approach till they commenced firing. They fired right into the hospital, at the same time shouting and yelling at a terrific rate. The negro men ran and got out of their way as quickly as they could. A number of the citizens were shot at and some captured; all are now released.[13]

One of our patients, Mr. Black, a Kentuckian, who was stopping at a farm-house, was roused from his bed and made a prisoner. He was

[13] As the only fighting of which she had a direct knowledge this action loomed large in Miss Cumming's personal history of the War. As a part of the campaigns around Atlanta it was a minor incident. General Joseph Wheeler described his victory over General Edward M. McCook in his official report of October 9, 1864. U. S. War Department, *War of the Rebellion: A Compilation of the Official Records of the Union and Confederate Armies* (Washington, 1880–1901), Ser. I, XXXVIII, pt. 3, 954-57. Cited hereinafter as *Official Records* (Army).

with them when they heard Wheeler and Roddy were after them, and says he never saw men so badly frightened. They treated him well, as they knew the tables would soon be turned.

Many of them told him, and indeed I have heard it from others, that when they came here they felt confident that they would be captured. Their time would be out in a week; they would then be of no service to the United States government. By sending them on this raid they would draw cavalry from our army.

My wonder is, that the enemy fight as they do, when they are treated with such inhumanity by their own people.

Dr. Henderson has come back from the army, and has started for Mobile. I expect he will have a hard time in getting there, as the road between Opelika, and Montgomery is reported to be torn up by the late raiders.

August 1.—I have had a visit from my old friend, Dr. P. Thornton, who is in General Wharton's command. I told him all I had heard against General Wheeler. He says General Wheeler has no taste for raiding or running after raiders. His forte is in defending the rear of the army in a retreat, and in that capacity he can not be excelled. Dr. Thornton also says that nearly all the men were exhausted, as they have been chasing these raiders since last Tuesday.

On Saturday General Wheeler ordered General Anderson, who had fresh men, to hurry and intercept the enemy at a place called Corinth, where there is a good crossing on the river. He had failed to get up in time, but the doctor thinks few of them will escape. He thinks we have captured and killed at least eight or nine hundred, and they still continue to be brought in, and not an hour in the day but droves of horses are driven past.

Dr. Wellford has nearly all the wounded to attend, as Dr. Reese has gone to the front, and Dr. Burks is very sick; and, to add to our distress, many of our best nurses have been sent to the front, and among them Dr. Wellford's head nurse, Mr. Martin, from South Carolina, one of the best nurses we had; his health is bad. I think it is sinful to take such men away from these poor sufferers.

Dr. Henderson told me he was at the receiving field hospital when some of these same men were sent back from the army; and our surgeons got a few blessings from the doctors, as they had enough to do without taking care of such sick men.

August 6.—The prisoners still continue to come in. A few days ago I saw about sixty in a crowd, and a more deplorable sight I never beheld; they were barefooted and bareheaded.

Mr. Holt, who has charge of the linen-room, gave them all the hats and shoes he could collect.

We sent them about two gallons of nice soup and what bread we could procure. Many of the men told me they would do without,

218

and give their share to the prisoners. It would be some time before they could get food cooked at the prison.

On looking at these poor creatures, I thought what a pity it was that the men in Washington could not be made to take their places; if this was done, I think we should have peace.

A few days ago I visited the wounded prisoners, in company with Mrs. Bigby and Mrs. Berry. In one of the wards nearly all were men from the southern states—Kentucky, Tennessee, North Alabama, and North Mississippi, were there represented. I have far less respect for these men than I have for a real Yankee. To me it has always been a mystery how any man born on southern soil can have any affinity with the enemy.

We had a little boy with us, about two years old, whom the men tried to get to speak to them, but he would not go near them. One of them said he thought it strange. I told him I did not, as instinct had taught the child who its worst enemies were. He said, " Why, we never hurt children! " I answered, that burning their homes and destroying their food was not hurting them! Many of them answered, " We never do these things, and would shoot a man as soon as you would, who would do so." I asked them if any one had been shot for setting fire to Palmetto? They answered no; they could not find out who had done it. I told them that I expected they never would.

They told us a good deal about how well the women of Georgia had treated them; they said they had given them food, and been very kind in every way. At this they need not feel at all flattered, as doubtless news had reached those ladies of the inhumanity with which many had been treated in North Georgia, and they thought it but wisdom, when in the lion's jaw, to extricate themselves as easily as possible.

I know of many in this place who, as soon as they heard of the enemy coming, went to work to cook for them. We all know that this was not for love.

There was a Captain Shortz of Iowa, who had one of his hands cut off, and the other badly wounded. He was a pitiful sight. I told him I had more sympathy for him than I had for our own men. He asked me why. I answered, his conscience could not be at rest, like theirs. He said that was a difference of opinion. All the men there told us the same old story—they were fighting for the Union.

In another ward one of them, from New York, but a native of Cornwall, England, was nursing. I told him I was perfectly astonished to see one of his nation aiding the oppressor. He answered, that he was ashamed of his native country for sympathizing with us as it had done. He was an abolitionist, and the first I had met.

He said the main thing he disliked in being a prisoner was, that his time had expired, and had he been free he would have been home. I asked him if all went home when their time was up. He said yes; there was nothing for them to do, as they had three reserves, and we had only been fighting the first.

219

We have certainly a bright prospect ahead of us, if we have the other two reserves yet to fight!

I think the Federal government very inhuman. Why do they not send all the reserves to fight us at once, and not have their men killed piecemeal, as they are now doing? The prisoners, one and all, told us that they could not be better treated.

Some of our wounded have died lately. Mr. Hull, a fine-looking lad, was one. I think he was a member of Ross's Texas Cavalry. His brother was with him. A lieutenant, whose name I have forgotten, told me that Captain Hailey is really killed. This gentleman was a particular friend of Captain Hailey; they had been school-boys together. He says a nobler or better man never lived.

Knives, forks, and spoons are still scarce. I do dislike to see the men eat, as many are compelled to eat, with their fingers. Some few have knives and forks of their own. We have cups, plates, bowls, and pitchers made at a factory near; they are common brown earthen-ware, but we are glad to get them.

We have heard that Mobile has been attacked in reality this time. I shall be anxious till I hear from there.

I have made the acquaintance of an excellent family by the name of Taylor, refugees from the northern portion of this state. A member of their family died lately. He had been captured some time ago, at one of the battles in Virginia. His mother, hearing that he was in the last stage of consumption, sent a letter by flag of truce to Stanton, or some of the other leading men of the North, stating his case, and begging his release—which request was granted. He came home in a dying condition; but it was a great consolation to both himself and family to breathe his last amid the endearments of home. I went to see him, but he was too far gone to speak to me.

August 11.—A few days ago we received orders to pack up for a move.[14] We were told to send the worst wounded to the Coweta House. As we have learned to do every thing with dispatch, all was ready for removal in a very short time. The cars were waiting for us, and the wounded who could be moved were put aboard. They disliked being left so much, that many pretended they were better than they really were. After every thing was in readiness, about dark, I went to the Coweta House to bid the patients good-by. The men had been sent from the Bragg, Gamble, and our hospitals. The galleries, halls, and rooms were full, and there were no nurses, no lights, and nothing to eat or drink, not even water. I met Dr. Wellford, who had gone over for the same purpose as myself. Never were two persons

[14] Dr. Wible had informed Dr. Stout from Newnan on July 23: " I have all the Surplus hospital property packed up ready for shipment and wagons engaged to transport them if the trains should fail. I will have the Surplus property shipped to a safe place the first opportunity—By wagons if the danger should seem pressing. Convalescents will march away on foot. Those too sick to go will be collected in one hospital and supplies provided for them." ALs, Stout Papers (Emory).

more joyfully received than we were. One poor boy was crying like a child. Dr. Wellford came back home with me, and we procured some of the nurses, and, taking some of the rations which we had cooked, and making a quantity of toddy, we carried all over. The men did not eat much, but the toddy seemed to revive them. We had also taken candles with us. I remained as long as I could be of any service. I believe Dr. Wellford was there till 12 o'clock that night.

The next morning I went to see them, and found they had no breakfast; and there was little prospect of their getting any. No one seemed to have them in charge. I was told that Dr. Smith, one of the surgeons of the place, was to take care of them, but he was not there then.

I heard no little grumbling, which was not much wonder. Many said they did not care how soon the enemy had them; that they could not use them worse than our own people had done.

I looked around, and discovered that there were no dishes, and no utensils in which to cook, even if we had any thing to cook. There were no changes of clothing for the men, and no rags for their wounds. I told Mrs. Williamson the plight the men were in, and she said she would remain with them and run the risk of being captured. We sent for Dr. Hughes, and he gave his consent for her to stay. I then asked him to send at least a change of clothing for the men who had left our hospital. He said he could not without orders. He left us, and after awhile some clothes were sent, and a lot of eggs and butter. The steward came, and asked us what kind of dishes we wished. I gave him a list, and he tried to get them, but was unable to do so, as they were packed away in boxes, which were in the car, and could not be got at.

Sallie (a little girl who was in the hospital with us) and I got on one of the box-cars along with the ladies of the Gamble Hospital, Miss Rigby and Mrs. Dr. Wildman. We were just about starting when we were informed that our hospital would not leave before next morning. Sallie and I got off, and remained all that night at Mrs. Dougherty's, who, as usual, was very kind.

Mrs. Williamson stayed at the Coweta House, and by daylight next morning she came to me in great distress, saying she had not slept any all night, she had been kept awake by the groans of the men. And on trying to get something for them for breakfast, and finding nothing, had become sick at heart, and sick in reality. I sent over a large can filled with edibles, and Mrs. Dougherty sent a nice breakfast for about six. I then went to the hospital, and, between us, we managed to get enough food for all. The men from the Gamble Hospital had been provided for; but there were not more than six or seven of them, so their things did not add much to the stock on hand.

I resolved not to leave Mrs. Williamson, as she was quite sick. I told the post surgeon I would like to remain. He informed me that I could not please him better than by so doing; that he had been disappointed in procuring the assistance of some of the ladies of the place. He expected Dr. Smith would have taken charge of the patients before that time, and see that they were properly cared for. There had been some misunderstanding about the matter. In the hurry of evacuating a post, as was the case with us, oversights are unavoidable. Dr. Wible had issued an order to the surgeon in charge of each hospital to turn over, for the benefit of the patients, medicines, liquors, and money; which order was complied with. Such is the strict discipline in our medical department, that, as he did not specify any of the other necessaries, they were not left. The mistake was not found out until too late to retrieve it, as every thing had been packed up and sent off on the cars.

Dr. Gore, who remained a little while after the hospitals left, gave us a large box full of things which had been sent to him as a donation for the wounded. There were some nice wines and many other useful articles in it. Dr. Gore did his best to induce the citizens to lend us their assistance.

As many men as could be spared were sent around to the citizens, asking them to send us cooked provisions. Drs. Divine and Wellford were to be left as long as there was no sign of the approach of the enemy.

I spent the most of the day going around among the people, begging them for the loan of almost anything. Mrs. Berry gave me a washboiler; Mrs. Dr. Redwine, a wash-tub; and Mrs. McKinly, a negro woman, to wash, and a small tub in which to bathe the men's wounds.

Dishes of all kinds being very scarce, I could not even borrow any. By dinnertime the people commenced sending in all kinds of good things to eat, but we were in a dilemma, as we had nothing on which to put them. We managed after awhile to have them stored away until they would be consumed. We had to economize, as we were not certain when we would get any more. Mrs. Brooks intends sending food to six, which will be a great help.

I am completely worn out, as the day has been very warm. We do not know the moment the enemy may be on us, but we will have to make the best of it if they come. Our clothes have all gone with the hospitals, so we have nothing but ourselves to care for now.

Mr. Moore remained to help take care of the wounded, and he has done his part in procuring food; he has got a friend to send us some milk.

Sunday, August 14.—We expected to leave to-day, but the cars did not come down from Atlanta. Mrs. Johnston and Mrs. Ashcraft have taken the men under their care, and Mrs. Captain Nutt, who is very kind to the wounded, will also do her part. Dr. Smith is surgeon in charge, and is having every thing put in order. The ladies of the place have been very kind, and have sent the men all kinds of nice things.

I have spent a portion of the day with the young lad who cried so much the first night I came over here. He is wounded in the foot, has gangrene, and suffers excruciating pain. His name is Morgan, and he is from Mississippi. A Mrs. Ross has kindly offered to take sole charge of him. He has begged Mrs. Williamson and me to take him with us.

Mrs. Williamson has been very busy; she does not know what I have been doing, nor I of her doings.

A Lieutenant Sommerlin, from Covington, Georgia, is here, badly wounded; his wife, a lovely woman, is taking care of him.

She told me she was in Covington when the raiders passed through there, and that they committed some terrible outrages; among others was the shooting of a Captain Daniel, a cousin of Miss Womack, of whom I had heard her often speak. He was in the state service, and the vandals made believe they thought him a bushwhacker. He has left a large family of motherless children to mourn for him. He was a man of a highly cultivated mind, and stood well in the estimation of all.

They went to the house of an old man, and as he knew they had come with designs on his life, he sold it dearly. He fought manfully, and killed some half dozen before he fell.

Several of our attendants have come back; they had been sent for the bunks and other things that our folks were not able to take with them.

The hospitals went to Macon by Atlanta, and one of the men has informed me that while passing there the shells flew all around the train, and one struck within a few feet of them.

Atlanta is closely besieged. General Hood is now in command of this army. I believe Johnston is in Macon. There have been many conjectures as to this change of commanders, but no one can tell exactly the why or the wherefore.

Last evening Mrs. Brooks and myself went up to the College Hospital, in which are many of the wounded, besides the prisoners. Among our men I found two Scotchmen, very badly wounded. The wounded Federal captain that I had seen before was here, and looked badly. The prisoners are in much better quarters in this hospital than our men at the Coweta House.

All have fared much better than they have with us, as Mr. Kellogg, the steward, owns the building and has all of his own furniture. There are two ladies who take care of the patients—Mrs. Kellogg and Mrs. Alexander—both kind and excellent women.

We have had a few false alarms about the enemy coming, but they have always turned out to be our own cavalry.

We are leaving many good friends in Newnan; Mr. Dougherty's family and many others have been very kind to us. As we have been much engaged, we have visited little. I spent a very pleasant evening at the house of Dr. Reese; Mrs. Reese is an excellent lady, and her daughters are highly educated young ladies and accomplished musicians.

Some time ago we all spent a delightful evening at the house of Mr. Bigby. We had a very fine supper, and all on the table was of home production, with the exception of the tea. But the supper was the least of the entertainment. Mrs. Bigby is a most charming lady, is a poetess, and is called the Mrs. Browning of the South. Lately she published a poem in the Field and Fireside, called *Judith*.[15] She was earnestly requested by Dr. Hughes to read it, and did so. It was certainly a treat, for she lent to the "rhyme of the poet the music of her voice."

Mr. Bigby is a lawyer and a polished gentleman. Their residence is in a romantic part of the city, is a handsome building, inclosed in a very pretty garden filled with choice flowers.

There are some very nice residences in this place, and many very beautiful flower-gardens, laid out with a great deal of taste.

The people here seem to regret our leaving the post, though I am told the quartermaster owes many of them money for house rent, etc. I know that Mr. Dougherty has not reecived one dollar from the government, and we have cut down quantities of timber on his land.

Our post surgeons have been careful to respect the rights of private citizens, and with the exception of taking the churches when we first came here, I believe there have been no buildings taken for hospital purposes without the consent of the owners. In Chattanooga we were constantly coming in collision with the people for taking their property for government purposes. I do not know who was to blame, but I do know that such was the case.

[15] Mrs. Mary Catherine (Dougherty) Bigby's poem was the winner of a competition sponsored by *The Southern Field and Fireside* of Augusta and was published in its issue of July 2, 1864.

IX: WEST POINT, AMERICUS, MACON

✝✝

August 19, 1864.—We started from Newnan on the 15th instant, and very much to our regret, as we had to leave so many of our old patients behind. Mr. Morgan cried like a child; but, child-like, I suppose he has forgotten all about us ere this.

Mr. Williams of the Ninth Kentucky, one of our old patients, tried to procure a permit to come with us, but he did not succeed. We were very sorry, as he was anxious to get away from Newnan for fear of being captured. He had been in the country at the time the hospital was moved.

Many of the ladies of the place called on us before we left, and promised to do all in their power for the wounded.

As we have very little money, Dr. Wellford insisted on our taking some from him. He said we did not know what we were about, to think of starting in these times with the small amount we had; and he was about right, as the sequel proved.

We arrived at West Point about sundown the same day. Dr. Wellford had put us under the care of the conductor, and he took us to a small hotel—the Exchange. The landlord was moving, but informed us we might lodge there for the night, as we had provisions with us; that was all for which we cared. He gave us a room without even a wash-bowl or pitcher in it; for the privilege of remaining in this delightful room we paid the moderate sum of ten dollars.

There was a large brick hotel in the place, but as we had such a short time to remain, we thought it would be useless to change.

We walked around the place; it is like many other of our small towns—in a forlorn condition. There are in it some very nice private dwellings, but no one seems, in these war times, to care how their property is kept.

There is quite a formidable fort built on a high hill, and from it we had a very fine view of the surrounding country. The fort is garrisoned by Massingale's battery, the men of which very politely showed us all its mysteries.

An accident occurred in it but a short time since. A lieutenant of Massingale's battery and one of the men were standing near a caisson, when a shell exploded, killing the lieutenant instantly and wounding some of the men. The former was from Macon, and had been but a short time married.

We had a pleasant walk on the bridge which the enemy were so desirous of destroying. I believe the guard on it were Governor Brown's men. In the late raid through this portion of the country, the enemy's object was the destruction of this bridge, as it is a very important one to us. By its destruction we would lose one of the communications with the Gulf States, and at present they are the granary of the Tennessee army; and, besides that, all communication between these states and both armies would be hindered, at least for awhile. The river at this point is very wide.

The late raiders did not come any further than Opelika, which is not many miles distant. There they destroyed a large portion of the railroad and government property.

We stopped at a small farm-house, to try and procure some milk; we were unsuccessful, but the lady of the house gave us a watermelon, for which she would take no money.

We asked her what she intended doing in the event of a battle being fought there. She said she did not know, but supposed she would have to remain.

We next visited the hospital. Dr. Oslin, the post surgeon, we knew well from reputation. We introduced ourselves to him. His personal appearance did not belie the high encomiums we had often heard passed on him. I am told he is not only a kind-hearted and polished gentleman, but a Christian. He has no ladies in his hospital, Miss Womack's sister having never come. He told us that our friend, Miss Womack, who is living near, would take charge of one if we would remain there with her. This we felt very much tempted to do, as we should be much nearer the army there than where we were going.

We went around the hospitals; they were filled with badly wounded and sick; there were a number of erysipelas cases in a ward by themselves.

If the enemy should attack the place, I do not know what would become of all these poor fellows.

We were informed that morning that the Federals had cut the road between that point and Atlanta, and as the train did not come in at its usual time, we were confident the report was true, but the arrival of the train proved it false. We left about 4 P.M. on the 16th.

When a few miles beyond Opelika, the locomotive ran off the track, and we came near having a very serious accident. I was reading, and knew nothing of it until I heard some ladies scream. I then felt a motion as if the train was about to upset. I saw several of the cars ahead of us plunge off the road, and men jumping from them; many took to the woods, as they were fearful of an explosion.

We remained on the car all night. Next morning men who had come from Opelika were at work trying to clear the track, but the job looked like an endless one. Every car excepting the one we were on (it being the last) was off the track. Had we gone a very little further, we would have been thrown down quite a precipice, and no doubt many of us sent into eternity.

One of our old patients made us some coffee, and we, like all the rest, ate our breakfast on the roadside. We were in the woods, and no sign of a habitation near. As there was little or no hope of our leaving there for some time, a gentleman who had found an empty house a little ways back came and took his party, Mrs. Williamson, and myself to it. We found it quite a nice retreat. It had been a schoolhouse, and the benches and desks were left standing. We had books, and altogether had quite a pleasant day. Our gentleman friend was Senator Hill, of Lagrange, Georgia. With him were two nice young ladies, the Misses Leach, who were on their way to their homes in New York. They had been spending some few years in the South. Senator Hill informed us that the ladies of Lagrange had undertaken the care of the wounded left there, and his daughter, a girl of sixteen, had special charge of six. I was much pleased to hear this, and only hope the ladies of Newnan will do the same. Mr. Hill gave us some nice biscuit and ham, his servant made our coffee for dinner, and altogether we had a most delightful repast.

Miss Evans, the authoress, was on the train, going to Columbus, where she has a badly wounded brother. From her I learned that all was quiet in Mobile, although we have had a naval battle, and Forts Morgan, Powell, and Gaines were taken. The battle was a desperate one, and we have lost our splendid ram, the *Tennessee*. Admiral Buchanan was severely wounded; himself and whole crew are prisoners. I believe we have lost several gun-boats. We were attacked by a fleet of war ships, and instead of retiring, as would have been policy, fought them. The act was a bold and daring one, but showed a lack of wisdom. We have too much of this spirit among us, and I think it would be much better every way had we less of it and more discretion.

About 3 P. M., a wood-car came from Columbus, on which we all got. We cut branches of trees and held them over us for protection from the sun, and I have no doubt, as we went along, that many thought that "Birnam wood" was coming. We reached Columbus without further accident in time to catch the Macon train. We arrived at the latter place about 4 A. M., the 17th. Went to a hotel and paid ten dollars for a bed, and as much more for breakfast. We called on Drs. Bemiss and Stout, and learned from them that our hospital had gone to Americus, Georgia. These two gentlemen were low-spirited; they do not like the idea of coming so far South at this season, and think it will be deleterious to the wounded.

Miss Leach took the address of some of my relatives in Europe, promising to write and let them know of having met me. As com-

227

munication with foreign parts is uncertain, we take advantage of every opportunity of sending letters through the lines. The train to Americus had already gone, and Mrs. Williamson, being fearful that if we remained in the hotel another day our exchequer would be empty, we called on our old friend, Dr. Cannon, who has charge of the Wayside Home. I knew he could tell us where we could procure a boarding-house more suited to our means. His two daughters were with him, and were keeping house in *two* rooms, refugee style; one of the rooms was parlor, bed-room, and dining-room, the other a kind of dressing-room. It astonishes me to see how well every body manages now-a-days; they put up with inconveniences as if they had been used to them all their lives. The war seems to have raised the minds of many above common every-day annoyances. Dr. Cannon insisted on us remaining with his family, and as Mrs. Williamson was half sick, and we were both worn out, we were only too thankful to accept the kind invitation. The family seem to be perfectly happy, as much so, I expect, as they ever were in their home in Tennessee. I shall never forget the cup of coffee I drank there; it put me in mind of New Orleans.

Dr. Nagle and an officer who is stationed at Andersonville, where the prisoners are kept, spent the evening with us. The prisoners and their behavior was the principle topic of conversation, and from all we could learn we did not like the prospect of being so near them. (Americus is ten miles below Andersonville.) This officer informed us that no less than a hundred died daily. He said they were the most desperate set of men that he had ever seen. There are two parties among them, the black republicans and the copperheads, and they often have desperate fights, and kill each other. This officer said it was revolting to be near such men, and did not like his position.

Dr. Cannon sent us to the depot on the 19th in an ambulance. The train stopped a little while at Fort Valley, where the Buckner and Gamble Hospitals, of our post, have remained. There we saw a few familiar faces. The train remained about a half an hour at Andersonville, so we had time for a good view of the prisoners' quarters. I must say that my antipathy for prison-life was any thing but removed by the sight. My heart sank within me at seeing so many human beings crowded so closely together. I asked a gentleman near why we had so many in one place. He answered that we would not have men enough to guard them were they scattered. O, how I thought of him who is the cause of all this woe on his fellow-countrymen—Abraham Lincoln. What kind of a heart can he have, to leave these poor wretches here? It is truly awful to think about. But, as sure as there is a just God, his day of reckoning will come for the crimes of which he has been guilty against his own countrymen alone. To think of how often we have begged for exchange; but this unfeeling man knows what a terrible punishment it is for our men to be in northern prisons, and how

228

valuable every one of them is to us. For this reason he sacrifices thousands of his own. May Heaven help us all! But war is terrible.[1]

Arrived at Americus to-day, the 19th. We can not tell how we shall like the place. It is quite a large village, and from all appearances we are going to have a very nice hospital, but none of us liked being compelled to come to it. We are far south-west, near the Florida line, and the weather is very warm; I think much warmer than in Mobile, as there we have the sea breeze. The town is in Sumter County, on the South-western Railroad. It is one hundred miles south-west of Milledgeville.

I have a number of letters from various points, one from a young man, a member of an Alabama battery, shows that, with all our re-treating, our soldiers are not down-hearted:

BIVOUAC, 11 MILES WEST OF ATLANTA,
August 4, 1864.

Your kind favor of the 19th ultimo came to hand. I can tell you I was delighted at receiving it. Since last writing you, there has been many a hard fight, in which, I am happy to say, I was a participant.

The Yankees are broken of charging rebel breastworks. They keep shelling all the time; but, thanks be to God, there is not much damage done. It is astonishing to see two armies drawn up confronting each other for hours and hours; every thing is as still as a mouse, when all at once, men rush to arms. Then commences the booming of artillery and the heavy roar of musketry.

This kind of fighting has been going on for the last eighty-six or eighty-seven days, more or less, much to the detriment of Sherman and his hirelings. Poor old Sherman! he has had a hard road to travel, and in my opinion he will never reach Atlanta as long as *Sergeant* Hood intends keeping him out.

We have just been relieved from a position on the left of our division, where we did some good firing, and came here this morning. The Yankee sharp-shooters are very troublesome, and have been so all through this trip, at least this campaign.

Last night, while sleeping along side of our guns, I was awoke by heavy moaning; on inquiry, I found that an infantryman had been shot by a sharp-shooter while sleeping, thinking of no danger. Poor fellow! I pitied him. There were two or three others hit at the same time, but, thank God, none were killed.

On the 26th or 27th—I have forgotten which—General Hood issued

---

[1] At Macon in September 1864 President Davis told a Confederate audience: "Your prisoners are kept as a sort of Yankee capital. I have heard that one of their Generals [Grant, according to C. C. Anderson in an article in the Macon *Telegraph* reprinted in the *Confederate Veteran*, XXIX (1921), 168] said that their exchange would defeat Sherman. I have tried every means, conceded everything to effect an exchange[,] to no purpose. . . . We want our soldiers in the field, and we want the sick and wounded to return home." Richmond *Examiner*, September 29, 1864.

orders for every man on the line to have a musket in his hands, excepting only those who were needed to work the guns of artillery.

I took a musket, and on the 28th the Yankees pitched into our pickets, and such another cheering and rattling of small arms I never heard for picketing. I gathered up my ammunition, and took my gun and ran into the ditch along side of the infantry, expecting the Yankees to charge, but it was only a feint on their part.

The sound of small arms to me has become monotonous; you may think I am callous, but I am not. I am determined not to do any thing that is inconsistent with my duty, and, through God's assistance, I intend doing that to the letter.

You must excuse me for not answering your last sooner, for we have been marching, digging, and fighting all the time. I must close and smoke my pipe.

Yours, etc.,   J.

In papers received from Mobile, I see that General Maury is begging the people to leave the city, but I do not expect the appeal is heeded. Governor Shorter has had sheds built for the people to live in, so they have no excuse.

The planters are still holding on to their corn, and will not sell it to those who have the best right to it.

August 28.—We have become a little settled, and think we shall like the place very well. I never had such a nice kitchen.

Dr. Wellford has been here. He was ordered away from Newnan, as the enemy were expected. He brought word that our patients were doing pretty well; a few of them had gone to their long homes. He has been sent back, as it was a false alarm, and there are many wounded there yet.

Dr. Reese has returned from the front. He is very sanguine of our success; says that the Yankee pickets exchange tobacco and newspapers with ours, and have told them that Sherman is nearly exhausted, and will have to give up soon.

I should like to believe this, but am afraid it is too good to be true. I see by the papers that we have had a great deal of fighting in Missouri and Kentucky.

Lieutenant Haskill of Garrity's battery was killed on the 7th. He is much regretted.

We have quite a number of sick. The ladies of the place have called on us, and seem very anxious to assist us. I am very glad of this, as we have little or nothing of our own to give the patients. The paymaster has not been around lately; so Dr. Hughes, like all here, is entirely out of funds.

This is said to be a very wealthy place; and were we to judge from the carriages and fine horses we see, I should think the impressing officer had not been down this way for some time.

September 1.—Last night our hospital was burned to the ground, and with it much valuable property belonging to the town.

About 5 P. M., while on my way to visit some sick men, a cry of fire was raised, and on looking in the direction it came from, saw a large cotton warehouse in a blaze. The sight was fearful, as it covered the whole square, and the cotton seemed to have ignited all at the same time. Had I not known how inflammable cotton is, I should have thought it was covered with turpentine. The flames spread with great rapidity, and it was not long before two whole squares were entirely consumed.

We have saved very little. A number of buildings were blown up; by this we lost much more than we otherwise should have done.

Our hospital occupied three sides of a square; out of this there is one two-story brick building saved.

The people have been very kind, and many came in from miles in the country, and took the patients to their houses.

Mrs. Williamson and I remained with a very nice lady, who was very kind to us. We are now in a small room, about twelve feet square, in which are all our stores, and besides we have two patients, who come and eat with us. It is just as much as we can do to turn around.

Our men have put up stoves in an open field, which they use for their kitchen. All this is very disheartening, and I feel as if I never would assist to fix up a hospital again.

It is estimated that three or four million dollars will not cover the loss. Thousands of bales of cotton were destroyed; it had been sent here from every portion of the state, to be out of the way of the enemy. The fire originated from a small piece of lighted paper, thrown down by a little negro boy. We all feel confident that it was accidental.

Sept. 7.—Atlanta has been evacuated. We have had some very heavy fighting in that direction. Atlanta was important on account of its position. I hear few regret the loss of the city itself, not even Georgians, as they say it was the most wicked place in the world.

A lady writes from Newnan, that the wounded are all doing well, and that the ladies are very kind to them. She says Newnan is almost entirely deserted—every body having left for fear of the enemy; many of them are here.

The Bragg and Foard are the only hospitals here. The Bragg is very large, and has a ward about a mile in the country, in a beautiful spot. A large brick college is its main building.[2] Dr. Adams, Mrs. Harrison, and Mrs. Harris are there.

We have numbers of wounded men, who have been sent home on furloughs; while there, their wounds break out again, and as there were no experienced surgeons to attend them, they are worse than

[2] Sherwood lists a Female Institute at Americus. *A Gazetteer of Georgia . . .* , 122.

ever. A great deal of mischief is done in this way. This is one of the reasons why surgeons are so unwilling to give furloughs.

The public square opposite to us is filled with tents, which are full of gangrene cases. One lad suffers so much we can hear him scream for two squares off.

After the fire, several of the ladies called on us, and asked us what they could do in the way of feeding our men. We told them, if they would give the worst cases their dinner, we should be very grateful; which they have done.

September 16.—We have a truce of ten days. It has been given to let the people get out of Atlanta. Sherman has ordered every one to leave that place. Refugees are coming out by the thousand, perfectly destitute, as they are not permitted to bring any thing with them.

The authorities in the South are doing every thing to alleviate the sufferings of these unfortunates. There are people here separated from their families, and with no idea where they have gone.

The great chieftain, General John Morgan, is no more. This brave man did not have the honor of falling on the battle-field. It is said he was betrayed by a woman, and that after he surrendered he was brutally murdered, and that indignities of all kinds were heaped on his lifeless body; but his " country conquers with his martyrdom."

Alas! how fleeting is every thing in this world; it seems but yesterday that he took for his bride one of Tennessee's fairest daughters. She is now bereft of her all . . . He was brave, chivalrous, and patriotic. He will never die in the hearts of his countrymen. He has fallen in a great cause—a nobler death he could not have wished for. " His spirit will walk abroad, and never rest till the great cause triumphs."

September 19.—I received a letter from my brother, saying he had lost all his clothes except what he had on, and wishing me to procure more. As they could not be obtained here, I went up to Macon on the 17th, in company with Captain Tomlinson. He and his family are refugees from Tennessee.

He told me that Governor Brown was out with a proclamation, warning the people against refugees and runaway negroes. I think he must be deranged, as I do not think a man in his senses could be guilty of outraging the feelings of the people, as he does. We all know that there have been bad people, who have taken advantage of their being refugees, to impose on good people. But that is no reason why the good and patriotic, who have been driven from their quiet homes by the ruthless foe, should be insulted in this manner. I really think that the character of the good people of Georgia has suffered from this half-distracted governor.

On arriving at Macon, I went to Dr. Cannon's, and one of his daughters accompanied me to Major Fairbanks, quarter-master, and one of the best men we have in the service. I told him my errand.

232

232

It is against orders to get clothes from a quartermaster without a descriptive list, so I was uncertain about getting them. Major Fairbanks said, if my brother was as good a soldier as myself, he could have them. I answered, he was a much better one, as he never grumbled at any thing.

We then called on Mrs. General Anderson, who was in town with her husband, he having been badly wounded near Atlanta. He was not at home, but we saw the general's mother, and she said he was improving.

A lady friend in Macon told me that one of her daughters had gone through the lines to Memphis, proceeded to New York, and returned by Fortress Monroe. She went to Washington to procure a pass from Stanton, which he refused to give, but she received one from Lincoln. On reaching Fortress Monroe, General Butler disregarded her pass, and had her arrested as a spy, and she was imprisoned for six weeks. Before her trial could come off she had to send to Richmond for Colonel Breckinridge to act as witness in her defense. He had been at Fortress Monroe when she first arrived there. She was arrested on the charge of having spoken treason to him.

There is a young man stopping at Dr. Cannon's, by the name of Stone. He has just come from Arkansas in company with recruits from that state for our army.

On Sunday, 18th, I went to church with Miss Cannon, my old friend Mr. Stickney, and Captain Prendergast. The last has again been wounded, and was then on his way to Mississippi. He does not like Hood as a commander, and gave us a description of the terrible work in the army since that general took command. They have had to march all day, throw up intrenchments at night, and fight incessantly! He says they have suffered almost beyond human endurance.

Macon is a beautiful place; the streets are very wide, and the buildings lofty. It is the third town in importance in Georgia, and is one hundred miles south-east of Atlanta. The Ocamulgee [Ocmulgee] River runs through it. It is a very patriotic place; the citizens have done much for the cause. The Wayside Home, of which Dr. Cannon has charge, is entirely supported by them. I only wish there was one at every place where our soldiers are likely to be detained. I think it one of the most useful institutions we have. When the soldiers get furloughs from the army or hospital, on their way home they are often detained at stopping-places, waiting for cars. They generally have no money, and nothing to eat, so they come to the Wayside Home, lodge there, and get their meals.[3]

[3] Wayside Homes were small hospitals, usually supported outside official Confederate channels and staffed by volunteers, " which sprang into existence at almost every railroad junction . . . to care for the numerous sick and wounded men who were dumped off or left stranded by the inefficient railroad service." Francis B. Simkins and James W. Patton, The Women of the Confederacy (Richmond, New York, 1936) , 95.

Several months ago Macon was attacked by a large raiding party, but it was driven off by our troops. I have been told by eye-witnesses that the enemy threw shells promiscuously, and some of them fell into the hospitals.

I got a very nice lot of clothes for my brother. Besides what I procured from Major Fairbanks, Dr. Cannon procured me some from the Georgia Relief Association, and also took the parcel and got the same society to send it on. I shall ever remember the kindness of Dr. Cannon and his charming daughters with heartfelt pleasure.

The morning I left Macon I met my two kind friends, Drs. Gamble and Bemiss. Dr. Gamble is now post surgeon of Macon. Dr. Bemiss is anxious to get back to the hospital again; he says it is much more gratifying to wait on patients than what he is doing.

Lieutenant Bond, a member of Garrity's battery, is killed. He had been wounded, and was on his way home, when the train met with an accident, and he was killed instantly. This is the third lieutenant that company has lost in the last three months.

September 24.—Newnan is now the head-quarters of the army. Hood is moving West. No one can tell what will be done next. Sherman is still in Atlanta. Every thing is quiet.

I have received a letter from my friend, Dr. Burt, who is now at Cuthbert, twenty miles below this place. The way the hospitals move from place to place puts me in mind of the contra-dance, where the head couple are always taking a jump to the foot. Some time ago I wished to go to the hospital which Dr. Burt is in, because it was so near the army, but now he is way below me. He gives an account of two raids which visited Oxford, near Covington, while he was there. He says the enemy infested the place twice; but, thanks to high weeds and green grass, he was not captured. He also says he is completely demoralized with what he has gone through and the fear of other raids, and that any thing *blue*, even the blue of heaven, gives him an unpleasant feeling.

We are getting the hospital put to rights again. On the square where the fire was new buildings are being erected. The latter is one of the things I do not like to see; for, like Dr. Burt and the blue, the sight of new lumber gives me an unpleasant feeling, as it is always a sure sign of our exodus. We are having a fine bakery built—I believe the eighth one our baker has had to put up since the war.

October 9.—Mr. Alexander Nixon died last night. He was a member of the Third Mississippi Regiment. He died perfectly happy, and intended to have joined the Methodist Church if he had lived till today. Mrs. Williamson was very attentive to him. She intends writing to his wife. His death is the only one we have had here, except that of a man who died the night of the fire. His father being with him, I took no pains to learn his name.

We have few dishes, knives, forks, or spoons, which annoys me not a little. We have two officers who eat with knives and forks which they have made themselves, out of wood. The last time I was at Macon I tried to procure some of those articles, but my efforts were fruitless.

November 20.—Paper is scarce, and money is scarcer; and, having neither, I have been unable to keep a record of past events; so I will sum up all I can recollect.

I paid five dollars for ten common hair-pins, and three dollars for a ball of common homespun thread.

I do not feel well, and have been taking horseback rides for my health, as I did in Chattanooga. I have been twice on foraging expeditions, with Mr. Yerby. He has a little wagon in which he drives out every day, and procures butter, buttermilk, and eggs. The days I went with him he took Sallie and Mrs. Smith's two children. I rode horseback, and we had quite a delightful time.

We visited the country people; they all seemed pleased to see us, and had a smile of welcome for Mr. Yerby. One lady gave me some nice cake and home-made wine.

Sorghum grows very plentifully in these regions; we saw fields of it, and the process of making the molasses.

Mr. Yerby gets quantities of buttermilk; butter and eggs are not quite so plentiful, as the foragers from Andersonville buy up every thing of that kind for the hospitals there. We use at least ten gallons of buttermilk per day.

I had another ride, in company with one of Dr. Cross's daughters and Mr. Moore. We visited Mrs. General Anderson, who is now here with her husband.

Many of our nurses have been sent to the army by an examining board. I know few of them are fit for field service. A Mr. Chandler could scarcely walk, from his wound; he was one of our best nurses. One hand of Mr. Holt, who had charge of the linen department, was useless, from the same cause. Many others have been sent off in like condition. If we can not do without such men, I think the country is badly off indeed.

I have made several nice acquaintances, and as we have few patients, I have spent two or three evenings in their company, practicing for our church choir. There is an Episcopal parish here, although there is no church. We have the use of the Presbyterian Church in the afternoons. Rev. Mr. Staley, an excellent preacher, officiates once a month. When he is not here, Dr. Adams has prayers, and sometimes preaches.

The ladies do not feed the men now, as we are doing very well in that respect ourselves. I told them they could do much good by mending the men's clothes, which they did once or twice; they also made a number of haversacks for the men, who have gone to the front.

We have two wounded officers from General Strahl's staff; one is

Lieutenant Kelly, the other Lieutenant Dupree. The latter is wounded in his leg and foot; he has suffered much from neuralgia. I gave him some of the lotion we had received from Mrs. Dr. Pierce, and it relieved him almost instantly. Mrs. Pierce has sent as a donation a dozen bottles of it, and we find it invaluable.

We have had a call from Dr. Hunter. The Newsom Hospital has been here, along with many others; all are moving in this direction. The Newsom has gone on to Mississippi.

A number of hospitals from North Georgia are encamped near the depot; the ladies with them are in tents, and I am told that they are more comfortable than our rooms. This I can well believe, as our sitting-room has so many openings that the wind rushes through it in every direction, and in the evenings we find it impossible to prevent our lights being blown out.

A clerk of one of the hospitals called on me the other day, and told me that the steward of his hospital was a young Scotchman, named Ross. He had been but six weeks in the country when the war broke out, and he enlisted in a Louisiana regiment, and lately has been a hospital steward. My friend lauded him very highly, and told me he had had it in his power to make at least fifty thousand dollars in the hospital, but he would not do it. I asked how this could be done, as I had often heard of stewards making fortunes, but could not exactly understand how they managed it. He informed me that men were sent out foraging; the country people, thinking they were giving it to the suffering, and for the cause, let them have their produce at a much lower rate than they sell it to the citizens. The stewards buy the food in this way, and speculate on it.

We have had several days of terror, to be long remembered. It was rumored that a raid had taken Columbus and Macon, and were marching down to free the prisoners at Andersonville, and set them loose to do their worst on us, but it was merely a rumor. I hear the prisoners are being moved away from Andersonville, which news has rejoiced us not a little. There is a good deal of talk about their treatment.[4]

[4] The fear of prisoners escaping from Camp Sumter, the prison stockade at Andersonville, was a constant one. The most complete record of conditions there is *Trial of Henry Wirz.*

Dr. Stout defended the location of the prison, declaring that he had previously decided to establish a hospital there but deferred to the desire of General Bragg to have a healthy place for a prison. Dr. Stout attributed the evils of the prison to overcrowding. He claimed that the Federals' refusal to permit exchanges and their declaration of medicine and surgical instruments as contraband led to the defeat of humane policy. "The inhumanity of their own government towards Federals in Southern prisons, must forever remain a blot upon the reputation of the authorities that refused to relieve its suffering prisoners of war, even at one time declining when invited to do so, to send its own surgeons with medicines and food suitable to the palates of the sick, to treat them and to administer to them." Stout, "An Address . . . ," *Southern Practitioner,* XXIV (1902), 450-51.

Dr. Hughes informed me that a friend of his—Lieutenant Allen—who is stationed there, and a young man of undoubted veracity, told him that in general the treatment of the prisoners was as good as our means would admit of. There is much suffering among them, but we can expect nothing else; it would be the same if as many of our own men were thrown together where supplies were exhausted. They get the same rations as our own men. The scurvy has broken out among them, but I am told that the country people around here are sending them quantities of vegetables.[5]

I see by the papers, that some who were exchanged, and sent to Atlanta, told their sufferings to their comrades, and they were about to wreak their vengeance on the prisoners in their hands.

Dr. Abernathy, one of our surgeons, asked them to hear him, and they did. He told them they must not blame our people, but their own, who would not have them exchanged. The crowd quietly dispersed, evidently fully convinced that we were not to blame.

How can they expect us to feed their people, when we can scarcely feed our own? They have destroyed our provisions whenever they have had an opportunity. Sherman, and many of their generals, have issued orders not only to destroy food, but garden implements. And then only think that no entreaties will make them exchange them! Lincoln and his minions have this sin on their consciences.

Some of the exchanged prisoners have held a meeting in Savannah, and denounced their own government for leaving them with us, and fully exonerate ours from all blame.

Dr. Hughes's youngest son has been to see him, and paid us a visit. He is a fine-looking young man, and a true southerner. He was at school when the clarion of war was sounded through the land; he cast aside his books and entered the army, determined to battle for the right. He is now with General Wheeler, and is very hopeful of our success. He told us that the army had gone into Tennessee, and that ere long we would hear of brilliant exploits being done by it in that

[5] Dr. Jones testified at Wirz's trial: "They had plenty of food in one sense, but it was not of the proper character for sick men." He treated the prevalence of scurvy at length in his report and recommended that the best treatment for it and for gangrene would be "to furnish liberal supplies of well-cured meat, together with fresh beef and vegetables, and to enforce a rigid system of hygiene." Though he blamed much on the prisoners themselves and their unsanitary habits, and though he maintained that the ration at Andersonville was equal to that of the Confederate guards, he was fully aware of the horrible conditions in the prison. He concluded his recommendations: "This gigantic mass of human misery calls loudly for relief, not only for the sake of suffering humanity, but also on account of our own brave soldiers now captives in the hands of the federal government. Strict justice to the gallant men of the confederate armies, who have been or who may be, so unfortunate as to be compelled to surrender in battle, demands that the confederate government should adopt that course which will best secure their health and comfort in captivity; or at least leave their enemies without a shadow of an excuse for any violation of the rules of civilized warfare in the treatment of prisoners." *Trial of Henry Wirz*, 641, 639.

quarter. I asked him what was to be done with Sherman, as he is not disposed of? He answered, that if he attempted to march through Georgia, our cavalry was to march before him, and destroy all the food, and his army would be starved out.

I do not know any thing about military matters, but it does seem to me that there might be a better plan adopted than that to rid the country of this marauder.

We hear little or nothing of what is being done in the rest of the Confederacy. I remarked this to a friend in Macon, who said he would like to live here, as he was wearied with listening to war stories. But we hear plenty of reports. Dame Rumor, with her many tongues, is ever on the go.

We have been told that Forrest and Wheeler have Sherman hemmed in, and numerous other things that we can place no dependence upon.

We attended the wedding of Miss Kate Furlough [Furlow], one of the *elite* of the town, which took place in the Methodist Church. There were about eighteen young ladies who stood up with the bride, but no gentleman with the groom, as there are none scarcely in the town. The wedding-party was quite a pretty sight.

Dr. Estell, an assistant surgeon in the Bragg Hospital, died lately. He was in his seventy-fifth year, and a most princely-looking man. He was attended by his bosom friends, Drs. Cross and Hughes, who resorted to every means that experienced skill could bring to bear to restore him to health and usefulness, but all in vain; he sank under his disease, and departed this life beloved and regretted by all who knew him.

Colonel Colyar, whom I met in Newnan, is his son-in-law. His daughter, Mrs. Colyar, and his son, Colonel F. Estell, were with him during his illness.

He was from Tennessee, and joined the army at the outbreak of the war, and had served in it ever since. His home is in the hands of the enemy, and his invalid wife was turned out of doors, and has since died. . . .

I went to see him, but he could scarcely speak. He pressed my hand, and murmured faintly, " I am happy." He was a man of highly cultivated mind and polished address.

One of the ladies, Mrs. Byrom, in the same hospital, lost her husband. He lived a Christian, and died one. He was from Tennessee, and was in that army through the late campaign. After he came here, all thought he only required rest; but not so: he sank under the disease, and death claimed him as his own.

His wife has been in the hospital service for some time. She came out from Tennessee with her parents, who are now living in North Georgia, so she is again separated from them.

A little while ago I met a brother of hers, Dr. Powell, who had just come from Atlanta. He told us that in some instances the Federal soldiers had behaved shamefully to the inhabitants, and he did not think Sherman had it in his power to restrain them.

I suppose, as we have had so little to do, that we have had a better chance of hearing what " they say " than we had before. The good people of this place have fallen into an error that we poor mortals are very apt to commit; that is, talking thoughtlessly about what we are totally ignorant of, and thus doing gross injustice to persons' characters, and hurting their feelings without ever intending it. Scarcely a day passes that we do not hear some slander against the attachees of the hospitals: all suffer.

We are told that the surgeons had better be at the front, as they kill more than they cure; and that they drink all the liquor and eat all the good things provided for the soldiers.

I can not keep from laughing at all this, although we ladies come in for a share of the scandal. But I am like the Quaker whom the man called a liar. He said, " Friend, prove it; if thee can, I am one; if thee can not, then thee is one."

Dr. Gore, formerly surgeon of the Bragg Hospital, was an eminent physician in Bloomfield, Kentucky. He gave up every thing for the cause, and since his entering the army has been devoted to his country. Dr. Cross, his successor, was one of the wealthiest men in North Alabama, and is a high-toned gentleman. He joined the army at the outbreak of the war, and has nobly done his duty.

One of his assistant surgeons was Dr. Estell, of whom I have already made mention. Dr. Redwine, another of his assistant surgeons, is a refined gentleman, and was also a man of wealth. Dr. Adams is the third assistant surgeon; of his worldly goods, I am unable to give an account, but I can say that he is rich in all that constitutes true riches. He is a Christian, and an humble and devout one. I feel confident that he never had a patient who would not gladly give him all of his " good things " any day, just to see him eat them, as his health is so bad.

I have already spoken of the surgeons in the Foard; they are on a par with those of the Bragg.

I wonder if it ever strikes these good people, who give such open expression to their views, that surely these gentlemen did not sacrifice so much to come into a hospital, just for the purpose of drinking the liquors and eating the poor diet of the patients.

The first is so bad that I do not believe any of our surgeons could be paid to drink it. And do not these good people know that the surgeons, with the exception of Dr. Adams, who is a patient, all board away from the hospital, and get plenty to eat at their boarding-houses.

Our post chaplain, when we first came here, requested me to see if some of the citizens would not take him to board.

None that I spoke to would do so. After awhile a rich man, and one of his own persuasion, took him. The first month's board was, I believe, two hundred dollars; the next was to be three hundred. I think his pay from the government is eighty dollars per month, and he does not get all of that, unless he is more fortunate than the rest of us.

As we know him to be a man who, like ourselves, does not care what kind of food he gets, so it is eatable, we asked him to come and board with us. Besides giving his rations, he could pay his board, and that could go into the hospital fund. Dr. Hughes would not give his consent to this arrangement. He said it would be a breach of the hospital regulations.

Mr. Moore found a boarding-house with a family, I believe refugees, where he has his rations cooked, and pays what he can afford.

The term " hospital rat " I have often heard applied to our hospital attendants. When I hear men, whom I have known suffer so much as many of our men have done, called by such an odious name, I can not help being indignant.

Mr. Dyson from Kentucky, was severely wounded in battle, and is in bad health. He is one of our head nurses. Mr. Catlet, our baggage-master, is from Kentucky. I believe he served under Morgan, and received a severe wound in battle, from the effects of which I fear he will never recover.

Mr. Williams of Tennessee, our commissary, from all appearances, is a stout, hearty man; but he was wounded badly at Murfreesboro; a ball entered his lungs, and is still lodged there. He can not walk any distance without suffering.

Mr. Bohannon from Georgia assists me in giving the men their meals, and is as good as any lady in that respect. He has little or no use of one of his hands, from a wound.

I could give many more just such examples of our " hospital rats." Have these men not endured enough, and are they not serving their country now? They are gentlemen, and have not been used to the menial labor they do here; but they do it cheerfully, knowing it is for their country's good. . . .[6]

As a whole, the people have been very kind. We have received more assistance from them than at any other place where we have been. Several ladies send us a pitcher of sweet milk daily. A lady, on my telling her that one of our men could not go to church for want of clothes, gave him a nice new suit. And the ladies' society had a pair of shoes made for a soldier who was barefooted. We are living in a part of a small cottage; the owner, Mrs. Smith, a very nice lady, in the other:

[6] " The Hospital Rat," however, was an object of general Confederate derision. George Dunn & Company of Richmond published a comic valentine on the theme in 1863 with a contemptuous illustration and verse on the idea " I'll take your physic, but not take the field." But the true hospital rats were not the attendants in the hospitals but those who " if sent to the field one week . . . would be sure to be back the next, on some trifling pretext of sickness or disability." Pember, *A Southern Woman's Story*, 181.

her husband has gone to the army. The house is a poor one, clap-boarded inside, with daylight peeping through portions of it. The floors of our sleeping-rooms have seams in them at least an inch in width. We have nothing of which to complain in the way of ventilation.

There is a Baptist, Methodist, and Presbyterian Church here, and on last fast-day they all united and had prayers, but no preaching. Many a solemn prayer was offered up to Him who sitteth in the heavens, in behalf of our foes. The Presbyterian and Methodist ministers have been to call on us. The former has service very often in the hospital, and the men like him very much.

November 26.—We are all ready to make another move. Our hospitals are ordered to Gainesville, Alabama. The base of our army is changed. This will be a long, tedious trip, as we have to change cars very often. Well, there is no use in grumbling.

We have been packed up for some time. We are leaving a nice bake-house, the best the baker has yet put up, a new dining-room and kitchen, and the nicest kind of a distributing-room. I knew when I saw them going up that our doom was sealed as to remaining here.

There has been quite a battle near Macon,[7] and we have had some wounded from it; but I have not seen them. They are militia.

I hear the men telling a good many jokes on them. One poor boy, when he came to the hospital, said the battle was the most *terrible* of the war. It was quite a severe fight. The enemy set a trap, and the unsophisticated militia were caught in it. I believe there were at least one hundred killed and many wounded, and I am told they were nearly all old men. The *veterans* whom I have heard speak of the fight say that old soldiers never would have rushed in as the militia did.

" Joe Brown's Pets " have done much better than any one expected; they have fought well when they have had it to do.

We have some wounded men, who were with General Early in his late disastrous campaign. I have heard some of them blame General Early for not marching right up to Washington, as they think he could have taken it.

[7] Miss Cumming received exaggerated reports from " Joe Brown's Pets." Frederick H. Dyer in his *A Compendium of the War of the Rebellion* (Des Moines, 1908), 721, classifies the actions near Macon on November 20 and 21 as skirmishes.

✠✠✠

X: MOBILE

✠✠✠

December 12, 1864.—Left Americus on Sunday, the 27th ult. We had a very nice box-car. Mrs. Williamson, not being very well, had a bunk put up in one corner, and we had a curtain hung across, making quite a snug little room. In the afternoon we stopped at a place called Butler, where we were detained all night. It was bleak and barren-looking, and had very deep sand. Dr. Hughes and myself went to service, which was held in a small building. We heard a very good sermon preached by a chaplain. There were numbers of soldiers there; and, as usual, all listened with profound attention. The preacher told us that the war would not cease until Christians lived more up to what they professed than they did now, and that they had much to answer for in this matter.

The Bragg Hospital was on the train with us. Miss Burford and Mrs. Byrom, the matrons, and Dr. Cross's family were with it, which made the trip much pleasanter for us. Dr. Cross was a man of wealth, and when he joined the army left his family well provided for. They lived near Tuscumbia, in the northern portion of Alabama.. When the enemy went there they took every thing that Mrs. Cross had: upward of seventy negroes, twenty-five thousand pounds of meat, all her live stock, and a large amount of grain, and a large supply of groceries for family use. After they took all of these things, they *politely* asked Mrs. Cross to leave the house, as they intended burning it. They would not give her time to get a change of clothes for her children. Her old father was an invalid, and had to hobble out on crutches. After getting through with her house, they went to a neighbor's and did the same. The officer in command made a great fuss talking; but, as usual, did nothing to restore what was lost. I have been intimate with this amiable family some time, and their uncomplaining endurance of their wrongs has excited my unbounded admiration. I have never heard a complaint from any of them. Mrs. Cross tells me that, since she has lost every thing, nothing annoys her. Miss Cross is a highly educated and refined young lady, and has traveled in Europe.

We left Butler on the 28th, and arrived at Columbus the same day. There we met some of our Newnan friends, who had gone there for fear of the enemy.

Columbus is quite a pretty place; the streets are very wide, and the houses handsome; many of them had very beautiful flower-gardens around them. I noticed some very magnificent public buildings. It is on the Chattahoochee River, ninety miles west south-west of Macon, one hundred and twenty-eight miles west south-west of Milledgeville, and two hundred and ninety miles west of Savannah. The river is the dividing state line; a handsome bridge extends across it to the village of Gerad [Girard], in Alabama, which is well fortified in case of raids. At this point it is navigable for steamboats to the Gulf of Mexico during eight months of the year. Large quantities of cotton were shipped from here annually, and at this time it is filled with that staple, sent from various points, to be out of the way of the enemy. It is the terminus of the Moscogee [Muscogee] Railroad, and a branch of the West Point.

We left Columbus on the 30th, about 8 A. M.; arrived in Montgomery the same day. I learned that the trains were not running to Mobile, as something had happened to the railroad; and as I had no money to pay my passage on the boat, I was compelled to remain in Montgomery, with the hope of soon getting on with the hospital. Montgomery was filled with hospitals, moving in the same direction as ourselves; so there was a prospect of a lengthy sojourn at that place.

We were given possession of an empty car that had been set aside for refugees, which I named " Refugee Hall." We did very well, considering every thing. We had our cooking done outside, and the weather was very fine. I shall not have so much sympathy for refugees I see in cars again. But we were not in it long enough for the novelty to wear off.

On Sunday, the 4th inst., I went to the church of the " Holy Comforter." The rector, Dr. Scott, preached an excellent sermon. The Bragg Hospital had left to go to Gainesville, by the way of Selma.

On Monday, the 5th, I called to see Dr. Scott on business, and he very kindly gave me aid. He introduced me to a friend, Judge Jordan (another refugee from Florida) , who transacted my business with dispatch. I am much indebted to him for his kindness.

I saw little prospect of the hospital getting away from Montgomery, as the boats were busy and so few. I concluded to come on by myself, and pay my way, as we were told that if we went at government expense we would have to take a *deck passage*. Dr. Hughes very kindly loaned me $200; so on Tuesday, the 6th, I left Montgomery on a steamer for Selma. On the boat I met Bishop Wilmer of Alabama; with him, a highly accomplished lady, Mrs. Irwin, who was on her way to Tuscaloosa, Alabama, to become a deaconess.

I have no doubt that this order in the church, will be the means of accomplishing much good. Since the war we have felt the necessity of such an organization, to teach our women the art of nursing.

There are to be church homes for the benefit of the aged and helpless, orphan asylums, and schools, under their supervision. Bishop Wilmer is fortunate in having an excellent lady, Miss Hewitt of Baltimore, as chief deaconess. She is a woman of energy, intelligence, and devout piety.

Bishop Wilmer has been but a few years bishop of Alabama. He is a Virginian. He is the youngest-looking bishop I ever saw; he has nothing of the "venerable" in his appearance. He is very fine-looking—is a man of energy and ability, and is much beloved in his diocese.

We arrived at Selma on the 7th; there I saw Dr. Jackson, and learned that the Bragg Hospital was still in Selma. He sent a telegram for ours to come and go the same route. I had a little girl with me, for whom the clerk of the boat had charged full price. I sent for the captain (Finnigan) ; informed him of the circumstance, and that the child was a soldier's orphan. He immediately refunded all the money.

We took another boat at 12 A. M., and started en route for Mobile. We had a very pleasant party on board; among them many of the citizens of Mobile returning home, who had *refugeed* from fear of an attack. I heard many say that they did not care what might happen, they would not run again.

Captain Curran, whom I little expected to see alive at this time, was on board. He is still helpless from his wound. There was also a very sick doctor, by the name of Holmes, whom I visited. Poor fellow! he did not look as if he was long for this world. He had been on duty with my friend, Dr. Divine, at Macon.

A young lady, Miss M., one of the handsomest women in Mobile, sat near me at table, and when I told her how I had been employed since the war, she said she had often wished to do the same. I wondered what hindered her.

I made the acquaintance of Rev. Dr. Hamilton of the Methodist Church; his wife and daughter were with him. I knew him well by reputation as an eminent preacher, and a particular friend of Mrs. Williamson's.

I was introduced to Major Hester of the Twenty-second Alabama Regiment. We had a long talk about the times. He was on his way to the army; had been in the service ever since the commencement of the war. He said, when he saw so many men as there are at home making fortunes, who had never been in the service, that his patriotism cooled a little. He informed me that Montgomery was full of such. He has a relative, a Scotchman, who had run the blockade, and was daily expected back. I believe he was on government business. Scotland was a theme of conversation with us. Major Hester was an enthusiastic admirer of "Auld Scotia," as nearly all I have met in the South are.

I met an old friend, who was going to Mobile, in company with a bridal party, as even in these war times people "marry and are given in marriage." The groom is a soldier. The bride was pretty, as all brides are, and we were much indebted to her for helping to while away the time, by discoursing " sweet music," although the time did not hang heavy on my hands, as I had a copy of Joseph the Second— a charming work, by Muhlbach, translated from the German, by one of our literary stars—Mrs. Chaudron.[1]

We arrived at Mobile on the 9th, and found every thing pretty much as usual, and the enemy still expected.

Sunday, September 11.—The alarm-bell rang early this morning—a sure sign that " the enemy had come this time." All the home guards turned out, with them the " burly British Guard," and their " venerable " Captain Wheeler. In the guard are a few more " venerables," one being a paternal relative of mine. The women folks went to church, but I know that their thoughts often wandered to the intrenchments.

It has been one of the coldest days we have experienced this season. About 10 P. M. one of the " venerables " came from the intrenchments, and informed us that it was another " wolf " alarm. So " Richard is himself again "—" till next time."

December 20.—We have heard rumor after rumor about the battle in Tennessee, which was fought last month at Franklin. It is now confirmed that we have gained a victory, and that our army is closely investing Nashville. As usual with our victories, a darkened shadow hangs over them, that veils their brightness. It is the vision of the terrible carnage, and the spirits of the mighty dead, but

> " Is't death to fall for freedom's right?
> He's dead alone that lacks her right! "

We have been told that at the battle our dead lay in heaps; our men stormed and took every breastwork that the foe had. Many a brave spirit has winged its flight to regions above. The gallant Cleburne is among the slain, General Strahl, and many others of our best men. Mobile, as usual, is a loser. In a letter received from my brother, he informs me of the death of two members of his company, Mr. N. Leonard and Mr. M. Kavanaugh, and of many being wounded.

The battle was fought on the 30th November, commencing at 3 P.M., and raging until 3 next morning. It is said that the scene presented when day dawned was appalling; rider and horse lay in the trenches, one lifeless mass. Well, God alone knows what is best. We can but say, " Thy will be done."

December 25.—Christmas day—the nativity of our Lord and Savior; the day he left his throne on high, and came in his humility to dwell on earth, and on which was sung in heaven

[1] [Clara Mundt,] *Joseph II. and His Court, an Historical Novel*, by L. Mühlbach [*pseud.*]; from the German by Adelaide de V. Chaudron . . . (4 vols., Mobile, 1864).

"Gloria in excelsis! peace! to man
Good will! . . ."

"Good will to man!" Many of our enemies profess to believe these precious words, and yet how little of it they manifest for us.

What visions of cheer does not the sound of "Merry Christmas" bring in review—happiness, plenty, and a forgetting for a few short hours the cares of this weary world! This one has been any thing but merry to us; a gloom has hung over all, that, do what we will, we can not dispel. Our thoughts, whether we will or no, wander to where our armies are struggling to maintain our rights against fearful odds. Alas! when will this strife and bloodshed cease? When will we have peace? "Sweet peace is in her grave!"

The weather is very inclement; too much so for us to attend the services of the sanctuary. Last evening I visited St. John's Church. It was very beautifully dressed with evergreens, I thought more so than I had ever seen it before. I am told that all the Episcopal Churches in the city are decorated the same.

December 31.—The last day of '64, and much coveted peace seemingly as distant as ever. If it were not for the knowledge that there is an end to all things, and that some day there will be an end to this, it would be unbearable. The past year has equaled any of its predecessors for carnage and bloodshed. Our land is drenched with the blood of martyrs! Her fair hills and valleys, lit by blazing homesteads, and echoing to the booming of artillery and the roar of musketry. The very air is rent with the groans of the wounded and dying, and the wail of the widow and orphan. Lord, turn not thy face from us, and save, O, save us from this terrible scourge! "Let not our sins now cry against us for vengeance! Hear us, Jehovah, for mercy imploring: from thy dread displeasure, O, bid us be free!"

Although woe and desolation stare at us every way we turn, the heart of the patriot is as firm as ever, and determined that, come what may, he will never yield. There is no doubt but we have some among us whose love of self forbids their minds to rise above the dank sod upon which they tread; men who have never known what it is to experience a thrill of pleasure, when listening to the " patriot's moving story, shedding for freemen's rights his generous blood." Such we have among us; but, thank the Giver of all good, they are in the minority. . . .

The brave army of Virginia is defending Richmond as gallantly as ever.

Any news we hear from Tennessee is uncertain, as the railroad for many miles between Corinth and Nashville is destroyed. The last heard from there our army was besieging Nashville.

Charleston, heroic Charleston, has proved a very Charybdis to the invader. Our champions on the water are doing us good service by

246

destroying the enemy's commerce. Their very names strike terror to the heart of the foe. The army, with the valiant Kirby Smith at its head, is keeping the enemy in check in Louisiana.

But O, my heart sickens when I think of the many, many valiant heroes who have left us, never more to return. . . .

God grant that their lives have not been offered up in vain, and that the time is not far distant when triumphant peace will spread her wings over this now distracted land.

January 5, 1865.—Our hospitals have all been ordered to Tennessee.[2] I am highly delighted at this new move, as it shows that our army is still triumphant. The Foard has changed surgeons. Dr. Hughes had several of his ribs fractured by a fall from the cars, while in Montgomery. He has resigned until he recruits in health. Dr. de Yampert of Alabama has taken his place.

At a party a short time ago I met a friend, Mrs. Payne, who had just come from Enterprise, Mississippi. She was there at the time of Sherman's raid. As we do not know the moment when we may be *honored* by a visit from the enemy, we were all eager to know how she had done, as she fared much better than many others. She informed us that when the enemy came into the town, they commenced firing promiscuously, and her little daughter, who was in the yard at the time, came very near being shot. About twenty-five of these marauders entered her house at one time. She had no one with her but the children. The sight of such a mob of lawless men filled her with dismay, but she did not lose her presence of mind, and tried to appear perfectly collected. She remarked to them that in such a crowd there must be at least one or two gentlemen, and if there were any among them, she called on them to come forward and protect her. After this speech she burst into tears. These two appeals were too much for even these vandals, and she thinks they looked ashamed of themselves, and one stepped forward, saying he would protect her. He remained with her while the others ransacked her house, from the garret to the cellar. They broke open her trunks, drawers, and pantries. She offered them her keys, but they laughed at her, saying they had no use for them. They took every little trinket that they came across, and did not even leave her scissors and thimble.

The vandals remained at Enterprise some four or five days, but she

[2] From Auburn, Alabama, Dr. Dudley D. Saunders had written to Dr. Stout on October 25 with great enthusiasm for Hood's campaign into Tennessee. "Friday night Genl Hood, Beauregard & Lt Gen [Stephen D.] Lee addressed the troops. The former told them by the first snow his Army would confront Nashville. . . . Lt Genl Lee said that Genl Sherman was demoralized & that by the time he could get up with us in Middle Tennessee he would have no army to fight with. . . . Make your arrangements to go with my Corps to Huntsville Ala some time next month & the month after to Nashville. Our army is represented as being men wild with enthusiasm & seem to think they can whip the whole Yankee nation, now that the order is forward march towards Nashville." ALs, Stout papers (Emory).

was not further molested by them, as she had the protection of one of the officers. He called on her, and offered her his aid, as she had been very kind to a young lady cousin of his some few years before. The cousin had requested him, in case of their meeting, to protect her.

This lady's negroes all deserted her in her hour of trial, with the exception of one, and told the enemy about some valuables she had hid away. Nearly the whole town was laid in ashes, but it only shared the fate of every other town in Mississippi which the vandals visited. I am told that nearly every house in Okolona is leveled with the ground.

Mobile is gayer than ever; it seems as if the people have become reckless.[3] I am told that there was as much visiting on New Year's day as there usually is in peace times. The city is filled with military, which is one cause of the gayety.

There is no necessity of our discussing war or politics (I mean the ladies), as we have an all-absorbing topic in the matter of dress and " something to eat " " How do you manage to live? " or, " What have you got to wear? " is the first question on meeting a friend, no matter where. The answer as to the eating is usually, " We live on peas, corn meal, and bacon." These are the staples, and the rule; the exceptions are flour, tea, coffee, and sugar, and they are all at famine prices.

The scarcity of coffee seems to affect the spirits of the people more than any thing else. I have noticed that some who did not touch it before the war, talk as gravely about its loss as if their very existence depended upon it, and indeed they are quite melancholy about it. It is amusing to see how seriously it is discussed. I have said jestingly that I do believe it will yet be the means of subjugating us. When invited any place, if we are certain of getting a cup of pure coffee, or even a cup of that which " cheers," there is no sending " regrets " to that invitation.

The enemy have deprived us of one great luxury since taking possession of the bay; that is, oysters. They are not to be had, unless at an exorbitant price. With all this " starving," people look well. I am told that there is less dyspepsia than was ever known before. The poor do not suffer as much as one would think. Work of all kinds seems to be plentiful, and the Supply Association is still in operation.

In the matter of dress we are pretty " hard up," and if the war lasts much longer, I for one will have " nothing to wear." We have a good many kinds of homespun for dresses; but it makes a very expensive dress. I have heard many say that they would rather have one good calico than three homespuns.

We have a very excellent home-made cloth for gentlemen's clothing.

[3] This phenomenon of approaching defeat was remarked in Richmond by Miss Pember who commented: " To thinking people this recklessness was ominous." " All this winter of '64," she wrote, " the city had been unusually gay. Besides parties, private theatricals and tableaux were constantly exhibited." *A Southern Woman's Story*, 164, 163.

I have seen some, made with a mixture of cow's hair and cotton, which was really nice, and I am told that it is water-proof. I had no idea our people were so ingenious.

A friend showed me a nice pair of gloves she had made from the ravelings of scraps of silk, worked in with a little cotton. The same lady makes all the shoes worn by her household.

Dyeing old clothes is about the most fashionable thing done; those who can not afford to pay for it do it themselves. The materials used are to be found in the woods.

Gentlemen's and ladies' hats are made out of saw palmetto. The ladies braid it, and use it to trim their dresses, and it makes a very pretty trimming.

We have any amount of shoe establishments, and very nice boots and shoes are made in them. An excellent pair of ladies' calf-skin bootees can be bought for one hundred dollars, and men's are one hundred and fifty.

The gentlemen talk a good deal about the ladies dressing extravagantly, but I do not think they do so. We have learned the art of making " auld claes look amaist as weel's the new." All the rag-bags have been emptied, and dresses turned and cut into all kinds of shapes. Any and every thing is the fashion; nothing is lost. The old scraps of worsted and flannel are carefully unraveled, carded, and spun, for making capes and nubias. The fact is, it is a kind of disgrace to have plenty of clothes. If any one has on a new silk or calico dress, kid gloves, or any thing that is foreign, they have to give an account of how they came by it.

The Confederate oil is much improved; but we can only buy a very little at a time, as it becomes gummy by standing, and will not burn. Alabama abounds in coal, and yet we find it almost impossible to get any, and wood is from sixty to seventy dollars per cord.

There is nothing cheap. I sometimes think we will be charged for the light of heaven and the air we breathe. We expect after awhile to have to pay for merely asking for a sight of goods. Well, these are things that we can afford to laugh at, as we know they will not last forever.

I have been visiting in the suburbs, and really it is a sad sight to see how desolate every place is. The fine shrubbery, trees, and beautiful flower-gardens, once the boast of Mobile, are now laid waste by the military authorities in preparing for the defense of the city. Every tree, fruit and shade, has been demolished, and even rose-bushes have been destroyed. All houses near the intrenchments are ordered to be fired on the approach of the enemy.

We have excellent public schools, and, much to the gratification and surprise of many, they are still in operation. I was certain that the war would close them; but, as a rule, our citizens have been very energetic and liberal in money matters.

249

January 7.—I have just returned from paying a visit to Bienville Square; a very fine band of music plays there some two or three times a week, and makes it a very pleasant place of resort.

While there, we heard that the men of the Twenty-first Alabama Regiment, who have been for some time prisoners at Ship Island, are exchanged, and have returned home. I am told that they received shocking treatment at the hands of their jailer.

We have bad news from Tennessee; the particulars have not yet come, but it is believed that General Hood has met with a great repulse, and is retreating.

January 8.—To-day I visited a friend, Mr. Henry Griffin, one of the Ship Island prisoners, and a member of the Twenty-first Alabama Regiment. I never saw such an emaciated frame as his. He is completely prostrated from disease and starvation.

Many of our men who were captured when the Mobile forts were taken were sent to New Orleans, and from thence to Ship Island. They were placed under negro guards, and every possible indignity heaped upon them. They had to walk many miles for every stick of wood they used, and if they showed the least disposition to lay down their load, they had a bayonet stuck into them by the guard.

When sick, they were put on straw right on the ground, and Mr. Griffin says, on putting your hand down with a slight pressure, the water would gush up.

When I listened to this recital, and thought of the humane treatment I had seen their men receive, my blood boiled with indignation. Our surgeons would not allow a nurse or any one to say an unbecoming word to them; and many a time while in Chattanooga I have received the strictest orders concerning what I must prepare for them.

Surely these wrongs will benefit our people, and stimulate them to more exertion than ever before. I think that is why they are allowed. I have been told by more than Mr. Griffin, that a lad named Dunklin, from Alabama, was shot dead by a negro guard, while putting a potato on the stove to cook.* Well, there is a time for all things. . . . I feel

* Joseph Dunklin, a private of Company K, Lockhart's batallion, aged sixteen years, was shot dead by a negro soldier, at half-past 3 o'clock, P. M., December 15, 1864, on Ship Island, under the following circumstances:
Dunklin had been sick, and was recovering. A lot of sweet potatoes (which were a rarity to us) had been sent by the citizens of Mobile to the prisoners; the little fellow, thinking he would like one roasted, asked permission of the sentinel then on duty to cook it on the stove, which permission was granted, (this always being done after regular meals had been served up.) The sentinels in the mean time were changed, and he went near the stove, and asked the cook to please give him the potato. As the cook was in the act of handing it to him, he saw the sentinel cocking his gun, and aiming it at the little boy; the cook said to him, "Look out, he is going to shoot!" and immediately the sentinel fired, shooting him through the heart, and killing him instantly. He then loaded his gun again, remarking, "I have killed one of the damned rebels, and I'll kill another if I can get a chance!" Not a word of precaution was given Dunklin before the sentinel

as confident that in time our wrongs will be redressed, as I am that I am living. In listening to all these tales of wrong and insult, I can not but think that our sins must have been great to have deserved them.

January 12.—The late bad news from Tennessee is confirmed. A friend—one of our most influential citizens—has received a letter from his young son, which gives a graphic description of the retreat of our brave but unfortunate army from before Nashville. I give it as it is written, knowing the writer's veracity to be beyond a doubt:

CAMP WAGON-TRAIN, TRUEHEART'S BATTERY,

NEAR FRANKLIN, TENNESSEE,

December 16, 1864.

MY DEAR FATHER—Before this reaches you, the news of our defeat yesterday will have been received. As you will be anxious, let me say, in the first place, that I came through without a scratch.

Yesterday morning early the enemy began sharp-shooting in our front; that is, the front of Stewart's corps, which was the extreme left of Hood's line. We soon received orders—that is, our ordnance train and forage wagons, which are under command of the batallion quartermaster, Captain Spindle, with whom I am detailed as clerk—to be ready to move at any moment. This must have been about 2 o'clock, and was the first notice we received that there was any danger. No one had any idea that the enemy were then massing on our left. The firing soon became heavy, and our infantry commenced moving to the right—our right, but really the center of Hood's line.

Major Trueheart being in the line, Captain Spindle dispatched a courier to him, to know whether he would move his train out or not, as the enemy's shells began to fall pretty thick. Before the courier returned, Captain Spindle decided to move all his train, except the ordnance, further to the rear, and ordered me to go with him.

I started, and got upon a high hill, where I could see the Yankees moving on our left, and preparing to charge Lumsden's battery.

And here, in order that you may understand the whole affair better, I will give you a description of our position, as far as I saw it, from the left toward the right.

It was in the form of a half circle, the center about a mile and a half from the Yankee line around Nashville. Cheatham was on the

---

fired, except by the cook, and all he could do then was to draw his shoulders up, and was immediately killed. Dr. Robinson was immediately sent for, and said, " This boy has been brutally murdered, and he intended to report it immediately." He entered the death on his hospital record, " Shot dead by a sentinel! " The sentinel said that orders were given him by Lieutenant W. C. Abby, 74th U. S. C. I., then officer of the guard, to allow no one to go to the stove but the cook. Colonel C. D. Anderson, Twenty-first Alabama Regiment, demanded an investigation, but was told by Colonel Holmstedt, commanding the post, that this was a right that " prisoners of war could not demand! "

EYE-WITNESS.

right, Lee in the center, and Stewart on the left. Walthall's division of Stewart's corps was on the extreme left of our corps. Our battalion was with Walthall's division, Lumsden's battery being on the left; one section of Tarrant's battery came next; one of ours (Seldon's battery) about a half mile further to the right; the other section of Tarrant's battery came next, and the remaining two guns of our battery on the extreme of Walthall's division.

The enemy, as I stated above, first flanked and took Lumsden's battery, the captain and most of his men making their escape. They immediately turned our guns on us, and took Tarrant's two guns. About this time I succeeded in getting to the section of our battery to which my gun belongs. I saw the enemy advance and take Lumsden's battery. On getting to my piece, I took a *blow*, and then went to work. I found Major Storrs in charge of the section.

The enemy soon began to appear in two lines of battle on our immediate front, and we poured shell and solid shot on them very heavily, causing them to halt. Our ammunition getting scarce, the major ordered us to reserve our fire. Our infantry support, consisting of about one hundred men of Sayre's brigade (the general himself in our works) continued to fire a few rounds now and then. The Yankees about this time commenced a furious cannonading, and we had to remain idle behind our works.

We received orders about this time to hitch up and save our guns, as the enemy was now seen coming up the pike, in our rear, and at the same time charging in two or three lines of battle (I am not quite sure which) on our front and right flank.

We got our two pieces about four hundred yards from our works, in a muddy field, where we had to abandon one of them; two of the horses being shot, leaving only four, and they were not able to pull it. Our other gun and our ammunition wagon we brought off. Just as we arrived in this field, the last brigade, either Shelly's (Canty's [Cantey's] old brigade) or Renold's [Reynold's], being flanked, and the Yankees two hundred yards, in two lines of battle, on their left and rear, broke, General Walthall himself giving the order. From this time it was one perfect stampede for a mile. As I came out, I saw a pony rearing and pitching, and being nearly worn out, went back and got him. But after doing this I got so far behind, and the shells and minies came so thick and fast, I could not mount the pony until I reached a skirt of wood. As soon as I got on him I felt so relieved that I did not care much what came. I was so nearly worn out, that had I not got the horse I do not know what I should have done.

After falling back nearly a mile (I may not be correct in the distance, as the fatigue made it seem much longer than it really was, I suppose) we formed a second line of battle, and there I left the front, as my piece had gone on, and we had no ammunition with which to fire any longer. As I had nothing to eat, and no blanket, I

252

started to find our wagons, which I did after walking three or four miles, *en route* for this place. Being tired out, I got in a wagon and remained in it till we reached our present camp, which is a mile and a half south of Franklin. We reached here about 1 or 2 o'clock in the morning; I am not certain whether this is the 15th, 16th, or 17th; I think it is Friday, the 16th.

I am so tired and sleepy that I can scarcely write, and only do so because an opportunity of sending a letter to-morrow offers, and I know you will want to hear from me. I fear many of our infantry were captured. All of Trueheart's battalion of artillery, except Sergeant Riddle's piece (eleven out of twelve), to which I belong, was taken. I gave myself up once or twice, and felt sure that by this morning I would be on my way to some Yankee prison; but, God be thanked, I am safe and sound.

Our last news from Sherman was good; viz: that he had been compelled to fortify about eighty miles from Port Royal, South Carolina. Is this news?

When I left the front, about 8 P. M., no one knew whether we were going to stand and form a new line, or fall back to this point. I never had such a fine view of the enemy approaching before. If we had only had some works; but even without these, had we only been reinforced, we might have done better, for it was very evident to every one that the Yankees had massed on the extreme left.

Give my sincere love to mother, sisters, and all the family, and many kisses to the little ones. God grant that we may yet be victorious, and that peace may soon spread her balmy wings over this troubled land.

The country we are in is a rich one, and we have been doing well. We had no idea we would so soon be made to leave our winter-quarters. I had sent Bill down to Columbia to pay a visit. We had chimneys to our tents, and were doing finely.

I do not know how General Hood intended to protect his flank; I do not see how he could have expected to do so, but I am no general. If he does not take some stronger position than he has at present, I fear the enemy will do him more damage yet, by taking possession of the pike, and cutting him off entirely.

If any thing happens, I will add before closing. With much love, etc.,   H.

P. S.—Two of our men have just come in from the front; they report the Yankees advancing down a pike which intersects the Nashville and Franklin pike, between our position and Franklin. I hope this is not so.

January 20.—Hood's army is really demoralized; our loss in every thing has been very great, and had it not been for our brave cavalry, scarcely a man would have been left to tell the tale. We have lost nearly all of our artillery. The company of which my brother is a member—Garrity's battery—lost one man (Edward Haggerty) and all their guns, excepting one.

253

My brother writes, that the scene on leaving Tennessee was extremely distressing. On their entering it, the ladies received them joyfully, and were ready to do any thing in the world for them. When they left, the grief exhibited was enough to melt a heart of stone. He says the recollection of them makes him miserable. We have been told by many that the devotion of the women to the wounded at the battle of Franklin is beyond all praise. They gave clothes of all kinds to the well soldiers.

I have heard nothing before this to equal the sufferings of the men on this last retreat. Many of them were without shoes, and the snow was lying heavily on the ground. The flesh actually dropped from their feet. I heard of one man who has been compelled to have both feet amputated from this cause.

Every way we turn there is trouble and woe. A lady told me the other day that her young son in the Virginia army had suffered so much lately, that his hair is turning white. The army there have much to endure from the cold. The men are many of them from the South, and are not used to such weather.

In a letter received a few days ago from Rev. Mr. Clute, in Okolona, Mississippi, he says the enemy have destroyed the place, and robbed the people of every thing. They have even taken his children's clothes; and he writes that he was himself in borrowed clothes.

Well, though every thing looks dark at present, that is nothing. The sun is often obscured with clouds, only to shine out more resplendent than ever. . . .

February 4.—While getting ready to go back to the hospital, my father came in overjoyed, and told me that my work was over, and that we are to have peace at last. Lincoln has agreed to receive peace commissioners, and three of our ablest men, Vice-president Stephens, Judge Campbell, and Senator Hunter, have gone on the mission.

Many think the northerners are going to war with France, and expect us to assist them, but I know that none of our people will be mad enough to do that; indeed, I am certain that they will not. Let the northern people fight their own battles; we will be neutral.

All seem much pleased with the selection which has been made in our commissioners. I hope Stephens is satisfied now that he has gone on the mission for which he has so long wished.

February 8.—More woe and sorrow in store for us! The Egyptian will not let us go! Our commissioners have returned unsuccessful! No peace for us without going back to the Union! . . .

What castle-building we have had in the last few days! The thought of such a thing as our enemy asking us back to the Union never once entered our heads. I really did think that they had come to their senses, and resolved to let us go. Well,

"We'll but to prouder pitch wind up our souls,"

and commence again.

February 20.--Since my return I have visited three of the hospitals; they have very few patients. The Levert (so called in honor of the late Dr. Levert of this place) is set apart for officers. Our old patient, Captain Curran, is in it, and, much to my astonishment, is recovering.

This hospital is a small one, but seems perfect in every department. The surgeon—Dr. Redwood—was captured at Shiloh, and was for some time practicing in prisons in the North, and has his hospital arranged as they have them there. A hospital like his is all very well in a place like Mobile; but I am afraid, if he had a few runs like we have had, it would not be quite so nice. Captain Curran asked me if I would not like to be in such a one. I answered him no; for then I might forget we had a war on hand, with all these nice things around me. There is one room trimmed with blue, another with yellow, etc. The whole hospital is not as large as one of our wards. I asked Captain Curran what he thought would become of all these " pretty things," if some few hundreds of wounded were brought in from the field, as we have had them many a time. I think the blue and yellow spreads would be *slightly soiled.*

On one of my visits there, Captain Curran informed me that the day previous his surgeon had neglected to state what was to be his diet, and he had to fast all day, as the matron could not give him any thing not prescribed. To think of a wounded man, who is convalescing, fasting a whole day! I think I should have broken the rules that day. I believe in discipline; but, as I heard a friend say, we need not break the rules, just bend them a little.

A good many jokes are told on Dr. Redwood, on account of his strict discipline. It is said, one day when the examining board met there, and one of the surgeons was taken suddenly ill, Dr. Redwood could not procure whiskey for him until he put his name down as a patient.

The other hospital (the Cantey, so called in honor of General Cantey) is in a very handsome building. It was the city hospital, and part of it is still reserved for the use of the sick citizens. The Sisters of Charity are its matrons, and we all know what they are in hospitals. And, by the way, why can we not imitate them in this respect, during these war times? Here one of them is a druggist; another acts the part of steward; and, in fact, they could take charge of the whole hospital, with the exception of the medical department.

My friend, Dr. Henderson, is surgeon of this hospital; he kindly took us all through it. He is making great improvements, in the way of chicken-houses, etc., but somehow I never look at these things now without thinking we are doing all this work for our foes.

Dr. Henderson related an anecdote about the quartermaster. He was in want of lumber, and had tried fair means about getting it till he was tired; so he made it a rule to spend every spare hour he had in the quartermaster's office, till the latter gave him as much lumber and other material as he wanted.

I tell the surgeons here that they do not know any thing about the war, compared with those in the field, and near it. There is one thing that I have remarked: they have many more privileges than those near the front. Nearly every surgeon in Mobile boards in the hospital; whereas, with us, they were on no account permitted to do so.

The Ross Hospital, so called in honor of Dr. Ross of this place, is, like the others, *perfait* in every respect. Dr. Needlet [Nidelet] of Missouri is surgeon, and Mrs. Crocker matron.

The surgeon-general, Dr. Moore, is constantly issuing orders to the medical department, and the order of one day contradicts that of the day previous. The surgeons are a good deal annoyed at these orders.

While visiting the Ross Hospital, Mrs. Crocker showed me a book large enough to keep all of the records of the Confederacy, in which she was to note every mouthful eaten by the patients, and every drop of whiskey that they drank. According to the rules in this book, she will be compelled to keep some half dozen of assistants. On looking at its size, I could not but think that paper must be much more plentiful than we thought for. The diet-lists are amusing to read. We know there are such articles as those named in them, from having seen them in good old peace times, but that is about all we know of them. The lists always put me in mind of the receipt, "First catch your hare, and then make your pie."

February 26.—All is at a stand-still again. Our people seem to have revived after our late disasters. The Tennessee army has scattered— many of its troops are here. As nearly all of its cannon were lost, many of the men of the batteries are here drilling as infantry; among them Garrity's battery.

I am told that there is a good deal of dissatisfaction on account of this, as artillerymen do not like being taken from their guns. A lady friend told me the other day, that two or three members of a Louisiana battery had deserted on this account.

Fenner's battery, from New Orleans, is here. It has been in active service nearly throughout the whole war, and has suffered much. On the retreat from Dalton three brothers in it were killed; two were shot down, at one time, along side of the third; and, as it was in the heat of battle, he could not leave his post to go to their rescue. Not long afterward he also fell, a martyr for his country. Alas! we have many such self-immolations to record in the pages of our history; and what more glory do we need than such records? None. These martyrs shall live in future story, and ages yet unborn shall sing their requiem. Youths shall listen, with quivering lip and glistening eye, to gray-haired sires, recounting their deeds of heroism, and tell how nobly freemen shed their blood in defense of liberty.

It is reported that General Johnston has taken command of the Tennessee army, or rather what is left of it. This has given universal satisfaction, but no one can tell for how long, as that hydra-headed monster—the people—is a little inclined to be fickle. I have been told that before General Hood took command, the people of Georgia sent many a petition to the president, asking him to remove General Johnston, as he was permitting the enemy to lay waste the country.

There is scarcely a town in the Confederacy where there has not been a meeting held, approving of the answer given by the peace commissioners, and passing resolutions never to yield while there is one man left to strike a blow.

Mobile has had a very large, enthusiastic meeting; and I see by the papers that Newnan has not been behind any in this respect. It is rumored that vice-president Stephens has said he is fully convinced that there is but one way to have peace, and that is to conquer it.

Mobile never was as gay as it is at present; not a night passes but some large ball or party is given. Same old excuse: that they are for the benefit of the soldiers; and indeed the soldiers seem to enjoy them.

The city is filled with the veterans of many battles. I have attended several of the parties, and at them the gray jackets were conspicuous. A few were in citizen's clothes, but it was because they had lost their uniforms.

The Alabama troops are dressed so fine that we scarcely recognize them. A large steamer, laden with clothes, ran the blockade lately, from Limerick, Ireland.

Notwithstanding the gayety, nearly all the churches are daily opened for special prayers, imploring the Most High to look down in pity on us, and free us from this fearful scourge. . . .

February 27.—Our hospitals have taken another exodus, and gone back to Georgia. We have all become real cosmopolites.[4]

The surgeons of the Foard and the chaplain spent the evening with us. They spoke highly of Gainesville, and said there was plenty of all kinds of food there, but they suffered for want of wood, as they had no teams to haul it. The winter so far has been a very severe one. We have all suffered from the cold, and clothing of all kinds is scarce. We have given nearly every thing in the way of bed-clothing to the soldiers, and at night the only way we keep warm is by heaping on us the piano and table covers, and in many instances all kinds of clothing. Many have cut up their carpets for blankets for the soldiers.

Mrs. Williamson has been confined to her bed ever since we came back, and is unable to go to the hospital. I have tried to get a lady to take her place, but in vain. I am half inclined not to go myself, and would not were our cause less gloomy.

Dr. de Yampert sent a gentleman to escort Mrs. Williamson and

[4] After moving west to Mississippi the hospitals were represented in December 1864 as far north as Pulaski, Tennessee. On January 3, 1865, they removed in part to Meridian, Mississippi, and on January 25 back to Columbus, Georgia. Atlanta once again became headquarters in April and the last order of record was dated there on April 27, 1865. Flewellen Hospital. Manuscript Order Book.

myself on the journey; but I have let him return without me, as I thought I might prevail on some lady to accompany me. And we are more independent traveling by ourselves than we have ever been, as the men are nearly all in the service. There is a lady in the hospital already, so I will have some company.

It has been hard work to move the hospitals this time, as the weather has been so very cold. Many of the hospitals have been encamped on our wharves for weeks, and ladies with them. It is useless to think of going to hotels now; a person must be rolling in wealth to even stay a few days at one.

I intend leaving to-morrow, and it is with a sad heart, as God alone knows what may be the fate of Mobile ere many days have elapsed; for it is no feint this time. The enemy means something now; of that all are confident.

As I walk along, every brick and paving stone is sacred; I never thought Mobile was half so pretty as it is now. My brother is still here, but I have not the least idea that we will be able to hold Mobile; so he, along with the rest of the army, will be sent out.

It is rumored that General Johnston has gone after Sherman. That despoiler is laying the whole country in his track a perfect waste. He has marched through Georgia with his *invincible* army, and they encountered *perils* of all kinds in defenseless old age, women, and children. But that kind of warfare seems to suit these *chivalrous knights,* and one they are certain to triumph in.

The very name of Sherman brings up woe and desolation before us. The beautiful city of Columbia, South Carolina, has been laid in ruins by him and his hirelings. Bands of marauders, black and white, are sent through the country to do their worst on the helpless inhabitants.

We are told that he warned some ladies who were coming South, from one of the towns in Georgia, not to go to South Carolina, as there he did not intend being so lenient as he had been in Georgia. He has made his threat good, and poor South Carolina has indeed been scourged.

This was done because they say she was a sinner above all the rest. She committed the unpardonable offense of being the first to leave the " best government the world ever saw." But there is a day of reckoning for the evil-doer. " Lord, how long shall the wicked triumph, and all the workers of iniquity boast themselves! They slay the widow and the stranger, and murder the fatherless."

✝✝✝

XI: GRIFFIN

✝✝✝

March 9, 1865.—I arrived at Griffin, Georgia, yesterday, having left Mobile on the steamer *Southern Republic*, one of the largest and finest boats on the river. Major Berry, quartermaster, was at the wharf, and very kindly made arrangements with the captain to take me on my transportation ticket.

I felt very sad at leaving Mobile, as I have no idea when I shall see it again. I left many of my friends in sadness and tears, in anticipation of woe soon to fall on the city. All are confident that the enemy means something this time, and I am certain that nearly all think that we can not possibly hold the city. If we only had the seaboard to protect, Mobile could stand a siege of years, but the enemy can come in by Florida, North Alabama, and Mississippi, and we all know that we have no forces to keep them back.

For once in my life I wished to give the military authorities advice. That would have been to abandon Mobile, send all the forces to Selma, and try and save that portion of the country.

Heretofore I have wished that Mobile would be laid in ashes before the foe would be permitted to desecrate it, but now I think it would be but policy to give it up, and try and save towns in the interior, which will be of more use to us.

On my way down to the boat I saw the provost guard taking all the cotton out of the warehouses, and searching garrets and cellars for it. They were taking it to the public square, to be fired in case the enemy reaches the city.

The river was higher than it had been for years. We saw whole towns submerged: Cahaba, which is on a high bluff, was in some places covered with water four or five feet deep. Many of the people were sailing about in boats. There was a large warehouse on the bank of the river, filled with prisoners, whose spirits, if we were to judge by their actions and the noise they made, had not been dampened by prison life. They seemed rather pleased than otherwise with their chances for *aquatic sports.*

As wood was scarce, the captain helped himself to the fences of the river banks. At one place the owner of the wood came after the boat had left it and seemed very angry. He was told by the men on the

259

boat to send his bill to the *quartermaster*, which suggestion did not seem to afford him much satisfaction.

One morning, on waking up, I found the branches of trees very near my state-room window; I supposed we were on a cane-brake. There were two women on the boat, who had been to the camp of instruction—Camp Watts—near Montgomery, to try and bring their sons back—two boys who had been sent there by a conscript officer. One of the women had a cancer on her face, and the other one told me that the son of this unfortunate woman had been sent to camp, and that one of his eyes is eaten out by the same disease. How can our people be guilty of such outrages! There is no punishment too severe for those thus guilty. But I have known conscript officers to take men from their homes whom the surgeons had discharged many times, and send them to camp. We have had them die in our hospital before reaching the army. These women had gone from Montgomery to Mobile by railroad, and had to come up the river before they could reach their homes; and to judge from their appearance, they could ill afford this expense. Colonel Phillips, whose wife has been such an eyesore to the Federals, was on board. He is a very dignified and courteous gentleman. He informed me that his sister-in-law was in a hospital in Virginia, and has been in one since the commencement of the war.

Among the passengers was a wealthy widow, who owned a plantation on the river. I heard her tell a gentleman that, in case of the enemy coming, she intended setting fire to her house rather than they should have the benefit of it.

There were some ladies on board who had been to Mobile to visit their relatives, who are stationed there. The principal topic of conversation was Sherman's barbarities, and the outrages in general of which the enemy have been guilty lately. They were any thing but pleasant to listen to, and filled me with dread of the future. In many places the enemy are acting with a barbarity almost equal to any thing of which the Sepoys were guilty. Negro regiments, officered by men with white skins, but with hearts as black as night, have been turned loose on the helpless inhabitants, and encouraged to do their worst. And all of this is done by a people calling themselves Christians. But we need not wonder when we think of who their teacher is— Ward Beecher, that sectional fire-brand, who has made God's house a den of thieves, and polluted the holy sanctuary with his impious ravings. How can these people ever expect us to forget these fearful wrongs? How hard it is for us to feel any thing but the most deadly hate toward our foes, when justice calls aloud to us for vengeance! God is indeed trying us with the refiner's fire; may we come out of it purified.

I heard more about the dissipation of Mobile after leaving it than I did all the time I was there. I had no idea it was such a wicked place and that the people were so much demoralized.

I paid a visit to some friends in Selma, and they were a good deal alarmed at the prospect of the enemy coming there. The fare on the boat was very good, and I was much indebted to one of the officers—Mr. Scott—for sending me a tumbler of milk at each meal, which was very acceptable, as the substitute for coffee was any thing but nice.

We arrived at Montgomery on the 4th, at 1 P. M. I remained all night at the house of Rev. Dr. Scott. There I met some ladies from Florida, who, like many others, had been driven from their homes by the enemy. The refugees are very clannish; it seems to be great consolation for them to get together and talk over by-gones. Dr. Scott has a church in Montgomery, I believe, wholly supported by refugees. Mrs. Scott is a refined and intellectual lady, such as I have found nearly all of our better class of women to be, and she is a true southerner. The doctor and she were both very kind and before I left in the morning, which was very early, they had a delightful cup of pure coffee made for me, and an old negro man drove me to the train in their buggy.

While in Montgomery I met Dr. Anderson of Mobile (medical purveyor), packing up his drugs, having been ordered to Macon. I am told that the military department head-quarters has been ordered to the same place. Dr. Anderson informed me that he had sent his family to Mobile for safety. I heard of many others doing the same; it being considered the safest, whether it falls or not, and no one seems to think there will be any fighting in the city.

I left Montgomery on the 5th, at 7 A. M., in company with Lieutenant Edwards and his wife, who were on their way to Florida, and arrived at Columbus, Georgia, the same day, at 5 A. M.

On the way to Columbus I met one of my old Chattanooga patients, Lieutenant Blair of Texas. I did not recollect having ever seen him, but he had not forgotten me. He inquired after Mrs. Williamson, and he told me that to our attention in Chattanooga he owed his life. We are often told this, and although knowing it is not true, can not help feeling gratified at hearing it. Poor fellow! since I last saw him he has lost a leg in one of the battles near Atlanta. He said that while lying wounded he had often thought about Mrs. Williamson and myself.

In Columbus we put up at the Cook House; at supper the table *actually groaned*. I have not seen as many good things since the war. There were cold turkey, sausages, roast pork, biscuit, hot rolls, cornbread; and I could scarcely believe my senses when I saw cake. We had a substitute for coffee, which was very nice, and plenty of hot milk and sugar.

My friends were going to Florida by the Chattahooche River, so I left early next morning for Macon. I had some pure coffee, which a waiter had made and brought to me, with milk, sugar, and buttered toast. I paid ten dollars for lodging, and ten for supper.

In this hotel was a very nice-looking girl, who seemed to be acting

261

as head chambermaid. I knew from her accent that she was from the "land of cakes." She is from Glasgow, and has been a number of years in this country. She is the first Scotch woman I have met in the South in that position.

We were all invited to witness a wedding (a runaway match); the couple had come from Montgomery on the cars with us; they were quite young looking. I believe the drawback was the young lady's cruel father. A chaplain performed the ceremony.

After witnessing the wedding, Lieutenant Edwards, his wife, and myself called on Mr. Stickney, chaplain of the post. He is a native of Mobile, and was a chaplain at one of the forts in New Orleans at the time of its surrender, and had to leave there in a hurry, losing nearly all of his worldly possessions. Mrs. Stickney is a daughter of Rev. Dr. Hedges of New Orleans, who left that city as a registered enemy to the United States.

They are living, refugee-style, in two rooms. Mrs. Stickney is an enthusiastic southerner, and seems to glory in living as she does. But she is much better off than many others, who would be thankful to have her place. Many of the richest people in the country are living in tents or old sheds. . . .

On the cars from Columbus I met my old friend, Mrs. Newsom. She has been to Arkansas since I last saw her, and brought out a young sister, who has been assisting her in the hospitals. She had very little trouble from the Federal authorities in going through the lines, though she made no secret of how she had been employed in the Confederacy. She has left the hospital service for awhile, as her duties in Atlanta injured her health. The patients were in tents there, and the weather bad. The Sisters of Charity previously in the hospital could not stand the work and exposure, and had left. Miss Monroe of Kentucky had assisted Mrs. Newsom in one of the hospitals, and she spoke highly of her kindness to the suffering, and of her abilities in managing the duties incidental to a hospital.

We reached Macon on the 6th, and I went to the Blind School Hospital, where my friend, Miss Rigby, is matron. It is a new hospital, and the building had been a school for the blind. It stands on a very elevated spot, and the view of the city from it is very fine.

Miss Rigby is a member of the Episcopal Church, and an excellent lady. She is very devoted to the patients, and at present, although there are but few in the hospital, she finds it difficult to get food for them.

I saw Dr. Gamble, who is post surgeon, and is having all the hospitals fixed up again as if there was no such thing as making another move. I met a number of my old friends in Macon; I think all are getting worn out with this wandering kind of life; or, as I heard a surgeon say, this *inspecting* the railroads.

I left Macon on the 8th; Dr. Mellon, an assistant surgeon in the hospital, very kindly escorted me to the cars. The receiving hospital for Macon is at the depot, and is under the care of Surgeon King; I am told he is an excellent gentleman. The bunks were in the car shed, and all looked very neat. This arrangement saves a good deal of extra moving for the sufferers.

I think I never saw rain until to-day; it is actually pouring in torrents. Yesterday, when I arrived at the depot, it was raining very hard, and when I looked out of the car at the crowd of men, and saw no familiar face, I felt a little homesick. In the depot I met Dr. Steele, who sent word to the hospital that I had arrived. I did not have long to wait; Mr. Catlet came for me, and as it was still raining, and the hospital some half a mile distant, I went to a hotel opposite. Dr. de Yampert had sent some one after me every day for a week, and had concluded I was not coming. At the hotel I found some Chattanooga friends, Mr. Rawlings, the proprietor, and his family. Although I had never met Mrs. Rawlings before, we were like old friends. The daughter of Dr. Taylor, who was so kind to us in Chattanooga, was there. Her father is a prisoner, and has not been heard from for a long time; many think he is dead. I was glad to learn something concerning the many kind friends I left in Chattanooga. They were scattered all over the Confederacy; quite a number are in this place.

After I had remained there some hours, Mr. Catlet brought a buggy and took me to the hospital, where I received a hearty welcome from Dr. Reese, who introduced me to Miss S., my assistant. I felt very gloomy, and had no good, kind Mrs. Williamson to say, in her quiet manner, " Have patience the Lord will bring all right." Left wholly to myself, I felt that all my boasted determination to remain in the hospital till the war was over, or as long as I could be of service to the suffering, would now be put to the test.

Mr. Moore and Dr. Burks called, and were glad to see me, as were all in the hospital. Not even the warm welcome I received served to dispel the gloom; I was completely *demoralized*. So much for remaining so long at home. Dr. Reese kindly invited me to dinner, and, although I had eaten nothing that day, I refused.

Dr. de Yampert, who had been with the medical board, after awhile came to see me. As it had ceased raining, I went with him to visit the hospital. The main part is to be in tents or sheds. We have one large building, formerly a young ladies' college,[1] and which was the Quintard Hospital last year. There were a few out-houses, put up in hospital style, which were used for kitchen, dining-room, bakery, etc. Dr. Burks showed me where the foundation of the college was crumbling, and the pillars in front giving way; but, as we did not intend giving a ball, where the gyrations of the performers on the light fantastic toe might give it a shake, I did not see that we had much danger to apprehend. There will be one nice, large ward in the upper

[1] There were two female colleges in Griffin: Griffin Female College and the Synodical Female College. Sherwood, *A Gazetteer of Georgia* . . . , 120.

room. There are many rooms down-stairs, one a fine linen-room. I was well pleased with the manner in which Dr. de Yampert was having every thing arranged. I did not know till now that he fixed up the nice one the Sisters of Charity were in at Corinth. I tried to enter into his ambitious plans with as much zeal as I could muster; but visions of raids and army movements causing us to make hasty retreats, leaving the fruits of our labor behind us to be destroyed by the foe, would rise up before me. To save my life I could scarcely utter one enthusiastic word of praise, though I could not but admire his perseverance, as he has had almost as much running to do as myself. He says he has made up his mind that the war will last ten years, and he is preparing accordingly. There was no use in my saying I thought that it would be impossible for us to hold out so long, as three years ago we were certain we could not keep up another year. In a tent I found Mrs. Love and her family, who seemed rejoiced at my return.

Dr. de Yampert told me, as I had had so much experience, I knew better what to do than he could tell me; that he wished me to overlook all the domestic arrangements. He wishes to have three more ladies. We are to have three wards, with separate kitchens. He does not like the idea of having the patients in tents (I find there are few surgeons who do), and is going to try and build sheds. I always feel nervous when I see them go up. From what little experience I have had of tents, I like them for patients, although it is impossible to keep bedding as clean as in rooms. They have another drawback, like Jonah's gourd, what the night before was a nice shelter, by the next morning has fallen and become a heap of canvas. Still with all this, the men improve in them much faster than in houses. I have never lived in a tent myself, or perhaps I should not like them for others. I think we are generally in favor of what we like best ourselves. I have often noticed that surgeons order for their patients what they like and what best agrees with themselves. When a doctor requests me to send no buttermilk to his ward, and another no greens, and another no onions, etc., I set it down that these are things they are not fond of.

I have become much better reconciled of every thing since I have seen Dr. de Yampert. He seems to have no aim but to do every thing for the good of the patients, and I can ask for nothing more. He was a wealthy planter in Alabama, and enlisted as a private at the commencement of the war. He was soon promoted, and for some time was on General Bragg's staff, and served in the field until lately.

To-day, feeling that I would like to have something to eat, I found corn meal and beef of the leanest kind to be all of which our commissary could boast. I have often said that I did not wish to live otherwise than the soldiers, with the exception of corn-bread and bacon, which are things I thought I would have to starve before I could eat (I suppose I must have inherited this dislike from my foreign origin) ; but I have found that starving will not do. When we get bacon we do not get beef. This is the beef week; and there is not fat enough on it to fry it with. I sent a note to a lady, requesting her to lend me some lard to put in bread, though I have no idea when I shall be able to return it; but I can pay her in money. I made the bread, and stewed the beef, and with corn coffee, minus milk or sugar, made a very good meal.

Fast-day, March 10.—Went to the Presbyterian Church with Dr. Reese, and was well pleased with the discourse. The church was the dirtiest I have ever been in; I was shocked to see a house dedicated to the worship of God in such a state. I am told that the rector, Dr. Patterson, has a day-school in it, as his school-house was last year taken for a hospital, and has since been burned. I miss greatly in this place " the sound of the church-going bell." On making inquiries, I was informed that all the bells had been taken to make cannon. Griffin is a nice little place, but not so pretty as Newnan. It is in Pike County, Georgia,[2] on the Macon and Western Railroad, fifty-eight miles north-west of Macon. It is said to be very healthy, and is noted for its excellent water.

The day is bitter cold, and wood is scarce. I thought it bad enough to have so little to eat; but we have no candles or light of any kind, not even light wood. I am compelled to retire at dark, which is a severe trial, as the days are short. I do not believe that even Mark Tapley could be " jolly " under these circumstances. The only consolation I have is comparing my lot with that of the men in the field— I know they are so much worse off.

March 13.—A bright, beautiful day. A woman has been here with a young child, begging me to give her any kind of work, as she has nothing for herself and child to eat. She had just come from Atlanta, and represents the distress there as being very great. I am sorry that we have no work for her. We have many negroes, and nothing for them to do but sewing, as we have no patients. After this woman left, two others came and begged me to give them work just for their shelter and food. How sad all of this is! I have not been long in finding out that there are many worse off than myself.

A number of negro women are at work quilting comforts. Dr. de Yampert wished to have the cloth for them dyed; but most of the Confederate dye does not stand. The comforts are made out of unbleached homespun, and the raw cotton is put in them in lumps, and they are tacked about a foot apart; when washed they are not fit to use.

Cotton goods of all kinds are very high; but I am told that the government manufactories in Georgia, and, I believe, in the other

---

[2] Griffin is not in Pike County but in Spalding, which had been laid out from Pike and Henry some years before the War. *Ibid.*

states, sell goods to soldiers' relatives for nearly one fourth what they can be bought for in the stores.

Sunday, March 19.—Went to the Episcopal Church. The services were held in a small brick house, which was not much cleaner than the Presbyterian. Captain Hicks, one of our patients, and his wife went with me—the first time they were ever in a church of that denomination. They were both delighted with the music. They live about twenty miles from here. Captain Hicks is from Alabama, and was wounded in one of the battles around Richmond. He can not rejoin his regiment, as he is not able to walk the distance, namely, one hundred miles, Sherman having torn up that much of the railroad track near Augusta.

March 25.—A very beautiful day. I feel very low-spirited regarding our cause. A friend, Dr. [Young] has just called, and has not served to dispel the gloom. He denounced President Davis, and said that, in putting negroes into the field, he should have given them not only their own freedom but that of their families. He added, that Davis's last proclamation was the essence of despair, and that he and all in congress know that our cause is gone, and that we soon shall be subjugated. I contended against him to the best of my ability, and said, that if even both our armies were scattered we would not give up. I could not help feeling there might be some truth in what Dr. [Young] said.

We seem to be completely hemmed in on all sides. I hear that the long-expected attack on Mobile has at last begun, and that a large force is moving against Selma and Montgomery. One of the largest armies yet massed by the North is investing Richmond; Sherman and his vandals are in the very heart of the country, and a large army coming in by Wilmington—which is now in their hands; Charleston is closely besieged. Not one ray of light gleams from any quarter. It seems like hoping against hope; but my strong faith in the justice of our cause makes failure to me an impossibility. I know we shall have much yet to suffer before the end. I have seen only extracts from the president's message, and must say I do not like the tone of them. He is still urging the people to do their duty; but says, if we fail, we must bow with submission to the decree of an all-wise Providence. I do not like the word "fail" at all. While we have one spark of hope left, one breath of submission ought not to be breathed by any one, much less by our chief magistrate.

Sunday, March 26.—I went to the Episcopal Church, and, after the morning service, the rector, Mr. Thomas, introduced me to his wife, Mrs. Bector, and Mrs. Mitchell. Mrs. Mitchell told me she had a son in Massindorf's battery, which is now stationed in Mobile, and that he is much pleased with the place. Last year, at the retreat from Dalton, Griffin was filled with wounded. Mrs. Mitchell's house was full. Bishop Lay and Dr. Quintard visited the place then, and the rite of confirmation was administered to many. One of our old patients, Lieutenant Dupree, was confirmed while lying, badly wounded, at the house of Mrs. Mitchell. I am told that the ladies of the place did a great deal for the sufferers.

March 29.—We have scarcely any patients, as the road between Augusta and Atlanta is not yet finished. There is rumor on rumor of battles in the direction of the army. I only wish we could get the wounded to take care of. Dr. de Yampert is busy getting every thing ready for the reception of patients. The large ward is nicely white-washed, and he has had comfortable cotton mattresses made by a regular mattress-maker. A new bakery, wash-house, and every thing else necessary are being put up, just as if there was no such thing as moving again. I am kept quite busy attending to the sewing. The thread, bought in bunches, has to be doubled, twisted and reeled. We have no wheel of our own, but borrow, as every house in the neighbor-hood has one. Mrs. Love's two little girls stay with me a great deal. In the evenings I teach them to read. Neither their father or mother know how to read. They are from Tennessee.

We have a vegetable garden in cultivation next to our house, and another large one, "*the plantation,*" about two miles in the country, of which Mr. Yerby has charge. I have a flower garden, and Mr. Moore has procured me some very nice plants. After awhile, I have no doubt, I shall have flowers enough to delight our patients.

April 1.—I have just been told that Spanish Fort is closely besieged. The day is very beautiful, but I can not enjoy it on account of the bad news. I wish, now, I had remained at home, so as to help take care of the wounded.

April 3.—Have a very nice lady, Mrs. Fyffe, assisting me. She is a refugee from Chattanooga. She came out of Chattanooga on a visit to some friends a few miles in the country; while she was there our army took possession of Lookout Mountain, and she found herself within our lines and cut off from her family. She tried very hard to get back, as she had left her house and in it an only child, a married daughter, very sick, but her entreaties were of no avail. Rosecrans had given orders on no account to permit any woman to cross the lines, as they were worse rebels than the men. Mrs. Fyffe remained on the mountain, living in a house about half-way up, for some weeks, within sight of her daughter's home, and between the firing of both armies. Finding she could not get into Chattanooga, she came South. She is now in great distress, having heard but once from her daughter since she left.

The citizens of Chattanooga have suffered all kinds of indignities from the Federals. I have been told that Mrs. Whiteside has been sent North, and that herself and family are now in prison. I knew

267

Mrs. Whitesides well; she was a perfect lady. I had heard her say before I left Chattanooga, that if the enemy should come there she intended remaining, as she had a family of seven children, and could not leave her home with them. She felt certain that the Federals would not molest her if she kept quiet; but it appears she has given them more credit for philanthropy than they deserved. I can not understand this, as I believed as she did about remaining quiet.

I have thought, if I should ever be so unfortunate as to be in the "enemy's lines," that by taking little or no notice of them I should be unmolested; as I think many of our ladies have been in fault, by giving a warm and open expression to their feelings, when silence would have much better become them, and spoken more eloquently their wrongs. "Discretion is the better part of valor," in this as well as in other cases. When we are in the lion's gripe, it is no sign of cowardice to use every means that wisdom can suggest to extricate ourselves. I feel confident that neither we nor our cause have ever gained any thing by walking around the flag instead of under it, or using insulting language when silence would have much better become us. A flag is nothing but a symbol, and walking around it can not take away the reality of being under it. And we much oftener lower ourselves by insulting language than the person whom we abuse.

I have been told that it was on account of Mrs. Whiteside's wealth that she and her children have been imprisoned, but the enemy could have taken that without such harsh measures.

April 5.—News has come that Selma is in the hands of the enemy, who have destroyed it, and are *en route* for Montgomery. Dr. de Yampert's home is near Selma, and he has no doubt that it is now in their possession. He says he does not care, as he expected to lose his all.

Dr. Bemiss is here on a tour of inspection; I am much pleased to see him again; it is like seeing a very old friend to meet any of our former surgeons. He is low-spirited, and it is not much wonder, as he has been separated from his wife and children a long time, and there seems little chance at present of his seeing them soon; and, what adds to the trouble, communication through the lines is very uncertain. These are things we try not to think about.

Mrs. Newsom arrived to-day. She does not intend remaining, but is trying to reach the army in North Carolina, as her brother is there. She is leaving two of her negroes, a man and his wife, with Dr. de Yampert.

April 6.—We have just heard that Richmond has fallen; and I am not sorry, as I feel certain we shall never have peace until the enemy has possession of all our large towns, and then they will see that they have work still before them to conquer the South.[3]

---

[3] Optimistic to the last ditch Dr. Saunders wrote on receipt of the news this same day: " The evacuation of Richmond seems to have been precipitate & I fear Grant

Mrs. Newsom has gone to visit Mrs. Dr. Porter, an old friend from Tennessee. She is as lovely as ever, but her health is very bad. I have nothing to give her to eat but bacon and corn-bread; we have very little milk. I have got so that I can eat corn-bread as well as any southerner.

Mrs. Fyffe finds the living very hard, and the doctors grumble not a little. I tell them it is all for the good of the cause. Our attendants do not get near enough of such food as we have; I have seen them many a time dining on less than an ounce of bacon, and a piece of corn-bread half an inch thick and about six inches square. We have one very sick man, who can not eat that. I have very little coffee, and every now and again make him a cup of it. I went to see Mrs. Ware,[4] whom I met at Ringgold. Her son is now quite well, and going about on crutches. She informed me that the people here, with few exceptions, do not fare any better than we do, and that many of them do not get as much.

Sunday, April 10.—Mrs. Newsom's sister is here, and we had a hearty laugh at dinner, as I told them it was an extra one. Our corn-bread had in it lard, soda, and a *whole* egg. Mrs. Newsom told us of a friend of hers, now living in Marietta, who could scarcely get enough of corn meal for herself and children.

April 11.—We can hear little or nothing from Mobile, but I have no idea that our people will try to hold it, now that Selma has gone. I suppose by this time our army has left it. We have evidently had some hard fighting at Spanish Fort. On looking over the list of killed and wounded in a Macon paper, among the killed the first name I saw was a son of Mrs. Mitchell of this place. He is the second or third she has lost in this war; she has my heartfelt sympathy.

Mrs. Newsom and her sister have left to-day. They expect to be able to go to North Carolina.

Good Friday, April 14.—A gloomy day. I went to church in the morning, and listened to one of the finest sermons I ever heard. The text was " and the people stood beholding." The vocal music was excellent; the voices were very sweet, and the contralto is one of the finest I ever listened to. Captain Hicks and his wife went with me, and were more charmed than ever with the music.

Easter Sunday, April 16.—A most beautiful day—one that speaks of peace and good will toward men. On my way to church a feeling of sadness came over me, when I remembered the sunny Easter Sundays I had spent with many now gone forever. The little church, I was glad to see, had been all nicely whitewashed, and thoroughly cleaned, and a beautiful bouquet of flowers was on the communion table—an

---

gained some advantage over Lee, but I still think old Bob will whip him." ALs, Stout Papers (Emory).

⁴ Miss Cumming earlier rendered this lady's name as " Weir."

emblem of the resurrection. The church was crowded, and I noticed that Mr. Thomas did not dismiss the congregation before communion, as is common with us, but went on with the communion service as the Methodists do. I felt like thanking the singers for the good music. It took me right back home, as the tunes were all familiar ones. They sang the sixty-ninth Easter hymn, one I had listened to many a time on that day, and one which my father sung, when a boy, in "auld Scotia."

Mr. Thomas's text was, "I am Alpha and Omega," and an excellent sermon he preached from it. He is an able logician, and a concise and fluent speaker. He is a native of Wales, but was raised in Georgia. For many years he was a chaplain in the United States navy. When the war broke out he joined our army. Lately he has been living here on his farm, and I have been told that General Wheeler's commissary took every grain of corn which he had, leaving him and his family starving. He receives little or nothing for his services, and has to earn his living by manual labor.

Mrs. Fyffe and myself spend an hour or two every evening trying to teach our negro women to read. I have almost given up in despair of their ever learning. We teach them their A B C's, and think, well, they know that much; but the next time it is all forgotten.

Mrs. Newsom had been teaching her woman some time before she came here, but we find her the dullest of all. I think the African is capable of learning but very little; many may learn to read and write, but I feel confident, as a rule, they will not go much further. I have taught them before, and find that in learning hymns and prayers orally they do pretty well.

I have just received a letter from Mrs. Newsom, who is in Athens, Georgia. She says that some members of congress had just passed through Covington on their way to Atlanta. They reported that Richmond had been given up in a hurry, and that the public archives and other valuables were left. The congressmen were still hopeful of our success, as is also Mrs. Newsom.

It is reported that Atlanta or Macon is to be the seat of government, but I can not see how that can be, as we have no army in either place, and the enemy is now all around us, and our railroads torn up in every direction.[5] All this puzzles me so much that I intend to give over thinking about it, and await the issue.

A day or two ago word was brought that our hospitals were to make another exodus; they are to go to North Carolina. I dislike leaving this nice place, but shall be glad to get near the army. But I scarcely think they will let us ladies go, as at least for a hundred miles of the road every thing will have to be moved on teams.

[5] In his letter of April 6 Dr. Saunders had stated that he presumed the hospitals would again be moved and that Macon would be established as a hospital center and the seat of government. He predicted that the Confederacy would establish the Savannah River as a line of defense. Stout Papers (Emory).

April 17.—Mr. Moore came in to-day and told us very calmly that Lee and his whole army were captured.[6] I was mute with astonishment, and looked at Mr. Moore, thinking I had seen our people take disasters coolly, but had never seen any thing to equal his coolness in telling of such a terrible one. After awhile he laughed, and said he had frightened us enough; that such news had come by a lady from Chattanooga; she had seen it in the northern papers. He said it was one of the tales invented by the enemy to dismay us, but we were not to be so easily frightened.

After Mr. Moore had left us, I commenced thinking over the news, and concluded that it probably might be true. I had just read an account of the last three days' fighting around Petersburg, and it had filled me with dismay. How our men ever withstood such a host is a perfect miracle. They were behind breastworks, but the enemy came on them eight deep, and as fast as one line was mowed down another took its place. It is said that in these three days at least sixty thousand of the enemy were killed; and that our loss was nothing in comparison, but God knows it was enough. General Lee did not have fifty thousand in his army, and the enemy at least two hundred and fifty thousand. It seems like downright murder attempting to oppose such a force. O, how terrible is this cruel, cruel war! When will it cease?

When I saw Mr. Moore again, I told him I had made up my mind to try and think that our late disaster might possibly be true. Perhaps General Lee had been overwhelmed by numbers, and compelled to surrender with his handful of men. We seem to have forgotten that he is mortal, and liable to failures like all others.

Mr. Moore would not listen to me, and said that such a thing was a moral impossibility. We can hear nothing reliable. It seems as if we were shut out from the whole world.

This evening we went to the Methodist Church; a chaplain, Rev. Dr. Baird, a Presbyterian, preached. Quite a number of children were admitted on probation and some were baptized. The sight was quite an interesting one.

April 18.—This afternoon I went to the citizens' graveyard, in company with Mrs. and Captain Hicks. I lost a very important article —my vail [veil]—a serious loss, as I have no idea where I am to get another. I was delighted with the graveyard. Every thing about it was in the greatest order, and it was a perfect flower garden. A few soldiers were buried in it. I saw the graves of five or six colonels side by side;

---

[6] A Federal hospital matron in Virginia recorded the news of General Lee's surrender: " Oh, such joyful news! *Lee has surrendered*, and the rebel capital is in our hands. Oh! soon we shall go home now—the war must be at its close. Such cheering from the men was never heard. Every man able to get out of his bed is following after the drum, and the cripples have hoisted their crutches, and put their tattered hats upon them for banners, and the whole camp is wild with clatter." S. A. Palmer, *The Story of Aunt Beckey's Hospital Life* (New York, 1888 [c. 1867]) , 188.

I think they were all Tennesseeans. The soldiers' graveyard is a little ways from the citizens'; I visited it a few days ago. The ladies of the place have displayed a great deal of taste on it; each grave was neatly trimmed with shells, stones, and flowers. I counted nearly five hundred graves; they were principally those of men who had been wounded at the battles near Atlanta.

Georgia has a greater variety and more beautiful roses than I have ever seen; and here they seem to be more luxurious and fragrant than anywhere else. But there is a great lack of shade-trees; I tried the other day to get some cedar to dress our wards, but failed. How often I think of the grand old woods of Tennessee and North Georgia.

On reaching home we found great excitement in expectation of the enemy. We packed up as usual. I was asked to go to two or three places, but Mrs. Fyffe and myself have concluded that we had better remain where we are. Captain Hicks has taken his wife to a relative, five miles in the country, and walked the distance.

Dr. Bemiss is here, having rode all the way from Columbus on horseback. He is a good deal worried about his books, as they were on the Macon train, which it is said the enemy have burned. He is very low-spirited, and says he feels like the man who was chased by a snake, who, after running till he was exhausted, laid down to let the snake do its worst, and found he had been running from a piece of rope hung to the tail of his coat.

Columbus is now in the hands of the enemy. After capturing Montgomery, they marched on to Columbus. Dr. Bemiss says the militia fought manfully in its defense; they had at least ten to one to contend with.

He describes the scenes along the road as distressing, but at the same time ludicrous. There was a perfect panic at the cry that " the Yankees are coming! " At one place the women and children were running through the streets like people deranged, and men, with mules and wagons, driving in every direction. At that time the enemy was not within miles of the place.

Dr. Stout has gone to North Carolina, and Dr. Bemiss intends following in the morning.[7] He advises us to keep quiet, as, from all he can learn, the enemy are not hurting private property. We are to make believe that our house is a private one, although our rooms are filled with government property. All the valuables are committed

[7] From Charlotte, North Carolina, Surgeon General S. P. Moore had addressed a special order to Dr. Stout on April 6: " [Surgeon Stout] will without delay select from the corps of medical officers serving under him the most efficient medical officers in charge of hospital posts, and their most efficient assistants in charge of hospitals, and report with them to this place, bringing with them all the hospital stores, furniture, bedding, tents, etc., for which transportation can be obtained, and turning over the remainder to Surgeon S. M. Bemiss, who, without further orders, will assume control of that hospital department as medical director." Stout, " An Address . . . ," Southern Practitioner, XXIV (1902) , 453.

to our care, and we are to be very busy quilting if the enemy should *honor* us with a visit.

Nearly all the men have taken to the woods. Dr. de Yampert is at his post, although we have begged him to leave; he says it is his duty to remain. Dr. Burks says he has run all he intends to, and, like the man with the snake, has made up his mind to let them come on and do their worst. Our two barrels of whisky have been taken to the woods.

Well, we are all ready for the enemy. Mrs. Fyffe knows more about them than I do, and is not quite as calm. I see no way of escape, and am making the best of it. I am thinking it is at such times that we need all our coolness and caution. I will do what I can, and leave the rest to God. He has protected me thus far, why should I doubt him now?

April 19.—The enemy did not come last night; but I expect they will *honor* us to-day. We are ready to receive them. Dr. Bemiss has gone to Atlanta. I could scarcely bid him good-by; it seems so sad to think of a man like him running from such wretches.

Mrs. Fyffe has tried her best to frighten me; but the more terrible her stories, the stronger my nerves become. This I can not account for. I opened a prayer-book, and my eye fell on the twenty-seventh psalm: " The Lord is my light and my salvation; whom then shall I fear," etc. I read it aloud, and from it we both gained strength. I do not think it was accident made me turn to those appropriate and comforting words—however some may laugh and say so. My faith is strong in the belief that there is an unseen hand directing all our ways.

Dr. Horton called this morning with a young lady, Miss Bailey, who requested Mrs. Fyffe and myself to go and stay with her, as she was in a large house, and no one with her but negroes. If she left it, it would be certain to be destroyed by the enemy. Neither of us could go. I felt very sorry for her, as she can get no one in the place to go with her. All are remaining at home to take care of their property. Her parents are on a visit to South-west Georgia; and so, like many other families, they are separated.

Night—The enemy marched in about 5 P. M. I have just been on the gallery, watching the burning of the warehouse, and the sad work of destruction is still going on. We hear the sound of axes, and suppose they are tearing up the railroad track. I thank the Giver of all good that I have been enabled to look calmly on the destruction without one feeling of revenge. I gaze up at the heavy columns of smoke ascending to heaven as if pleading in our behalf; I felt that it was incense rising from a sacrifice, and ascended with the prayers of the saints, which I knew had been offered up on every altar from the Potomac to the Rio Grande in behalf of our down-trodden and desolated land—and that God in his own good time would avenge our wrongs.

One of the enemy rode coolly through the place with his rifle in front of his saddle. I could not but admire his daring, for he was at least a quarter of a mile away from his band, and if any of our men had felt disposed, they might have made way with him, and his comrades never have known what became of him. I wonder if that would be called murder or self-defense? He came here to kill and rob, and all have a right to defend themselves and property as best they can. This man called at the back door of a house near by, and asked the negro servant for something to eat, which was given him. After awhile an officer galloped past us and rode up to the college, where Dr. de Yampert and Dr. Burks sat, like stoics, ready to receive their *distinguished* visitor. Dr. de Yampert rose on his approach, and conversed with him awhile. He then rode off, looking behind every now and again, as if expecting a stray bullet from some concealed musket.

Mrs. Fyffe and I wondered what he had said to Dr. de Yampert. We made up our minds he had come to order the sick away, as he meant to fire the building; or, perhaps, with the *pleasing* information that Dr. de Yampert and all the rest of the men were prisoners. We were left to conjecture, for Dr. de Yampert did not have the least *pity* upon us. He certainly knew that we had inherited at least a little of mother Eve's frailty.

I went over to the hospital to view the fire from the upper gallery. I asked Dr. de Yampert if they were going to burn the building; if so, our house would not escape, and we wished to move our clothes. He said he did not know what the enemy intended doing, but advised us not to do any thing, it being too late, as our doing so would attract attention.

This evening Dr. Burks called, and told us that the Federal officer merely asked how many patients we had, and passed the compliments of the day. I *know* they were *reciprocated*.

April 20.—The enemy are gone. I have no idea but that they will be back soon. Mrs. Fyffe and myself lay awake all night, expecting to hear them returning. They have done little or no damage to the place. They burned a large warehouse, filled with private and government stores, and gave the contents to the negroes and poor people. They fired the turning-table, which is still burning; they were in the act of setting fire to the ticket office, when Mrs. Rawlings implored the commanding officer not to do so, as her house would be burned too. He told her, if it would benefit the United States Government ten thousand dollars, and destroy ten cents worth of private property, it should not be burned. So much goodness looks suspicious. They beat and knocked down some of the negroes, and told the people they were the worst behaved negroes they had met anywhere.

One of the stories afloat is, that they had no idea of coming here; but the mayor and some of the citizens met them some miles from town, and offered to surrender the city if they would spare private property.

There were not more than one hundred. They were a detachment from the main body, who have gone on to capture Macon. I am told that the captain boasted that, last year, when Sherman went through the eastern portion of this state, he, along with many others, had come to Griffin, dressed in Confederate uniform, calling themselves Wheeler's men. They then broke open stores and took out what they pleased. They said they had often done so. This will, likely, account for the bad repute of Wheeler's men.

April 22.—There is much excitement in town. News has just come that there is an armistice, and that we had been recognized by France, England, Spain, and Austria; Lincoln has been assassinated, and Seward badly wounded. I was going down town when I heard great hurrahing: as we had heard that there was another raid coming, I was terribly alarmed, thinking it was the enemy coming in triumph, but was informed that it was a car filled with our men and Federals hurrying up to Atlanta, with a flag of truce, to let all know about the armistice. None of our people believe any of the rumors, thinking them as mythical as the surrender of General Lee's army. They look upon it as a plot to deceive the people. Many think that Governor Brown has sold the state. There is evidently a crisis in our affairs.

Sunday, April 23.—All are yet in doubt as to the rumors afloat.[8] One gentleman is so confident that Governor Brown had sold the state, that he would not be at all surprised if an order was to come by the next train to have all the men put under arrest.

April 26.—We have just heard that the French fleet has had a battle with the Federal fleet, and whipped it, and taken New Orleans. All are much rejoiced. There is really an armistice.

April 29.—This evening Miss King, Mrs. Newsom's sister, brought us word that peace is really declared, but she could not tell us on what terms. All the rumors have been confirmed excepting the one about recognition.

One of my Kentucky friends called the other day, and he was bitter against our own people, and says we are subjugated, and that we are alone to blame; and that the enemy have raised all of these recognition rumors to blind us until the rope is fairly round our necks, just as they deluded the poor people in Kentucky. He was resolved never to see Kentucky again, and was going to South America.

I can not believe that we are subjugated, after enduring so much; but it is useless to be miserable about an uncertainty.

April 30.—This morning Mr. Thomas preached a very fine sermon from the text, " Thy will be done." It fell upon our saddened ears with a mournful cadence, as if warning us to prepare for some

[8] Confederate communications had broken down and rumors replaced news in the interior of the South. As late as April 25 General Nathan Bedford Forrest was still declaring to his troops that no credence should be placed on the reports of Lee's surrender. *Official Records* (Army), Ser. I, XLIX, 1263.

calamity soon to come, and telling us that, no matter what befell us, we must bow in meekness to "Him who doeth all things well." "For whom the Lord loveth he chasteneth, and scourgeth every son whom he receiveth: that the trial of our faith, being much more precious than of gold that perisheth, though it be tried by fire, might be found unto praise, and honor, and glory at the appearing of Jesus Christ."

In the evening, Miss King, Mr. Moore, and myself went to the Baptist Church, and heard an excellent sermon. The text was, "And a man shall be a hiding-place from the wind, and a covert from the tempest." A very earnest prayer was offered up in behalf of our fugitive president, in which I know every one joined heartily. I did not know he was a fugitive, but the truth is gradually dawning on us that we are really subjugated, and our beloved president is fleeing from—what? Not justice, for he has committed no crime. I knew we had peace—how, I did not understand; but certainly thought we were independent. This is a severe ordeal; may God in his mercy give us comfort through it.

May 1.—A lovely day; spring is silently working her great Creator's will, and arraying herself in all her glories. Meadow and woodland is brilliant with her gorgeous robes. There is a mellowness breathing in the air, which fills one as with an undefinable feeling of perfect tranquility. O, how welcome it comes to our troubled spirits! How bountifully God has showered his blessings on us, if we would only receive them!

Miss King, Mr. Moore, and myself rode out in Dr. Porter's carriage, to see Mr. Thomas; when half-way there we met him going to town. He remarked that no doubt the church would suffer by the revolution which had shaken the land, and that he was prepared to earn his living, as he was then doing, by the sweat of his brow.

I do think it is disgraceful that a man with Mr. Thomas's education and talents should not at least earn a living at his calling. His is no isolated case. I have heard of some of our clergymen in the cities, who were so bad off that they did not know from day to day where they would get the money to buy bread for their households. . . .

Mr. Thomas's house is situated in a lovely and romantic spot. There is a fine grove of trees in front of the house, of nature's planting. I was rather hasty when I said there were no woods in this place; I had not seen one half of its beauty. Mrs. Thomas gave us a hearty welcome. She told us that many of General Lee's men had passed there; some of them she had entertained. She said they seemed to take their defeat with a serious dignity, as if they were confident they had done their duty as the defenders of their country and cause; had failed, and were accepting the issue, like all do who feel they have "left no blot on their name," and can "look proudly to heaven from the death-bed of fame." It is only those who have sold their country and honor for their own selfish ends who have cause now to mourn.

It is now rumored that France has recognized us. We conversed about her coming to aid us at the eleventh hour. Mrs. Thomas and I said we would much rather it had been Great Britain; the others preferred France, as she had always shown herself our friend. I asked them in what way; for I had never seen or heard of any benefit we had received from her. True, she now and then gave us a few words of pity, to let us know we were remembered. She had an idea that some day we might be her neighbors, and it was wiser to make friends of us than foes. It is said she requested Great Britain to join her in recognizing us; but has she become so poor;

> " Is she steeped so low
> In poverty, crest-fallen, and palsied so,
> That she must sit, much wroth, but timorous more; "

and knock at Britain's doors, asking her aid to stay this fratricidal bloodshed? Has the land of the immortal Lafayette really sunk so far that she could not have raised her hand and helped us without the aid of other nations? Who was her ally when she helped the colonies? And, by the way, I do not suppose the colonies would ever have gained their independence without her. Since then we all know she has not sunk in power, but is much greater in all that constitutes true national greatness; I look on her present ruler as a wiser and a better one than his great uncle; for by his rule he has brought prosperity to his people, where his uncle brought the reverse.

A lady asked me why I took the part of England, as it had sub-jugated Scotland. To this I need scarcely give my answer—that not even the august Cæsar, whose boast was he had conquered the world, had subjugated Scotland; and that, when he conquered England, he had to build a wall to protect his people from the " daring Cale-donian." To be sure she was under the yoke of England through treachery for awhile, but her brave sons, with their dauntless daring, threw off that yoke, and now the Scot

> " Wanders as free as the wind o'er [winds of] his mountain,
> Save love's willing fetters, the charms o' his Jean." [9]

This is not the first time I have heard the southern people speak thus of France; although I have heard many of them say that the government of Great Britain is the best in the world, and wish we had such a one here.

I think the reason they lean so much to France is because she aided in the revolution of '76. If she has indeed stepped in just now to help us (which seems at rather a strange time) it is because she wishes us to aid her in keeping Mexico.

Dr. Young is here with the medical stores. Dr. Porter and I tried to get him to give us some of the medicines; he would not; he says

[9] Burns, " Their Groves o' Sweet Myrtle," Stanza 2, ll. 7-8.

they were intrusted to his keeping, and he will not give them to any one without orders. We proposed that he should give us a *hint* of where they were, and we could help ourselves; but even this he would not do.

We have received orders to have every thing packed to hand over to the United States Government, or some one—we do not exactly know who. I asked our post surgeon, Dr. Foster, if we could not keep some of the hospital stores, as we had no money (excepting dear old Confederate) to pay our way home, and we thought we could sell some of the hospital goods. Dr. Foster said "No"; that it was like a dead man's estate, and he, as trustee, was bound in honor to give it up. I must confess that this is a little more honesty than I think at all necessary. Many of our men have not even a change of clothes, and have not been paid for months; and here we are giving hundreds of suits to the United States Government. It seems to me by rights they belong to the men.

Dr. Foster is a high-toned, cultivated gentleman. He thinks we are conquered, and speaks calmly on the subject. He is from Tennessee, and intends going back; and if he finds he can not live there, will leave. He has traveled much on the continent of Europe.

The Tennesseeans, as a whole, seem to dislike President Johnson; but I heard a very intelligent one say he was a man of much more ability than he got credit for, and that he had a good deal of tact, and his aim would be to please the people; so from policy might make a very good ruler.

May 4.—I heard yesterday that there are no cars running south of West Point, the raiders having destroyed the bridges in that section. I intend going to Newnan, as I may have a chance of getting a conveyance from there home.

I have made up my mind to *rob* the United States Government of a few things; namely, the bedding I have used since I have been in the hospital, and a few other articles. We have the two barrels of whisky, and I also intend appropriating some of that.

To-day I tried, at quite a number of places, to see if they would not barter some sheets or whisky for flour, as I can not take cold cornbread to travel with; but I did not succeed. This evening a friend of Mrs. Fyffe's, a refugee, sent me a little, and also a few eggs, so I feel quite rich. I have forgotten Mrs. Ware, who also sent me some flour.

Mrs. Fyffe has no idea how she is to get home, as at least one hundred miles of the railroad track is torn up between here and Chattanooga. She is grieving very much about her daughter. Since she has been here, the last word at night, and the first thing in the morning is, "My dear child, is she living or not?"

My kind friend Mr. Yerby, is in the country, and I shall not see him before leaving; I feel very sorry for him; he has lost nearly his all in this war. He was at his home last winter; the enemy had been to his house, and had taken every thing that his wife had, not leaving her even a cooking utensil; but that did not make much matter as she had nothing to cook. Since the enemy was there, she and her children have been living on what their neighbors have given them, and they had little to spare. All this distresses Mr. Yerby, he says his wife was the picture of despair.

He informed me that the tales which had been told him of the enemy's atrocities in Mississippi, were truly awful. It was a common thing for them to kill negro children, so as to carry off the parents with greater facility; and that many a negro child had been left to starve in the woods.

I am told that the enemy is behaving badly in Macon. A few days ago a lady took shelter with us from the rain; she was just from Macon, and was there when the enemy arrived. She has come up here to remain until something like law and order is restored.

The armistice was proclaimed before Wilson's army reached Macon. The mayor and a number of citizens met the army some miles from the city, and informed General Wilson of the armistice, and begged him not to come any further; but he pretended not to believe it, and marched his troops right in. Robbery and scenes of violence are as common as if peace had not been restored.

This lady knew of a gentleman who had killed a Federal in self-defense, and scarcely any notice was taken of it. Her house had been searched many times by bands of the vandals. They took her gold watch and her mother's, and made a great fuss because they could not get any more. These ladies thought, like others, that an armistice meant peace, and were not prepared for any thing of this kind. Their house is in the suburbs, and all there share the same fate. She says she does not think that General Wilson has it in his power to restrain his men, but he had no right having them there at all. They use the negroes shamefully, and kill them on the least provocation.

This lady's name is Gordon; she is a relative of General Gordon, of Virginia fame. Her brother, a member of Massindorf's battery, is now lying wounded in Mobile.

I see by the northern papers that General Canby, who captured Mobile, says he has received a heartier welcome from the Mobilians than he has any place he has yet taken. How can the people there so soon forget their dead? Why, even the enemy can not respect us when we can be guilty of such heartlessness.

XII: NEWNAN

May 5, 1865.—I arrived at Newnan to-day at 11 A. M., having left Griffin yesterday. On the train to Atlanta I met my friend, Dr. Hughes, on his way to this place; also Dr. Archer. The latter had been an assistant surgeon in one of the hospitals at this post. He is from Maryland, and like many others, since our failure, does not relish the idea of going back.

Major Fleming, inspector of the Mobile and Ohio Railroad, was on the train. He had left Mobile before the attack, on his way to Richmond, to collect some millions of dollars, which the government owed the railroad company. He turned back, as Richmond had fallen. He had just come from North Carolina, and informed us that Mrs. General J. E. Johnston and Mrs. Jeff Davis had gone, under his charge, to [Charlotte], N. C. Mrs. Davis had her children with her; the youngest, an infant, some few months old. On arriving at [Charlotte] every house was thrown open to receive Mrs. Johnston, but he had gone from house to house with Mrs. Davis and not one door would open to receive her; after awhile he prevailed on a Jewish lady to take her in. "Alas! how the mighty have fallen." Does not this recital fill the mind with pity, for poor frail humanity? Scarcely one, in this whole town, brave enough to receive the wife of him who but a short time ago "all delighted to honor," but now a houseless wanderer in the land which he has presided over with a wisdom, dignity, and statesmanship which has perhaps never been excelled.

Major Fleming also told us that it was believed President Davis, accompanied by a number of troops, was trying to make his escape, and cross the Mississippi, to join Kirby Smith's army, who were in Louisiana. Many say, had the latter been on this side of the Mississippi, we should not be in the position in which we now are.

From Jonesboro to Atlanta was one scene of desolation. There, day after day, the brave men of our army had struggled to maintain their rights, against overwhelming numbers. The woods showed how desperately each side had fought for mastery. Large oaks were riven asunder, their branches broken, and scattered all around. Ever and anon we saw the intrenchments which our brave fellows had thrown up; many a time wörking all night long, after fighting and marching.

We saw many a field hospital. The bunks, made of the branches of trees, were left standing where the poor sufferers had lain, and where numbers of them had breathed their last. Near the hospital, the graveyards were to be seen, where, side by side, lay friend and foe. . . .

As we neared Atlanta, the scene was one of desolation and ruin. As far as the eye could reach, pile after pile of blackened brick could be seen, where once had stood stately mansions. I had no idea that Atlanta was so large a place as it is. There being few or no buildings, trees, or any thing else left standing, we had a full view of its extent.

We had to remain in Atlanta all night, and as there were no hotels, stayed at the house of Dr. Powell, Mrs. Byrom's brother; she had just arrived from a hospital in Macon. Mrs. Dr. Powell had also just returned. She, like others, had been driven from her home by the remorseless Sherman. Their house had not been treated as badly as the others. It had been the head-quarters of one of the generals. The *glorious* star-spangled banner had been sketched on all its walls.

This morning, when we came down to the depot, it was almost impossible to find where it had been. I never expected to see such utter destruction as we there beheld[1] The meanest building on that street—the old Gate City Hospital—was left untouched. It served as a mark, to show us where we were. Opposite it, formerly the Front [Trout] House, the Atlanta Hotel, the banks, and many other large buildings had stood, of which not one stone is now left upon another. In the front yard of where the Atlanta Hotel once stood were some graves.

My heart sickened as I looked around, for every thing bespoke the malignity of the foe. The modern Tartars had done their work well. They will reap their reward.

There had been no Federal troops there since Sherman left. A garrison of them had just arrived, and were about to plant the stars and stripes over the city, or rather the ruins.

There were many Confederate soldiers there, returning to their homes. They treated the Federals with perfect indifference.

At the depot we met Dr. Burks and Mr. Catlet. They were on their way to Kentucky. Both have suffered much. Dr. Burks spent quite a fortune in the Confederate cause. Mr. Catlet told me that some of our men, on the trains to Atlanta, had quarreled with the Federals; and no wonder. I advised him, and all I saw, to treat them with perfect

---

[1] Mrs. Smith passed through Atlanta three weeks later returning to her home in Memphis. " This city," she reported, " like much of the good old State, was completely ruined by the ruthless hand of that merciless tyrant chieftain and his band of outlaws. None but those in whose midst, and over whose rights, the band of far worse than savages swept as a tornado, can give the most faint idea, or description, of what this noble Gate City and its vicinity, suffered, and the great contrast between its former and present appearance." *The Soldier's Friend*, 188.

indifference, as we were in their power, and none but *cowards* would taunt a fallen foe. If we quarreled with them, we put ourselves on their level.

Mrs. Byrom came down to the depot with us. I felt sad at bidding her, and the rest of my friends good-by. We had been associated with each other through much tribulation, little thinking that it would amount to nothing.

On the road to Newnan the cars were densely crowded with our soldiers. I noticed Senators Clay and Wigfall. I had just read an article written by the latter, in defense of General Johnston, which I much admired.

I found my Newnan friends, Mr. Dougherty's family, well, with the exception of one, an old lady, who is supposed to be at the point of death.

Sunday, May 7.—This is one of the gloomiest days I have spent since the war. The enemy have offered a reward of one hundred thousand dollars for the apprehension of our president. There are also rewards offered for many others of our leading men.[2]

I do hope and pray that Davis will get off. I am so afraid that some of our men will be tempted to betray him for the love of gain. If they should, it will be no more than others have done before them. Wallace was betrayed by one of his own countrymen; Charles I likewise. Some of our people are condemning Davis's administration. I have even heard him called a despot. If his detractors could see themselves in the proper light, perhaps they would hear a voice whispering, "He that is without sin, let him cast the first stone."

If Davis has committed errors, they have been, as even those who condemn him say, errors of judgment, for a truer patriot never lived. Can his defamers say the same?

Davis did not bring on secession, but accepted it, like many others, as the issue of a people's decision, and did what he felt was his duty when he found the rights of his country imperiled.

> "War, war to the knife, be enthralled or ye die,
>   Was the echo that woke in his land!
> But it was not his voice that promoted the cry,
>   Nor his madness that kindled the brand.
> He raised not his arm, he defied not his foes,
>   While a leaf of the olive remained;
> Till, goaded by insult, his spirit arose
>   Like a long baited lion unchained."

The reward is offered on the plea that he was accessory to the

[2] There are extant copies of two broadsides offering such a reward for Davis. One is for Davis only and was issued at Macon May 6 by General J. H. Wilson, whose troops captured the fugitive President on May 10. The other adds the names of Senator Clement Clay and four others and offers rewards totalling $360,000. It was issued at Athens, Georgia, on May 9.

murder of Lincoln, but we all know that not even the enemy believe that.[3] They only make this a plea so as to capture him, should he get to a foreign country. The placards, when put up here, were immediately torn down by some of the citizens.

Since my arrival here I have been told that some time after the armistice a report was brought to town that a large army of the enemy were advancing on it. The citizens, forming themselves in a body, went and met them some few miles from the town, and informed them of the armistice. Instead of the enemy remaining where they were, they marched right in.

The general commanding this army, and indeed nearly all of the officers and men, made a boast, which, I think, were it known, would be scorned and contemned by their own people, as well as by us. They said, had it not been for the armistice, Newnan would have been laid in ashes; and the General had some half-dozen ladies' names written down, whom he intended making examples of, by punishing most ignominiously, in revenge for some ill-natured remarks they had made to the prisoners who were captured near here last year. I believe one of the ladies committed the *unpardonable sin* of refusing some of them apples and water. She was a refugee, and had lost her all by some of these men, so it was not much wonder if she was embittered against them. Another cause of complaint was, that a man, or some men, living a few miles from here, had hunted some of them with blood-hounds, and I know that this is false. I am certain these are all their wrongs, unless I add Generals Roddy and Wheeler having the *daring* to *rout* the whole command who came here with the kind intentions then, so we thought, of laying Newnan in ashes, before the *terrible* wrongs, I have just narrated had been committed.

I visited the wounded prisoners, and they all spoke highly of their treatment. I was told of one lady, Mrs. Dr. ——, who, when the well prisoners passed her house, abused them. Some of us were shocked to think she could so far forget herself, as a lady and a Christian, to insult the helpless. But when we remembered that this lady and her children had been left in the world without shelter or food—these vandals having robbed her and set fire to her house, she being compelled to stand by, looking helplessly on the destruction, without even the liberty of remonstrating—when we thought of this, we concluded that perhaps, had we been like treated, we might have done the same.

Have the northern people really become such arbiters of all things, that every woman who makes use of the only weapon she has, when wronged beyond human endurance, is to be punished with degradation worse than that which even Haynau visited on the unhappy

[3] The Athens broadside declares: " The President of the United States has issued his proclamation announcing that the Bureau of Military Justice have reported upon indubitable evidence, that Jefferson Davis, Clement Clay, Jacob Thompson, George N. Saunders, Beverley Tucker and W. C. Cleary, incited and concerted the assassination of Mr. Lincoln and the attempt on Mr. Seward."

Hungarians; and for this *terrible offense* is a whole town to be laid in ashes? I believe, notwithstanding all the woe and inhumanity perpetrated on our unfortunate people by the enemy, that there is still manhood enough among them to condemn this officer to whom they have intrusted their honor.

Those things may do in barbarous lands, but they ill become the boasted descendants of the great and good men who were the followers of the immortal Washington.

This general kept his men in the place till many a lady's wardrobe was lessened, and many a little trinket stolen. Mrs. Myers gave me a description of one band who came to her house. They took every thing they could carry away. After they left she sat down in despair, where a door hid her, when in walked a Dutchman, who commenced turning over what few things had been left in her drawers and trunks. Seeing her, he said, "Madam they have treated you very badly." He meant *himself*, for nothing was left for him. She answered, "Yes; what do you want?" He begged her for some clothes, saying he was badly in want of them. She told him she had none, or else he should have them, for his politeness in asking.

Sunday, May 14.—President Davis has been captured, and I am glad of it, as he can clear his fair fame from the aspersion cast upon it.

I have been told that, on hearing of the reward offered, and the accusation against him, he did not try to get away.

One thing, in connection with him, has made me feel prouder of our people than any thing else. At this time the country is filled with lawless men, whom defeat has made reckless. They steal from friend and foe. It seems that bands of these men came across Davis, but on finding out who he was did not molest him.

The patriot is now a prisoner, for devotion to freedom and his country's good. He has the consolation of religion to support him, and also the consciousness of having done his duty to his country. . . .

Quite a number of Federal cavalry have been here. They went to Mr. Dougherty's corn-crib, broke down the doors, and took all his corn and fodder, without giving him any thing for it.

A number of paroled prisoners have passed through here. Many of them stayed a day or two at Mr. Dougherty's. Some of them go quietly away, saying nothing, while others have the war spirit still in them. All have behaved gentlemanly, with the exception of two Texans, who had been on a general's staff. Mr. Dougherty had closed his house, as he could not afford to buy provisions and get nothing but Confederate money for board. These men told him they had greenbacks and silver. They have been here some time. To-day they told Mr. Dougherty that if he did not take Confederate money he would have to do without; and said that they had been fighting for four years to save his property, and had a right to what he had given them.

284

My good friend, Mrs. Dougherty's sister, who was so very ill when I first came here, is getting better.

I have received much kindness from all my old friends. Many have called and invited me to make their houses my home. But with all this, I am very anxious to get to Mobile.

I called on Mrs. Judge Hopkins, of Mobile, now here, to see if she knew of any way of my getting there, but was disappointed. Mrs. Hopkins has nobly done her duty in the cause. She went into the hospital service at the commencement of the war, and had charge of some two or three Alabama hospitals, in Richmond. She left that place some time before it fell, as the hospital department was ordered away. Since then she has been at a post near Montgomery, and came here from fear of Wilson's raid.

She told me she had nothing to eat but corn-bread and bacon, and that she had drawn from our commissary. Judge Hopkins is with her, and is in very feeble health, caused mainly by his poor diet, and were it not for a little coffee and sugar they have, Mrs. Hopkins thinks he would have died.

Before the war he was one of the richest men in Alabama. She spoke very highly of the lady she was staying with; says they all fare alike.

My friend, Mrs. Captain Nutt, and her children, are here. They intend leaving in a few days for Louisiana. I could go with them, but should be compelled to leave my baggage, which I am unwilling to do.

This evening Mr. and Mrs. Brooks went with me to a Mrs. Barnett's, whose husband is going as far as Montgomery in a wagon. I asked her if he could not take my baggage, but he had no room. There we met a fine-looking lady, Mrs. General Fry, who has spent much of her time in Richmond, and related to us some incidents in high life there.

One of them I will notice, which occurred in an Episcopal Church, as I have witnessed the like more than once in our own churches—in Mobile—and which I think reflects little credit, not only on Christians, but on all who claim to have a sense of true politeness.

It seems that the wife of one of our generals, who is high in command, and a member of one of the most aristocratic families in Virginia, was dressed very plainly, as true greatness needs no adorning. She went to one of the churches, I suppose a stranger there, took her seat in the pew of one who she thought would make her welcome, when a member of his family, a young lady fashionably dressed, came to the pew, and judging of the occupant from appearances, ordered her out, and did not find out her mistake until too late to retrieve it, and until a dozen of the pew doors were flung open to receive Mrs. General ———.

May [1]5.—Since my return here, I have received a letter from a young lady in Texas, thanking me, in grateful terms, for some little attention

285

I paid her brother, Mr. Angel, while in the Foard Hospital, wounded. She also says she is certain that, next to my own state, I cared most for Texas, as I wore a star on my hat while waiting on the Texas soldiers.

This caring for one state more than another is a feeling I have never experienced, and, indeed, I expect that, many a time, I have been guilty of slighting men from my own, as it had never been overrun by the enemy, and the men from it could communicate with their families, and so receive their aid.

I never approved of state hospitals, situated as we were. They would do with the northern people, where there was no foe, taking state after state from them, thereby shutting out all communication with homes and friends; but not here, where it was the duty of the more favored to aid their sister states in adversity.

I have often observed the spirit of rivalry existing between men from the different states. In many instances it has been made a subject for jesting; in others, it has been exhibited by a spirit of bitter prejudice.[4] I have found a mixture of good and evil in them all.

The lowest and most degraded people I have ever met were in Tennessee, and the best educated and most polished men were also from that state.

The most unruly and dastardly in our hospitals have been from Louisiana; and yet, to be a Roman, in the palmiest days of that ancient republic, was no higher honor than to be a citizen of that state. The men from it have won laurels for bravery and heroism, that will long live in story.

We all know what it is to be reputed a Virginian, a descendant of the ancient cavaliers and the nobles of France, who, rather than submit to a power that they thought had no right over them, left wealth, home, their native land, and emigrated where they could enjoy that

" Eternal spirit of the chainless mind," [5]

as best suited them.

[4] Miss Pember wrote: " The wounded wards would be noisily gay with singing, laughing, fighting battles o'er and o'er again, and playfully chatting with each other by decrying the troops from different States, each man applauding his own. When listening to them one would suppose that the whole Southern army with the exception of a few companies from the speaker's section of country were cowards. The up-country soldiers, born in the same States as those they derided, went even further and decried ' them fellows from the seaboard, who let us do all the fighting.' The Georgians would romance of how the South Carolinians laid down at such a battle, refusing to charge, and how they had to ' charge right over them.' The Mississippians of the backwardness of the Tennessee troops, who ' would never go into action unless led by their commanding general.' The Virginians told bitter stories of the rowdyism of the Maryland volunteers, who were ' always spreeing it in the city, and dancing attendance on the women,' and the North Carolinians caught it on all sides, though their record is certainly a gallant one." *A Southern Woman's Story,* 77-78.
[5] George Gordon Byron, " The Prisoner of Chillon: A Fable," l. 1.

The great Lee was deserted in his last extremity by hundreds of the Virginians.

I have often remarked that the men from Kentucky and Missouri were more intelligent and finer-looking, as a whole, than the men from the states further south. I have thought the reason was, that as a rule, none came from those states excepting the better class, and men who left their homes for pure patriotism, while from the other states we had all classes.

These two states were represented in our army by some of the noblest and most dauntless of men; and yet I could relate instances where some of them strayed widely from the right path.

Texans and Arkansians I can say but little about, excepting what we all know—their faultless bravery on every battle-field. I may say the same of South Carolinians and Marylanders, who boast of their descent from the same ancient lineage as the Virginians.

But I have forgotten an incident which happened to me some time ago. I was in company with an officer from South Carolina, whose actions I did not think entitled him to the name of gentleman. I related the circumstance to a friend, a native of the same state, and jestingly told her I was done with it forever. She asked me if I would cast aside a roll of bank bills because it had a counterfeit in it.

Mississippi I have heard abused for every thing that was contemptible, and yet, when the history of this war is written, no pages in it will boast of brighter stars than the names of the gallant men from that state. And in all the places I have been I have never seen any thing to equal the enthusiasm and patriotism which I met there.

Georgia, poor abused Georgia! no state in the Confederacy came forward with more alacrity than she did at every call for troops, and I expect none has surpassed her for liberality in providing for the sick and wounded. In this respect Atlanta can vie with any city. The ladies of it have worked assiduously, year after year, for the sufferers. It was a hospital from the evacuation of Bowling Green until the time of its fall.

North Carolina and Florida, like others, had lights and shadows. Of the former I know but little, excepting the records of the deeds of bravery of her noble sons on the battle-field. Florida, being a small state, could send fewer troops to the field, but did not send fewer in proportion to her population. She can compete with any of them in every thing that is good and gallant.

Of my own state, Alabama, I need say but little, as acts speak louder than words, and I have already recorded enough of them to tell how her people have suffered, and what their character has been.

There are no Federal troops sent here yet to garrison the town. We all think that their presence would be of benefit, as all southern rule is now *dead*, and we have no law.

Scarcely a day passes without our hearing of some outrage committed by men calling themselves returned Confederates. The other day a band of them went to the house of a gentleman living near here, who had some gold and silver. They told him if he did not give it up they would hang him. He stoutly refused; they took his wife and commenced hanging her before his eyes. So he gave them every cent he had. They were closely disguised.

Another case, but one more excusable, happened in town. Some poor women, headed by one or two men, went to the house of a lady, and demanded some commissary stores which they thought she had, as they said they were starving. There were men enough in the house to prevent them doing any harm.

Many laugh at the idea of these people starving. I do not. One of the men who headed this party is Mr. Love, who once had charge of our wash-house. I have been to see his family, and found him an invalid, and his family on the very brink of starvation. I could do nothing for them, so did not go back. God pity them and all such! Mr. Love was in the Cherokee Hospital before I went to it; was a quiet, inoffensive and truly honest man.

A little while before the war closed, when there was a call for troops, Dr. de Yampert, thinking Mr. Love was fit for field service, sent him to the army. His wife and children had to leave with him. As our government had not paid any one in months, they had no money. A few of the good people of Griffin gave them some; Dr. de Yampert also gave them a little out of the hospital fund.

Mr. Love brought his family here, and joined the army, I believe, at Macon. He had not marched far when his old disease, the dropsy, came back; and when I saw him his feet were so swollen that he could not walk. He was one of the " hospital rats."

I am told that the people of Georgia are collecting provisions and money for the destitute in their state, and that the Federals are giving them rations.

Some Federals have been here from Atlanta; they came for the purpose of visiting their relatives' graves, men who were killed near here last summer; some of their comrades had marked the graves. These men behaved very gentlemanly.

Mrs. Bell, a relative of Mrs. Dougherty's, a warm-hearted southerner and an excellent lady, has been here lately. The battle near here last year was not far from her farm. And at the present time one of our men, Rev. Mr. Hudson, is lying in her house, helpless from a wound near the spine, received then. He is a Presbyterian minister, and was a chaplain in Ross's Texas cavalry. Mrs. Bell says he is as helpless as a child, and one of his companions has been with him all the time nursing him. She says his patience and endurance are above all praise.

Newnan, like every other town in the confederacy, has her array of martyrs. The war has cast the mantle of sorrow over many households. The whole country has lost heavily. Mr. S. Martin, who is over sixty years of age, entered the service at the commencement of the war, along with four or five sons. Two or three of them are now sleeping their last sleep, and another has lost his arm in the service. Mr. Thurmond and Mr. Brown have each lost two sons; Major Kendrick, whom I have heard spoken of as being a good citizen and a brave soldier, was killed. It would be useless for me to mention them all, as there is scarcely a family in the whole country but that has to mourn the loss of a loved one.

My friend, Captain Brooks, had a brother killed, and has another who lost an arm in the service. Captain Brooks was in the state service, and had a very narrow escape in a battle near Macon. Mrs. Brooks showed me a shawl that he had on at the time, which is completely riddled with bullets, and he did not receive a scratch.

Colonel Berry, whom I met one evening at Mr. Dougherty's, a relative of Mr. Dougherty's, is now suffering from his sixth or seventh wound, and it is supposed he is a cripple for life.

There is a gentleman and his family here who have just come from Auburn, Alabama, and report great difficulty in getting on, as every bridge between West Point and Montgomery has been destroyed. He has just returned from a long sojourn in a northern prison, and gives horrible accounts of the ill-treatment of himself and companions. His feelings against the North are very bitter. He is a highly intelligent man; I believe was editor of a newspaper in Atlanta.[6] We hear many recitals from returned prisoners, such as this gentleman has given us.

One gentleman told me that he had seen as many as six carried from their bunks at one time, frozen to death. At night a sentinel went round, and if they had more than one blanket on, no matter how cold the night, it was taken from them. Another told me that they had been kept for days without food or water, and a table filled with all kinds of dainties set so they could see it, and told if they would take the oath of allegiance to the United States they could have them. He knew of one poor fellow who did take the oath, but says his mind was almost gone, and when he got the food, his tongue was so swollen for want of water, that he could not eat.

One young man, who was confined at Camp Douglas, told me that it was common for them, whenever they heard of their army being defeated, to keep the prisoners for days without food or water. And he knew of one young man who went out and picked up a handful of snow to put to his parched lips, when a sentinel shot him dead. My narrator told me he helped to carry in the young man's body. These are only a few of the evils which were inflicted on our men. How hard it is to suppress feelings of hate for our enemy! I feel as confident as I am living, that God, in his own good time, will avenge our wrongs. When I think of the kind treatment that our people be-

---

[6] James Pinkney Hambleton, sometime editor of the Atlanta *Southern Confederacy*. A portion of Hambleton's private papers are preserved in the Emory University Library.

stowed on the prisoners here, bad off for food as we were, did I think otherwise, it would be contrary to the faith I have in the justice of God.

A few days ago a speech was published in the papers, made by President Johnson to the Indiana delegation. It seems to have struck dismay to many a heart, and if he carries out what he says in it, I am confident the war is not over yet, for I have watched the countenances of some men, who I have been told never favored the war or secession, and I think they expressed a determination that, if there should be another war, they would assist in it, heart and soul.

If President Johnson wants the southern people to be more inimical to the North than even this war has made them, he will carry out the policy indicated in that speech; but, if he wishes the North and South to be united in spirit, as well as in the form, he will adopt another.

" God has implanted a desire to resist oppression in the nature of every man," and " even the smallest worm will turn, being trodden on."

What wound was ever healed by continual irritation. Have we not been wounded? God knows how terribly! Grant that we were in the wrong, are we the only people who have erred? . . . We are of the same indomitable race as himself. We have not been conquered, for that would be a disgrace to him, as well as us; but we have been overpowered by numbers, and in no craven spirit would I tell him, for we and all we have are in his power, that forbearance and magnanimity are godlike virtues, while cruelty and revenge characterize the dastard; and that if he wishes to make a name for himself, such as mortal man has never had before, by bringing two such adverse spirits together, in peace and harmony, it will never be done by oppression. History gives us no such examples.

O, if I had the ability to write to him, as did the lamented Bishop Otey to Seward, at the out-break of the war, and plead with him, in earnest tones, to let dove-eyed peace reign where cruel war has been sole monarch—with the hope that my appeal would not be in vain as was Bishop Otey's—how earnestly I would pray to him to have peace, and peace alone, as his sole aim!

God grant that some wise and able advocate may rise in our behalf, and that ere long, peace, with all its blessings, may reign over our now distracted land!

To the people of the South I would also say a few words. Our doom is sealed; we are in the power of the North. Our representative man a prisoner; our armies vanquished—or, those which are not soon will be. Have we done our duty? Have the planters given of the abundance of their harvests to the poor women and children of soldiers who were fighting to save their wealth? But I should not say poor, for that is not the word; none were poor whose husbands, sons, and brothers offered up their lives a sacrifice for liberty! No money can buy such riches.

Have no native southern men remained at home, when their country had need of their strong arms, speculating on what the planters charged so much for, doubly taking the bread out of these same poor, yet rich, soldiers' families' mouths?

Have no native southern quartermasters and commissaries robbed these *poor*, yet *rich* soldiers, who walked boldly up to the cannon's mouth, regardless of consequences? They have starved, gone ragged and bare-footed through burning suns and chilling frosts, while these delinquent commissaries and quartermasters have lived on the best of the land, and worn the finest clothes to be had.

Have the examining surgeons conscientiously worked, sending none to the field but those who were fit for field service? And none who would have served their country better and more effectively had they been left at home to till the ground, thereby making food for the army and themselves?

Have the conscript officers taken none for the army, that the surgeons had discharged some three or four times, and sent them to the field; they dying before it was ever reached?

Have the stewards and foragers, in hospitals, never speculated on food sold them, much cheaper by the farmers, because it was for the soldiers and the cause; and have they never robbed the government of the money appropriated by it to buy food for the wounded and sick soldiers?

Have there been no officers, to whose keeping mothers have entrusted their young sons—they promising to guide and protect them; but who, as soon as away from all restraint, forgot all obligations, and took advantage of the position the war had given to them to act the tyrant in a thousand petty ways, inducing many of the men to do what they would otherwise never have thought of?

Have all the young native southerners who cried *secession*, and *war to the knife*, before the war broke out, gone into the field when their country was bleeding at every pore?

Have all the Christian and refined women of the South, who had no household duties to attend, gone into the hospitals, nursed the wounded and sick, preparing little delicacies, which no man has ever been able to do, for the poor bed-ridden soldier, who had lost all but honor for his country; and, when his hours were numbered, stood by his bedside when no wife, mother, or sister was there, to soothe his last moments and lift his thoughts to the Cross whereon his Redeemer had died, and to that heaven where he was waiting with open arms to receive the departing spirit?

Have the women of the South never passed by, in disdain, a ragged and wounded soldier, who had suffered more than words can express? In a word, have the women of the South done their whole duty; and can the southern people, as a whole, say they have fully done their duty?

It is all over with, some will say, and why bring those things in

291

review before us, as it can do no good. It is not all over with. Men and women of the South, there is much yet to be done.

" What are monuments of bravery
Where no public virtues bloom? "

What though we had gained our independence, while all these sins were crying out against us, could we have expected, as a nation, to go on in them and prosper? Never! We should have worked our own downfall as we have now done.

Had we been true to our God and country, with all the blessings of this glorious, sunny land, I believe we could have kept the North, with all her power, at bay for twenty years.

What I would ask now, is for the southern people to look to themselves, forgetting all the wrongs inflicted on us by our foe in the knowledge that we have sinned against each other. I do not mean that we should forget all we have suffered, for that would dishonor the glorious dead. I mean, to stop all useless recriminations. They will do us no good now. Let us look to ourselves; " raise monuments where public virtues bloom." Let us leave the North to itself, with all its isms, to answer for its own sins. I think we have as many as we can see to.

To professed Christians, north and south, I would say, much, very much, depends on you. If you quarrel with each other, in the name of every thing that is good and holy, what will become of us? . . .

292

✠✠

XIII: MOBILE

✠✠

May 29, 1865.—I arrived in Mobile on the 27th, having left Newnan on the 17th instant, in company with Captain Nutt, his wife and three children. Captain Cloud, one of General Morgan's squadron, and about six of Captain Nutt's men, were of the party. I regretted leaving Newnan, as I have many good and true friends there; among them my kind friend, Dr. Hughes. He intends starting for his home in Kentucky in a few days. The failure of our cause has been a sad blow to him. He is one of those who was willing to suffer much more than he had already, so we had gained our independence.

I had concluded to go to Atlanta, and see if the Federal commander there knew of any way to send me on, as I had been told they were sending refugees back to their homes. While getting ready, Captain Nutt, and Captain Butler, our old commissary, called and told me, if I wished, I could go with Captain Nutt and his family; they were going to West Point in the cars, and Captain Butler would have a wagon waiting there to take them to Montgomery. I was only too thankful to accept the kind offer. Dr. Hughes very kindly disposed of my whiskey, and received three dollars and fifty cents, all the money I had in my possession, with the exception of a one dollar greenback that Dr. Bateman had given me as a memento; he had picked it up on the battle-field of Chickamauga.

As we were to be some time on the road, I set my wits to work to see what I could hunt up in the way of provisions. I went to Mrs. Dr. Redwine, and she promised to give me what she could. I then tried to get some eggs, and other things, for the sheets I had with me, but did not succeed. I found it impossible to sell them, as there was no money about. Bartering was the order of the day.

I went to see Mrs. Nutt, and had a hearty laugh at her; she was so earnest, bartering away for food every little house-hold article she had. One calico dress, which she was trying to dispose of, she paid the moderate sum of five hundred dollars for. A friend told me she had paid five hundred dollars for a calico dress, six hundred for a pair of cotton cards, and twenty for a bar of brown soap.

The morning I started, Mrs. Brooks had some nice ham, cake, and biscuit ready for me. Mrs. Redwine sent the same. Mrs. Dr. Reese brought me a present of some cakes and eggs; Dr. Berry, some ham. On the whole I was pretty well supplied, considering the times.

Many of my friends came to see me off; Miss Taylor, her sister, Mrs. Brooks, and Dr. Hughes. I remarked that I should ever remember Newnan with pleasure, as every one had been so kind. A friend answered me, saying that my opinion was different from that of some soldiers lately there; they said it was the meanest place on the earth.

A little while before the armistice, our cavalry, passing through there, begged corn for their horses, but got none. As soon as the enemy came on their last raid, the same people who refused our men sold corn to the Federals; but perhaps the people were very much in want of the money.

We got on the freight train, and after starting, the conductor came for our fare. He charged me four dollars to go to West Point; that took all the money I had except fifty cents. I forgot for the moment that I had been in the *service*, and did not tell the conductor, or, I expect he would not have charged any thing.

We reached West Point about two hours before sunset, and such a scene as I saw there I never shall forget. The river was gliding as smoothly as if the enemy had never been there to disturb the quiet. The fine bridge that spanned it had been destroyed, and every way the eye turned was ruin and desolation. The depot and warehouse were a pile of blackened bricks. The banks were covered with the men of our army returning to their homes. The faded gray uniform was seen every-where. There were some half a dozen " blue-coats " standing by themselves, as much alone as if they had been in the Desert of Sahara, instead of in the midst of a people whom they claimed to have conquered. I almost pitied their loneliness. I thought they looked ashamed of themselves; or, rather, as if they had been guilty of a wrong for which they were sorry.

We had to remain some few hours on the banks of the river, as there was nothing to take us across but a flat and a few small boats. The scene was a most impressive one. I wish I had been gifted with the pencil of an artist, so I could have drawn a picture. Nature never looked more beautiful to me, and when the setting sun flung his rays over the grand old trees and scattered groups, as if to remind us that there was something more than the present, which no foe could take away . . .

The last time I was there we were suffering, but free. Some other families and ourselves were the last to cross over. In the crowd were two young ladies, who seemed to be returning home. They evidently had run with their valuables from some of the raids; with them were two negro women, who had charge of their trunks. A Federal officer, who seems to be the post commandant, was standing near this group. One of the young ladies pointed to a trunk, and told the servant to take care of it, as it was filled with silver. The negro said to her, please speak lower, as the Yankees will hear you, and steal it. I looked at the officer, but he never raised his head. Perhaps the remark hit him!

We put up at a large hotel, which we were told the enemy had left standing in pity for the proprietor, Mr. Camp, who had both of his eyes shot out while helping to defend the place at the time of its capture. I have been told that at that time the garrison in the fort consisted of seventy-five men of Massingale's battery. The citizens, old men and boys, amounting to about forty, joined them. They defended it manfully, for six hours, against twenty-five hundred of the enemy. We lost fifteen in killed, and some wounded. The enemy destroyed two bridges, the depot, some very valuable flour mills, and other property.

My money being all gone, Captain Nutt kindly offered to pay my expenses. He had got his money by selling two horses. Some of the *rebels* kept up a great noise all night, singing " Dixie," and hurrahing for Jeff. Davis. I thought they would have to be informed that they were " *whipped*," as they did not seem to be aware of the fact.

The next morning, the 18th, we were aroused by the information that we could go a few miles further on a wood-car. As the expected wagon was not there, Captain Nutt resolved to take the car. In the hurry of leaving, woman-like, Mrs. Nutt forgot a very precious bottle of camphor, and I took a coffee-pot full of coffee, and ran with it. When the conductor came for our fare, I told him who I was; he said, all right, and passed on. We had quite a pleasant ride, as we had the full benefit of the breeze.

Our next stopping-place was on the banks of a creek or river. The bridge having shared the fate of the others, we had to cross in a small boat. The owner would take nothing but Confederate money as ferriage, and charged seventy dollars. Captain Cloud said he felt like giving three cheers for the Confederacy, as there still seemed to be a spot of it left.

We climed a very steep hill, which was hard on the children. Captain Nutt's men carried my baggage, which consisted of a trunk and a large bundle. Mrs. Nutt, like a *true soldier*, had none but what she could carry in her hand.

After walking about a mile, we came to a house inside of a very pretty park. We went into the park, and remained there nearly all day. The house was large, and some two or three hundred yards from the road. The trees around it were magnificent, and put me in mind of dear old Tennessee. The sun was in a cloud, and the breeze blew delightfully through the trees, which had a very soothing effect after our hot walk. The park was filled with other stragglers besides ourselves, *rebels* returning to their homes. Many of them stretched themselves on the grass to rest, as they had doubtless done many times in camp. We looked like a real band of gipsies; Captain Cloud and myself called Mrs. Nutt the queen. As we knew no way of getting on, we were " trusting to luck," for something to " turn up."

Captain Cloud is a Kentuckian, and was outlawed by the governor of that state. He seemed much grieved because he could not go home to see his mother and sisters.

He related many an incident about his late general, John Morgan; said he arrived at the place where the general was killed a little while after the deed was done. When the men heard of their general's death, they wept like children . . . Not even the noble Douglas himself had the hearts of his countrymen more than had this dauntless chief.

Captain Nutt was a lawyer in Shreveport, Louisiana, and entered the army at the first call of his country. He commanded a company of scouts, and saw service in the Virginia and Tennessee armies; he was wounded and a good while a prisoner. His wife went through the lines and remained with him until he was released. She told me that, on arriving at Richmond on her return south, the ladies crowded around her, she expecting the first question to be, how is our cause progressing in the North? but no, the fashions were all they cared for. She became so thoroughly disgusted with them that she wrote a letter to Vice-president Stephens on the subject, asking him to comment on it, and have the whole published; but she had looked in vain for the appearance of the article in the papers.

Mrs. Nutt is a true southern woman, and when she had the good of the cause in view, could not be daunted. I could not but compare her to the wife of Pantheus, that noble Spartan woman who followed her husband to Africa, and after his death met hers with so much fortitude.

We commented a good deal upon a report that was going the rounds: It seems that before the surrender of Richmond the dead-letter bag was opened, and on reading the letters from the soldiers' wives, nearly all were begging the men to desert! Many of the gentlemen now are blaming the women for our failure. I do not altogether agree with them, for I think if the truth was wholly known, the rich people who remained at home and did nothing for the soldiers' families, are greatly to blame. In the afternoon the gentlemen managed to procure a wagon which took all the baggage and the children.

There was a party from Helena, Arkansas, who, like ourselves, were trying to get home. The wife and child of one of the gentlemen rode in the wagon; Mrs. Nutt and myself preferred walking.

A little while before dark we reached a small town, called Cussetta. There was but one hotel in the place, and it has left an indelible impression on my mind time will never efface. It was in a most dilapidated condition, and when the children walked on the upper gallery they ran the risk of falling into the street. We were given two rooms which opened on the gallery. The floors were so covered with tobacco spit and other filth, that even to walk on them with thick shoes was disagreeable. As it was the only shelter here we had to put up with it. We had our own edibles with us, so got along pretty well.

Our Arkansas friends were at the same *hotel* with us. They told me that the loyal people of Arkansas had suffered much by the war. The lady had an aunt who was an invalid, and lived in a beautiful house surrounded by all the comforts of home. Some of the enemy went to her house, and without any provocation, except her southern proclivities, carried her out, and fired her house. Such things were quite common.

Riding one day with a very beautiful young lady from that state, she told me that many a time she had stood at her room window, and saw our troops shoot down these vandals, and with great vehemence she said, " I clapped my hands with delight, when I saw the robbers fall." I looked at her, as she spoke, in wonder that any one so gentle and lovely could feel such hate, and I made a few remarks on the subject. She said, " Yes, it is all very well for you to talk thus, you who have never known the wrongs that we have had to endure; you know nothing about the war." She was about right; for as much trouble as I have seen, I have been spared the evil of ever coming in contact with the enemy except as prisoners.

Hundreds of *rebels* passed and re-passed all the time. Some were from Lee's army, going south, others from the Mississippi and Gulf department, going north. They were much quieter than might have been supposed. One band of them occupied an empty store, near us, and sang hymns nearly all night. General Allen and his staff, with some wagons, passed. I bought two ounces of coffee from a woman who had a pound of it, and paid her twenty cents in silver. Captain Nutt replenished his larder. He bought some nice fried chickens from a farmer, who also gave us a pitcher of sweet milk. We left this *delectable* place, in a wagon, on the 20th, much relieved to get away from it. Arrived at Opelika the same day, and was disappointed at finding no way of getting on further. General Bragg and his staff stopped awhile there. As they were to pass through Tuskeega [Tuskegee] they kindly offered to take my baggage in their wagon. They would have taken us, but their horses were almost broken down, having come so far. Captain Nutt's men then left us, as we had no idea when we should get away from there, and they were anxious to return to their homes. They were all from Louisiana, and had been with the captain through the whole campaign. They fairly venerated him, and told me that he had cared for them as if they had been his relatives. I was grateful for their kindness to me on this trip. I found them, as I have nearly always found the southern soldiers, true gentlemen. Opelika is sixty-seven miles from Montgomery; is a post village of Russell county. A railroad runs from there to Columbus, Georgia. The enemy seemed to have done little damage there in the way of destroying private property. The depot and warehouses were in ruins; and we saw the remains of a number of cars; their ruins were to be seen all along the road.

We took a walk in the afternoon around the fortifications. Quite a large fort commanded the Columbus and Montgomery road. As far as the eye could reach, the trees had been cut down to prevent the enemy from having a cover. We saw another fort; it enclosed a very pretty house. There are three or four churches there: the Episcopal, Methodist, Baptist, and I believe, a Presbyterian. Dr. Hedges, of New Orleans, lives near there, and has charge of the Episcopal Church. He had an appointment elsewhere, so the church was closed on Sunday the 21st.

I spoke to some men returning from Mississippi. They looked weary and sick. One had been wounded in his foot. They had been with the army in Mobile, and told me there had been no fighting in the city; which information relieved my mind a good deal.

Many Confederate soldiers passed us, with their clothes in rags, and almost barefooted. At any time, on looking down the road, these poor fellows could be seen, wending their weary way home. The sad remnant of a brave but unfortunate army.

The hotel we put up at was a great contrast to the one we had just left, as all about it was neat and clean.

On the 22d a locomotive and tender came from Columbus, Georgia, to take us a little further. While getting ready to start, the gentleman told Mrs. Nutt and myself to hurry, or we should not get a place, as there were so many soldiers going, and southern chivalry was played out. But they were mistaken; for as soon as we made our appearance the soldiers made room for us.

We crowded the engineer so much that he could scarcely work the engine. After going a short distance we came across two freight cars, and coupled them on the engine—fortunate for us, as in a few minutes afterward a heavy shower of rain fell. In the car were a number of officers, Mississippians.

It was quite amusing to hear all giving their opinions as to the cause of our failure; each having his own ideas on the subject. The merits and demerits of our generals were fully discussed; and as to forming an opinion of them from what we hear, is simply out of the question. I have heard some say that *Lee* was no general, and that Johnston was much his superior. Another says the reverse; and some, that *Morgan* did us more harm than good. I repeated the remark of a friend, that he believed General Bragg was one of our best generals; and a gentleman answered, that my friend must be deranged. I replied, that perhaps he would say the same of him.

Our conversation next turned on Napoleon. From some remark I made about him, a friend said, he did not think I liked him. I answered, that I could not glorify him as I heard many do, though no one could help being struck with awe and admiration at his meteor-like genius. But I could not like any man who made ambition his god, and every thing subservient to his love of power; and one who had broken the most sacred tie on earth, and waded through the best blood of his countrymen to gain it; thereby bringing woe and desolation where, had he loved glory less, and his country more, would have been peace and prosperity. I might have told him that I disliked him for the same reason that the children of to-day, in after years, may hate the Federals; as my mother's father was imprisoned by him many years. And when I thought of our hatred toward our enemy of to-day, another circumstance came up before me: The forefathers of perhaps all those about me then, had fought against mine; and my fraternal grandfather, when a midshipman, was captured by the redoubtable Paul Jones. By the way, here is another proof that the colonies had foreign aid, for Paul Jones was a Scotchman, and his familiarity with the rocks and shoals around his native coast made him the successful privateer that he was there.

After we had gone some few miles we came to a creek, and got out. The bridge here had been a very large one. In its destruction the main portion of it had fallen into the water which made a pathway for us to go on. We met some soldiers, who carried the children over. They were fine-looking men from Missouri. They were outlawed by their own state, and were on their way to join Kirby Smith. Mrs. Nutt and myself remained on the bank of the creek while Captain Nutt went in search of a conveyance to take us to Tuskegee, some four miles distant. The name of this place was Chehaw. In wandering along the banks I came across two springs of delightful, cool water, which was a great treat, as the day was very warm. Near the springs was a pathway over which the trees and shrubbery made a dense covering, which the sun's rays could scarcely penetrate. The whole scene was wild and solemn. I gazed at the ruins the enemy had made round it, and thought how beautiful were all of God's works till man defaced them!

Mrs. Nutt and I were so much pleased with the prospect, that we concluded to remain there all night if the captain failed to get a conveyance, as we were both going home without having ever "camped out." The grass was so green and fresh-looking, compared with the floors of the hotel at Cuscetta, that the fear of getting into another such a house made us firmer in our resolution. After staying there some few hours, Captain Nutt came back, unsuccessful, but said there was a small house near, where we could go. In vain we protested against leaving our rural retreat, but the captain was inexorable, and said if we remained there all night we would have chills by next morning, so we had to obey our *commander*, pack up our "truck," and go. The sun was very hot, and we had some quarter of a mile to walk. The children, three little girls, (the oldest eight years of age,) stood the journey like *soldiers*, with the exception of the youngest, (a little beauty, named Nannie,) who broke down when half way to the house. Her mother told her that she was no "*rebel*" if she cried in that way. We remained at that house some few hours. There was no one in it except one or two negroes, who were in the kitchen. The *rebels* were still on the go, returning to their respective homes. One, from Lee's army, a fine-looking young man, badly wounded in the arm, came into the house to rest. The merits of our respective generals was again the subject of discussion. When the young man heard General Lee disparaged, I thought we were going to have a battle; but it was only one of words, and did no harm. The young man said, the first thing he intended doing, after he arrived home, was to get married. I heard many of the soldiers say the same.

At a little before sundown, Captain Nutt procured a wagon. The children, Captain Cloud, (who was suffering from the effects of an old wound, and could scarcely walk,) and myself got in. Mrs. and Captain Nutt walked. We went, at what is termed, " snail's pace." There were three mules drawing us, that had been on the go all day. When half way on the road we stopped at a very pretty place. The inmates were refugees, from Kentucky, old friends of Captain Nutt's. They came out to see us, and brought us some nice fresh water. Our driver was a good old negro man, and a member of the Methodist Church, and seemed very religious. We arrived at Tuskegee about 10 o'clock at night. As we entered the town we were greeted by the perfume of the cape jasmine, which filled the air. We put up at a nice hotel, where we had pure coffee, and, in fact, the table was supplied with every thing to be had in peace times. It was kept by an excellent gentleman, Mr. Kelly, whose son had just returned from General Forrest's army. Captain Cloud and he were old friends.

On the 23d, the gentleman tried to get a wagon to take us the rest of our journey, but failed; so we had to make the best of our lot, and remained contented, hoping that some good genius would send us a conveyance.

Tuskegee is the capital of Macon county, Alabama, and is forty miles east-by-north from Montgomery. It is a pretty town, and has some very fine buildings in it, and an excellent college for the education of young ladies. The flower gardens exceeded every thing for beauty I had ever beheld. I never saw the cape jasmine in such profusion.

I walked through the place with our host's daughter, and I think I met more pretty girls than I had ever seen before, and they were very gaily dressed. The people there have felt the war very little. Raiders passed through the town, from Montgomery, on their way to Columbus, Georgia, just before the war closed, but did little or no damage to the place, as they were in a hurry to reach Columbus. Some of the citizens, it seemed, had sent a petition to the commandant at Montgomery, requesting him to send Federal troops there to garrison the town. The windows of my room were near where a knot of men were seated. As I sat by it I could not help hearing their conversation. The majority of them were condemning the senders of the petition, as this was a quiet little town, and had no need of the garrison. One of the group was accused of having signed it, which he stoutly denied, but said he had never favored secession or the war.

While Captain Cloud and myself were in the parlor, looking over some books, a lady called on Miss Kelly; in the course of conversation the latter informed her that the Federals were expected to garrison the town. The lady replied, " I am so glad, as it will be such a nice change." I looked at Captain Cloud; the blood mounted to his face, and he muttered between his teeth, " Is this the kind of woman I have been fighting for? "

I called on Mrs. John Battle of Mobile, who has been living there for some years, to see if she could tell me anything about Mobile, or if she knew of any conveyance for us. She could give me no information, excepting that the enemy were behaving very well to the citizens of Mobile. She had suffered by the late raid. On hearing that they were coming, she had sent her carriage horses and other valuables into the woods; the horses and the negro man with them were captured; the negro made his escape, and brought the intelligence that the Federals could not get the horses to work under the saddle, and had shot them.

We left Tuskegee on the 26th, in a wagon without a cover; but we had two very large umbrellas. We started about an hour before sunrise, and the first thing that greeted our sight, on leaving the town, was the Federal encampment; they had arrived the night before, and were busy getting breakfast. I looked at them through curiosity, as this was the first camp of them I had seen, excepting as prisoners. The rest of the party gazed into vacancy rather than look at them. They had some negro women and children with them, the most squalid and miserable-looking creatures I ever beheld. We met some few negro men going to join them. The negro boy that drove us made a good deal of fun of them for going, and told them they had better keep away, as the Yankees were hanging all the darkies they could catch; and that we had just seen some hanging as we passed. We met an old man hobbling to them; the owner of the wagon was with us, and told us that this old man had been treated by his owner as one of his own family.

About 12 o'clock A. M., we stopped at a charming spot, where there was a delightful grove of oaks. There we alighted, for the purpose of taking dinner and resting in the shade. I went to a house near, and the lady of it gave me the privilege of making coffee. She also gave us a large pitcher of sweet milk, for which she would take no money. I think her name was Elder. She related a horrible tragedy that had lately happened near there. A negro woman killed her little child so that she might with greater facility go to the Federals; her negro companions, without trial, burned her.

After resting for awhile we started on our journey, and two or three times came near having a disaster, the mules taking fright at the dead horses and cattle of all kinds that strewed the way; the enemy had killed what they had no use for. Some parts of the road were very bad, and we could scarcely drag through it.

We met hundreds of negro men, women, and children, returning to their homes from Montgomery, where they had been with the Federals, and had had a taste of freedom; and to judge from their looks it had brought them any thing else but happiness. As we journeyed along we sang the laments of Ireland, as they best accorded with our feelings. Moore's and Campbell's songs were duly appreciated. We felt that the " Exile of Erin " and " Tara's Halls " described realities. Our conversation was not at all cheerful. We spoke of the terrible past and the gloomy future. Some say that it is a disgrace to be living after our country has gone.

Even the wind had a melancholy sound, and seemed to sigh and moan through the woods as if lamenting with us o'er our buried hopes, and the graves of that unconquered band of heroes, whose names are radiant with immortality . . .

We commented on the cause of our failure; first one thing was blamed for it, then another. There is no doubt but we as a whole might have done better, but it would only have prolonged the war, for the North, with a determination which seemed demoniacal, was bent on our subversion. Why the enemy were permitted to work their fiendish purposes, is still in oblivion. The unfolding future will lift the vail which is enveloping us, and then, I trust, all shall be revealed. " God is his own interpreter." Let us trust him for his grace, and remember that " no chastening for the present seemeth to be joyous, but grievous: nevertheless, afterward it yieldeth the peaceable fruit of righteousness unto them which are exercised thereby."

As we neared Montgomery the country presented a rich appearance. We passed quite a number of plantations, with very neat houses on them, and luxuriant flower gardens; some few of the houses were magnificent buildings. The whole wore an air of prosperity; the evil effects of the war had certainly not been felt there.

We had heard so much about the ladies of Montgomery and Mobile having given the Federals a warm reception, that we were disposed to accuse every lady we met on the road of the same *crime*, and take every man we met for a Yankee.

Some members of our party were bitter against the Alabama girls for acting as report said they had done. A very beautiful girl passed us on horseback, accompanied by a fine-looking young man. They were certain the latter was a Yankee. To be sure of it, they stopped and asked a lady and gentleman who were passing, and were told that he had been a Confederate staff officer. We next passed a company of ladies and gentlemen, who seemed to be a bridal party. They concluded directly that an Alabama girl had been marrying a Yankee. I found it useless to try and defend the women of my state against such *ocular proof* of their *guilt*.

The woods and roadside were filled with wild flowers; we saw numbers of the sensitive plant in full bloom, and the flower of it is very beautiful. We saw many trees with the same leaf and flower, only much larger. We pulled some of the branches, and found that the leaves did not close like the plant's. This tree in full bloom was gorgeous.

At dark we stopped at a house about twelve miles from Montgomery. It was untenanted, but we found some negroes in the kitchen who gave us an unfurnished room to lodge in for the night. An old negress brought us in a mattress from her own bed and put it on the floor. Mrs. Nutt spread a blanket for the children; the gentlemen lodged in the hall. I did not like the idea of sleeping on the mattress, but Mrs. Nutt did not seem to mind it; as it was the best we could get, and we were weary with our days jolting, we wrapped ourselves in our shawls and slept on it very soundly.

We got up at 4 o'clock the next morning, 27th instant—it was dark as Erebus—and started on our journey. When within a short distance of Montgomery, we came to the Federal encampment, and the head-quarters of the commanding general, where the gentlemen had to have their paroles inspected. They did not remain long, and on their return said they were politely treated.

The Federals displayed good taste in selecting their camp ground. It was on a slight eminence and amidst the finest forest of trees I ever beheld. The sun was an hour high, and its golden rays came glimmering through the trees, mantling them with a flood of glory. As we rode on, camp after camp came in view, filled with the mighty host, who had taken this fair heritage from us. The men with us said little or nothing. They seemed to be trying to keep from giving utterance to the indignation they felt at seeing their native land in the hands of the conqueror.

O, I felt so sad! visions of the terrible past would rise in review before me—the days, weeks and months of suffering I had witnessed—and all for naught. Many a boyish and manly face, in the full hey-day of life and hope, now lying in the silent tomb. But it is not the dead we must think of now . . .

We were a solemn company as we rode into Montgomery, and the sights greeting us there did not by any means dispel the gloom. The stars and stripes were floating over many of the large buildings. Federal officers and privates were standing in groups and thronging the streets.

We stopped at the Exchange Hotel, and found in the parlor quite a number of refugees—French people—returning to New Orleans. With all the characteristics of that light-hearted people, they were playing the piano and singing, apparently enjoying themselves, just as if there never had been one dark hour in our sunny land. I do not know but that this cheerfulness displayed a good deal of wisdom. They had done their duty—had failed—found it was vain to repine for what was already gone, and were

303

"Acting [Act, act] in the living present,
Heart within and God o'erhead."[1]

Captain Nutt concluded to go to Mobile by the river. I made up my mind to take the cars, being much the quickest way. I was very anxious to reach home, as I had not heard from there for three months. To add to my anxiety, news had reached Montgomery of a terrible gunpowder explosion in Mobile. Captain Nutt had paid out a good deal of money on my account, and I wished to repay him before leaving. I had an order for transportation, with which I hoped to get a ticket from the Federals to take me on the cars. Handing my order to Capt. Nutt, I called on Mrs. Dr. Scott to see if I could not borrow enough to pay my debts, but I found her as poor as myself. She had been in the possession of five dollars, made from selling vegetables, but had given it to the doctor, who had gone to Pensacola, with naught but that *large amount* to pay his way.

She introduced me to Colonel Jones, superintendent of the Pensacola road, who told me if I could not get my passage from the Federals, he would give me a note to Mr. Jourden, the superintendent of the Mobile and Great Northern Railroad, and I could pay him on my arrival in that city.

Mrs. Scott told me that the people in Montgomery had suffered much by the Federal soldiers.

She had been nearly frightened to death by a negro soldier. He demanded all her valuables; and when she refused, he cursed her, and held his drawn sword over her head, threatening to kill her. She thinks, had it not been for her seeming bravery and a negro servant-woman who stood by and protected her, he would have done so. She had a guard around her house for days afterward. A horse was stolen from her by some of the soldiers. On informing the commanding general, he gave her another in return. She has lost a great deal by the war, but she has only shared the fate of many, many others.

I was told there was a great deal of destitution in the city. People that were wealthy before the close of the war were then living on rations drawn from the Federals.

From all I heard and saw I do not believe that the ladies of Montgomery were accepting any attentions from the Federals. I scarcely saw one while there, and the last time I passed through the streets were thronged with them.

I believe there was little or no fighting at the capture of Montgomery; so it did not suffer like Selma, which I am told is in ruins. The Presbyterian clergyman of that place was killed in the trenches, and many other citizens. Mr. Ticknor, the Episcopal clergyman, was wounded, and a friend told me that, after the place had been surrendered, the enemy went to Mr. Ticknor's house and demanded some

[1] Henry Wadsworth Longfellow, "A Poem of Life," stanza 6.

valuables that Mrs. Ticknor had laid away, and whipped her till she was compelled to give them up. They did the same to many other ladies. The same friend told me that she saw the blood running in streams through the streets of Selma, from hundreds of slaughtered cattle. The enemy killed those they did not need, so we would have none to use for farming purposes.

Captain Nutt failed in getting transportation for me, so Colonel Jones very kindly gave me the order which he had promised. I went back to the hotel as empty-handed as I left it, so I could not pay my kind friend what I owed him.

I looked at my roll of Confederate money, and put it away with a sigh. Memories of what it once was came crowding upon me. Now

> " Representing nothing in God's earth below,
>   And naught in the water beneath [below] it;
> As the pledge of a nation that's dead and gone,
>   Keep it, dear captain, and show it;
> Show it to those who will lend an ear
>   To the tale that this paper can tell—
> Of liberty born, of the patriot's dream,
>   Of a storm-cradled nation that fell. . . ." [2]

I left Montgomery on the 26th, and the roads were so bad that I thought at one time we should never get to the end of our journey. It was a dreary trip to me, as, being left alone to my sad thoughts, I could more fully realize than ever before the state of our affairs. As we neared Mobile my heart sank within me at the desolate appearance of every thing. The explosion had laid whole squares in ruins, and destroyed a number of steamboats. Instead of the carriages and crowds of familiar faces that used to grace the landing on the approach of the steamer, nothing was to be seen but "blue coats," cannon, and ammunition of all kinds.

On reaching home I found my family all well. My brother, along with his company, had done good service at Spanish Fort. The company lost, in killed, James W. Sampson, a brave youth who was a native of Mobile, and W. B. Anderson, an excellent young Scotchman, and also had several wounded. The Twenty-first Alabama Regiment lost, in killed, Fitz Ripley, William Martin, William Hartenett, and others.

The fort at Blakely and Spanish Fort, on the eastern shore, were erected after the fall of the forts on the lower bay for the defense of Appalachee River. General St. John Liddell, under General Maury, had command of those forts at the time of the siege. They were manned by veteran troops of Missouri, Texas, Arkansas, Georgia, Mississippi—indeed, nearly every state in the Confederacy was repre-

---

[2] Here Miss Cumming included the full text of " The Confederate Note." This poem was written just after the close of the War by Major Samuel Alroy Jonas of General Stephen D. Lee's staff. It has been reprinted many, many times.

sented in them. The garrison was a mere handful of men, who withstood manfully, for seventeen days, the assaults of more than ten times
their number, besides the fire of a formible fleet of gun-boats.

We lost heavily, but did not yield until our ammunition was nearly
exhausted and our forces almost surrounded. Colonel William E.
Burnett of Texas, chief of artillery, was killed in Spanish Fort. He
is spoken of in the highest terms as having been a good and brave
soldier. General Gibson, with his galant band of Louisianians, was
the last to leave the forts. I have been told that, after the surrender,
the negro troops acted like demons, and slaughtered our troops on all
sides; the white Federal soldiers had to turn on them and shoot them
before they would desist. But we must draw a mantle over these
horrors.

Many of our men waded through the sloppy marshes, and when they
reached the city they were covered with mud, and many of them with
blood. During the siege the people did all in their power to render
assistance to the garrison, and many of the old men went over with
refreshments for the men, and to take care of the wounded.

Mobile has acted nobly in this contest. The main portion of her
arms-bearing citizens were in the field, and those who were incapable
of taking the field worked assiduously in relieving the wants of those
who were in it, and they did every thing that could be done for the
relief of the poor in the city. Her hallowed dead can be numbered by
the score; scarcely a family but is enshrouded by affliction for the loss
of one or more loved ones. She has given up the very flower of her
youth and manhood as an oblation on the altar of freedom. The
history of Mobile is, I expect, the history of every city in the South.

I found that the people of Mobile had been sadly misrepresented,
and that instead of the joyful welcome given by the citizens to the
triumphant army, the town had the quietness of the grave. Scarcely
a soul was to be seen in the streets, excepting negroes. Every blind
was closed, and the whole place looked more as if the plague had
entered it, instead of its deliverers, as they call themselves.

Since then, there are but two or three ladies who have countenanced
the enemy in any way, and now their old friends will have nothing to
say to them. The ladies take no more notice of the Federal officers
than if they were invisible, and a friend told me that they say they
would much rather that the ladies would give them impertinence than
treat them as they do.[3] They have a fine band of music, which plays

[3] Personal reconciliation to defeat did not come easy. As late as 1867 Augusta
Jane Evans wrote a friend: " Officers of high rank have brought me letters of
introduction, but I have *invariably refused* to receive the bearers, and have
assigned as my reason for doing so, a determination to hold no social intercourse
with persons who drew their swords against *a cause,*—for which, I would gladly
have sacrificed my life. Having been an ardent and *conscientious Secessionist*, and
indulging still, an unwavering faith in the justice and sanctity of the principles
for which we fought and prayed so devotedly, I of course could not find it agreeable
to associate with those, who were arrayed in arms against my own section and

on the public square; have reviews, and display their fine trappings; give receptions; but all has been in vain; with few exceptions, the ladies are true to their dead. The color of blue is wholly ignored. I heard one little girl crying bitterly because her mother was going to put a blue ribbon on her hat. She said the Yankees might take her for one of them.

The negroes are free: and the poor creatures are acting like children out on a frolic. The main portion of the women do little else than walk the streets, dressed in all kinds of gaudy attire. All are doing their own work, as a negro can not be hired at any price. But they have behaved much beter than we had any right to expect, as they have been put up to all kinds of mischief by the enemy. Many of them seem to despise the Federals, and it is not much wonder, as they treat them so badly.

A lady told me that they robbed a poor old woman, that she had left in her house in the country of every thing that she had. They have treated all who fell into their hands in the same way.

As a rule the Federal soldiers have behaved very well to the citizens; they are any thing but exultant—and they need not be, when they consider that they succeeded by overwhelming numbers alone. They found that they could gain nothing by fighting themselves, so they hired foreigners, and at last had to take the *darky*; and Sambo boasts that the *rebels* could not be conquered until he took the field. Many think if we had put negroes into the army at the start, that we should have had another tale to tell to-day; and I am confident that if we had freed the negro, we would have had the aid of foreign powers. I believe now that Great Britain was consistent in her hatred to slavery. And she dreaded bringing war upon her people, as she knew more about its horrors than we did. In this I can not blame her. We all know that the majority of her people sympathized with us, and did much to render us aid. To be sure the northerners got men and ammunition from her, but then they had money, which is a lever even with Britons. But all is gone now, and we must try and " let the dead past bury its dead! "

This year has developed the fate of the South. Time has revealed the utter loss of all our hopes. A change must pass over every political and social idea, custom, and relation. The consummation makes the year just passed ever memorable in our annals. In it gathers all the interest of the bloody tragedy; from it begins a new era, midst poverty, tears, and sad memories of the past. O, may we learn the lesson that all of this is designed to teach; that all things sublunary are transient and fleeting, and lift our souls to that which is alone ever-during and immutable—God and eternity! And forgetting the past, save in the lessons which it teaches, let us . . . redeem the time, live humbly, and trust God for future good. . . .

---

people." ALs dated Mobile, January 13, 1867, now at the Alderman Library of the University of Virginia.

INDEX

This is an index to the personal and place names in Miss Cumming's narrative. It is not a subject index, and it does not include references to material added to the narrative by the present editor.

Bears, ———, 111
Beauregard, Gen. Pierre Gustave Toutant, 33, 47, 51–52, 76, 82, 205
Bector, Mrs., 266
Beecher, Henry Ward, 260
Beers, ———, 194
Beers, Mrs. Fannie A., 64, 194, 195
Bell, Mrs., 288
Bell brothers, 47
Bemiss, Dr. Samuel Merriford, 126–29, 131, 137, 138, 143, 163, 169, 199, 227, 234, 268, 272, 273
Benedict, Dr., 37
Benedict, Samuel, 159–61
Benton, Decatur, 30
Berry, Dr., 294
Berry, Maj., 259
Berry, Mrs. Andrew J., 219, 222
Berry, Col. I. T., 188, 289
Bibia, Mrs., 160
Bigby, John S., 224
Bigby, Mrs. Mary Catherine (Dougherty), 219, 224
Birch, Mrs., 156
Black, ———, 217–18
Blackie, Dr. George Stodart, 188
Blair, Lt., 260
Blind School Hospital, Macon, Ga., 262
Blythe, Col. Green L., 12
Bohannon, ———, 203, 240
Bolt, Robert, 109, 124
Bond, Lt. David, 150, 234
Booneville, Miss., 43
Booth, Lt., 70
Booth, Miss, 13
Boullemet, Milton, 55
Bradley, ———, 187
Bragg, Gen. Braxton, 33, 47–48, 61, 71, 73, 78, 83, 96, 101, 103, 111, 115–17, 119, 122, 123, 129–31, 139, 140, 142, 145, 148, 159, 161, 163, 165, 171, 181, 182, 207, 297, 298
Bragg, Mrs. Braxton, 129–30, 136
Bragg Hospital, Americus, Ga., 231, 239

Bragg Hospital, Chattanooga, Tenn., 64
Bragg Hospital, Cherokee Springs, Ga., 126
Bragg Hospital, Newnan, Ga., 156, 220
Bragg Hospital, Ringgold, Ga., 146
Bragg Hospital, Selma, Ala., 244
Bragg Hospital (without location), 242, 243
Brannegan, Lt., 53
Brazelton, S., 179
Breckinridge, Gen. John Cabell, 104, 163
Brennan, ———, 35–36
Brewer, ———, 87, 88, 117
Brewer, Mrs., 79–81, 85, 87, 105, 109, 117
Brewster, Maj. William R., 165
Brookhaven, Miss., 40
Brooks, ———, 285
Brooks, Capt., 289
Brooks, Mrs., 79, 81, 203, 222, 223, 285, 289, 293, 294
Brown, ———, 151, 212, 289
Brown, Gen., 154
Brown, Gov. Joseph Emerson, 187, 204, 226, 232, 275
Brown, Gov. Neal, 149
Brown's Brigade Hospital, 154
Bryant, Mrs., 70
Bryson, ———, 131
Buchanan, Adm. Franklin, 227
Buck, Col. William A., 76
Buckner, Gen. Simon Bolivar, 88, 121
Buckner Hospital, Chattanooga, Tenn., 64
Buckner Hospital, Fort Valley, Ga., 228
Buckner Hospital, Newnan, Ga., 185, 200, 217
Buell, Gen. Don Carlos, 42, 71, 72
Burford, Miss, 126, 242
Burgess, ———, 83
Burks, Dr. David Johnson, 182, 186, 193, 218, 263, 273, 274, 281
Burnett, Col. William E., 306

311

Elliott, William G., 169
Ellis, Miss, 108, 116, 121, 122
Ellis, Mrs., 148
Ellis, Capt. Henry, 52
Enterprise, Miss., 247
Epperson, Frank, 54
Ernest, ———, 39
Estell, F., 238
Estell, Dr. Wallace, 238, 239
Etowah River, 122
Evans, Mrs., 4, 62, 64, 146–48
Evans, Augusta Jane, 64, 227
Evergreen, Ala., 87
Exchange Hotel, Montgomery, Ala., 59, 89, 90, 303

Fairbanks, Maj. George E., 232–34
Fairbanks, Mrs. George E., 160
Farmer, ———, 23
Farragut, Adm. David Glasgow, 29
Farrow, Charles, 11, 70–71
Faught, Jesse H., 22
Ferrell, Jesse, 163
Finnegan, Capt., 88, 244
Fleming, Maj., 280
Flewellen, Dr. Ed. Archelaus, 61, 69, 152
Floyd, Gen. John Buchanan, 35
Foard, Dr. A. J., 17, 20, 97, 152, 212
Foard Hospital, Americus, Ga., 231, 239
Foard Hospital, Chattanooga, Tenn., 76, 96
Foard Hospital, Ringgold, Ga., 129
Foard Hospital (without location), 247, 257
Fogle, ———, 59
Ford, Thomas, 76
Forney, Gen. John H., 58
Forrest, Gen. Nathan Bedford, 104, 122, 142, 184, 206, 238
Fort Blakely, 305
Fort Donelson, 70, 71
Fort Gaines, 227
Fort Morgan, 37, 77, 227
Fort Powell, 227

Fort Sumter, 12, 172
Fort Valley, Ga., 228
Foster, Dr., 21
Foster, Dr. Robert C., 278
Fowler, John, 48, 51
Fowler, Capt. W. P., 48, 50, 51, 118
Franklin, battle of, 245
Franklin, Tenn., 253
Frémont, Gen. John Charles, 24, 25
Fry, Mrs., 116
Fry, Mrs. J. Eber, 285
Fuquet, Isaac, 25
Furlow, Kate, 238
Fyffe, Mrs., 267, 269, 270, 272–74, 278

Gainesville, Ala., 241, 243, 257
Gaither, Col., 126
Gamble, Dr. Carey B., 126, 129, 141, 156, 157, 160, 171, 188, 197, 234, 262
Gamble, Mrs. Carey B., 129, 136, 188, 194
Gamble Hospital, Fort Valley, Ga., 228
Gamble Hospital, Newnan, Ga., 197, 213, 217, 220, 221
Garner Hospital, Mobile, Ala., 57
Gate City Hospital, Atlanta, Ga., 197, 201, 281
General Hospital, Mobile, Ala., 54
Georgia Aid Society, 152
Georgia Relief Association, 234
Georgia Relief Committee, 148
Georgia Relief Society, 154
Gettysburg, battle of, 115
Gibbs, Dr. John H., 150
Gibson, Gen. Randall Lee, 306
Gilmer, Mrs. William P., 4, 23, 86, 95
Gilmer Hospital, Chattanooga, Tenn., 95, 96, 100, 104, 124
Gilmer Hospital, Marietta, Ga., 159, 160
Girard, Ala., 243
Gladden, Gen. Addley H., 12

313

Hudson, ———, 288
Hudson, Lt., 76
Hughes, ———, 67
Hughes, Dr. J. N., 169–72, 181, 186, 193, 194, 203, 210, 216, 221, 230, 237, 238, 240, 242, 243, 247, 280, 293, 294
Hughes, Dr. William, 22, 43–45, 51, 53, 96
Huldah (Negro cook), 69
Hull, ———, 220
Hunt, ———, 150
Hunt, Miss, 150–53
Hunt, Mrs., 153
Hunt, Col. Thomas Hart, 45
Hunter, Mrs., 12, 13
Hunter, Dr. Alexander, 63, 67, 69, 72, 74, 79, 80, 93, 95, 96, 98, 103, 104, 112, 113, 116, 123, 236
Hunter, Mrs. Alexander, 103, 116
Hunter, Robert M. T., 254
Huntley, Lt., 70
Husten, Rev., 145

Ingraham, Joseph Holt, 65
Insey, Capt., 171
Irwin, Mrs., 243
Iuka, Miss., 71

Jackson, Dr. Robert D., 198, 244
Jackson, Gen. Thomas Jonathan "Stonewall," 54, 82, 101, 103, 188
Jackson, Miss., 103, 106
James, W., 79
Jarboe, Mrs., 41
Jarvis, D. W., 68
Jewitt, Maj. Origen Sibley, 144
Johnson, ———, 27, 30, 108
Johnson, President Andrew, 278, 290
Johnston, Mrs., 143–45, 169, 186, 222
Johnston, Gen. Albert Sidney, 11–12
Johnston, Gen. Joseph Eggleston, 7, 52, 80, 83, 94, 96, 195, 200, 201, 205, 206, 208–11, 223, 256–58, 280, 282, 298

Johnston, Mrs. Joseph Eggleston, 81
Jole, H. C., 73
Jones, ———, 26, 32, 74
Jones, Col., 304, 305
Jones, Allen, 68
Jones, Brittle, 92
Jones, Watt, 68
Jones, William, 55
Jonesboro, Ga., 214, 280
Jordan, ———, 243
Jourden, ———, 304

Kavanaugh, M., 245
Kay, James, 171
Keeler, Charles, 55
Keith, Lt., 85
Kellogg, M. P., 223
Kellogg, Mrs. M. P., 223
Kelly, ———, 60, 61
Kelly (hotel keeper), 300
Kelly, Lt., 236
Kelly, Miss, 301
Kenesaw Mountain, 159
Kennedy, Josh, 53
Ketchum, William H., 10
Keyes, Gen. Erasmus D., 52
King, Miss, 262, 269, 275, 276
King, Dr. John W., 263
Kingston, Ga., 116, 120, 122, 125, 201
Kingston Hospital, Kingston, Ga., 170
Kirwin, William, 181
Knoxville, Tenn., 193
Kratz, Dr. O., 87

Labuzan, ———, 191
Labuzan, Catesby, 182, 191
Lagrange Relief Society, 156
Lambert, ———, 210
Laramar, ———, 199
Latta, ———, 213
Laws, Frank, 130, 205
Laws brothers, 205
Lay, Bishop Henry C., 197, 267
Leach, Misses, 227
Leadbetter, Gen. Danville, 64
Ledyard, ———, 12
Ledyard, W. I., 55

315

Lee, Gen. Robert Edward, 7, 52, 54, 82, 101, 115, 142, 271, 275, 276, 287, 298, 300
Lee, Gen. Stephen Dill, 252
Leonard, N., 245
Leslie, ———, 201
Lessel, Edwin, 107
Leuseine, T., 55
Levert Hospital, Mobile, Ala., 255
Lick Creek, 193
Liddell, Gen. St. John, 305
Lincoln, President Abraham, 17, 108, 174, 183, 228, 233, 237, 254, 275, 283
Little, J. B., 79
Little, Dr. William G., 17
Lockwood, H. S., 55
Lomax, Col. Tennent, 55
Longstreet, Augustus Baldwin, 66
Longstreet, Gen. James, 54, 55, 82, 203
Lookout Mountain, 68, 102, 109, 165, 172, 173, 267
Loughrey brothers, 53
Love, ———, 128, 288
Love, Mrs., 128, 264, 267
Lovell, Gen. Mansfield, 29
Lowe, Mrs., 170
Lowe, Julia, 156, 170, 179
Lowenthall, Mrs., 199
Lyle, Dr. William D., 19
Lyons, Mrs., 19, 21
Lyons, John, 22, 212

McAllister, Dr. William Thomas, 64, 143
McCook, Gen. Alexander McDowell, 217
McCown, Gen., 106, 109
McCoy, Mrs., 60
McCullough, ———, 101
McFarland, Mrs., 112
McFerrin, ———, 195
McHenry, ———, 158
McKinly, Mrs. Ann, 222
McKinstry, Alexander, 73
McLean, ———, 91
McLean, J. M., 31, 32, 79, 86, 191
McNair, Col., 101

Macon, Ga., 223, 227, 232–34, 236, 241, 261–63, 270, 275, 279
Macon and Western Railroad, 87, 265
McVoy, ———, 65
Maffitt, Capt. John Newland, 184
Maguire, Charles, 106
Maguire, John, 11, 12
Malvern Hill, battle of, 54
Manigault's Brigade Hospital, 150, 156
Marietta, Ga., 159, 160, 207
Marks, Miss, 37, 39, 45
Marryatt, Frederick, 158
Marshall, ———, 12
Martin, ———, 218
Martin, S., 288
Martin, William, 305
Mary Wilson (steamer), 59
Mashburn, Col. Elisha, 207
Massinger, ———, 110, 124
Maury, Gen. Dabney Herndon, 190, 230, 305
May, Mrs., 31, 59, 61–63, 65, 67, 68, 70, 72, 110
Medical College Hospital, Atlanta, Ga., 200
Mellon, Dr., 262
Memphis, Tenn., 14, 41
Memphis and Charleston Railroad, 14
Michel, Dr. Charles Eugene, 96
Military Aid Society, Mobile, Ala., 55, 74 ,79, 106
Miller, ———, 109–110, 214
Miller, Benjamin M., 9, 10, 14, 16, 19, 44, 48, 62, 114, 191
Millward, Mrs., 31
Minor, ———, 23
Missionary Ridge, Ga., 165, 173, 177
Mitchell, Dr., 137
Mitchell, Mrs., 266, 267, 269
Mitchell, John M., 89
Mobile, Ala., 9–14, 16, 37, 39, 51, 52, 55, 88, 101, 109, 121, 177, 189–91, 195, 227, 245, 259, 260, 266, 269, 279, 293, 301, 304, 306
Mobile *Advertiser and Register*, 132

Mobile and Great Northern Railroad, 304
Mobile and Ohio Railroad, 9, 14, 280
Mobile Bay, 89, 189
Mobile River, 89
Monro, Edward, 155
Monroe, Miss., 5, 262
Monterey, Miss., 25
Montgomery, Ala., 59, 87–89, 243, 260, 266, 268, 272, 289, 293, 302–304
Moore, ———, 164, 192
Moore (chaplain), 174, 179, 180, 182, 187, 206, 213, 222, 235, 240, 263, 267, 271, 276
Moore, Mrs., 73, 92
Moore, Dr. Samuel Preston, 256
Mordecai, Dr., 53
Mordecai, Lt., 52–53
Morgan, ———, 223, 225
Morgan, Maj., 96
Morgan, Gen. John Hunt, 39, 41–42, 47, 82, 96, 132, 189, 232, 295, 298
Morton, Joseph, 104
Mulden, Capt., 76
Munroe, John, 170
Murdoch, ———, 45
Murfreesboro, Tenn., 76, 120
Murfreesboro, battle of, 83, 84
Murphy, ———, 111
Murphy, Miss, 31
Murray, ———, 93
Murray, Alfred R., 153
Murray, James, 71
Muscogee Railroad, 243
Myers, Mrs., 284

Nagle, Dr. J. E., 228
Nashville, battle of, 251–53
Nashville, Tenn., 13, 245, 246, 251
Nashville and Chattanooga Railroad, 62, 165, 171
Neligen, ———, 170
Neptune Fire Company, Mobile, Ala., 12
New, ———, 151

New Hope Church, battle of, 205, 209
Newbern, ———, 74
Newnan, Ga., 140, 149, 156, 178, 189, 198, 200, 208, 225, 230, 231, 257, 265, 278, 280, 283, 288, 294
New Orleans, 26, 29
Newsom, Mrs. Ella (King), 4, 39–40, 63, 76–79, 86, 87, 95, 96, 125, 130, 159, 262, 268, 270, 275
Newsom Hospital, Americus, Ga., 236
Newsom Hospital, Chattanooga, Tenn., 63, 67, 96, 123–24, 134, 154
Newsom Hospital, Cleveland, Tenn., 116, 136
Nidelet, Dr. S. R., 256
Nichol, Dr. W. L., 113
Nickajack cave, 107
Nixon, Alexander, 234
Noland, ———, 60, 61
Noland, Mrs., 26, 62
Norton, ———, 57
Nott, ———, 17
Nott, Dr. Josiah Clark, 12, 39
Nutt, Capt., 38, 293, 295–97, 299, 300, 304, 305
Nutt, Mrs., 213, 222, 285, 293, 295, 298–300, 303

O'Brien, ———, 116, 144, 151
Ocmulgee River, 233
Ogden, ———, 30
Ogden, Mrs., 13, 14, 16, 19, 31, 38, 43, 44, 46, 48, 79, 186
Okolona, Miss., 10, 39–41, 248
Oliver, ———, 44, 48–49, 53
O'Neal, Dr. Seaborn King, 100
Ooostanaula, River, 122
Opelika, Ala., 226, 297
O'Rear, Capt. E. O., 202
Orr, ———, 213
Ortella, John, 11
Osborne, Capt., 172
Oslin, Dr. John Wimbish, 192, 226
Otey, Bishop James Henry, 290
Otis, Mrs., 83, 191
Oxford, Ga., 234

317

Palmer, Mrs., 40
Palmer, Benjamin Morgan, 131
Palmer, Col. Joseph B., 116
Palmetto, Ga., 214, 219
Patterson, Dr., 98, 100, 103, 265
Patterson, John, 206
Payne, Lt., 137, 139, 165, 173
Payne, Maj., 173
Payne, Mrs., 247
Pemberton, Gen. John C., 106, 113, 121
Pensacola Railroad, 304
Perryville, battle of, 72
Petersburg, Va., 203, 271
Phillips, ———, 60
Phillips, Col., 260
Pickett, ———, 147, 163
Pierce, Bishop Henry Niles, 21, 57, 59
Pierce, Mrs. Henry Niles, 208, 236
Pike, ———, 103
Pim, Dr. L. T., 208
Pinkerton, ———, 25
Polk, Gen. Leonidas, 22, 30, 117, 145, 159, 205, 206
Port Hudson, Miss., 107, 121
Porter, Dr., 276, 277
Porter, Mrs., 269
Posey, Capt. Ben Lane, 201
Powell, Dr. Thomas J., 238, 281
Powell, Mrs. Thomas J., 281
Prendergast, Capt., 160, 233
Price, Gen. Sterling, 25, 27, 28, 31, 35, 41, 56, 71, 72, 82
Pritchard, ———, 101
Proctor, Maj., 46, 47, 140
Pullet, ———, 212–13
Pursley, Dr. George F., 199

Quintard, Dr. Charles Todd, 113–14, 116, 117, 125, 126, 129, 131, 196, 197, 205, 206, 267
Quintard Hospital, Griffin, Ga., 263
Quintard Hospital, Rome, Ga., 122

Rabbit, ———, 214
Raccoon Mountain, 171
Rally, ———, 78

Ransom, ———, 179
Rawlings, ———, 274
Rawlings, Mrs., 263
Read, ———, 111
Redwine, Dr., 239, 255
Redwine, Mrs., 222, 293
Redwood, Dr. George Edward, 14, 64, 255
Redwood, Tyler, 55
Reese, ———, 199
Reese, Dr. Joseph E., 182, 186, 212, 218, 223, 230, 263, 265
Reese, Mrs. Joseph E., 156, 165, 223, 293
Regan, ———, 18, 20–21
Renfruit, ———, 76
Rhea, Dr., 130, 137, 143, 150, 154, 156
Richmond, Capt., 189
Richmond, Maj. W. B., 80, 145, 189
Richmond, Va., 203, 266, 268, 280
Richmond Fund, Mobile, Ala., 94
Riddle, ———, 253
Rienzi, Miss., 31, 33, 38
Rigby, Miss, 197, 221, 262
Ringgold, Ga., 59, 124–26, 137, 142, 146, 150, 152, 156–58, 161, 171, 177, 196
Ripley, Fitz, 305
Robbins, ———, 75, 164, 166
Roberts, ———, 163
Robertson, ———, 180
Robinson, ———, 166
Robinson, Dr., 251
Robinson, Lt., 101, 106
Rock City, Lookout Mountain, 109
Roddy, Gen. Philip Dole, 215, 217
Rogers, Charles, 204
Rome, Ga., 121–22, 201, 209
Rosecrans, Gen. William Starke, 79, 111, 131, 160, 161, 165
Ross, ———, 236
Ross, Mrs., 223
Ross, D. F. A., 256
Ross Hospital, Mobile, Ala., 256
Roy, Thomas Benton, 77